The Criminal Justice System and Blacks

The Criminal Justice System and Blacks

Edited and Compiled by

Daniel Georges-Abeyie

Clark Boardman Company, Ltd.
New York, New York
1984

Library of Congress Cataloging in Publication Data
Main entry under title:

The Criminal justice system and Blacks.

1. Criminal justice, Administration of—United States—Addresses,
essays, lectures. 2. Discrimination in criminal justice
administration—United States—Addresses, essays, lectures.
3. Afro-American criminals—Addresses, essays, lectures.
4. Afro-Americans—Crimes against—Addresses, essays, lectures.
I. Georges-Abeyie, Daniel E., 1948-
HV9950.C75 1984   364'.973'08996073   84-9437
ISBN 0-87632-438-3

List of Contributors

Roy L. Austin
Arthur Black
Scott Christianson
George W. Crockett, Jr.
Alfred W. Dean
Bruce C. Frederick
Lynne Goodstein
Keith D. Harries
Michael J. Hindelang
Doris Layton MacKenzie

Joan Petersilia
Michael Philip, Jr.
Carl E. Pope
Marc Riedel
Harold Rose
Barry C. Sample
Howard Stewart
Vernetta D. Young
Bruce McM. Wright
Sherwood Zimmerman

About the Editor

DANIEL GEORGES-ABEYIE has a Ph.D. in Urban Social Geography from Syracuse University, New York. He is a member of the graduate faculty in Administration of Justice at The Pennsylvania State University. He teaches in both law enforcement and academic settings and has published in numerous social science journals, monographic series, and edited volumes. Recent publications include: *Crime: A Spatial Perspective,* co-edited with Keith Harries; "Propaganda by Deed: Defining Terrorism" in *The Justice Reporter;* "Terrorism and the Liberal State: A Reasonable Response" and "Toward the Development and Application of a Terrorism Severity Index" in the *Journal of Police Studies;* "The Social Ecology of Bomb Threats: Dallas, Texas" in *The Journal of Black Studies;* "Political Crime and Terrorism" in Graeme Newman's *Deviance and Crime: A Comparative Perspective;* "Toward the Development of a Realistic Approach to the Study of Black Crime" in Paul and Patricia Brantingham's *Environmental Criminology;* and "Women as Terrorists" in Lawrence Freedman and Yonah Alexander's *Perspectives on Terrorism.* He specializes in the study of blacks and criminal justice and in political, criminal, and collective violence. He has held academic appointments at The City University of New York, The Johns Hopkins University, The University of Texas at Arlington, The State University of New York at Albany, and The Southern Illinois University at Carbondale and is a member of the 1984 American Society of Criminology Program Committee.

About the Contributors

ROY L. AUSTIN is an Associate Professor in the Department of Sociology, The Pennsylvania State University. He specializes in criminology, deviancy, race, ethnic relations, and the sociology of the Caribbean. He received his Ph.D. in Sociology from the University of Washington. His recent publications include "Women's Liberation and Increases in Minor, Major, and Occupational Offenses" in the journal *Criminology* and "The Colonial Model: Subcultural Theory and Intra-Group Violence" in *The Journal of Criminal Justice.*

ARTHUR BLACK, a black penologist and correctional educator, is the Education Administrator for the Illinois Youth Center at Harrisburg. He has also served as the Associate Superintendent in Charge of Adult Education, The Illinois Department of Corrections (School District #428). His Ph.D. in Education Administration was awarded by Southern Illinois University at Carbondale.

SCOTT CHRISTIANSON is the Executive Assistant to the Director of Criminal Justice of the State of New York. His recent publications include *Index to Minorities and Criminal Justice* and "Our Black Prisons" in the *Journal of Crime and Delinquency.* He received his Ph.D. in Criminal Justice from The School of Criminal Justice, The State University of New York at Albany.

GEORGE W. CROCKETT is a member of the U.S. House of Representatives. He was the presiding judge of the Recorder's (Criminal) Court in Detroit. He has long contended that racism and classism permeate the American criminal justice system at all levels as well as at all levels of civilian government and American society in general. He holds an A.B. degree from Morehouse College and an LL.B. degree from the Detroit College of Law.

ALFRED W. DEAN is the Director of Public Safety for the city of Harrisburg, Pennsylvania, and was a Lieutenant in the Philadelphia, Pennsylvania, police force. His Master of Social Work degree was awarded by Temple University.

BRUCE C. FREDERICK is Chief of Research and Evaluation, The New York State Division of Criminal Justice Services. His Ph.D. is in Educational Psychology and Statistics, The State University of New York at Albany.

LYNNE GOODSTEIN is an Assistant Professor of Administration of Justice at The Pennsylvania State University. She received her Ph.D. in Social Psychology from the Graduate School of the City University of New York. Dr. Goodstein has conducted a number of studies on the impact of determinate sentencing on inmate adjustment to prison and the correctional system. Her most recent work on this topic is *Determinate Sentencing and the Correctional Process*. She has published numerous articles on this topic and the subject of inmate adjustment to prison in general in such journals as *Journal of Research on Crime and Delinquency, Criminology*, and *Justice Quarterly*. She is also interested in the social definition of rape and bystander responses to crime and has published articles on these subjects in such journals as *Social Psychology Quarterly* and *Victimology*.

KEITH D. HARRIES is an acclaimed scholar in the spatial-environmental crime specialty area. His recent books include *The Geography of Laws and Justice* (co-authored by Stanley Brunn); *Crime and Environment, The Geography of Crime and Justice*, and *Crime: A Spatial Perspective*. His Ph.D. in Geography was awarded by The University of California at Los Angeles.

MICHAEL J. HINDELANG was a prolific scholar in the study of the processing of minority race suspects. He was the founder of the Albany Center for Criminal Justice Research and the *Sourcebook for Criminal Justice Statistics*. The article reprinted in this volume was one of his last publications. Professor Hindelang died March 29, 1982.

DORIS LAYTON MACKENZIE is an Assistant Professor of Experimental Statistics at The Louisiana State University. She specializes in the study of stress and inmate adjustment to prison. One of her recent publications was "Personal Control and Inmate Adjustment to Prison" the *Journal of Criminology*.

JOAN PETERSILIA is a senior researcher in the Rand Corporation Criminal Justice Program. Her most recent books include *Implementing Change in Criminal Justice Agencies, Age, Crime and Sanctions, Criminal Careers of Habitual Felons*, and *The Criminal Investigation Process*.

MICHAEL PHILIP, JR., is Staff Attorney of the Office of Policy Analysis, Research, and Statistical Services, New York State Division of Criminal Justice Services.

CARL E. POPE is a Professor of Criminal Justice at The University of Wisconsin at Milwaukee. He is a well-known academic writer in the area of race and crime. His recent publications include "Race and Juvenile Court

Dispositions: An Examination of Initial Screening Decisions," in the *Journal of Criminal Justice and Behavior* and *Race, Crime, and Criminal Justice.*

MARC RIEDEL is an Associate Professor of Criminal Justice, the Center for the Study of Crime, Delinquency, and Corrections, Southern Illinois University at Carbondale. He specializes in the study of homicide and the imposition of the death sentence. He is currently completing *Stranger Violence: A Theoretical Inquiry* to be published in the fall of 1984. His most recent publications include "National Versus Local Data Sources in the Study of Homicide: Do They Agree?" in Gordon P. Waldo's, *Measurement Issues in Criminal Justice* and "The Effectiveness of Correctional Treatment—Another Look" in Gerald Cooke, *The Role of the Forensic Psychologist.* He received his Ph.D. in Sociology from the University of Pennsylvania and was the recipient of a major grant funded by The National Institute of Law Enforcement and Criminal Justice to study the "Nature and Patterns of American Homicide."

HAROLD ROSE is a Professor of Geography and Urban Affairs at the University of Wisconsin-Milwaukee. He is a prolific, scholarly contributor to the literature on black urbanism. His 1971 book, *The Black Ghetto,* helped to introduce a generation of geographers and social ecologists to the intricacies of blacks and urban existence. He has recently completed a study of "Black Homicide and the Urban Environment" funded by the Center for Minority Group Mental Health Programs, the National Institute of Mental Health. He is a former president of the Association of American Geographers. He received his Ph.D. in Geography from Ohio State University.

BARRY C. SAMPLE is Bureau Chief of Program Development and Planning, New York State Division for Criminal Justice Services. He served as the Program Coordinator at The State University of New York at Albany Center on Minorities and Criminal Justice. His M.A. is from the School of Criminal Justice, The State University of New York at Albany.

HOWARD STEWART is an Assistant District Attorney for Dauphin County, Pennsylvania. His B.A. is from Millersville State University. His J.D. degree is from Dickinson School of Law.

VERNETTA D. YOUNG is one of America's first black women Ph.D.s in Criminal Justice. She specializes in the study of sex, race, and criminal justice. She is a graduate of The State University of New York at Albany, School of Criminal Justice. She is an Assistant Professor of Criminal Justice at the University of Maryland, and has also taught at the American University in Washington, D.C.

BRUCE McM. WRIGHT is a member of the New York City Supreme Bench. He is one of America's most outspoken and uncompromising jurists on issues that concern bias against defendants with minority race, ethnic, or poverty characteristics. Judge Wright was graduated from Lincoln University and The New York University Law School.

SHERWOOD ZIMMERMAN is Deputy Commissioner for the Office of Policy Analysis, Research and Statistical Services, New York State Division of Criminal Justice Services. He received his Ph.D. in Criminal Justice from The School of Criminal Justice, The State University of New York at Albany. His most recent academic appointment was at The Center for the Study of Crime, Delinquency, and Corrections, the Southern Illinois University at Carbondale. He has also served as a parole officer in the state of Colorado. His recent Sage publication, *Corrections at the Crossroads,* has received critical acclaim. He held a two-year post-doctoral fellowship at the Urban Systems Institute, Carnegie-Mellon University.

Foreword

Each contributor to this fine collection of essays, classic articles, and interviews shares most of the same concerns regarding crime and criminal justice. Each represents either a distinct black perspective on some aspect of crime and criminal justice or a scholarly concern with the adequacy and accuracy of research on blacks and the law. And each writer conveys the belief that crimes must be dealt with through actions that do not compromise justice. A common recognition exists that any actions that are taken to make society more secure, must be the result of cool logic, responsible analysis, and a strong sense of justice.

Many of the views presented in this volume are strong. But by attacking various criminal justice practices and standards, these authors force the reader to review his or her own assumptions and biases. And the problems they address—discrimination, inequity, and a blatant disregard for justice —are so urgent and complex that researchers and students cannot afford to limit their vision to the confines of their own experience or to the most popular ideology of the moment, which today might be appropriately labeled "justice with a vengeance."

There is no question that the 1980s are witnessing a resurgence of "retributive justice." Individuals are being executed at a frightening rate, the exclusionary rule is being tampered with, and many inmates may soon face a future without the hope of parole. The nation seems almost eager to avenge itself against violence and crime, which are now regarded by many as "objective evils," rather than as acts primarily borne out of poverty, class struggles, and the effects of social rejection and deep-seated prejudice. But before this country goes too far in its "war" against crime, which will not be waged necessarily with justice as its banner, the black experience in America must be revealed in its most realistic light.

This volume will make a substantial contribution to black studies by offering the most comprehensive coverage available on all aspects of blacks in relation to criminality, victimization, and criminal justice. *The Criminal Justice System and Blacks* brings together the many ways in which the black experience must be considered before scientists, policy makers, and politicians can conscientiously attack the problem of crime with justice on their side.

LESLIE T. WILKINS
1984

Preface

Few topics in the social sciences stir the conscience or incite the passions of people as much as those of race, crime, and criminal justice. French social observer Alexis de Tocqueville, as early as the nineteenth century, noted that law and order without justice was normative in an America that legally and extra-legally subjugated its black population. De Tocqueville warned of the inevitability of racial confrontation as a result of racial injustice and minority race subjugation. De Tocqueville's predictions have obviously been realized—witness the race riots in New York in 1863, East St. Louis in 1917, Chicago in 1919, Tulsa in 1921, Detroit in 1943, Los Angeles in 1965, and the numerous ghetto revolts in American cities during the 1964-1970 Viet Nam era and Miami in 1980, 1982, and 1984, as well as the mutiny of black American military units such as the 24th Infantry in Houston, Texas in 1917 which resulted in a fire fight between black troopers and white civilians and other dramatic black-white racial confrontations involving black troopers and white civilians in Texas, such as in Brownsville in 1906 and along Concho the river at San Angelo in 1881.

The Criminal Justice System and Blacks explores many of the issues noted in De Tocqueville's nineteenth century social science classics, *Democracy in America* and *On the Penitentiary System in the United States and Its Application in France*. Within this volume are original works and classic reprints by some of America's most prominent black academicians and practitioners, such as New York State Criminal Justice researcher-planner Barry Sample; University of Wisconsin-Milwaukee's Harold M. Rose, homicide specialist and former president of the Association of American Geographers; University of Maryland crime and race specialist Vernetta D. Young; Pennsylvania State University criminologist Roy Austin; the outspoken, uncompromising, and controversial New York City Supreme Court Justice Bruce McM. Wright; U.S. House of Representatives and former Detroit Recorder's Court (Criminal Court) Justice George W. Crockett; Harrisburg, Pennsylvania, Director of Public Safety Alfred W. Dean; Dauphin County, Pennsylvania (Harrisburg), Assistant District Attorney Howard Stewart; and Illinois penologist and correctional educator Arthur Black.

This volume also contains original and reprinted articles and executive summaries of the most current research findings in race, crime, and criminal justice conducted by prominent majority race scholars, such as, Southern Illinois University criminologist Marc Riedel; juvenile justice scholar and researcher Carl E. Pope of the University of Wisconsin at Milwaukee; New York State criminal justice researcher-planners Michael Philip and Bruce Frederick; New York State Deputy Commissioner for the Office of Policy Analysis, Research and Statistical Services, New York State Division of Criminal Justice Services Sherwood Zimmerman; Pennsylvania State penologist-criminologist Lynne Goodstein; New York State penologist, criminal justice researcher, and planner Scott Christianson; Rand Corporation criminal justice researcher Joan Petersilia; Oklahoma State University geographer Keith Harries, an acclaimed scholar in the spatial-environmental crime speciality area; Louisiana State University penologist-statistician Doris Layton MacKenzie; and the late Michael J. Hindelang of the State University of New York at Albany.

The Criminal Justice System and Blacks provides an in-depth look at the theory and practice of criminal justice research on crime, race, and justice. It offers insight into black criminality and criminal victimization while addressing the less than objective criminal justice system processing of black defendants and felony crime arrestees. It is hoped that this volume elucidates what is fact and myth in the controversies that surround black criminality, criminal victimization, and the criminal justice system.

Table of Contents

PART 3: BLACKS IN PRISON

CONCLUSION

PART 1

Blacks and Crime

Introduction

The year was 1940 when Richard Wright's novel of restive black men scorned by their nation and sentenced to slum-ghetto environments was personified in *Native Son* in the immortal character of Bigger Thomas.[1] In Bigger, Wright portrayed a youth filled with hate and rage swept into a torrent of violence, murder, assault, rape, and alleged rape. Through Bigger, Wright spoke of black men who drifted into a world of crime, of black men who rationalized their violence, crimes, and distrust of others through a personalized racial ideology. Wright portrayed a criminal justice system that placed the burden of "guilty until proven innocent" upon the shoulders of any black unlucky enough to be caught up in a white system of so-called justice.

Lynn A. Curtis, a culture conflict theorist very much influenced by Marvin Wolfgang's subculture of violence thesis, also saw a slum-ghetto world very much like Richard Wright's *Native Son.*[2] Curtis's slum-ghetto residents were doomed to an anomic world of norms and beliefs in conflict. These were the men doomed to violent encounters among themselves and their associates, men for whom jail was an inevitability, for whom death waited in the form of sanctioned executions or violent death on some deserted or crowded slum-ghetto street corner.

Wright's and Curtis's violent world of anomie,[3] clashing with a criminal justice system that stresses crime suppression rather than justice, is reflected in the various chapters that appear in this volume. This is a world where crime and violence may be instrumental and normative. This is a world studied by many of America's foremost social scientists yet understood by few.

Part 1 reviews the best of recent studies of black criminality and offers insights into the dynamics and social parameters of the juvenile justice system; women and crime; black criminality and criminal victimization; perspectives on race-oriented crime research and criminal justice planning; and a relatively new social plague, black-on-black homicide, which has become the number one cause of death for black men aged 16 to 25.

The authors of Part 1 constitute a new generation of criminal justice and criminology researchers. Daniel Georges-Abeyie, author of Chapters 1 and 9 acknowledges in Chapter 1 the reality of a disproportionate black crime and criminal victimization rate, yet questions the validity or reliability of

3

criminological research that often confuses race for ethnicity. This chapter explores as well a number of definitional issues that are relevant to the student of minority crime, victimization, and criminal justice. Chapter 9 provides a thorough overview of those research efforts that seek to demonstrate the existence of racism in law enforcement and in the courts and those studies that deny racism's role in criminal justice decision making.

Barry Sample and Michael Philip, Jr., New York state researchers, review five of the most important and frequently applied theoretical orientations in the area of race-related crime studies: individual theories, social disorganization theories, subculture theories, radical theories, and the colonial theory. Keith Harries, one of the foremost geographers of crime today, examines data on black crime and criminal victimizations, noting what blacks and whites think about crime as well as providing a review of the official picture of black crime. Marc Riedel, a former student of Marvin Wolfgang, offers insight into how and why black youths appear to be killing each other at such a high rate.

Harold Rose's chapter is the summary of an important study of black-on-black homicides, the urban environment, and violence. Ways to reduce this subculture of violence, to lower black homicide and victimization rates, are discussed to demonstrate research directions for the future. Carl Pope examines the role of discretion in the processing of black juvenile offenders, concluding that "what ultimately happens to juvenile offenders may be a function of what one has done, who one is, and how one is processed." Vernetta Young reexamines and consequently rejects Dr. Freda Adler's thesis that patterns of female criminality differ by race because of differential opportunities historically available to the offender. The late Michael Hindelang's "Variations in Sex-Race-Age-Specific Incidence Rates of Offending" is a demographically oriented study that serves as a guide to race-related criminal justice research.

Notes

[1] Nathan Wright, *Native Son* (New York: Harper and Row, 1966).

[2] Lynn A. Curtis, *Violence, Race and Culture* (Lexington, MA: Lexington-Heath, 1975).

[3] Curtis, *Violence, Race and Culture,* defines anomie as norms in conflict, whereas Emile Durkheim uses the term to refer to normlessness. See Emile Durkheim, *Suicide* (New York: Free Press, 1951). Thus, for Curtis, the anomic situation refers to a situation in which rules of behavior conflict while for Durkheim the anomic situation is one in which there are no well-defined rules of behavior.

1

Definitional Issues: Race, Ethnicity, and Official Crime/Victimization Statistics

Daniel Georges-Abeyie

For many, crime and race are one—the activity of slum-ghetto black and hispanic youth. But how accurate is this image? What factors complicate and possibly invalidate the reams of race and ethnically identifiable offender and victim statistics reported, for instance, in the FBI's Crime in the United States—The Uniform Crime Reports or the U.S. Department of Justice's Sourcebook of Criminal Justice Statistics and Criminal Victimization in the United States? To answer this and related questions, this chapter provides a brief introduction to the social, cultural, and biological significance of race and ethnic-based data commonly associated with offender and victimization statistics.

WHAT IS CRIME? WHO IS A CRIMINAL?

Before minority criminality or criminal victimization can be discussed rationally, the political, social, and cultural biases hidden in crime definitions must be identified. Few would argue that the prevailing schools of thought—the conservative, liberal, radical, and critical perspectives—color definitional issues and interpretations of criminals and criminality. The hidden biases contained within these orientations need to be examined in order to understand the significance of race and ethnicity to more general notions concerning criminal propensity and victimization.

Crime is both a social and legal reality to the conservative criminologist who believes that crimes are violations of "conduct norms" or well-established behavior patterns (Thorsten Sellin, 1938). The conservative criminologist believes that these conduct norms need not be written into a nation's or a state's criminal code as expected and proper behavior because "normal" people automatically or ritualistically obey, and thus, act out, these behaviors. The conservative criminologist specifically believes that crime is—

(1) A violation of expected behavior (i.e., the violation of a conduct norm)
(2) An act of deviance or a failure to act
(3) An action harmful to society in general, some segment of society in particular, or an individual
(4) A public wrong
(5) "Violations of the fundamental morality underlying a particular society" (Sykes, 1978:48)
(6) "Acts deeply repugnant to the members of a society, arousing vengeance for expiation through punishment" (Sykes, 1978:49)
(7) Improper behavior
(8) A forbidden act or omission
(9) A sinful or ethically blameworthy behavior

The social reality of crime from the conservative criminological perspective need not have the same meaning as the legal or political reality of crime. Paul Tappan (1960) sociologist-lawyer provides a simple but comprehensive definition of the legal reality of crime:

> Crime is an intentional act or omission in violation of criminal law (statutory and case law), committed without defense or justification, and sanctioned by the state as a felony or misdemeanor.

In brief, from the conservative perspective, the legal reality of crime is a behavior or non-behavior ("omission") that is in violation of a criminal code. From this perspective, the legal reality of crime is well-defined and declared through a complex criminal justice procedure. For the conservative criminologist, the crime is both the violation of a conduct norm as well as the violation of a law clearly defined by a political and judicial process; the criminal is an individual who acts in violation of law and social custom.

The liberal criminological perspective encompasses Tappan's social-legal definition of crime. The liberal criminologist would also agree with the conservative belief that legal definitions of crime reflect conduct norms. Thus, for the liberal and conservative criminologists alike, crime is the legal codification and sanctioning of societal norms.

The liberal perspective, however, might question how realistic societal norms and goals are and whether unrealistic norms and goals may predestine certain individuals to the likelihood of criminality. The criminal from this perspective is a rule or law breaker who violates the law in an attempt to attain culturally and socially supported goals.

The radical and critical perspectives reflect the belief that there are no universally approved conduct norms that are not challenged by some facet of society. To these criminologists, opposition is inevitable since the law acts solely in the interest of the capitalist ruling class, which has either managed to write the laws in its own interest and thus legislate the legality of its acts or omissions, or has persuaded members of other social classes to compose, legislate, support, and enforce laws in the interest of the ruling class—laws directly in opposition to their own class interests.

From the radical criminological perspective, then, crime is not the mere violation of generally or universally accepted conduct norms which have been legally codified into law, but is rather the codification of the production and distribution of goods and services. For the radical criminologist, law is the codification of economic vested interest; it is the codification of the following processes noted and discussed by Quinney (1979):

(1) The *definition of law*, that is, the legal sanctioning of the act and omissions by or in the interest of the capitalist ruling class.

(2) The *process* by which so-called conduct norms are codified into legally proscribed and sanctioned actions.

(3) The *enforcement* of the vested interest of a small sector of the population currently existent under a profit motivated economy, that is, the enforcement of the vested interest of the capitalist ruling class.

The critical or non-radical (non-Marxist) criminologist would agree with the radical (Marxist) contention that crime is merely a code word for the codification of vested interests and privileges. The question for the critical criminologist is whether this vested interest and privilege can be equated with the guaranteed interest and privilege amassed by the monopoly capitalists: Can it be equated with one's economic class, one's position in the capitalist, socioeconomic political order?

The complexity that surrounds the definitional issues of crime and criminality are further complicated by the issues of race and ethnicity, poverty, urbanization, urbanism, and ghettoization. For example, unemployment and underemployment, high rates of infant mortality and morbidity coupled with inadequate housing are the trademarks of the black slum-ghetto. Thus, the prime issue for some criminologists concerned with minority criminality and criminal victimization is not simply whether or not non-whites are disproportionately represented among the ranks of the criminal and the victimized, but rather what role race, ethnicity, and poverty play in this complex relationship.

COMPLEXITIES SURROUNDING THE CONCEPTS
OF RACE AND ETHNICITY

Most Americans have witnessed, if not participated in, racial and ethnic stereotyping of crime and criminals. The news media and mass entertainment media are rife with examples of racial and ethnic stereotypes, from portrayals of Italian gangsters, to Jewish loan sharks, to black rapists and armed robbers.

More objective pictures of minority members are purportedly offered by federal, state, and local municipalities that frequently collect crime-related data cross tabulated by various demographic characteristics, including race and ethnicity. For example, the FBI's *Crime in the United States, 1982* (1983) includes racial and ethnic data tabulated by arrests (by offense) by race and ethnicity as well as racial and ethnic data on murder victims (see Tables 1 and 2 respectively).

Table 1, "Total Arrests, Distribution by Race, 1982, for Crime Index Offenses" reveals that more whites than non-whites were charged and arrested for aggravated assault, burglary, larceny-theft, motor vehicle theft, and arson. However, non-whites, especially blacks, were disproportionately represented among persons charged and arrested for all of the crimes included in the FBI Crime Index. Blacks were also more numerous among those arrested and charged with murder and non-negligent manslaughter, forcible rape, and robbery.

Official criminal justice agency data on murder victims in 1982 (FBI, 1983) (see Table 2) reveals 42.3 percent of the murder victims were black, while 1980 criminal victimization data for the crimes of rape, robbery, assault, and theft reveal the following race and ethnic-based findings (Paez, 1982):

— Blacks experienced violent crime at an overall rate higher than that for whites but not significantly higher than members of other minority races. There was also no significant difference between the rates for whites or members of other races.
— The difference in vulnerability for whites and blacks chiefly was the result of a high robbery rate among blacks.
— The difference in victimization for whites and blacks reveals that personal contact during the victimization is more common for blacks than whites.

In considering victimization rates, the differential in rate of blacks and whites reporting crimes and criminal victimization needs to be considered. This differential rate of reporting appears to be affected by socioeconomic factors such as income and homeownership versus rentership. Lynn A.

Curtis (1975) and the U.S. Department of Justices' national crime survey, *Criminal Victimization in the United States, 1980* (1982:72-77) also note that the rate of victim reporting is affected by the belief that—

(1) Nothing could be done
(2) Evidence of victimization was lacking
(3) The victim believed that he or she was not important enough to report
(4) The police would not want to be bothered
(5) The reporting procedure was too inconvenient or time consuming
(6) The victimization was the result of a private or personal matter
(7) The report could result in a reprisal (possibly even by the police)
(8) The victimization was reported to someone else

What does all of this mean? Are blacks just slightly more crime and victimization prone than their non-black racial and ethnic counterparts? If so, is this crime and victimization proneness a true racial factor, that is, a genetic factor, rather than a cultural variable associated with poverty and urbanism?

THE SOCIAL AND BIOLOGICAL SIGNIFICANCE OF RACE AND ETHNICITY

Race

There is no single universally accepted definition of race. Thus, most blacks do not fit any single ideal racial construct. By social definition, most people probably identify racial groups by means of rather crude and at times vague "racial" characteristics of one or more other races, such as dark complexioned Arabs or kinky-haired Jews and Latins. The most common racial identifiers, and thus definitions of race, often rely on biological characteristics socially and culturally prescribed as the overt physical characteristics of given ethnic and racial groups. These racial identifiers are the legacy of custom and are often tied to varied conditions of social, economic, and political defense and power. For example, in some countries the most basic determinant of race is the race of the mother (the legacy of slavery—slavery status was passed from generation to generation, regardless of the race of the father). A classic American application of the significance of maternal race classification is the usual non-white or black social classification of such seemingly white people as Delaware Whites (Delaware), Jackson Whites (New York), and Creoles (Louisiana). One should also note that the Census Bureau has allowed for self-classifying, as in

1970 and 1980 censuses, while its agents were the determiners of race during previous census interviews. It is also obvious that such vital statistics as birth records are frequently suspect as to accurate racial classification. These statistics are, in part, faulty because one or both of the parents are unavailable at the time of the child's birth to declare race, or one or both parents intentionally falsifies the declared racial declaration. It should also be noted that some countries, such as Cuba, no longer collect official racial data; yet their citizens frequently immigrate to countries which do tabulate racial and ethnic data.

What is race? The *Dictionary of Sociology* (Fairchild, 1966: 25) defines race as follows:

> A biological subdivision based upon similarity of ancestry and consequent physical kinship . . . The ideal race is a group of organisms all descended from a single ancestor, or pair of ancestors, without the introduction of any external germ plasm during the entire series of generations.

However, Gordon (1964: 27) defines race as—

> . . . differential concentrations of gene frequencies responsible for traits which, so far as we know, are confined to physical manifestations such as skin color or hair form; it has no connection with cultural patterns and institutions.

These characteristics seem to cancel any attempt to link racial characteristics directly to evolution and crime proneness. Nonetheless, such an attempt to associate race with atavism, physical degeneracy, and crime proneness has been and continues to be a social reality.

For the social scientist, racial and evolutionary crime causation arguments have not stood the test of empiricism or sound logic, which would call for the testing of the following questions (paraphrased from those asked in *Crimes of Violence* (1969):

(1) Of all those who commit criminal acts, what percent exhibits possibly relevant racial and/or evolutionary features?

(2) Of all those who have a racial or evolutionary feature possibly relevant to criminal behavior, what percent commit criminal acts?

(3) Of all those who do not commit criminal acts, what percent exhibit the racial or evolutionary feature presumably relevant to criminal behavior?

(4) Of all those who do not have a racial or evolutionary feature relevant to criminal behavior, what percent commit criminal behavior?

In sum, biological and social definitions of race have—

(1) Designated 3 of 5 racial categories based on a people's location on earth (i.e., spatial location); this is often referred to as "geographical races" (Campbell, 1976)
(2) Stressed physical characteristics such as skin color, nasal index, hair texture, head form, hair and eye color, facial index, and stature
(3) Stressed perceived intelligence
(4) Stressed the legacy of culture and historical circumstance
(5) Stressed superficial differences in internal physiology

Yet scientists and non-scientists alike often confuse social and cultural realities for biological realities. This confusion is largely due to spurious associations and faulty inferential procedures. For example, note that the U.S. Department of Justice's *Criminal Victimization in the United States, 1980* allowed the interviewer to define the interviewees' race upon observation and to ask only about persons not related to the head of the household who were not present at the time of the interview. The racial categories distinguished were grouped into three broad categories: white, black, and other, with "other" referring mainly to American Indians and persons of Asian ancestry (FBI, 1980:97). Obviously, this gross method of categorization can promote major misconceptions when crime and victimization rates are broken down by race.

Ethnicity

One of the most frequently misused social identifiers is ethnicity. Like race, there is no universally accepted definition of ethnicity. In fact, the terms race and ethnicity are often used interchangeably, such as when one's nationality is used as a racial classifier. For instance, the appellation "Puerto Rican" seems to be used more as a racial rather than an ethnic identifier.

What is ethnicity? The term appears to be derived from the Greek word for people, "ethnos." Three classic definitions of ethnicity follow:

(1) . . . the unity of both race and nationality (Fairchild, 1966:109).
(2) ". . . common ties of race or nationality or culture" (Morris, 1968:-167).
(3) ". . . any group which is defined or set off by race, religion, or national origin, or some combination of these categories" (Gordon, 1964:27).

Ethnicity can be defined, then, as the intersection of race, culture, and place of origin. From a more abstract perspective, ethnicity is the foundation for the sense of "weness" or self-identification that unites a culture and society.

There can be little argument that this "weness," based on a strong cultural identification, is demeaned by wholesale references that mistake race for nationality. Consider the misconceptions that are perpetrated by the U.S. Department of Justice's *Criminal Victimization in the United States, 1980* when it delineates ethnicity simply as "a distinction between Hispanic and non-Hispanic respondents, regardless of race." Subsequently, Hispanics are defined as "persons who report themselves as Mexican-American, Chicano, Mexican, Mexicano, Puerto Rican, Cuban, Central or South American, or other Spanish culture or origin, regardless of race" (Paez, 1982:96). Again, how can data based on such broad and misleading definitions of ethnicity and a concomitant disregard for race contribute to realistic efforts to understand and control crime in society?

CONCLUSION

There can be little doubt that blacks commit a disproportionate number of FBI Crime Index offenses, and are in turn, disproportionately victimized by crimes involving physical contact. Nonetheless, the issue of who is "black" and what is meant by the terms race and ethnicity remain serious social science questions. These questions need to be answered since racial and ethnic demographic data associated with crime and victimization rates include major inaccuracies due to typing offenders and victims by race and ethnicity. These inaccuracies probably affect crime data at all levels, from records of police response to calls, to that of arrest, conviction, and incarceration. This reality of confused or vague racial and ethnic identification is exemplified by the description of the 1981 New York City "Slasher" victims. These victims were initially identified by the mass media as black. Later media reports identified some of the victims as black, presumably black American, others as hispanics—a succinct illustration of how irresponsible media coverage can serve the belief that blacks are more prone to being victims of crime than other racial and ethnic groups.

Still, conscientious social scientists, researchers, or criminal justice practitioners can be misled by stereotypical notions of race and criminal involvement. Inaccurate labeling, as reflected in official statistics, or irresponsible reportage, as presented in sensational newspaper coverages of crimes, lead to serious misconceptions which mask the social and biological dynamics that underlie criminal behavior. In addition, the belief that certain racial and ethnic groups are biologically predestined to commit crime has dangerous implications for the future of criminal justice: if individuals are biologically motivated to commit crime, recommended reforms based on addressing the pressing needs of the poor, must be dismissed as irrelevant in fashioning crime control strategies. Such a reliance on biological theories can easily justify a retributive approach to justice as it can exonerate a society of all responsibility in placing blame for minority crime.

References

Campbell, Bernard G., ed. Human Kind Emergencing (2nd.), Boston: Little, Brown and Co., 1976.

Curtis, Lynn A. Violence, Race, and Culture. Lexington, MA: D.C. Heath and Co., 1975.

Fairchild, Henry Pratt, ed. Dictionary of Sociology. Totowa, NJ: Littlefield, Adams, and Co. 1966.

FBI Uniform Crime Reports for the United States, 1982. U.S. Department of Justice, Washington, D.C.: U.S. Government Printing Office, 1983.

Gordon, Milton. Assimilation in American Life. New York: Oxford University Press, 1964.

National Commission on the Causes and Prevention of Violence. Crimes of Violence, vol. 12—A Staff Report. Washington, D.C.: U.S. Government Printing Office, 1969.

Paez, Adolfo L. U.S. Department of Justice. Criminal Victimization in the United States, 1980. Washington, D.C.: U.S. Government Printing Office, 1982.

Quinney, Richard. Criminology (2nd ed.) Boston: Little, Brown and Co., 1979.

Sellin, Thorsten. "Culture, conflict, and crime," Bulletin #41. New York: Social Science Research Council, 1938.

Sykes, Gresham. Criminology. New York: Harcourt Brace Jovanovich, Inc., 1978.

Tappan, Paul. Crime, Justice and Correction. New York: McGraw-Hill, 1960.

Table 1   Total Arrests, Distribution by Race, 1982* for Crime Index Offenses

[9,789 agencies; 1982 estimated population 186,480,000]

Offense charged	Total arrests					Percent distribution**				
	Total	White	Black	American Indian or Alaskan Native	Asian or Pacific Islander	Total	White	Black	American Indian or Alaskan Native	Asian or Pacific Islander
TOTAL	10,000,078	7,070,374	2,777,145	91,845	60,714	100.0	70.7	27.8	.9	.6
Murder and nonnegligent manslaughter	18,475	9,008	9,174	141	152	100.0	48.8	49.7	.8	.8
Forcible rape	28,179	13,730	13,991	244	214	100.0	48.7	49.7	.9	.8
Robbery	137,562	52,480	83,522	629	931	100.0	38.2	60.7	.5	.7
Aggravated assault	257,607	154,035	99,842	2,264	1,466	100.0	59.8	38.8	.9	.6
Burglary	433,774	290,678	137,494	2,931	2,671	100.0	67.0	31.7	.7	.6
Larceny-theft	1,137,329	736,023	379,373	9,638	12,295	100.0	64.7	33.4	.8	1.1
Motor vehicle theft	108,279	72,466	33,989	946	878	100.0	66.9	31.4	.9	.8
Arson	16,810	12,446	4,159	147	58	100.0	74.0	24.7	.9	.3
Violent crime	441,823	229,253	206,529	3,278	2,763	100.0	51.9	46.7	.7	.6
Property crime	1,696,192	1,111,613	555,015	13,662	15,902	100.0	65.5	32.7	.8	.9
Crime Index total	2,138,015	1,340,866	761,544	16,490	18,665	100.0	62.7	35.6	.8	.9
Other assaults	448,166	286,492	155,125	3,664	2,885	100.0	63.9	34.6	.8	.6
Forgery and counterfeiting	79,722	50,564	28,475	422	261	100.0	63.4	35.7	.5	.3
Fraud	268,969	179,286	87,683	1,280	720	100.0	66.7	32.6	.5	.3
Embezzlement	7,288	5,448	1,743	30	67	100.0	74.8	23.9	.4	.9
Stolen property; buying, receiving, possessing	114,007	71,313	41,750	535	409	100.0	62.6	36.6	.5	.4
Vandalism	200,208	159,906	37,706	1,539	1,057	100.0	79.9	18.8	.8	.5
Weapons; carrying, possessing, etc.	163,461	100,805	60,865	863	928	100.0	61.7	37.2	.5	.6

Table 1 (Cont.)

[9,789 agencies; 1982 estimated population 186,480,000]

Offense charged	Total arrests					Percent distribution**				
	Total	White	Black	American Indian or Alaskan Native	Asian or Pacific Islander	Total	White	Black	American Indian or Alaskan Native	Asian or Pacific Islander
Prostitution and commercialized vice	110,713	56,209	53,112	457	935	100.0	50.8	48.0	.4	.8
Sex offenses (except forcible rape and prostitution)	66,083	51,348	13,700	595	440	100.0	77.7	20.7	.9	.7
Drug abuse violations	562,390	400,683	156,369	2,194	3,144	100.0	71.2	27.8	.4	.6
Gambling	36,539	12,831	22,287	34	1,387	100.0	35.1	61.0	.1	3.8
Offenses against family and children	45,260	28,511	16,292	380	77	100.0	63.0	36.0	.8	.2
Driving under the influence	1,379,180	1,209,679	148,221	13,761	7,519	100.0	87.7	10.7	1.0	.5
Liquor laws	402,690	356,379	37,395	7,167	1,749	100.0	88.5	9.3	1.8	.4
Drunkenness	1,033,385	848,265	162,387	21,031	1,702	100.0	82.1	15.7	2.0	.2
Disorderly conduct	760,687	449,230	303,164	6,293	2,000	100.0	59.1	39.9	.8	.3
Vagrancy	32,127	20,671	10,820	470	166	100.0	64.3	33.7	1.5	.5
All other offenses (except traffic)	1,949,405	1,285,642	636,461	12,843	14,459	100.0	66.0	32.6	.7	.7
Suspicion	8,885	6,876	1,740	35	234	100.0	77.4	19.6	.4	2.6
Curfew and loitering law violations	78,564	53,662	23,955	417	530	100.0	68.3	30.5	.5	.7
Runaways	114,334	95,708	16,351	895	1,380	100.0	83.7	14.3	.8	1.2

* Footnotes omitted.

** Percentages may not add to total because of rounding.

Source: F.B.I., *Crime in the United States, F.B.I. Uniform Crime Report, 1982,* U.S. Government Printing Office, Washington, D.C., 1983, p. 8.

Table 2   Age, Sex, Race, and Ethnic Orgin of Murder Victims, 1982

Age	Number	Percent*	Sex			Race				Ethnic Origin		
			Male	Female	Unknown	White	Black	Other	Unknown	Hispanic	Non-Hispanic	Unknown
Total	19,485	...	14,748	4,723	14	10,799	8,235	370	81	2,808	11,985	4,692
Percent	...	100.0	75.7	24.2	.1	55.4	42.3	1.9	.4	14.4	61.5	24.1
Infant (under 1)	228	1.2	121	106	1	134	82	9	3	25	151	52
1 to 4	352	1.8	183	169	...	195	147	8	2	34	224	94
5 to 9	158	.8	88	70	...	102	54	2	...	20	94	44
10 to 14	200	1.0	106	94	...	129	68	3	...	22	116	62
15 to 19	1,525	7.8	1,148	376	1	838	662	20	5	290	880	355
20 to 24	3,217	16.5	2,467	750	...	1,703	1,444	65	5	586	1,906	725
25 to 29	3,179	16.3	2,516	663	...	1,582	1,530	61	6	520	1,926	733
30 to 34	2,561	13.1	2,076	484	1	1,254	1,249	46	12	407	1,557	597
35 to 39	1,863	9.6	1,458	405	...	1,044	777	38	4	287	1,122	454
40 to 44	1,396	7.2	1,072	324	...	833	530	31	2	189	885	322
45 to 49	1,031	5.3	814	217	...	574	431	25	1	134	662	235
50 to 54	979	5.0	777	202	...	582	373	22	2	100	650	229
55 to 59	724	3.7	563	161	...	463	254	6	1	55	460	209
60 to 64	572	2.9	431	141	...	368	193	10	1	40	380	152
65 to 69	392	2.0	261	131	...	261	127	4	...	15	282	95
70 to 74	317	1.6	201	116	...	209	101	6	1	14	227	76
75 and over	484	2.5	237	247	...	354	118	11	1	11	350	123
Unknown	307	1.6	229	67	11	174	95	3	35	59	113	135

* Percentages may not add to total because of rounding.
Source: F.B.I., *Crime in the United States, F.B.I. Uniform Crime Report, 1982*, U.S. Government Printing Office, Washington, D.C., 1983, p. 8.

Table 3   Personal Crimes, 1980: Victimization Rates for Persons Age 12 and Over, by Type of Crime and Race of Victims

[Rate per 1,000 population age 12 and over]

Type of crime	White* (157,081,000)	Black* (19,691,000)	Other* (3,578,000)
Crimes of violence	32.2	40.2	36.8
Rape	0.9	1.1	1.0
Robbery	5.7	13.9	2.4
Robbery with injury	2.0	4.3	0.0
From serious assault	1.0	2.5	0.0
From minor assault	1.1	1.8	0.0
Robbery without injury	3.7	9.6	2.5
Assault	25.5	25.2	33.4
Aggravated assault	8.7	12.3	14.4
With injury	2.8	5.0	7.5
Attempted assault with weapon	5.9	7.3	6.9
Simple assault	16.9	12.9	19.0
With injury	4.7	3.8	5.0
Attempted assault without weapon	12.2	9.1	13.4
Crimes of theft	83.2	79.1	84.9
Personal larceny with contact	2.6	6.2	4.1
Purse snatching	0.9	2.8	1.1
Pocket picking	1.7	3.5	2.9
Personal larceny without contact	80.6	72.9	80.8

* Detail may not add to total shown because of rounding. Numbers in parentheses refer to population in the group. Estimate, based on approximately 10 or fewer sample cases, is statistically unreliable.

Source: National Criminal Justice Information and Statistics Service, *Criminal Victimization in the United States, 1980.* Government Printing Office, Washington, D.C., 1982, p. 25.

Table 4   Personal Crimes, 1980: Victimization Rates for Persons Age 12 and Over, by Type of Crime and Sex and Race of Victims

[Rate per 1,000 population age 12 and over]

	Male		Female	
Type of crime	White* (75,659,000)	Black* (8,864,000)	White* (31,421,000)	Black* (10,827,000)
Crimes of violence	43.1	52.3	22.0	30.3
Rape	0.3	0.2	1.5	1.8
Robbery	7.8	20.6	3.8	8.5
Robbery with injury	2.5	6.3	1.6	2.6
Robbery without injury	5.3	14.2	2.2	5.9
Assault	35.0	31.6	16.7	20.0
Aggravated assault	13.2	18.4	4.5	7.3
Simple assault	21.8	13.2	12.3	12.6
Crimes of theft	88.5	87.2	78.4	72.5
Personal larceny with contact	1.9	3.9	3.2	8.2
Personal larceny without contact	86.6	83.3	75.1	64.3

* Detail may not add to total shown because of rounding. Numbers in parentheses refer to population in the group. Estimate, based on approximately 10 or fewer sample cases, is statistically unreliable.

Source: National Criminal Justice Information and Statistics Service, *Criminal Victimization in the United States, 1980.* Government Printing Office, Washington, D.C., 1982, p. 25.

Table 5   Personal Crimes, 1980: Victimization Rates for Persons Age 12 and Over, by Type of Crime and Ethnicity of Victims

[Rate per 1,000 population age 12 and over]

Type of crime	Hispanic* (10,035,000)	Non-Hispanic* (167,137,000)
Crimes of violence	39.8	32.7
Rape	0.7	1.0
Robbery	11.9	6.2
Robbery with injury	3.4	2.2
From serious assault	1.9	1.1
From minor assault	1.6	1.1
Robbery without injury	8.6	4.0
Assault	27.2	25.5
Aggravated assault	12.8	9.0
With injury	4.7	3.1
Attempted assault with weapon	8.1	5.8
Simple assault	14.4	16.6
With injury	4.0	4.7
Attempted assault without weapon	10.4	11.9
Crimes of theft	75.9	83.4
Personal larceny with contact	5.4	2.9
Purse snatching	2.3	1.0
Pocket picking	3.1	1.9
Personal larceny without contact	70.5	80.5

* Detail may not add to total shown because of rounding. Numbers in parentheses refer to population in the group. Estimate, based on approximately 10 or fewer sample cases, is statistically unreliable.

Source: National Criminal Justice Information and Statistics Service, *Criminal Victimization in the United States, 1980.* Government Printing Office, Washington, D.C., 1982, p. 26.

2

Perspectives on Race and Crime in Research and Planning*

Barry C. Sample and Michael Philip, Jr.

Race consistently turns up as a major correlate of arrest, conviction, and incarceration. The inquiries of criminal justice researchers and planners in this area can result in lending scientific credence to various ideological positions on this emotionally charged issue. Their conclusions may also have implications for policy in the areas of race relations and social control. However, research in the area of race and crime has been criticized. Some have argued that an interest in correlations between race and crime is a form of racism and others have contended that the collection of statistics about the racial characteristics of offenders perpetuates errors and myths. One purpose of this chapter is to assess the validity of these and similar claims. In particular, the emphasis will be upon the operation of bias in race and crime research.

Bias can be grouped into two basic categories: overt bias and indirect bias. Overt bias involves placing or keeping persons in a position of subordination through the direct use of mechanisms related to their race. This deliberate form of bias has been inimical to the basic values traditionally held by researchers. Research grounded in overt bias axiomatically produces results that confirm the vested interest of researchers. Indirect bias is the unintentional assignment of persons to a position of subordination through the use of race. This bias can be found in the research techniques, political social beliefs, and the theoretical/substantive orientations of researchers and planners. Bias generated by the research technique can occur at numerous points in the research process, but it is particularly problematic when determining the appropriate questions to be asked. At this stage, an investigation can cease to be objective in any meaningful sense, and can unintentionally become an exercise in proving or disproving a position.[1]

---

* A version of this chapter was issued as a separate report by the Office of Program Development and Research, New York State Division of Criminal Justice Services. The authors would like to thank several colleagues for their contributions: Scott Christianson, Bruce Frederick, William Oliver, and Sherwood E. Zimmerman.

21

The research product is ultimately a reflection of the researchers' conception of what is important and worthy of examination and, by implication, what does not warrant consideration. Similarly, a researcher's quantitative training limits the way that research questions are addressed, and the methodology employed can influence research findings. For example, it is easier to identify discriminatory attitudes from a survey than it is to discern deliberately discriminatory behavior in a study of criminal justice processing.

Furthermore, the political and social beliefs of researchers and planners may also influence the research perspective. For example, Gunnar Myrdal notes a form of indirect bias in studies of racial discrimination that is related to a researcher's political perspective:

> The place of the individual scientist in the scale of radicalism-conservatism has always had, and still has, strong influences upon both the selection of research problems and the conclusions drawn from research. In a sense, it is the master scale of biases in the social sciences. Usually the more radical a scientist is in his political views, the more friendly to the Negro cause he will feel, and consequently, the more inclined he will be to undertake and carry out studies which favor the Negro cause.[2]

Finally, the conceptual framework or theory a researcher applies to a social question influences the ultimate findings. This issue is further complicated by the lack of confirmed social theory and the multiple theories available to explain social phenomenon. For example, what are now regarded by some as overtly racist theories of minority group crime were common—indeed normative—among criminologists of the nineteenth and early twentieth centuries.[3] However, aside from the efforts of a handful of more recent theorists,[4] whose work is generally regarded as a bit anachronistic, efforts to link criminality with racial characteristics seem to have gone the way of physical type theories generally.[5]

This final area of indirect bias, conceptual framework and theory, is the focus of this chapter,[6] which examines two competing schools of thought in race and crime research: those theories that focus upon internal influences and those that focus upon external constraints.[7]

INTERNAL INFLUENCES

Environmentally oriented theories have predominated studies of crime for the past three decades. However, from a cursory review of the literature on race and crime, it is evident that the internal influences orientation, or variants of it, was never entirely abandoned. Today, internal based theories have found new currency in the efforts of a growing number of researchers to isolate the personality characteristics that differentiate criminals from non-criminals. The studies produced examine personality differences among racial groups, and between criminals and non-criminals of the same race, in an effort to explain racial differences in criminal behavior.[8]

Individual Theories

Significant in this body of research is the relatively large number of studies that have examined racial variations in delinquency as a function of I.Q. and/or academic achievement. Hirschi, for instance, found that differences in academic achievement, as measured by Differential Aptitude Test verbal scores, explained much of the difference between blacks and whites in self-reported delinquent activity.[9] Wolfgang, Figlio, and Sellin in their Philadelphia cohort study found I.Q. to differentiate not only between delinquents and non-delinquents (as measured by recorded police contact) but between delinquents and non-delinquents within racially and socio-economically homogenous groups, and between blacks and whites overall.[10] Similar findings have been reported by other researchers.[11] Studies of personality differentials in delinquency among racial groups have examined such diverse aspects of personality as Interpersonal Maturity Level (I level),[12] self-concept,[13] achievement motivation,[14] locus of control,[15] frustration tolerance,[16] impulse control,[17] stimulus hunger,[18] future time perspective,[19] extroversion,[20] neuroticism,[21] trustworthiness,[22] mood states,[23] prejudice,[24] and alienation.[25]

Many of these studies are methodologically adequate and have internally valid findings; however, the conclusions drawn from them may be misleading. The studies start with the presumption that the causes of crime can be found in individual pathologies. Hence, when applied to the question of race and crime they tend to perpetuate the myth of racial inferiority. In part this is because systematic efforts to critically examine the theoretical foundations of such findings have been rare.[26] In addition, attempts to address cultural and other biases inherent in the measures used have been infrequent in studies of race and crime.

Specifically, the research discussed above is notable for its lack of attention to the role played by racial subordination and other environmental factors in personality formation. Also, there is little recognition by these researchers that crime is not a quality that is inherent in behavior; crime is a creation of law, and as such, is subject to all the vagaries of politics and custom. Personality traits may arguably predispose some individuals to aggressive, impulsive, and self-serving responses to situational factors. The transition from an aggressive or impulsive behavior to committing a criminal act requires not only the behavioral act, but also the existence of a law that comprehends that behavior and prohibits it. Variability in legal proscriptions and their enforcement is one of the intangibles that personality research has only superficially examined.[27] This failure to consider factors external to the individual creates the impression that personality exists independent of environment and that crime is the work of defective individuals. Hence, it is the focus of such research, rather than any conscious intent on the part of the researcher, that perpetuates stereotypes of racial inferiority.

It is not argued that personality has no influence on crime. Personal characteristics may be a factor in some crimes. Moreover, it does not seem unreasonable that the distribution of some of these characteristics may differ between racial groups. Two points, however, should be considered in this regard. First, the weight of anthropological and genetic research supports the view that any psychological attribute common to a given racial group is more likely to be due to a common social and historical background than to genetic factors. Recognizing this, a number of criminologists have begun to explore the possibility that certain aspects of personality, particularly self-esteem, may act as intervening variables between racial subordination on the one hand, and crime on the other.[28]

A second point requiring emphasis is that individual-level variables, (such as self-esteem, I.Q., and aggressiveness,) that are correlated with criminal behavior can be interpreted as factors that explain the fraction of crime not explained by external factors. Internal variables can be employed to explain differences in criminality among individuals who are similarly situated with respect to race, socioeconomic status, and other environmental factors. From this perspective, reference to individual differences may be misleading when interpreted as directly explaining differential crime rates among racial groups.[29]

Social Disorganization Theories

Several lines of reasoning have been explored within the broader context of the black ghetto environment. Many researchers have followed the lead of E. Franklin Frazier,[30] who examined the hypothesis that high rates of crime and delinquency among blacks can be attributed to the disorganization and instability of black family life. Patriarchal absence and an alleged matriarchal family structure have been prominent themes in this tradition. In 1965 the U.S. Department of Labor published a report that attributed a variety of socially undesirable behaviors, including disproportionate rates of crime and delinquency, to the alleged matriarchal structure of black families in the United States.[31] Empirical support for the existence of a black matriarchy has not been forthcoming.[32] Research has not demonstrated either the existence of a predominantly matriarchal family structure among blacks or a significant connection between female-dominated households and juvenile delinquency among black youth.[33]

The significance of the matriarchy hypothesis should not be underestimated, however, since it has generated considerable empirical research and has contributed to the development of a negative image of black families. The Labor Department study traced the origin of sex role reversal in the black family to the historical condition of slavery, which, it claimed, "destroy[ed] the Negro family" and "broke the will of the Negro people."[34] The importance of the historical antecedent—slavery—was lost in the concentration upon the "tangle of pathology"[35] that allegedly resulted from the reversal of sex roles. Thus, the emphasis in the Department of Labor report and in the ensuing literature is on the "pathology" resulting from female dominance rather than on slavery, and its impact upon family organization. The implication for research based on the matriarchy hypothesis was that black families, because of their domination by females, were pathological. The derivative areas for research became the extent to which black families are afflicted by this pathology, and the degree to which this pathological family structure contributes to crime and delinquency. Thus, the research, by the nature of the questions it asked, examined and located criminal pathology within the black family. Association of the term pathology with the black family also draws attention away from the disorganizing effects of slavery, and, in the process, may reinforce notions of racial inferiority.

Research into broader patterns of social disorganization in black ghettos, and the consequent breakdown of parental and community controls on behavior, have pervaded recent delinquency literature. The classic studies by Thrasher[36] and Shaw and McKay[37] have been supplemented by works that discuss the effects of deteriorated neighborhoods, inadequate housing, and recreational facilities on inhabitants of black ghettos.[38] The social disorganization tradition treats crime and delinquency in ghetto areas as a product of a breakdown of those institutions responsible for socialization. More specifically, this perspective focuses on the emergency of conflicting systems of values in impoverished neighborhoods and the consequent inability of the community to transmit to its young a consistent set of conventional values. While reference is made to the devastating effects of poverty on community organization, the primary concentration is on the failure of the community to socialize its youth adequately.

Adherents of this perspective have not explained the causes of social disorganization and its attendant institutional breakdowns. They have also failed to adequately examine the differential inability of blacks to overcome the allegedly disorganizing influences of poverty. Failure to examine external factors, such as racial discrimination and deprivation, results in placing the burden of crime on the black community and implicitly portraying it as pathological. Thus, despite the good intentions of these theorists and researchers, and even despite their occasional references to the black experience in America, racial inferiority can be, and has been, implied in their work.[39]

Subcultural Theories

The notion that crime is normative within the black community and that it is learned within the course of normal social interaction is another theoretical perspective that fails to avoid the inference of racial inferiority.

This perspective in its purest form[40] argues that patterns of violence are normative among large segments of the lower class black population. Residents of urban ghettos are viewed as developing favorable attitudes toward the use of violence as the result of normal learning processes.[41] This perspective stresses compulsive masculinity as a principal component and distinguishing feature of violent subcultures. Expressions of masculinity are viewed as means to attain acceptance and recognition in subcultures that value toughness and fighting ability.[42]

The question that remains unanswered, and that cannot be answered without stepping outside the subcultural perspective, is how to account for the emergence of subcultural patterns of violence in black communities. Traditions of violence can explain the persistence of violent norms, but they cannot explain their origin. For this purpose, many theorists who offer a subcultural interpretation of violence have found it necessary to step outside their perspective and introduce extra-subcultural factors to explain the importance of toughness in ghetto environments. Lynn Curtis, in what is probably the most cogent presentation of a violent contraculture thesis, rejects the notion that violent contracultural patterns can be explained without reference to contingencies external to the ghetto environment.[43] He argues that racial-economic constraints have causal primacy in determining black behavior, but that culture is a critical intervening variable.[44]

The subcultural approach has biases similar to those found in the approach that focuses upon individual differences. Just as looking only for individual-level differences between criminals and non-criminals ensures an individual-level explanation of behavioral differences, looking only at cultural-level factors ensures localization of the criminal pathology within the culture. By asking questions that can only elicit a cultural-level answer, this research infers that the issue is not where the pathology lies, or even whether the black community is pathological; instead the issue becomes the pervasiveness of the pathology within the culture.

EXTERNAL INFLUENCES

To avoid the implication that black criminality can be explained solely by factors existing within the black community, researchers should also look for factors external to the community. Numerous researchers have explored the ways in which deprivation and racial discrimination may affect crime rates of blacks.

Differential Processing

Thorsten Sellin was one of the first to raise the issue of whether the discrepancy between the crime rates of blacks and whites, as reflected in official criminal statistics, is a fair representation of differences in behavior or the result of differential treatment by agencies of criminal justice.[45] Sellin hesitated to answer this question, citing the inadequacies of data then available for an evaluation of the many factors involved.[46] Today, in spite of improvements in the kinds of statistics and measurement techniques researchers have at their disposal, the question remains unanswered. It has been suggested that racial discrimination in the justice system distorts the crime rates of blacks as reflected in official statistics.[47] However, the question of whether enforcement practices and policies account for a large portion of the discrepancy between black and white crime rates has not been resolved.

The weight of recent empirical evidence seems to support the view that racial differences in arrest rates are not entirely explained by discriminatory enforcement. The disparity in arrest rates also reflects the differential degree of involvement of blacks in the kinds of crime most likely to come to the attention of the police—(i.e., "street crime").[48] If measures of offenses less likely to be reported to, and acted on, by law enforcement authorities were available, the differential between black and white arrest rates would be reduced.[49]

Therefore, efforts to determine whether there is a connection between race and crime should examine the empirical evidence and the legal/historical material to determine the extent to which crime rates are affected by inequalities in legislation, law enforcement, and data collection. In addition to considering the justice system itself as one source of racial discrimination, other sources that affect minority group crime must be explored.

Relative Deprivation

Several lines of reasoning have been employed in examining the influence of racial and economic barriers on minority crime. One approach, following the logic of Robert Merton,[50] attempts to explain ghetto crime in terms of relative deprivation and the opportunity structure of American society. In this view barriers to achieving success through legitimate avenues result in the pursuit of illegal alternatives. This approach attributes high crime rates among blacks to employment, discrimination, and their low socioeconomic status.[51]

There may be appeal in the notion that crime is a product of unequal economic distribution. By focusing on relative deprivation and the inequities suffered by minorities, this approach attempts to avoid the inferences of racial inferiority implied in approaches that concentrate on pathologies of the community, the family, or the individual.[52] However, it contravenes the empirical evidence indicating that there are significant racial differences within socioeconomically homogeneous categories.[53] This evidence cannot be interpreted as proving there is no explanatory value in the relative deprivation thesis. It does caution against attempts to explain crime rate differences among races solely in terms of economic status and opportunity structures.

Colonial Theory

Colonial theory attributes disproportionate crime rates among blacks to the history of slavery and the persistent status of racial subordination. Blacks and other racial minorities are viewed as a colonized people whose economics and politics are controlled by white outsiders.[54] This perspective emphasizes the dehumanizing effect that racism has had upon black community life and self-esteem.[55] The most cogent presentation of the colonial perspective, as it relates to criminal activity, was presented by Frantz Fanon.[56] Fannon contended that racism was a product of most contemporary colonial relationships. He posited that blacks become hostile and suspicious as a result of racism. Criminal activity, particularly aggressive behavior, was viewed as a product of black hostility toward white society. The aggressive behavior is not initially directed against the colonizing power. It is turned inward and directed toward other blacks. Inevitably, however, the hostility and aggression is turned outward and directed against whites who are viewed as the ruling elite. In this context, crime is viewed as a revolutionary act and the shift from black-on-black crime toward black-on-white crime is seen as an evolutionary stage in the liberation struggle.

The primary limitation of the colonial perspective is the failure to realize that patterns of crime have differed among groups that have experienced colonization. Furthermore, the differences cannot be entirely explained by the variation that may exist in the experience with racism. Consequently, differences in the pattern of exploitation, history, geography, and culture are important factors that the colonial perspective does not adequately provide.

Radical Theory

The radical perspective has viewed crime as a byproduct of the capitalist mode of production and associated labor practices. Racial differences in crime are explained in terms of the historically conditioned relation of different ethnic groups to the means of production. According to this perspective, crime emerges as a rational response by individuals who are marginal to the production process. Rates of street crime are expected to be high among those groups in which institutionalized racism and capitalist exploitation have resulted in high levels of unemployment and demoralization, and low among groups in which these features have not been produced.[57] Such an analysis may seem peculiarly relevant to the study of race and crime. The radical perspective makes note of the differing kinds of economic exploitation suffered by racial groups and the possibility that this may have an effect upon the racial distribution of street crime. In addition, the radical theorist, particularly the Marxist theorist, has brought a sense of history to the study of crime that is largely absent in other approaches.

Most agree, however, that in general attempts by external theorists to draw causal connections between crime and the twin themes of discrimination and deprivation have not provided satisfactory explanations of minority group crime. Such approaches cannot explain within-group differences in criminal behavior, as can approaches that focus on the individual or the family. Nor can they explain differences between minority groups that have undergone similar discrimination and deprivation. Nevertheless, these approaches do provide valuable insight into important questions that do not arise in research focusing upon the pathology of racial groups. Consequently, an understanding of the role of discrimination and deprivation complements existing theory and research, rather than forming a competing paradigm.

CONCLUSION

A principal implication of the present review is that the relationship between race and crime is inadequately explained, and causal connections are inappropriate when the relationship is construed as the product of pathologies existing within the individual, the family, or the community. Rather, a satisfactory explanation of racial variations in crime should recognize the complex nature of the phenomenon it seeks to explain. The laws themselves may reflect racial biases, their enforcement may reflect discriminatory policing and, finally, their interpretation and application in the courts may compound any such biases, introduce new biases, or both.

However, discrimination may not influence the behaviors legally regarded as crimes. The relationship between race and crime may operate through a number of intervening variables. These include social disorganization, economic status, aspects of personality, effects on physical and biological characteristics, and subcultural or contracultural adaptations. Yet the incorporation of any of the above into an explanation of crime rate differences among races is not complete if it does not explore as well the possible antecedent effects of discrimination and deprivation. To this end, a historical and comparative analysis of the relationship between race and crime would be useful. Through such an analysis, individual and community characteristics may be transcended to develop a comprehensive theoretical explanation.

The foregoing is not intended as a comprehensive review of the literature on race and crime. Rather, what has been attempted is a critique of prominent themes within that body of literature. A value orientation toward race and race relations is implicit in each of the perspectives discussed, and none of these approaches provides, by itself, a complete explanation of the phenomenon. Therefore, although objectivity may be a desirable goal of research and planning, it is at best elusive, and at worst a stumbling block in the way of understanding. Adherence to a supposedly objective research paradigm may, in fact, result in failure to examine important causal relations and may, as observed in this chapter, lead to value-laden conclusions.

Notes

1 Alvin Gouldner, "Anti-Minotaur: The Myth of a Value-Free Sociology," *Social Problems* 9 (Winter 1962): 199-213. See also Alvin Gouldner, "The Sociologist as Partisan: Sociology and the Welfare State," *The American Sociologist* 3 (May 1968): 103-116.

2 Gunnar Myrdal, *An American Dilemma: The Negro Problem and Modern Democracy* (New York: Pantheon Books, 1944), p. 1038.

3 See, for example, Frederick L. Hoffman, *Race Traits and Tendencies of the American Negro* (New York: MacMillan, 1896), especially pp. 217-235; Cesare Lombroso, *Neue Verbrecher-Studien,* quoted in Willem Adrian Bonger, *Race and Crime* (Montclair, New Jersey: Patterson-Smith, 1969); David A. Orebough, *Crime, Degeneracy and Immigration* (Boston: Gorman Press, 1929). Discussions of typical theories of this period are included in Bonger, *Race and Crime,* this note. See also Charles H. McCord, *The American Negro as a Dependent, Defective and Delinquent* (Nashville: Press of Benson, 1914).

4 See, for example, William Schockley, "A 'Try Simplest Cases' Approach to the Heredity-Poverty-Crime Problem," *Proceedings of the National Academy of Sciences* 57 (June 1967): 1767-1774;

Robert A. Gordon, "Crime and Cognition: An Evolutionary Perspective," paper presented at the Second International Symposium on Criminology, International Center for Biological and Medico-Forensic Criminology, Sao Paulo, Brazil (1975).

5 Indeed, such efforts to co-opt scientific evidence into the service of such an enterprise were decried by no less an authority on physical type theories than E.A. Hooton, who commented in 1926 that "Certain writers on racial subjects, usually not professional anthropologists, associate cultural and psychological characteristics with physical types on wholly insufficient evidence. These race propagandists commonly attribute to the physical subdivision of mankind to which they imagine that they themselves belong all or most of the superior qualities of mankind, physical, mental and moral. They talk of the psychological characteristics of this or that race as if they were objective tangible properties, scientifically demonstrated. Starting from an *a priori* assumption that physical types have psychological correlates, they attempt to refer every manifestation of the psychological qualities assumed to be the exclusive property of this or that race to the physical type in question." E.A. Hooton, "Methods of Racial Analysis," *Science* 63 (1926):81.

6 Charles E. Reasons, ed., *The Criminologist, Crime and the Criminal* (Santa Monica, Calif.: Goodyear, 1974), p. 92.

7 Since black crime has received far more attention from criminologists than crime committed by other racial minorities in the United States, this chapter focuses in large part on a critique of that body of literature.

8 Most personality research has concentrated on differences between blacks and whites, although a few researchers have included other races in their analyses. The present review includes a variety of biological and psychological characteristics under the rubric of "personality." While this represents an oversimplification of the vast number of such characteristics that have been studied by criminologists, their inclusion within a single category is justified for the present purposes. Students of these correlates of crime have generally failed to trace social origins or to examine whether etiology may be social rather than individual or inherited.

9 Travis Hirschi, *Causes of Delinquency* (Berkley: University of California Press, 1969), p. 81.

10 Marvin Wolfgang, R.M. Figlio, and Thorsten Sellin, *Delinquency in a Birth Cohort* (Chicago: University of Chicago Press, 1972).

11 See, for example, Gordon, *Crime and Cognition,* note 6, supra; Albert J. Reiss, Jr. and Albert Louis Rhodes, "Are Educational Norms and Goals of Conforming, Truant and Delinquent Adolescents Influenced by Group Position in American Society?" *Journal of Negro Education* 3 (1959): 252-267; Vernon Fox, "Intelligence, Race and Age as Selective Factors in Crime," *Journal of Criminal Law, Criminology and Police Science* 37 (1946-1947): 141-152; Vernon Fox and Joann Volakakis, "The Negro Offender in a Northern Industrial Area," *Journal of Criminal Law, Criminology and Police Science* 46 (1956): 641-647; John J. Henning and Russell H. Levy, "Verbal-Performance IQ Differences of Negro Delinquents on the WISC and WAIS," *Journal of Clinical Psychology* 23 (1967): 164-168; R.J. Oldroyd and R.J. Howell, "Personality, Intellectual and Behavioral Differences Between Black, Chicano and White Prison Inmates in the Utah State Prison," *Psychological Reports* 4 (1977): 187-191; S.L. Boone and A. Montare, "Test of the Language-Aggression Hypothesis," *Psychological Reports* 39 (1976): 851-857. For review of the literature in this area, see Travis Hirschi and Michael J. Hindelang, "Intelligence and Delinquency," *American Sociological Review* 42 (1977): 571.

12 Herbert J. Cross and James J. Tracy, "Personality Factors in Delinquent Boys: Differences Between Blacks and Whites," *Journal of Research in Crime and Delinquency* 8 (1971): 10-22; Eric Werner, "Psychological and Ethnic Correlates of Interpersonal Maturity Among Delinquents," *British Journal of Criminology* 15 (1975): 51-67.

13 Douglas E. Wax, "Self-Concept in Negro and White Pre-Adolescent Delinquent Boys,"

British Journal of Criminology 14 (1974): 165-171; Anthony R. Harris, "Race, Commitment to Deviance and Spoiled Identity," *American Sociological Review* 41 (1976): 432-442; G.W. Healey and R.R. DeBlassie, "A Comparison of Negro, Anglo and Spanish-American Adolescents' Self-Concepts," *Adolescence,* 9(33): 15-24, (1974); Oldroyd and Howell, "Personality, Intellectual and Behavioral Differences," note 11, supra; Robert P. Daniel, "Personality Differences Between Delinquent and Non-Delinquent Negro Boys, *Journal of Negro Education* 1 (1932): 381-387; J.R. Lilly and R.A. Ball, "Norm Neutralization, Anomia and Self-Concept Among Institutionalized Female Delinquents," paper presented at the 28th Annual Meeting of the American Society of Criminology, Tucson, Arizona, 1976.

14 Frank H. Farley and Trevor Sewell, "Attribution and Achievement Motivation Differences Between Delinquent and Non-Delinquent Black Adolescents," *Adolescence* 10 (Fall 1975): 301-397.

15 Cross and Tracy, "Personality Factors," note 12, supra; Frank H. Farley and Trevor Sewell, "Test of an Arousal Theory of Delinquency: Stimulation-Seeking in Delinquent and Non-Delinquent Black Adolescents," *Criminal Justice and Behavior* 3 (1976): 315-320.

16 Ralph D. Norman and Gerald J. Kleinfeld, "Rosenzweig Picture—Frustration Study Results With Minority Group Juvenile Delinquents," *Journal of Genetic Psychology* 92 (1958): 61-67; Elmer Luchterland and Leonard Weller, "Effects of Class, Race, Sex, and Educational Status on Patterns of Aggression of Lower-Class Youth," *Journal of Youth and Adolescence* 5 (1976): 59-71; L. Wilson and R.W. Rogers, "The Fire This Time: Effects of Race of Target, Insult, and Potential Retaliation on Black Aggression," *Journal of Personality and Social Psychology* 32 (1975): 857-864; Gordon B. Forbes and Shirley Mitchell, "Attribution of Blame, Felling of Anger, and Direction of Aggression in Response to Interracial Frustration Among Poverty-Level Female Negro Adults," *Journal of Social Psychology* 83 (1971): 73-78; W.D. Gentry, "Bi-Racial Aggression: I. Effect of Verbal Attack and Sex of Victim," *Journal of Social Psychology* 88 (1972): 75-82.

17 Alfred B. Heilbrun and Kirk S. Heilbrun, "The Black Minority Criminal and Violent Crime: The Role of Self-Control," *The British Journal of Criminology* 17 (1977): 370-377.

18 Farley and Sewell, "Test of an Arousal Theory," note 15, supra.

19 Cross and Tracy, "Personality Factors," note 12, supra.

20 Daniel, "Personality Differences," note 13, supra.

21 Ibid.

22 Ibid.

23 T.J. Fagan and F.T. Lira, "Profile of Mood States: Racial Differences in Delinquent Population," *Psychological Reports* 43 (1978): 348-350.

24 R.W. Genther and S.P. Taylor, "Physical Aggression as a Function of Racial Prejudice and the Race of the Target," *Journal of Personality and Social Psychology* 27 (1973): 207-210.

25 Lilly and Ball, "Norm Neutralization," note 13, supra; R.A. Wilson, "Anomie in the Ghetto: A Study of Neighborhood Type, Race and Anomie," *American Journal of Sociology* 77 (1971): 66-88.

26 Exceptions to this include Hirschi, *Causes of Delinquency,* note 9, supra, who was, in any event, forced for reasons of unreliability to exclude blacks from most of his data analysis, and Gordon, "Crime and Cognition," note 4, supra, who attempts to demonstrate that blacks are genetically inferior to whites.

27 This argument, of course, does not apply to research that utilizes a dependent variable other than crime or delinquency.

28 John A. Davis, "Blacks, Crime, and American Culture," Annals of the *American Academy of Political and Social Sciences* 423 (1976): 89-98; Kenneth B. Clark, "Color, Class, Personality and Juvenile Delinquency," *Journal of Negro Education* 28 (1959): 240-251; Edward Byron Reuter, "Delinquency and Crime," in his *The American Race Problem* (New York: Thomas Y. Crowell

Co. 1970), pp. 315-337; W.E. Hulbary, "Race, Deprivation and Adolescent Self-Images," *Social Science Quarterly* 56 (1975): 105-114; Clemmont E. Vontress, "The Black Male Personality," *The Black Scholar*, 2(10): 10-16, 1971; W.T. Root, Jr., *A Psychological and Educational Survey of 1916 Prisoners in the Western Penitentiary of Pennsylvania* (Pittsburgh: Board of Trustees of the Western Penitentiary, 1927).

29 Bonger's argument is similar: "The circumstances in which the Negroes live are very different from those of the whites, and are strongly conducive to crime. . . . The influences of milieu on the Negroes in the United States are such that one has *a priori* no need to consider other factors." Bonger, *Race and Crime*, note 3, supra, pp. 45-47.

30 E. Franklin Frazier, "Crime and Delinquency," in his *The Negro in the United States*, (New York: MacMillan, 1965), pp. 638-653; E. Franklin Frazier, "Rebellious Youth," in his *The Negro Family in the United States* (Chicago: University of Chicago Press, 1973), pp. 268-280.

31 Daniel Patrick Moynihan, *The Negro Family: The Case for National Action*, Office of Policy Planning and Research, United States Department of Labor (Washington, D.C.: U.S. Government Printing Office, March, 1965).

32 For a review of the literature on compulsive masculinity and delinquency, see Ira J. Silverman and Simon Dinitz, "Compulsive Masculinity and Delinquency: An Empirical Investigation," *Criminology* 11 (February 1974): 498-515. See also Robert L. Perry, "The Black Matriarchy Controversy and Black Male Delinquency," *Journal of Afro-American Issues* 4 (1976): 362-372; L. Alex Swan, "A Methodological Critique of the Moynihan Report," *Black Scholar* 5(9): 18-24 (1974).

33 Roy L. Austin, "Race, Father-Absence and Female Delinquency," *Criminology* 57 (1978): 487-503; Alan S. Berger and William Simon, "Black Families and the Moynihan Report: A Research Evaluation," *Social Problems* 22 (1974): 146-161; Larry L. Hunt and Janet G. Hunt, "Race and the Father-Son Connection: The Conditional Relevance of Father Absence for the Orientations and Identities of Adolescent Boys," *Social Problems* 23 (1975): 35-52; D.B. Kandel, "Race, Maternal Authority and Adolescent Aspiration," *American Journal of Sociology* 76 (1971): 999-1020; Laurence Rosen, "Matriarchy and Lower Class Negro Male Delinquency," *Social Problems* 17 (1969): 175-186; Leonard D. Savitz, "Black Crime," in Kent S. Miller and Ralph Mason Dreger, eds., *Comparative Studies of Blacks and Whites in the United States* (New York: Seminar Press, 1973), pp. 467-516.

34 Moynihan, *The Negro Family*, note 32, supra, p. 30.

35 Ibid.

36 Frederick M. Thrasher, *The Gang: A Study of 1,313 Gangs in Chicago* (Chicago: University of Chicago Press, 1963). See especially Chapter X, "Race and Nationality in the Gang," pp. 130-154.

37 Clifford R. Shaw and Henry D. McKay, *Juvenile Delinquency and Urban Areas* (Chicago: University of Chicago Press, 1942), revised edition published 1972.

38 Chicago Commission on Race Relations, "Crime and Vicious Environment," in *The Negro in Chicago: A Study of Race Relations and a Race Riot in 1919* (New York: Arno Press and the New York Times, 1968), pp. 327-356 (orig. pub. 1919); Frazier, *The Negro in the United States*, note 31, supra; Oscar Handlin, *The Newcomers* (Garden City: Doubleday, 1959); Charles S. Johnson, *The Negro in American Civilization* (New York: Henry Holt and Co., 1930); Joseph D. Lohman, "Juvenile Delinquency: A Social Dimension," *Journal of Negro Education* 28 (1959): 286-299; James Edward McKeown, "Poverty, Race and Crime," *Journal of Criminal Law, Criminology and Police Science* 39 (1948): 480-484; Earl R. Moses, "Community Factors in Negro Delinquency," *Journal of Negro Education* 5 (1936): 220-227; Thomas F. Pettigrew, "Negro American Crime," in his *A Profile of the Negro American* (Princeton, N.J.: D. Van Nostrand Co., 1964), pp. 136-156; Reuter, "Delinquency and Crime," note 29, supra; Bernard F. Robinson, "Ethnic Factors in Crime," *Corrective Psychiatry and Journal of Social Therapy* 10(4): 191-201 (1964).

There has also been some attention in the literature to the effects of migration from rural areas to inner city slums. Typically, racial differences in patterns of migration is employed as partial explanation of black/white differences in arrest rate. The logic of this perspective is consistent with the social disorganization theme in that migration is believed to weaken interpersonal relations within the community (i.e., a community of recent immigrants is not characterized by close social bonds as are communities comprised of more established, long-time residents). For some examinations of the effects of migration, see Edward Green, "Race, Social Status and Criminal Arrest," *American Sociological Review* 35 (1970): 476-490; Vernon Fox and Joan Volakakis, "The Negro Offender," note 11, supra; Thomas F. Pettigrew and Rosalind Barclay Speir, "The Ecological Structure of Negro Homicide," *American Journal of Sociology* 67 (1962): 621-629.

39 See, for example, Moses, "Community Factors," note 39, supra; Pettigrew, "Negro American Crime," note 39, supra; Reuter, "Delinquency and Crime," note 29, supra.

40 See, for example, Edward C. Banfield, *The Unheavenly City* (Boston: Little, Brown and Company, 1968); Walter B. Miller, "Lower Class Culture as a Generating Milieu of Gang Delinquency," *Journal of Social Issues* 14 (1958): 5-19; Marvin E. Wolfgang and Franco Ferracuti, *The Subculture of Violence: Towards an Integrated Theory in Criminology* (London: Tavistock, 1967); Edwin Sutherland and Donald Cressey, *Criminology* (8th edition) (Philadelphia: J.B. Lippincott, 1970); Thorsten Sellin, *Culture Conflict and Crime* (New York: Social Science Research Council Bulletin 41, 1938).

41 An element of this perspective as applied to blacks may be found in P. Bohannon, *African Homicide and Suicide* (Princeton, N.J.: Princeton University Press, 1960). Quoted in Pettigrew, "Negro American Crime," note 39, supra; Walter Bromberg, "Delinquency Among Minorities: Afro-Americans," *Corrective Psychiatry and Journal of Social Therapy* 14 (1968): 209-212; Donald R. Cressey, "Crime," in R.K. Merton and R.A. Nisbet, eds., *Contemporary Social Problems* (New York: Harcourt, Brace and World, 1961); Lynn Curtis, *Violence, Race and Culture* (Lexington, Mass.: D.C. Heath, 1975); Mozell Hill, "The Metropolis and Juvenile Delinquency Among Negroes," *Journal of Negro Education* 28 (1959): 277-285; R.L. Nail, E.K.E. Gunderson and R.J. Arthur, "Black-White Differences in Social Background and Military Drug Abuse Patterns," *American Journal of Psychiatry* 131 (1974): 1097-1102; Pettigrew and Speir, "Ecological Structure," note 39, supra; Sutherland and Cressey, *Criminology,* note 41, supra, pp. 132-142. Traces of a subcultural perspective are also common in explanations of Hispanic-American crime (e.g., Norman and Kleinfeld, "Rosenzweig Picture," note 16, supra; and Native American crime (e.g., Jerrold E. Levy and Stephen J. Kunitz, "Indian Reservations, Anomie and Social Pathologies," *Southwestern Journal of Anthropology* 27 (1971): 97-128; Arthur S. Riffenburgh, "Cultural Influences and Crime Among Indian-Americans of the Southwest," *Federal Probation* 28 (1964): 38-46.

42 Miller, "Lower Class Culture," note 41, supra; Jackson Toby, "Violence and the Masculine Ideal: Some Qualitative Data," *Annals of the American Academy of Political and Social Sciences* 364 (1966): 19-27. Empirical studies of this phenomenon include Robert A. Gordon, James F. Short, Jr., Desmond S. Cartwright and Fred L. Strodtbeck, "Values and Gang Delinquency: A Study of Street Corner Groups," *American Journal of Sociology* 69 (1963): 109-128. See also Silverman and Dinitz, "Compulsive Masculinity," note 33, supra, for a review and critique of the literature on compulsive masculinity.

43 "Contracultures," as defined by Curtis, have values that are different from *and* in conflict with those of the dominant culture. Curtis, *Violence, Race and Culture,* note 41, supra, p. 8.

44 Ibid., p. 18.

45 Thorsten Sellin, "The Negro Criminal: A Statistical Note," *Annals of the American Academy of Political Social Sciences* 140 (1928): 52-64.

46 Ibid.; Thorsten Sellin, "The Negro and the Problem of Law Observance and Adminis-

tration in the Light of Social Research," in Johnson, *The Negro in American Civilization,* note 38, supra.

[47] See, for example, Michael J. Hindelang, "Race and Involvement in Common Law Personal Crimes," *American Sociological Review* 43 (1978): 93-109. Hindelang argues, with supporting data, that discrimination has some effect, but that it cannot account for *all* racial differences in official statistics; William Chambliss and Richard H. Nagasawa, "On the Validity of Official Statistics: A Comparative Study of White, Black, and Japanese High-School Boys," *Journal of Research in Crime and Delinquency* 6 (1969): 71-77.

[48] Hindelang, "Race and Involvement," note 47, supra; Michael J. Hindelang, Travis Hirschi and Joseph G. Weis, "Correlates of Delinquency: The Illusion of Discrepancy Between Self-Report and Offical Measures," *American Sociological Review* 44 (1979): 995-1014; Carl E. Pope, "Race and Crime Revisited," *Crime and Delinquency* (July 1979): 347-357. See also Morris A. Forslund, "A Comparison of Negro and White Crime Rates," *Journal of Criminal Law, Criminology and Police Science* 61 (1970): 214-217.

[49] For one perspective on reasons for the dearth of literature on white-collar crime, see Richard Peet, "The Geography of Crime: A Political Critique," *Professional Geographer* 27 (1975): 277-280.

[50] Robert Merton, "Social Structure and Anomie," *American Sociological Review* 3 (1938): 672-682.

[51] Lee P. Brown, "Causes of Crime," in Herrington J. Bryce, ed., *Black Crime: A Police View* (Washington, D.C.: Joint Center for Political Studies, 1977), pp. 37-66; Harold Finestone, "Cats, Kicks, and Color," *Social Problems* 5 (1957): 3-13; Murray Gruber, "The Nonculture of Poverty Among Black Youths," *Social Work,* Vol. 17, No. 3 (1972): 50-58; R.M. Jiobu, "City Characteristics and Racial Violence," *Social Science Quarterly,* Vol. 55, No. 1 (1974): 52-64; Boyd R. McCandless, Scott Persons III and Albert Roberts, "Perceived Opportunity, Delinquency, Race, and Body Build Among Delinquent Youth," *Journal of Consulting and Clinical Psychology* 38 (1972): 281-287; Earl R. Moses, "Differentials in Crime Rates Between Negroes and Whites, Based on Comparisons of Four Socio-Economically Equated Areas," *American Sociological Review* 12 (1947): 411-420; Pettigrew, "Negro American Crime" note 38, supra; Lonnie E. Mitchell, "Aspiration Levels of Negro Delinquent, Dependent, and Public School Boys," *Journal of Negro Education* 26 (1957): 80-85.

[52] Green, "Race, Social Status, Arrest," note 38, supra; John T. Blue, Jr., "The Relationship of Juvenile Delinquency, Race and Economic Status," *Journal of Negro Education* 17 (1948): 469-477; Moses, "Differentials in Crime Rates," note 51, supra.

[53] Marvin Wolfgang, R.M. Figlio, and Thorsten Sellin, *Delinquency in a Birth Cohort* (Chicago: University of Chicago Press, 1972): Moses, "Differentials in Crime Rates," note 51, supra; William Bates, "Caste, Class and Vandalism," *Social Problems* 9 (1962): 349-352; Blue, "Juvenile Delinquency," note 52, supra; Richard M. Stephenson and Frank R. Scarpitti, "Negro-White Differentials in Delinquency," *Journal of Research in Crime and Delinquency* 5 (1968): 122-133. For additional empirical critiques of this perspective, see Edgar G. Epps, "Socioeconomic Status, Race, Level of Aspiration and Juvenile Delinquency: A Limited Empirical Test of Merton's Conception of Deviation," *Phylon* 28 (1967): 16-27.

[54] Frantz Fanon, *The Wretched of The Earth,* (New York: Grove Press, 1963).

[55] Johnson, Guy B., "The Negro and Crime," *Annals of the American Academy of Political and Social Sciences,* 217 (1941: 93-104); Bonqer, *Race and Crime,* note 3, supra.

[56] Fanon, *Wretched of the Earth,* note 54, supra.

[57] Quinney, Richard, *The Social Reality of Crime* (Boston: Little Brown, 1970); Anthony Platt and Paul Takagi; "Behind the Guilded Ghetto: An Analysis of Race, Class and Crime in Chinatown," *Crime and Social Justice,* 9, (Spring-Summer 1978: 2-25).

3

Black Crime and Criminal Victimization

Keith D. Harries

This chapter is divided into three main parts. First, comparisons are made between the attitudes of blacks and whites toward crime and various criminal justice-related issues. The second and third sections of the chapter look at statistics on black crime from two perspectives, those of the FBI's Uniform Crime Reports (crimes reported to the police) and the National Crime Survey (data from questionnaires administered to the public). By illustrating what blacks and whites think about crimes and by setting out the "official" picture of black crime, a basis for comparisons is provided. This chapter should stimulate questioning and reasoning about why there are differences between the attitudes and crime experiences of blacks and whites.

BLACK AND WHITE ATTITUDES TOWARD CRIME

A review of the findings of public opinion surveys about crime reveals both similarities and differences with respect to the attitudes of blacks and whites. A word of caution is appropriate in connection with the discussion that follows. The survey results referred to are generally intended to be representative of attitudes across the United States, rather than in one specific locality. Furthermore, all surveys are subject to error, so minor differences in measured opinion between racial groups should not be given much attention.

Similar Perceptions

Blacks and whites appear to be more similar than dissimilar in regard to their perspectives on crime and criminal justice (Flanagan and McLoed, 1983:207-291) (see Table 1). It is especially interesting to note that most blacks and whites have not modified their mobility within their neighborhood (because of their fear of crime), i.e., 78 percent of whites and 66 percent of blacks, while they continue to believe that the courts have been too lenient in the sentencing of criminals (84 percent of whites and 77 percent of blacks), an attitude that apparently has resulted in only moderate confidence in the U.S. Supreme Court; only 27 percent of whites and 23 percent of blacks have "a great deal" of confidence in the Supreme Court. Also of significance is the fact that while most Americans say prison should be rehabilitative (73 percent) most Americans offer a retribution response (punishment advocacy) when asked if courts are too lenient or too severe; 83 percent of the respondents said the courts were "not harsh enough" with criminals. Other interesting points of similarity are on the morality issues of pornography control and legalization of marihuana, and the ownership of weapons, i.e., both whites and blacks wish to control more severely the distribution of pornography while continuing to criminalize marihuana use, only 6 percent of whites and 10 percent of the blacks polled favor no laws forbidding the distribution of pornography, 72 percent of whites and 71 percent of the blacks polled do not favor the legalization of marihuana, while only 25 percent of white households had someone who owned a handgun or pistol and 39 percent a long gun compared to 23 percent of the black households owning a pistol and 20 percent a long gun. Both blacks and whites while fearful of criminal victimization in general do not own a handgun, rifle or shot gun.

Different Perceptions

Black-white differences in perception are few but frequently profound. The most striking perceptual divergencies are in regard to (1) the striking of an adult male citizen by a police officer (76 percent of the whites versus 45 percent of the blacks surveyed said that it is sometimes acceptable) and (2) the imposition of capital punishment (70 percent of the whites favor the death penalty for persons convicted of murder compared to 40 percent of the black population polled).

While most blacks and whites polled favor a law requiring a police permit prior to a gun purchase blacks more strongly favor this law than their white counterpart (81 percent to 68 percent).

Sharp differences in black-white attitudes are also observed in regard to the perception of teenage gangs as a problem in the respondent's community; 55 percent of the whites polled compared to 32 percent of the blacks viewed it as "not a problem." Other areas of crime perception dissimilarity are noted in Table 2.

Blacks and whites differ in their perceptions of job performance by local, state and federal law enforcement officials. In general, whites view all levels of enforcement official job performance more favorably than do blacks, 65 percent versus 52 percent on the local level, 59 percent versus 47 percent on the state level and 49 versus 44 percent on the federal level.

Interpretation of Similarities and Differences

For the most part, the similarities and differences in black and white perceptions outlined above can be explained by several factors, individually or in combination.

— The nature of the question, including whether it was global in scope or referred more specifically to neighborhoods or individuals.

— The residential context or location of blacks compared to whites, particularly the inner city/suburb contrast. This may also be thought of as the 'geography of crime' explanation, and it has to do with the *skewed* distribution of victimization (Sparks, 1980) and of the location of crime. This will be explained further.

— Differences between blacks and whites in terms of cultural history and dominant values.

Although a comprehensive interpretation of each of the similarities and differences noted earlier will not be attempted, each of the explanatory factors will be discussed and illustrated in order to show in a general way how we may approach explanation of the differences observed.

The nature of the questions addressed to blacks and whites may relate to perception in different ways depending on whether the questions for respondents to perceive or evaluate their personal or local situation compared to the metropolis or the nation as a whole. For example, the media have consistently represented a picture of increasing crime in conformity to the increase in official crime rates in recent decades. Since this image is so constant and universal, it is not surprising that blacks and whites would respond to related questions with similar responses. On the other hand, when the questions refer to neighborhood or personal experience, blacks tend to perceive greater danger. Again, this is a rational response owing to the residential context factor referred to on the preceding page. Blacks, particularly poorer blacks, are still preponderantly located in an inner city context where crime rates are indeed high. Here we may discuss further the context of *skewness* introduced above. Skewness is an idea from the science of statistics, and it tells us that many phenomena do not necessarily occur in a normal pattern. *Normal* here has a special meaning. It refers to the idea of a normal or bell-shaped distribution.

When this concept is applied to crime, we find that it does indeed have a skewed distribution in two respects. First, victimization is skewed; in other words, few people are being victimized a lot. These people are disproportionately poor or black or both. Second, if we look at *where* crime occurs in cities on, say, a block-by-block basis, we find that relatively few blocks will have a great deal of crime, while many blocks will have, in a given year, little or no crime. Those blocks that are most heavily impacted are likely to be in the inner city, and such blocks are likely to be in minority neighborhoods. When blacks are asked about perceptions of crime in their neighborhoods and changes in behavior patterns due to perceptions of crime, it is not surprising that their reactions differ from those of whites.

Explanations of perception variations relating to black-white differences in cultural history and values are more speculative and perhaps less susceptible to convincing proof compared to the two factors mentioned above. What is being suggested is that the black experience in America has generated the development of values that are not necessarily shared to the same degree by whites. (For a comprehensive discussion, see Curtis, 1975.)

Differences in the black experience compared to the white show up in attitude differentials in connection with police performance and ways in which local police could improve. The history of policing is filled with examples of police harrassment of blacks, and police may be seen as an instrument through which whites have historically kept blacks "in their place." Particularly conspicuous is the expression by blacks of the need for police to be "more courteous, concerned." Another relevant point is that blacks tend to be underrepresented in police departments, with the result that police officers patrolling in black communities are likely to be white, are likely to feel insecure, and are perhaps more likely to react to crisis situations in an overly aggressive manner.

II. BLACK CRIME ACCORDING TO THE
FBI UNIFORM CRIME REPORTS

Some explanation is necessary at the start of this section to help the reader understand what the *Uniform Crime Reports (UCR)* are and why they have come to be regarded as a rather unreliable source of crime data. The UCR have existed since 1930, and until the recent availability of victimization data (discussed in the next section) the UCR were the sole "official" tabulation of crime statistics in the United States. The UCR contain crimes *reported to the police*. The problem, then, is immediately apparent—many crimes are *not* reported to the police, and the level of non-reporting varies across different groups in society. The heavily insured white middle-class home-owner may report the loss of a one dollar screwdriver. The uninsured ghetto dweller may not report the loss of a more valuable item because to do so would probably be pointless. Time spent with police would be wasted—recovery of the lost item is unlikely—and without insurance the rationale for not reporting is complete.

An additional problem is that some crimes are generally reported much more completely than others. Owing to victims' fears of embarrassment and humiliation, rape is greatly underreported, as are many minor events of larceny or theft. Homicide, on the other hand, is reported quite completely for obvious reasons. Concerning the interpretation of black crime in the *UCR*, it has been argued that it is exaggerated because of the general pattern of relationships between blacks and police. Owing to a high birth rate (common to poorer groups in society), the black population tends to be youthful. Since crowded housing conditions are also typical for poorer black families, it is natural that blacks would tend to gravitate to the streets for recreation and social contact. In the streets, blacks are then subject to police surveillance, and are more likely to be picked up for acts that might occur in private in a white middle-class neighborhood. Drug and alcohol use are examples; standing on a street corner in the inner city with a bottle (even in a brown paper sack) and/or a marihuana joint invites police interest, while similar conduct in private would not.

It is suggested, then, that black crime is inflated in the *UCR* because of this "surveillance effect"—people are not really behaving differently than elsewhere, they are just more likely to get caught. (This phenomenon, incidentally, has also been observed in Britain. See Stevens and Willis, 1979.) While there is unquestionably some merit to this argument, its validity should not be exaggerated. There is evidence from various sources suggesting that crime is indeed more prevalent (or at least more serious) in black neighborhoods. While the levels of black crime in the *UCR* can be discounted somewhat, it is not reasonable to dismiss the *UCR* data as entirely unfounded or to perceive them entirely as a product of exaggeration.

Arrests

Bearing in mind the imperfections of the *UCR*, we may now consider data on arrests of blacks. As a reference point, it should be noted that the population of the U.S. is about 13 percent black. If blacks are arrested in proportion to their numbers in the population, then, we should expect that about 13 percent of arrests in any particular crime category should be of blacks. According to the *UCR*, as Table 3 shows, the situation is quite different, with blacks actually being arrested anywhere from about twice the expected level (motor vehicle theft) to almost five times the expected level (robbery). Overall, blacks appear to be involved in violent crime at an extremely disproportionately high level, and in property crime to a somewhat lesser extent.

Homicide

The black experience with respect to homicide will be reviewed more closely for two reasons. First, the impact of homicide on American society is enormous. With over 20,000 victims a year, the emotional and economic losses are incalculable. Secondly, homicide is an offense not considered in the victimization surveys, discussed in the next section, (since homicide victims obviously cannot be interviewed). Table 3 showed that, on average, about half the arrests for homicide are of blacks. Table 4 indicates that about 45 percent of the homicide victims are black (FBI, 1976). Homicide is overwhelmingly intraracial. In 1982, in single victim/single offender situations, of 5,945 white victims, 566 (9.5 percent) were associated with black offenders. Of 5,386 black victims, 266 (4.9 percent) were associated with white offenders.

In some ways, the age distribution of murder victims is similar between blacks and whites. Victims cluster in the 15-34 age range with a slow but steady decrease in the homicide rate after the age of 34. One striking racial difference based on sex is the relatively greater involvement of black females. In 1982, for example, of 5,386 black victims (single victim/single offender situations), 1,079 offenders (20 percent of all black offenders) were female (FBI, 1983). Curtis (1975:59) has attributed this situation to "the cadence of ghetto life" which "may of necessity require a certain acceptance of violence, when the situation seems to demand it."

III. BLACK CRIME ACCORDING TO VICTIMIZATION SURVEYS

In contrast to the *UCR*, which tabulate only crimes reported to the police, the National Crime Survey (*NCS*) was established in 1972 in order to obtain data on *victims* of crime and on crimes not reported to the police. Data are obtained through interviews, measuring the victimization of persons aged 12 and over, households, and businesses. Crimes covered in *NCS* reports are: rape, robbery, assault, personal and household larceny, burglary, and motor vehicle theft (U.S. Department of Justice, 1982).

Data from the *NCS* show that an estimated 39.3 million criminal victimizations were incurred by individuals across the United States in 1980. Most of the crime experienced is non-violent, and according to one report, "*race appears to have less to do with exposure to crime than does income or place of residence*" (U.S. Department of Justice, 1981). However,

there was some indication that relatively more black households than white were victimized by crime during the 6-year period, but the differences were very small. In general, the percentage for both groups hovered around 30 throughout 1975-80. Black households were slightly more likely to have had a member who had been a victim of personal larceny without contact. On the whole, however, black and white patterns were remarkably similar (U.S. Department of Justice, 1981).

This remarkable overall similarity in criminal victimization does not hold as strongly for violent crime when 1980 criminal victimization data is examined carefully; in fact, blacks experienced violent crime at an overall rate higher than that for whites, but not significantly higher than members of other minorities; neither was there a significant difference between the rates for whites and other members of other races. The difference in vulnerability for whites and blacks chiefly was the result of a high robbery rate among blacks, a figure 2.4 times higher than that for whites (U.S. Department of Justice, 1982:5).

Thus, this general overview of the "households-touched-by-crime" indicator says nothing about the *seriousness* of crimes; in other words, a minor assault would count as much as a rape, robbery, or serious assault.

Personal Victimization

Personal victimizations encompass rape, robbery of persons, assault, personal larceny with contact, or personal larceny without contact. Blacks are victimized at higher rates than whites for rape (only slightly) and robbery, while there is no significant difference between black and white assault rates. Overall, black males and females are victims of personal crimes at appreciably higher rates than white males or females (Table 5) (U.S. Department of Justice, 1982). These *NCS* findings are consistent with the finding that blacks as offenders are strongly overrepresented in relation to their numbers in the population. Since most crime is intraracial, this would suggest that victims should also be strongly disproportionately black, and numerous studies have supported this observation.

Analysis based on the *seriousness* of personal victimizations suggests that the strongest relationships are to the age, sex, and race, respectively, of the victims. In general, the seriousness-weighted rates of personal victimization for blacks was higher than for whites. In other words, for a given number of victimizations, blacks would be more likely to suffer serious injuries compared to whites (U.S. Department of Justice, 1982:60-63).

Although the *NCS* shows a higher black than white involvement in personal crime, the difference is not as great as the *UCR* data in Table 3 would suggest. The explanation of this discrepancy apparently lies in part in the *type* of assaults reported by whites to the *NCS*. Whites reported more attempted or less serious assaults. If only serious assaults are considered, blacks have rates clearly higher than whites.

Other sources of explanation lie in the concepts, methods, and circumstances relating to the *NCS* interviews. Assault is a crime for which it may be difficult to distinguish "victims" from "offenders." Also, blacks may be assaulted by non-strangers more often than whites, and methodological studies have shown that such assaults are less likely to be recalled in a *NCS* interview. This could account for high levels of reported assault among young white males. Another possibility is that interviews in homes are often less than private, and young assault "victims" may not wish to admit to conflict within earshot of family members. Explanation also suggests that blacks involved in violent crime are more likely to evade interviewers (Hindelang, 1976:152-153). The weight of the available evidence suggests that blacks are indeed heavily disproportionately involved in violent crime, both as victims and offenders; the minimization of the difference between blacks and whites in the *NCS* would appear to be artifactual, at least to some extent.

The *NCS* data have tended to confirm the proposition that crime is *skewed* in terms of *place* of occurrence and *persons* victimized; it has been found that "area of residence may have a great influence on the likelihood of loss through a personal crime" (Hindelang, Gottfredson and Garofalo, 1978:-119). Furthermore, "victimizations are disproportionately concentrated among some segments of the population" and "persons residing in victimized households had substantially greater likelihoods of personal victimization than those residing in non-victimized households, e.g. income-related normative sub-cultures might increase or decrease the likelihood of certain types of victimizations.

The importance of place of residence as a factor in victimization is particularly critical for blacks who live in segregated *heterogeneous* housing areas, thus increasing the chances of class mixing in school or in the course of other social contacts. Thus it may be more difficult for young blacks to remove or isolate themselves from criminal involvement, compared to whites, who are more likely to live in socially *homogeneous* neighborhoods.

Household Victimization

Household victimizations are theft crimes including burglary, household larceny, and motor vehicle theft. *NCS* data have shown that burglary and motor vehicle theft rates for blacks exceed those for whites, while there were not significant differences among the rates at which household larcenies occurred (see Table 6).

One can speculate that sharp differences exists among cities in terms of household victimizations. Such differences would be due to various social and cultural differences between the cities, quite apart from the influence of the use of the incorporated city as the survey unit. This arbitrarily excludes interviewing of suburban residents and naturally gives the data a central city bias.

Victimization: Are Blacks Less Likely to Report to the Police?

Earlier in this chapter it was noted that a frequent basis for criticizing the UCR is the suggestion that various population groups may be less likely to report crimes to the police; a poor, uninsured person, for instance, may be less likely to report a burglary compared to a person with insurance. NCS data enabled an assessment of the extent to which crime victims failed to report to police, and it is possible to find out whether black victimization is less likely to be reported to police than white.

Data show that about two-thirds of all personal victimizations, and nearly 61 percent of household victimizations, are not reported. Racial differences in reporting are complex and inconsistent. In household victimizations, for example, whites and blacks reported crimes at virtually the same rate (U.S. Department of Justice, 1982:95). In crimes of violence blacks, in general, reported crimes at a higher rate than whites. However, for both crimes of violence and household victimizations factors such as age, sex of victim and specific criminal victimization also affected the rate of reporting. As early as 1976, Dr. Hindelang had contended that overall, when age and type of crime are taken into account, there are no clear racial differences in reporting crimes to the police (Hindelang, 1976:Chapter 14). Other research has shown that UCR and NCS crime rates are highly correlated for armed robbery and motor vehicle theft, somewhat correlated for burglary, and weakly correlated for unarmed robbery. Little or no relationship was observed for assault and rape (Nelson, 1980:84). The relationships between race and crime reporting and between the UCR and NCS are complex. Arguments suggesting that the official picture of black involvement in crime (as victims or offenders) has been totally unrepresentative and far too simplistic.

References

F.B.I. Uniform Crime Reports. Washington, D.C.: The Justice Department, Annual.

Flanagan, Timothy J. and Maureen McLoed. (eds). Sourcebook of Criminal Justice Statistics—1977. Washington, D.C.: U.S. Department of Justice, 1978.

Hindelang, Michael J. Criminal Victimization in Eight American Cities. Cambridge, MA: Ballinger Press, 1976.

U.S. Department of Justice, Criminal Victimization in the United States—1980, Washington, D.C.: U.S. Government Printing Office, Annual.

Table 1   Crime Issues Perceived Similarly by Blacks and Whites

Desire for a Neighborhood Crime Watch Program
Employment of Crime Prevention Measures
Restriction of Neighborhood Travel Due to the Crime Threat
Confidence in the U.S. Supreme Court
Severity of Courts in Own Area
Prison Sentences as a Deterrent to Crime
Objectives of Imprisonment
Reported Household Ownership of a Handgun or Pistol
Reported Knowing Victims of Child or Wife Abuse or Abuse of the Elderly
Rating the Problem of Wife Abuse, Abuse of the Elderly, Child Abuse [Slight Disagreement]
Legalization of Marihuana
Pornographic Material
Laws Regulating Distribution of Pornography

Source: Based on interpretation of tables contained in Timothy J. Flanagan and Maureen McLoed, eds. *Sourcebook of Criminal Justice Statistics—1982.* U.S. Department of Justice, Bureau of Justice Statistics. Washington, D.C.: U.S. Government Printing Office, 1983, pp. 207-291.

Table 2   Crime Issues Perceived Differently by Blacks and Whites

Neighborhood Safety (Night)
Fear of Specific Criminal Victimization
General Fear of Crime
Knowledge of Neighborhood Crime Watch Program
Teenage Gangs as a Problem in Own Neighborhood
Performance of Local and State Law Enforcement Officials
Police Striking an Adult Male Citizen
Capital Punishment for Persons Convicted of Murder

Source: Based on interpretation of tables contained in Timothy J. Flanagan and Maureen McLoed, eds. *Sourcebook of Criminal Justice Statistics—1982.* U.S. Department of Justice, Bureau of Justice Statistics. Washington, D.C. U.S. Government Printing Office, 1983, pp. 207-291.

Table 3   Blacks Arrested for UCR Index Offenses, 1975-79 (Percent of all arrests)

Offense	1975	1976	1977	1978	1979	1980	1981	1982	1975-1980 Average
Murder	54.5	53.5	51.0	49.4	47.7	47.9	50.5	49.7	50.5
Rape	45.4	46.6	47.3	48.3	47.7	47.7	57.8	49.7	48.8
Robbery	58.8	59.2	57.0	58.7	56.9	57.7	67.5	60.7	59.6
Assault	39.5	41.0	38.8	39.0	37.0	36.1	37.0	38.8	38.4
Burglary	28.4	29.2	28.9	29.0	28.7	29.1	26.0	31.7	28.9
Larceny-Theft	30.6	32.1	32.0	31.0	30.2	30.5	28.3	33.4	31.0
Motor Vehicle Theft	26.4	26.2	26.1	27.2	27.2	20.5	24.3	31.4	26.2
Violent Crime	47.1	47.5	45.7	46.2	44.1	44.1	53.4	46.7	46.9
Property Crime	29.6	30.9	30.6	30.7	29.4	29.9	27.1	32.7	30.1

Source: F.B.I., *Crime in the United States,* F.B.I. *Uniform Crime Reports, 1975-1982,* U.S. Government Printing Office, Washington, D.C., 1976-1983.

Table 4   Homicide Victims: Percent Black 1975-1982

1975	1976	1977	1978	1979	1980	1981	1982	1975-1980 Average
47.4	46.6	45.3	43.8	43.4	47.3	43.8	42.3	45

Source: F.B.I., *Uniform Crime Reports,* (1976-1982).

Table 5   Personal Crimes: Victimization Rate for Personage 12 and Over by Type of Crime and Sex and Race of Victims, 1980

(Rate per 1,000 population age 12 and over)

| | Male | | Female | |
Type of Crime	White (75,659,000)	Black (8,864,000)	White (81,421,000)	Black (10,827,000)
Crimes of violence	43.1	52.3	22.0	30.3
Rape	0.3	0.2	1.5	1.8
Robbery	7.8	20.6	3.8	8.5
Robbery with injury	2.5	6.3	1.6	2.6
Robbery without injury	5.3	14.2	2.2	5.9
Assault	35.0	31.6	16.7	20.0
Aggravated assault	13.2	18.4	4.5	7.3
Simple assault	21.8	13.2	12.3	12.6
Crimes of theft	88.5	87.2	78.4	72.5
Personal larceny with contact	1.9	3.9	3.2	8.2
Personal larceny without contact	86.6	83.3	75.1	64.3

Note: Patterns for other years are similar.

Source: U.S. Department of Justice, *Criminal Vicitimization in the United States—1980,* Washington, D.C.: U.S. Government Printing Office, 1982. Table 7, p. 25.

Table 6   Household Crimes: Victimization Rates, By Type of Crime and Race of Head

(Rate per 1,000 households)

Type of Crime	All races (80,977,000)	White (70,902,000)	Black (8,725,000)
Burglary	84.2	80.6	114.7
Forcible entry	29.7	26.9	52.8
Unlawful entry without force	36.7	36.9	34.6
Attempted forcible entry	17.8	16.7	27.3
Household larceny	126.5	125.2	133.7
Less than $50	61.2	62.8	47.7
$50 or more	50.2	48.3	63.0
Amount not available	6.1	5.6	10.1
Attempted larceny	9.1	8.6	12.8
Motor vehicle theft	16.7	15.6	25.1
Completed theft	11.4	10.7	16.4
Attempted theft	5.4	4.9	8.7

Note: Patterns for other years are similar.

Source: U.S. Department of Justice, *Criminal Vicitimization in the United States—1980,* Washington, D.C.: U.S. Government Printing Office, 1982. Table 21, p. 36.

4

Blacks and Homicide

Marc Riedel

This chapter discusses trends in black homicide, focusing on data gathered from 1968-1978. Important issues arise in the analysis of homicide trends, specifically the issue of policy options in light of the rather surprising finding that white, rather than black, homicides are on the increase. The sex and race of victims are also studied to determine which groups are most likely to be victimized by a criminal homicide. The data clearly show that while black males predominate as both victims and offenders, female blacks also stand a disproportionately high risk of being murder victims. Finally, the nature of intra- and interracial criminal homicides are examined to uncover relationships between victims and offenders.

TRENDS IN BLACK HOMICIDE

There were significant and substantial changes in the racial composition of criminal homicide in the United States from 1968 to 1978. Table 1 gives the rates per 100,000 population for the race of the victim and offender for an eleven year period.

Table 1 indicates that black offender rates and the rates at which black criminal homicide victimization occurred show a very different pattern from white offender and victim rates. For black victims and black offenders the rates increase to 1972; the rates then decline to 1978. For black victims, the increase is from 33.7 per 100,000 in 1968 to a peak of 43.4 per 100,000 in 1972; the rates then decline to 34.7 per 100,000 in 1978. For black offenders, the rates are from 25.9 per 100,000 in 1968 to 37.2 per 100,000 in 1972; the rates then decline to 34.8 per 100,000 in 1978.

The white victim and offender rates show a steady increase during the eleven year period. For white victims, the rates increased from 3.8 per 100,000 in 1968 to 5.9 per 100,000 in 1978. For white offenders, the rates more than doubled; in 1968, the white offender rate was 2.1 per 100,000, by 1978, the criminal homicide offender rate was 4.3 per 100,000.

It is important to recognize in Table 1 that there was a convergence in black and white offender and victim rates over the eleven year period. For

51

the victims, the black victim rate was more than eleven times the white victim rate (33.7 as compared to 3.8) in 1968. By 1978, the same comparison indicates that the black victim rate is less than seven times the whites victim rate (34.7 as compared to 5.9).

Similarly, in 1968 the black offender rate was more than twelve times the white offender rate (25.9 as compared to 2.1). By 1978, the black offender rate was less than nine times the white offender rates (34.8 as compared to 4.3). In both victim and offender rates, there has been a convergence in rates over the eleven year period.

The data in Table 1 raises two very different sets of policy implications for the prevention and reduction of criminal homicide. First, white victim and offender rates increased more in the eleven year period than black victim and offender rates. Indeed, much of the convergence in homicide rates discussed in the preceding paragraph is probably attributable more to an increase in white rates than a decline in black rates. If the latter interpretation is taken as a basis for social policy to reduce or prevent homicides, it is clear that more money and social programs should be focused on white rather than black criminal homicide. Second, regardless of the increase in rates among white victims and offenders, black victim and offender rates are still many times higher than similar white rates. As indicated earlier, the black victimization rate is about seven times the white victimization rate. From the latter policy perspective, money and social programs should continue to be directed toward the prevention and reduction of black criminal homicide. What the data reflect is a need for research designed to determine why black victim and offender rates have declined since 1972.

SEX AND AGE OF BLACK HOMICIDE

Victims and Offenders

The last section examined trends in black and white offender and victim rates. This section's concern is black and white homicides with respect to sex and age of victim and offender.

Table 2 lists the criminal homicide rates for males and females and five age groups in the United States for 1978. Keep in mind that the rates in Table 2, just as in Table 1, are compared with the appropriate population base. Thus, the number of black male homicides are divided by the number of black males in the United States in 1978. The results are multiplied by 100,000 to provide race and sex specific homicide rates for black males. Similarly, in Table 1 the number of black homicides is divided by the number of blacks in the population for a given year and the result multiplied by 100,000; this gives a race specific homicide rate per 100,000 population for black victims or offenders.

It is evident from Table 2 that black male victims and offenders have the highest rates of criminal homicide in the United States. The black male victim rate is 58.5 per 100,000 while the black male offender rate is 48.9 per 100,000.

It may be surprising to learn that the next highest rates for victims and offenders are not for white males but black females. In 1978 black female victims had a rate of 13.2 per 100,000 while black female offenders had a rate of 10.3 per 100,000. Nevertheless, among blacks, being a victim or offender of criminal homicide is clearly a male prerogative.

The rates that are most similar to black female rates are white male rates. For white male victims, the rate is 9.0 per 100,000 while for white male offenders, the rate is 6.7 per 100,000. The lowest rates occur for white females. For white female victims the rate is 2.9 per 100,000 while for white female offenders, the rate is only .9 per 100,000 population.

Table 2 demonstrates that criminal homicide is an offense in which black males predominate as both victims and offenders—some of the reasons for that predominance will be discussed in a subsequent section. The discussion here will focus on why black females have such a high victim and offender rate in comparison to white female rates.

In relation to homicide victimization, black females may be the victim of criminal homicides more frequently than white females because they are more frequently in situations where the risk of homicides are higher. Black females are the heads of households and are wage earners more frequently than white females. They are also more likely to have jobs that put them in high risk homicide situations. Thus, a black female who works late hours as a clerk in a convenience store exposes herself to the possibility of being victimized by a robbery, which could easily lead to a homicide in lower-class neighborhoods. Black females who work as domestics or cleaning personnel may be open to mugging, rape, robbery, and murder opportunities that are absent for the majority of white females.

In relation to white female victimization, the traditional role of the white female as wife and mother confined her activity to the home and suburban areas, both of which posed a low risk of being a victimized. In recent years, some authors have asserted that the women's liberation movement has been responsible for freeing women politically, socially, and economically from their subservient status to males. As these liberated women assume positions formerly open to men, their crime and victimization rates will begin to be more similar to that of males (Adler, 1975). But whatever effects the women's movement has had, they have been limited for the most part to white middle-class females. Historically, as a matter of economic necessity, the majority of black women have had to be principal wage earners and heads of the household; "liberation," in that sense, is something black women have known for a very long time (Simon, 1975).

Very little research has been devoted to the phenomena of black female crime. The irony here is that a group who suffers the problems of being the victim of prejudice associated with being black *and* being a woman is also the group whose relationship to criminal homicide is least researched.

Table 2 also gives the race of victim and offender rates for five different age groups. For both black victims and black offenders the highest rates are in the age range 25-29. For the black victim the criminal homicide rate is 82.3 per 100,000, while for black offenders the homicide rate is 70.0 per 100,000.

White victims and offenders, by comparison, show high rates at a younger age. For white victims, the rates for the age group 20-24 are as high as for the age group 25-29; the rate for both age groups is 8.8 per 100,000. With regard to white offenders, the age group 20-24 shows the highest rate—7.1 per 100,000 population.

For black and white victims and offenders the age groups from age 15-39, given in Table 2, represent the highest homicide rates. One explanation that has been suggested for high rates of violence in the 20-30 age group is that it is the consequence of a lifestyle that puts potential victims and offenders in frequent contact with one another. Hindelang, Gottfredson, and Garofalo (1978) suggest, for example, that young people spend more time in public locations where the risk of victimization is higher. Persons under age 19 are constrained more frequently by parental demands while those over age 29 are more likely to be concerned with family and activities that occur less frequently in public locations. While such an explanation is useful, it does not explicitly address the differences between black and white rates.

WEAPONS USED IN HOMICIDE

Table 3 provides us with the types of weapons used in criminal homicide in 1978 in the United States. For black offenders, the most frequently used homicide weapons are handguns (51.8%), followed by knives (20.5%), rifles and shotguns (13.7%) and other types of weapons. Like black offenders, the most frequently used weapon for white offenders are handguns (58.2%), followed by knives (16.4%), rifles and shotguns (6.3%), and other types of weapons. Among black offenders the use of handguns as a homicide weapon is slightly less (51.8%) than among white offenders (58.2%). On the other hand, black offenders favor knives and cutting instruments, rifles and shotguns, and personal weapons such as hands and feet more frequently than white offenders.

Over one-half of the criminal homicides in the United States in 1978 involved the use of handguns by both black and white offenders. Handguns are the most frequently used weapon because they are easy to conceal, lethal at a greater range than a weapon like a knife, and are not difficult to obtain, despite a plethora of laws designed to prevent easy availability.

While handgun use in homicide among black offenders lags behind white offenders when all types of weapons are considered, within the category of handguns we find that black offenders use them more frequently than white offenders. Examining Table 3 from a slightly different point of view, we find that among 6636 homicides where handguns were the weapon, 3697, or 55.7 percent, were used by black offenders, and 2938, or 44.3 percent, were used by white offenders.

What these results suggest is that in a society where handguns are not difficult to obtain, they may be more frequently used by black offenders. Black offenders, in turn, live more frequently in areas of the city where they perceive a need to carry a weapon for their own protection. In referring to the danger of being arrested with a weapon, one offender in a study cited by Curtis concluded, "I'd rather be caught by an officer with a weapon than to ever be caught by some of the folks on my street without it" (Curtis, 1975: 52).

VICTIM/OFFENDER RELATIONSHIPS AND HOMICIDES

Table 4 gives the relationship between victim and offender prior to the homicide. This table indicates that 19 percent of the homicide cases involving black victims were those in which the victim and offender were family members or relatives. Among white victims, approximately the same proportion involved family related homicides.

Almost one-half (43.4%) of the black victims were friends or acquaintances of the offender. A much smaller percent (39%) of the white victims were friends or acquaintances of the offender.

White victims, according to Table 4, are more frequently involved (15.9%) in homicides where they did not know the offender in contrast to black victims (10.1%). "Other known" relationships indicate that the victim was known to the offender, but the police could not specify the relationship.

What is most troubling about Table 4 is the large number of cases where the relationship could not be specified. For black victims, 25.5 percent of the cases had "unknown" victim/offender relationships while for white victims, the "unknown" category comprised 33.2 percent. Such a large percent of unknowns suggests the proportions reported in Table 4 may be severely biased.

In a unpublished study, Riedel (1981) compared the proportions of cases for several variables available from police data in Memphis, Tennessee from 1976-178 with data reported to the FBI. While the information from the Memphis police department on race, sex, age of victim and offender, and weapon, agreed with similar data available from the FBI, important discrepancies occurred with respect to victim/offender relationships.

The Memphis Police Department reported that from 1976-1978 65 homicides involved family members. The FBI data for the same period and city reported 61 homicides involved family members; the percentage difference was 2.6 percent. For friends and acquaintances, the Memphis Police Department reported 184 homicides while the FBI reported 168 homicides, a difference of 5.7 percent.

The major difference occurred, however, for homicides involving strangers. The Memphis Police Department reported 70 homicides involving strangers, while the FBI reported only 36 homicides involving strangers, a difference of 8.3 percent.

To understand why the Memphis Police Department reports significantly more stranger/friend/acquaintance homicides than the FBI reports, consider how the FBI collects information on homicides.

FBI Homicide Reports

Information on homicides reported by the FBI to the public and the research community is collected from individual police departments on a monthly basis through a system of voluntary cooperation with the Uniform Crime Reporting program (Uniform Crime Reports, 1978). In other words, the FBI can request, but cannot legally compel, over 3000 individual police departments to cooperate in reporting all types of crime. As may be imagined, such a voluntary system is vulnerable to numerous shortcomings, specifically in regard to reporting accurate data.

With respect to the reporting of victim/offender relationships to the FBI, there is no systematic follow-up of cases after the initial report is filed. Thus, when the police are notified of a homicide, the information is filed with the FBI. If the offender is arrested within a short period of time, information on victim/offender relationship is also filed. However, if the offender is arrested some weeks after the initial report is filed, information on victim/offender relationships may never be added and the initial report to the FBI simply records the victim/offender relationship as unknown.

For family related homicides, where the victim/offender relationship is known, 99.2 percent of the homicides were cleared within 24 hours by the arrest of one or more offenders. Approximately 85 percent of the friends and acquaintances homicides were cleared within 24 hours by the arrest of one or more offenders, but only 70.3 percent of the stranger homicides were cleared within that time period. In other words, if the type of homicide is one where the offender is easily found and arrested, as is true in family related homicides, victim/offender relationships are accurately reported to the FBI. If the offender requires more investigative time on the part of the police department, the reporting of victim/offender relationships to the FBI may be lost in the bureaucratic shuffle and never recorded. The latter explanation would therefore account for some of the unknowns reported in Table 4 (Riedel, 1981).

While results indicating an underreporting of stranger/friend/acquaintances/homicides is limited to a study of one city, similar results in other cities would support the conclusion that there are more homicides involving strangers than are currently being reported to the FBI. Since the FBI reports are of major interest to policymakers, researchers, and the general public, there may be a more frequent occurrence of stranger homicides than is currently recognized.

In regard to black homicide, stranger homicides are the major type of homicide that involves black offenders and white victims. Most criminal homicides are intraracial—either black offenders and victims or white offenders and victims. In the study of Memphis homicides, for example, 78.7 percent of the homicides involved black offenders and victims and 13.2 percent involved white victims and white offenders. Only 1.8 percent of the 555 Memphis homicides involved black victims and white offenders.

While only 6.3 percent of the homicides involved black offenders and white victims, they constituted over one-fourth (26.6%) of the stranger homicides. Among non-stranger victim/offender relationships, the black offender/white victim combination constituted only 2.2 percent. Interracial homicides, in other words, are comparatively rare but typically involve homicides among strangers (Riedel, 1981).

CONCLUSION

Criminal homicides involving friends and acquaintances appear to be the most frequent type of victim/offender relationships involving both black and white victims. Black victims, however, are more frequently involved in friends and acquaintance homicides than white victims.

The next most frequent type of victim/offender relationship involves family related homicides and black and white victims in almost equal proportions. There are more white victims involved in stranger homicides than black victims.

The validity of the FBI data presented in Table 4 was also examined by comparing that data with data gathered independently from homicides reported to the Memphis, Tennessee Police Department. The analysis suggests that information on stranger homicides is not being reported to the FBI. The latter finding leads to the conclusion that, nationally, there may be more stranger homicides than are currently being reported. It was also pointed out that stranger homicides represent a major category of interracial homicides; while most homicides are intraracial, over one-fourth of the stranger homicides studied in Memphis involve black offenders and white victims.

References

Adler, F. Sisters in Crime. New York: McGraw-Hill, 1975.

Curtis, L.A. Violence, Race, and Culture. Lexington, MA: Lexington-Heath, 1975.

Hindelang, M., M. Gottfredson, and J. Garofalo. Victims of Personal Crime. Cambridge, MA: Ballinger, 1978.

Riedel, M. "Stranger homicides in an American city." Unpublished paper, 1981.

Simon, R. Women and Crime. Lexington, MA: Lexington-Heath, 1975.

Uniform Crime Reports. Washington, DC: Federal Bureau of Investigation, 1978.

Table 1   Race of Victim and Offender Rates in the United States by Year (1968-1978)

Year	Race of Victim[1]		Race of Offender [2]	
	Black	White	Black	White
1968	33.7	3.8	25.9	2.1
1969	35.6	3.9	29.6	2.2
1970	38.3	4.3	29.7	2.5
1971	42.3	4.6	36.1	2.6
1972	43.4	4.9	37.2	3.0
1973	42.0	5.4	35.1	3.0
1974	42.6	5.7	33.1	3.1
1975	40.4	5.8	28.3	3.3
1976	40.4	5.4	30.8	3.4
1977	35.1	5.7	31.0	3.6
1978	34.7	5.9	34.8	4.3

[1] Data for victim rates taken from vital statistics tapes, *Nature and Patterns of American Homicide: Homicide Project,* National Institute of Law Enforcement and Criminal Justice, Oct. 1979-September 1981. Hereinafter referred to as *Homicide Project.*

[2] Data for offender rates taken from "Age, Sex, Race of Arrested Offender" tapes, *Homicide Project.*

Table 2   Race of Victim and Offender Rates in the United States by Age and Sex

		Race of Victim[1]		Race of Offender [2]	
		Black	White	Black	White
Sex					
	Males	58.5	9.0	48.9	6.7
	Females	13.2	2.9	10.3	.9
Age					
	15-19	21.5	5.1	26.7	4.6
	20-24	66.7	8.8	61.9	7.1
	25-29	82.3	8.8	70.0	6.3
	30-34	68.0	7.5	53.7	5.6
	35-39	62.2	7.5	48.3	4.9

[1] Data for victim's taken from vital statistics tapes, *Homicide Project.*

[2] Data for sex and age of offender taken from "Supplementary Homicide Report" tapes, *Homicide Project.*

Table 3 **Weapons Used in Criminal Homicides by Race of Offender[1]**

| | Black Offenders | | White Offenders | |
Weapon	Freq.	Percent	Freq.	Percent
Handguns	3697	51.8	2938	58.2
Rifles and Shotguns	978	13.7	316	6.3
Knives and Cutting Instruments	1461	20.5	828	16.4
Blunt Objects	289	4.0	282	5.6
Personal (Hands, Feet, etc.)	371	5.2	193	3.8
Strangulation and Asphyxiation	91	1.3	154	3.0
Other Weapons	292[2]	3.5	338[2]	6.7

[1] Data for weapon and race of offender taken from "Supplementary Homicide Report" tapes, *Homicide Report*.

[2] Includes 184 firearms for black offenders and 153 firearms for white offenders. Type of firearms could not be identified.

Table 4 **Victim/Offender Relationship by Race of Offender[1]**

| Victim/Offender Relationships | Black Victims | | White Victims | |
	Freq.	Percent	Freq.	Percent
Family Related	1572	19.0	2029	19.8
Friends and Acquaintances	3589	43.4	2976	29.0
Strangers	835	10.1	1640	15.9
Other Known	164	2.0	216	2.1
Unknown	2106	25.5	3406	33.2

[1] Data for victim/offender relationships and race of victim taken from "Supplementary Homicide Report" tapes, *Homicide Report*.

5

Black-on-Black Homicides: Overview and Recommendations*

Harold Rose

Life in large urban centers has been associated with economic gains for selected members of at least two generations of black migrants. During this interval blacks have made a major transition from living a predominately rural existence to comprising a significant numerical element in many of the nation's older and larger central cities. Although progress can be measured on a variety of indices, a number of serious problems have also accompanied this transition. This chapter is the concluding section of an important study of the greatest problem blacks face as urban residents: black-on-black homicide. The primary goal of Rose's research was to acquire a more precise understanding of the subculture of violence that pervades black urban communities and contributes to the high incidence of black homicides. According to Rose, more research is desperately needed to establish a precise set of relations that can be expected to increase the risk of victimization under certain identifiable circumstances. The recommendations that accompany this overview are specific suggestions, based on what is known at present about black homicide, for reducing the victimization level among blacks in urban environments.

CHANGING NATIONAL NORMS AND THE ROLE OF CULTURE ON HOMICIDE INCIDENCE

In a number of the earlier sections of this report, much emphasis was placed on changing national norms and on subsequent changes in the structure of American values. It was assumed that this represented a suitable overarching structure to be employed in understanding the increasing role of violence in American society in general and in the nation's larger black communities in particular. Such a framework would also facilitate an examination of the various theories, which relate to the role of culture on

* Reprint of Section 6, *Final Report, Black Homicide and the Urban Environment,* Center for Minority Group Mental Health Programs, National Institute of Mental Health, Jan. 5, 1981.

61

the propensity to commit acts of lethal violence, that have been put forth and that continue to find support in some quarters.

As the nation has moved from a period in which agrarian values dictated the roles of conduct in interpersonal relationships, to values chiefly fostered by industrial dominance, and finally to a period in which post-industrial values are beginning to gnaw away at previously held traditions, earlier notions regarding the appropriateness of using violence in specific contexts have also been altered. Throughout this report it has been assumed that interpersonal conduct leading to violent displays was culturally conditioned and that any changes in the cultural superstructure could possibly alter the pattern of violent responses in various ways. During the most recent fifteen-year period, violent deaths, such as homicides, suicides, and accidents, have emerged as the third leading cause of death in the nation (Holinger, 1980:472); and this in part has been attributed to a lack of respect for traditional values by young adults (Waldron and Eyer, 1975:383-396).

In almost all units in a national system of cities, there is growing evidence that certain socioeconomic changes have set the stage for increases in the risk of violent victimization in urban environments primarily occupied by a diverse black population. Moreover, in such instances, value shifts and subcultural explanations simply provide clues to the range of expected behavior under a prescribed set of circumstances. These circumstances evolve out of a combination of external determinants and internal responses.

HIGH HOMICIDE RISK ENVIRONMENTS AND THE PATTERN OF VICTIMIZATION

During the most recent period, the increasing complexity of circumstances in which individuals find themselves and the growing diffuseness regarding what might be considered normative responses often lead to behavior that is inimical to the best interest of the group and of the community of which it is a part. From the perspective of black youth, whose commitment to the values of their parents has been weakened by the emergence of new values, the incongruence between perceived and actual opportunity in the urban economy sets into motion a range of behaviors that were uncommon during a prior period. The incidence of black-on-black homicide is just one example of the behavioral manifestations of this situation that detracts from the quality of life available in large urban environments.

In an attempt to draw public attention to the homicide problem and to state more precisely its dimensions, our study focused exclusively on the growing seriousness of this problem in several of the nation's larger black communities. Few studies during the most recent upsurge in homicide frequency have devoted exclusive attention to the population at greatest risk of victimization—black Americans. Thus our effort, of necessity, had to rely on existing models as a means of attempting to unravel the various strands that account for blacks being both the principal victims and offenders in homicide transactions, at least on a per capita basis.

Another uncommon feature of this investigation was to assign a higher priority to the homicide environment than has usually been the case. It was found that the risk of homicide victimization varies greatly over space within the black community generally, but that the extent of the variation was partially related both to the nature of a given city's spatial configuration and to the sorting out of population along socioeconomic and lifestyle orientations. Varying combinations of environmental attributes obviously are associated with inherent risk-promoting features that are independent of external forces leading to variation in aggregate frequency of homicide within a specified time interval.

High risk environments were prevalent in each of our sample cities. Likewise, a set of stable high risk environments could often be identified. Nevertheless, the structure of victimization was observed to differ within specific high risk environments such that high-risk expressive and instrumental environments were likely to occur within different segments of the black community. A preliminary investigation has allowed us to target the location of this dual set of high risk environments and to consider ways that might be most appropriate in reducing risk in those areas which contribute most to raising the total level of victimization within some specified time interval. The presence of stable high risk environments seems to suggest the existence of a subculture of violence that is place specific. In those high risk environments where expressive violence represents the modal type, shades of the southern regional culture of violence predominate; and the cast of participants generally involves persons who have lost hope of ever escaping their marginal economic status.

High risk environments in which instrumentally motivated acts predominate are often place specific within the context of the black community. They tend more often to be found outside of the context of poverty neighborhoods, with working class neighborhoods more often representing the modal site. Such neighborhoods no doubt represent environments of greater opportunity for the commission of the type of felony in which the probability of a lethal response is heightened, such as armed robbery. Since the basic motivation associated with this dichotomous homicide pattern is different, one should also expect differences in the modal environment of victimization. Yet there is much evidence of overlapping spatial patterns and changes in modal dominance in specific neighborhood clusters over time. This we attribute to the population dynamics occurring within black communities, which frequently lead to alteration in neighborhood structure, both in terms of stage in the life cycle and in socioeconomic status.

Attempts to explain risk at the neighborhood scale, employing a set of structural variables, produced mixed results. The structural variables employed were less likely to explain risk in those environments where stress was low to intermediate than were they in high stress neighborhoods. High stress neighborhoods were much more likely to be environments dominated by expressive violence; instrumental violence was generally more commonplace in environments of intermediate stress, a situation indicating the juxtaposition of poor and non-poor populations. Only recently has more attention been devoted to this dichotomous set of homicide motivations.

Parker and Smith (1979:614-622) noted that the failure to recognize these motivational distinctions led to a weakness in accurately specifying the contribution of individual variables on homicide rates, as well as the strength of deterrence. At a much larger scale, that is, using states as units of analysis, previous writers produced findings similar to our own in terms of the strength of a common set of predictors to explain differential risk without acknowledging that homicide does not represent a unidimensional phenomenon. As those writers suggested, increased effort should be devoted to the specification of models that are more likely to predict risk of instrumental or non-primary homicides.

REGIONAL DIFFERENCES IN HOMICIDE PATTERN

Our interest in the role of value shifts resulted in the employment of life cycle stage and sex role differences as major points of departure in an effort to shed as much light as possible on this poorly understood phenomena. These variables were primarily examined through the use of statistics secured from public health departments and segments of the criminal justice system. This approach allowed us to simultaneously pursue the applicability of the two principal premises of the role of culture on the propensity for violence within a context of black residence in selected urban environments. Like many previous writers, we found weaknesses in both, but attempted to resolve the differences existing between the two on the basis of norms associated with the primary motivations for engaging in conflicts leading to death, which we agreed were regionally specific, at least at some point of temporal origin. Thus, a major premise extracted from the subculture of violence and southern regional culture of violence theses was that the former was predicated upon using violence to acquire some valued resource, whereas the latter was more likely to be related to preserving a valued position or relationship.

Blacks, we contend, were simply socialized in a context where one or the other principal motivation was operant. Because of both the black population's economic marginality and the environment's role upon their personality development, they were more likely to resort to violence when these dual norms suggested violence to be an appropriate response. We contend this led southern blacks to frequently engage in acts of expressive violence as a function of being socialized in an agrarian system, where honor and respect were primary themes associated with norms of conduct.

The desire for material resources on the part of blacks, who find these resources difficult to acquire through legitimate channels, leads to a willingness on the part of some group members to engage in violence to achieve such goals. The socialization process that provides legitimacy for this behavior is thought to have evolved in an urban industrial context, but has attained maturity in post-industrial settings. This leads to a much higher probability of primary or expressive homicide in large southern urban environments and the inverse in large northern environments. The mix of the black population in terms of regional socialization patterns, stage in the life cycle, economic marginality, and ability to successfully penetrate the legitimate economy are likely to greatly influence the expressive-instrumental mix in the pattern of homicide victimization within a given urban setting. The secondary data employed in this analysis provide some support for this position, but more scrutiny will be necessary in order to provide validation.

THE STRUCTURE OF THE STUDY

The two-tiered structure associated with this investigation has allowed us to view this issue both on a broad general level and on the basis of individual responses to specific items thought to be associated with a broad range of behaviors that influences the risk of victimization. Greater insight into the situations, ambitions, and feelings of individual actors, who were in some way associated with the homicidal drama, was gained through face-to-face contact.

Our survey data tapped a wide variety of responses to life in the black community. Although it would have been scientifically more meritorious to have captured a larger share of the randomly drawn sample, the nature of the sample population and the time constraint under which we were operating precluded that possibility. Nevertheless, the responses extracted from our several actor groups enable us to proceed cautiously in an attempt to specify those forces currently at work that prompt individuals with specific characteristics to behave in ways that heighten the risk of victimization. Another principal advantage of this approach was the ability to seek responses from offenders and representatives of victims. In the first tier of this investigation, little emphasis was placed on the offender's role because our primary focus was on the victim; that shortcoming was basically overcome in the second section of the report.

The nature of the survey responses enabled us to determine how well individual actors were functioning in the urban social economy, but failed to provide the desired insight into the direct contributions of the micro-environment to status and the threat of victimization. But the sample was not drawn in such a way that it could be sub-area specific within the context of the larger black community. The individual's perception of his or her environment was tapped, but the density of these responses did not allow for generalizations about the role of individual neighborhoods on a variety of elements thought to be important contributors to risk. Thus, our survey data largely enabled us to compile a set of personal histories and to deduce how those histories led to homicidal outcome.

Although our survey data did not shed much light on the role of the micro-environment on risk of victimization, it did reveal a strong association between self-image and community reputation on a broad spectrum of behavioral and attitudinal traits. These traits often served as significant predictors of behavior that had a high likelihood of proving troublesome for the respondent. The dichotomous hustler/non-hustler image forged by offenders often served as a critical variable in attempts to explain one's world view. This seems to represent a productive approach to aid in understanding current behavior. But it is obviously more important to learn what elements lead individuals to view themselves along the hustler/non-hustler continuum, for those forces are most important in influencing lifestyle preferences and the willingness to engage in a variety of activities to support those lifestyles.

This investigation brought that issue into sharper focus, at least as it relates to the risk of victimization; but much additional work is required in this area if we are expected to intervene in effectively reducing the risk of victimization and at the same time promoting the development of strong black communities. What information that is now currently available on this topic must be drawn from the spate of anecdotal works that have appeared within the last several years, but they all describe communities of despair rather than communities of hope.

Specific black populations were chosen as targets of this investigation. Residents of the central cities of Atlanta, St. Louis, and Detroit between 1970-75 constituted our primary population; and residents of Houston, Pittsburgh, and Los Angeles were our secondary target population. These places satisfied our several criteria related to patterns of black population growth, changing economies, and regional location. The attention given our secondary cities in this pilot effort was much less than originally planned. But the two-tier approach we chose to employ, in terms of data collection and analysis, left much less time and effort to be given to the latter group of places. Nevertheless, there appears to exist a series of comparative homicide trends. Among our sample cities, only Pittsburgh is without a well-matched counterpart, and we attribute that to its much smaller black population base.

The homicide trajectories, during the previously specified interval, were characterized by different slopes. By the end of the interval, the absolute level of black victimization was decreasing in Atlanta and Detroit, but increasing in St. Louis. Since the Atlanta and Detroit populations were projected to be growing more rapidly than the St. Louis population, we can conclude that risk of victimization was increasing in the latter city, while showing signs of decrease in the former. Among the secondary cities, homicide frequency was on the increase, except in Pittsburgh, where it showed signs of instability. The question of risk in Houston and Los Angeles is less clear, but it generally appears that risk is also rising.

KNOWLEDGE OF STRUCTURE OF VICTIMIZATION NECESSARY BASIS FOR RECOMMENDED INTERVENTION STRATEGIES

In order to be able to suggest place specific recommendations, however, the structure of victimization and the modal environment of greatest risk need to be understood. It was demonstrated that acquaintance homicides showed the greatest decline among young adult males in Atlanta; the inverse of this situation was true in St. Louis. In Detroit there was a downturn in the level of instrumental victimization during this interval. The crudeness of our measures of expressive and instrumental deaths, however, could lead to misclassifications, resulting in minor exaggerations in the structure of victimization at the individual city level. This was previously illustrated by citing the softness of the category defined as unknowns in calculating the level of instrumental death. Improved police clearance rates could shift a person from the unknown category to the acquaintance category, which would lead to the impression that instrumental deaths were decreasing, when in fact the opposite might be true. A case in point is the solving of deaths related to the control of the drug trade. Such deaths are clearly instrumentally motivated, but often bring together victims and offenders who are known to one another. It appears from our data that the possibility for the greatest misclassification might possibly have occurred in St. Louis during the interval between 1970-75.

The structure of victimization in the three city sample was city specific and influenced the micro-environment of risk in individual places. Expressive homicides clearly predominate in Atlanta; instrumental deaths take on greater relative importance in both Detroit and St. Louis. The extent to which the existing patterns continue to prevail appears to be directly related to the modal lifestyle orientation of young adult males, a situation largely influenced by the changing nature of the economy and by value shifts taking place within the larger society. Increased secularization and the growth of have-not populations with full knowledge of the cornucopia of goods to be consumed in American society have set the stage for the homicide epidemic in the nation's black communities during the previous decade.

The foregoing situation has promoted behavior that has increased the relative importance of homicide as a primary cause of death in the last decade and has at the same time seriously altered the structure of victimization. Although homicides occurring as an outgrowth of passion, jealousy, and quickness to anger are still commonplace, those associated with avarice and narcissism have evolved under a different set of conditions that threatens to erode any gains acquired by those holding onto the old values or developing the necessary skills to advance in a changing economy.

Young adult black males have been most seriously affected by this turn of events. Those least able to adapt to these changing circumstances are at the greatest risk of victimization. The number of life years lost among victims in our sample averaged 27. The major killer diseases are much less ruthless in that they strike their victims at higher average ages and thus lead to many fewer life years lost. The cohort of black males born since 1945 has become the group most subject to both the greatest likelihood of falling victim to homicide acts, as well as becoming victim to instrumentally motivated behavior. The younger age structure of the urban black population partially accounts for this phenomena; but in those cities with large elderly populations, they too have become increasingly vulnerable, although the absolute risk decreases with age. In his nine-year study of Chicago, Block points out that older black males experienced the highest percentage excess-increase in victimization among age-race-sex groups, and he largely attributes this to an increase in robbery homicides (Block, 1976: 504).

It has been demonstrated that homicide in the nation's larger urban environments is not a trivial cause of death. However, possibly because blacks and other low status persons have a history of a quick resort to violence, little concern has been exhibited during this recent epidemic because members of the larger society consider this to represent normative behavior for members of this population. This attitude is projected by Briggs-Bruce in his defense of the citizen's right to bear arms. In this context he states, "The great majority of these killings are among poor, restless, alcoholic, troubled people, usually with long criminal records. Applying the domestic homicide rate of these people to the presumably upstanding citizens whom they prey upon is seriously misleading" (Briggs-Bruce 1976: 40). But another response to this situation was expressed by Wolfgang. He indicates that "so long as the poor and blacks were raping, robbing, and killing one another, the general majority public concern with crimes of violence was minimal" (Wolfgang, 1978: 147). But the growing spillover of this behavior now threatens persons beyond the margins of the nation's black communities such that it is no longer what Briggs-Bruce simplistically refers to as the "niggertown Saturday night" phenomenon.

THE NEED TO PROMOTE ONGOING RESEARCH EFFORTS

As this study has emphasized throughout the report, homicide is not a unidimensional phenomenon. Like many other leading causes of death, it has a complex etiology and is thus not subject to an easy solution. Its many strains cannot be isolated in a laboratory setting as is true of disease-based killers, thereby making it even more difficult to explicate than the non-behavioral causes of death. Yet each of the major killer diseases attracts financial resources for research that is expected to lead to their eradication through foundations established for that purpose. Through continuous, costly, painstaking research, the American Cancer Society and the American Heart Association are making great strides toward reducing the risk of death from these diseases. Unfortunately, no such foundation exists to provide ongoing support of research that would lead to reducing homicide deaths. This is an indication that homicide is perceived to be only a minor contributor to the risk of dying, that it is too complex an issue to justify the investment that might be required to reduce its intensity, or that its disproportionate impact upon segments of the black population is inadequate to arouse sufficient national interest.

WHAT WILL IT COST TO BRING HOMICIDE RISK DOWN TO SOME ACCEPTABLE LEVEL?

It seems safe to conclude that the perceived benefits of such an investment do not justify the benefits to be derived. What represents an acceptable level of risk in this area? And, how much are we willing to pay to reduce the current risk to some to-be-determined acceptable risk? Such questions are seldom formally asked, but our ballooning health care costs tend to indicate that Americans are indeed willing to defray the expenditures associated with attempts to delay death, albeit even if it is through third party payment mechanisms. Dinman, in his discussion of risks on the expenditures necessary to reduce them, states: "Those risks that excite general concern are marked by a willingness to commit public resources to prevention are, per se, unacceptable" (1980: 1227).

A major goal of homicide research should be to make the current levels of risk unacceptable. But in order to do that, we must be able to specify what measures should be taken and what they would cost us. Whether we are willing to take the most effective measures depends upon how much segments of society are willing to sacrifice, and the level of reduced risk that might be expected by introducing various measures.

PUBLIC RESPONSE TO ONE SUGGESTED RISK LOWERING STRATEGY

Recommendations that are thought likely to lead to a reduction in the risk of victimization are highly varied and frequently seemingly infeasible, as evidenced by the public's response to them. This statement is partially predicated upon the call for an effective gun regulation policy and the strength of the efforts of countervailing forces to assure the public that this is either too high a price to pay for risk or that risk is not likely to be seriously altered in the high risk environments we have identified. Yet Farley thinks most of the recent increase in homicide deaths can be attributed to gun availability. He states unequivocally, "[W]ithin the non-white community, the increase in homicide results almost exclusively from murders by guns" (Farley, 1980: 184).

THE ROLE OF THE OPPORTUNITY STRUCTURE ON RISK

At this time, our most significant recommendations will focus on the opportunity structure and the need for more effective programs to enable a larger share of persons to escape the necessity of choosing lifestyles that are risk-promoting. Our data showed that more than one-half of all offenders and only slightly less than one-half of all victims were unemployed at the time of the incident. Unless persons, and particularly young persons, can identify productive outlets for their excess energy, the heavy burden of discretionary time is likely to prove troublesome. If we are unable to develop acceptable opportunities for such persons, the risk will remain high.

THE NEED FOR INNOVATIVE EDUCATIONAL PROGRAMS AS A RISK ABATEMENT STRATEGY

An individual's educational experience can also be related to whether that person may perpetrate or be victimized by a homicide. School suspensions, truancy, and an inability to find a role for themselves in the schools' extracurricular programs were all earmarks of persons likely to encounter risk-enhancing difficulties later in life. It is imperative, then, that we develop educational programs that can both educate and generate feelings of self-worth in persons whom the regular or traditional school programs tend to deny worth. If we are serious about producing potentially productive citizens out of persons who appear to be programmed for failure within the traditional school organizational structure, a major overhaul of our urban public school systems might be required. These persons can usually be identified very early in their school careers and should be candidates for programs designed to treat their specific problems.

Magnet schools have been designed to slow white flight from our school systems under court orders to desegregate, and they are usually outfitted with the most attractive programs conceivable. Thus, concepts of this sort must not only be employed to prevent white and upwardly mobile blacks from fleeing to the suburbs, but they should also be designed to prevent children who encounter difficulties in traditional programs from moving toward an early death. More than a decade ago, Robins indicated that school truancy was a good indicator of St. Louis schoolboys who would die at an early age (1968: 15-19), and our data found that this and other indices of school failure do indeed point in that direction.

THE NEED TO PROMOTE ALTERNATIVE LIFESTYLE ORIENTATIONS AS MEANS OF ALTERING RISK

As stated earlier, the hustler/non-hustler self-image that distinguished offenders turned out to be a primary determinant of lifestyle preferences and tastes that were risk promoting. In order to make the hustle a less viable option, or to at least direct those personalities with the inclination to devote creative energy toward survival into legitimate outlets, the opportunity structure in the nation's black communities must be expanded. Failing at this, a variety of sub-economies will emerge in which illicit activity will constitute an integral element.

INSTITUTIONAL RESPONSES TO RISK

These recommendations cited so far all revolve around attempts to forge local institutional structures that enhance one's chance of surviving in urban America rather than increase the risk of failure and the subsequent risk of an early death. In order to alter these risks, as a nation we must be unwilling to sacrifice a growing element of young adult blacks who indiscriminately choose lifestyles that are based on an overemphasis on consumerism—at the expense of longevity. Yet longevity, although a desired object in and of itself, must include a full and productive life.

Major institutions do not respond quickly to what is perceived as a non-crisis situation. But even if massive efforts of the sort discussed above were initiated, the benefits would probably be slow in coming. Nevertheless, they will be required if we wish to reduce the risk within a cohort by some specified ratio, such that a given cohort might be subject to the probability of an increase in its total life years. In the meantime, local programs which reflect the needs of local communities to treat the problem can be developed by organizations established for that purpose in conjunction with existing public agencies. The idea of establishing homicide prevention efforts, patterned after other preventive organizational efforts, appears to be new.

Nancy Allen, who is a health education specialist at UCLA and who has previous experience with other forms of life threatening behavior, recently published a book that suggests ways to initiate homicide prevention (Allen, 1980). This simply indicates that some interest is beginning to surface which attempts to foster or marshal efforts, at all levels, to come to grips with a serious form of life threatening behavior.

APPROACHES TO RISK REDUCTION ON THE BASIS OF SPECIFIC CONTRIBUTORS TO RISK

The preventive methods employed to curb one set of homicide motivations may not be effective for another set of motivations. Most attention is now focused on attempts to bring predatory behavior under control. In those environments where instrumental behavior adds appreciably to the risk of victimization, programs centered around drug education and abuse seem to be vital.

Efforts are underway in some communities to eliminate drug pushers actively promoting the distribution and sale of phencyclidine, known variously as angel dust or PCP. The black press in Los Angeles recently reported local efforts to rid the community of this dangerous drug. It was also recently reported in the *Journal of the National Medical Association* that PCP abusers treated at the Martin Luther King Jr. General Hospital in Los Angeles were predominantly black, even though the hospital's service population was 40 percent Mexican-American (Alexander, 1980: 849).

There is little question that drugs have played a role in the increased victimization, but we must gain a more precise knowledge of the role of individual drugs upon the incidence of violent death. The phencyclidine problem among sample cities surfaced only in Los Angeles. But drug abuse and drug apparatus were found to be considerable in both St. Louis and Detroit. A major effort is required to bring the illicit drug trade under control in those cities where it is known to heighten the risk of victimization, especially among young adult males.

Block suggests that the problem of robbery homicide could possibly be reduced by providing low-income, high-risk environment residents with a greater access to the cashless society (1977: 100). He is also a strong supporter of hardening the target through a variety of physical design innovations in high-risk communities. The latter strategy has been strongly promoted by Newman, whose work in this area has become well-known. In addressing himself to this issue in one of our sample cities, St. Louis, he partially attributes the high crime rate in the low-income black community to the design characteristics of some public housing units (Newman, 1980: 91-92).

In the past most persons have assumed that non-predatory homicides were outside the realm of public intervention as they most often occurred in private rather than public space. But as domestic disturbances continue to aggravate the risk of victimization, a few police departments have introduced family crisis intervention units to aid in amelioration of risk. Such a unit was placed into operation in Atlanta in 1976. This and other innovative techniques are required where domestic homicide rates reflect the need for intervention. Since most non-predatory homicides occur between friends and relatives, far less effort has been expended on formal programs that might lead to alleviation of risk.

References

Alexander, R. "Phencyclidine and chemical stroking." The Journal of the National Medical Association 72 (1980): 845-850.

Block, R. "Homicide in Chicago: a nine-year study (1965-1973)." Journal of Criminal Law and Criminology 66 (1976): 496-510.

Block, R. Violent Crime. Lexington, MA: Lexington-Heath, 1977.

Briggs-Bruce, B. "The great american gun war." The Public Interest (Fall 1976):37-60.

Dinman, B. "The reality of acceptance of risk." JAMA 244 (September 1980):1226-1228.

Farley, R. "Homicide trends in the United States." Demography 17 (May 1980):177-188.

Holinger, P. "Violent deaths as a leading cause of mortality: an epidemological study of suicide, homicide, and accidents." American Journal of Psychiatry 137 (April 1980):472-475.

Newman, O. Community of Interest. New York: Anchor Press/Doubleday, 1980.

Parker, R. and, M. Smith. "Deterrence poverty, and type of homicide." American Journal of Sociology 85(3) (1979): 614-624.

Robins, L. "Negro homicide victims—Who will they be?" Transaction (June 1968): 15-19.

Waldron, I. and Eyer, J. "Socio-economic causes of the recent rise in death rates for 15-24 year olds." Social Science and Medicine 9 (July 1975):383-396.

Wolfgang, M. "Real and perceived changes of crime and punishment." Daedalus 107 (Winter 1978):177-188.

6

Blacks and Juvenile Crime: A Review

Carl E. Pope

That juvenile crime continues to be a major problem is well documented. However, the extent and nature of juvenile crime is debatable especially as it reflects upon the black population. This chapter examines various trends and issues with regard to blacks and juvenile crime and reviews the nature and scope of the juvenile crime problem, various ways of measuring it, and some inherent problems in doing so. Since it is difficult, if not impossible, to examine juvenile delinquency apart from the way it is defined, sanctioned, and controlled, attention focuses on the juvenile court system, including the ways in which youth are funneled into that system. This review is intended to provide a basis for an assessment of juvenile crime and its relationship to America's black youth.

They started walking at dusk, two teenagers casually spreading the message that the streets of West Los Angeles were no longer safe. First they stopped Phillip Lerner and demanded money. Lerner had no cash, only his infant in a stroller. They let him pass and kept walking. They hailed Arkady and Rachel Muskin at a nearby intersection. The couple quickly handed over $8 and two wrist watches, and gratefully fled. Next the boys intercepted two elderly Chinese women and pulled out a pistol. When one woman tried to push the gun out of her face, ten bullets blazed out, killing both. The boys kept walking. They came upon a trio of friends out for an evening stroll. They took a watch and a few dollars and, without so much as a word, killed one of the three, a Frenchman visiting Los Angeles for the first time. The boys kept walking. At last they reached a drive-in restaurant where they found 76-year-old Leo Ocon walking on the sidewalk. They argued with him for less than a minute and then shot him down. Their evening over, they climbed into an old sedan and then, much as they had started, calmly went off into the night. (Copeland, et al., 1981).

The above scenario taken from *Newsweek* has been graphically repeated in most major metropolitan cities throughout the country and portrays a tale of violent juvenile crime with callous disregard for human life. Such incidents have increased the public's fear of crime generally, and especially with regard to violence among America's youthful population. Various opinion surveys, including Gallup, Harris, Roper, and victimization studies, have chronicled this increased fear, especially among the elderly population. For example, a 1975 survey conducted by the National Council on the Aging revealed that 23 percent of those elderly persons 65 years of age and over reported fear of crime as a major social problem (National Council on Aging, 1975). In many instances the elderly are afraid to venture outside their residences for fear of being mugged or otherwise brutalized. They are especially concerned about and vulnerable to gangs of juveniles who often prey upon the elderly as easy targets. Other age segments of the population express similar concern. The problem of violence within post-secondary schools has recently channeled public attention in this area. High school teachers frequently report repeated victimization by their students and are often afraid to venture onto the school grounds and into their classrooms.

Within the United States perceptions regarding both adult and juvenile crime are race specific (Pope and McNeely, 1981). That is, when utilizing official counts of criminal offenders, such as the arrest statistics contained in the Uniform Crime Reports (UCR), blacks are found to be overrepresented with respect to their population base. Across all age and offense categories, blacks are involved in 26 percent of all criminal incidents while they constitute approximately 12 percent of the population. Further, arrests for crimes of violence reveal a much higher disproportionate arrest rate for blacks (Skogan, 1979). It must be kept in mind, however, that these figures are derived from official tallies and may not be an accurate reflection of black/white crime rate differences. Official data and public perception regarding juvenile crime often focus on inner city areas where the severity of the problem is thought to be most pronounced (Swan, 1977). In sum, the problem of juvenile crime and official reactions to it frequently focus on black offenders within predominately black communities.

TRENDS AND MEASUREMENT OF BLACK YOUTH CRIME

Official Statistics

According to official statistics compiled in the UCR, arrests of persons aged 18 or under increased by 11.7 percent compared to a 9.5 percent increase for those aged 18 and older from 1969 to 1978 (Hindelang, et al., 1981). For the violent index offenses (murder, forcible rape, robbery, and aggravated assault) the arrest rate of persons under 18 years of age increased by approximately 44 percent, from 1969 to 1978. Comparable arrest figures for property index offenses (burglary, larceny-theft, and motor vehicle theft) reveal an approximate 23 percent rate increase.

These official arrest statistics document a substantial increase in criminal involvement of those under 18 years of age from 1969 to 1978, especially for crimes of a violent nature. In fact, for this nine year period, juvenile arrests for violent index offenses were up by 44 percent compared to a 41 percent increase for adults. In 1978, while persons under 18 years of age comprised 29 percent of the United States population, they accounted for 21 percent of all violent index crime and 46 percent of property index crime. Further, proportionate to their population composition, those under 18 years of age were overrepresented for the crimes of robbery, burglary, larceny-theft, and motor vehicle theft (Hindelang, et al., 1981).

With regard to race, the UCR data show that, for those under 18 years of age, blacks accounted for 23 percent of all arrests in 1978 (Hindelang, et al., 1981). Of those under 18 years of age, the proportion of black youths arrested for violent index offenses was 52 percent compared to an arrest rate of 44 percent for white youths. Again, for those under 18 years of age, black youth were arrested for 28 percent of all property index offenses compared to 69 percent for white youths. Proportionately more black youths were arrested for the crimes of forcible rape and robbery than were black adult offenders. In fact, for those offenses, blacks under 18 years of age have the highest arrest rates of any age/race grouping. (Hindelang, et al., 1981).

Official arrest statistics underscore the serious nature of juvenile crime, especially among the youthful black population. These data, however, are not without their problems and, as has often been argued, may provide an inaccurate picture of the crime problem. The UCR, as well as court statistics, prison counts, and similar tallies, have been criticized as being misleading, unreliable and fragmentary (Doleschal and Wilkins, 1972; Zeisel, 1971; Hindelang, 1974). Such data have also been accused of merely reflecting agency workload and thus are a more accurate statement regarding how agencies operate rather than a true representation of the crime problem. Perhaps more important, these official data are said to reflect "selection bias" associated with the criminal and juvenile justice systems. The argument here is that official arrest statistics are merely a reflection of the vagaries of individual officers in making an arrest, manpower deployment practices of various departments, police responsiveness to crime victims, and informal policy decisions to engage in aggressive patrol practices or proceed with less than full enforcement and similar factors. In fact, some critics have forcefully argued that the criminal and juvenile justice systems and their functionaries intentionally engage in discriminatory practices (Chambliss and Seidman, 1971). According to these critics certain population segments such as the poor, the unemployed, ethnic minorities, and those from lower class backgrounds are more likely to be arrested, convicted, and receive more severe sanctions. In an intensive study of juvenile offenders, Wolfgang and his colleagues maintained (1972:221):

. . . the rapidity with which the heavy volume of juvenile cases is handled, the initial absence of defense counsel for juveniles, and the weight of history strongly suggest that differential dispositions based upon race may be the result of discrimination, prejudice, bias.

Unfortunately, to date, the issue of selection bias remains unresolved. That is, some research findings across different sampling frames and with differing levels of methodological rigor support the above premise while others do not (Pope, 1979).

Self-Report Surveys

A major data source producing findings opposite to those in official statistics can be found in the results of self-report surveys where juveniles are asked to report or self-disclose their own involvement in delinquent activity. Self-report research began to gain prominence in the late 1950s and early 1960s partially as a result of concern regarding the methodological shortcomings of arrest statistics and as an attempt to test various sociological theories regarding the causes of delinquency. The majority of self-report findings reveal few differences between social classes and races among juveniles reporting their own involvement in delinquent activities (Chambliss and Nagasawa, 1969; Gould, 1966; Hirschi, 1969; Gold, 1970; Williams and Gold, 1972). For example, when white and black youth are asked to report their own degree of criminal involvement, the results tend to show that the differences are non-existent or much less than those found in official arrest statistics.

The critical question, of course, centers on the source of this discrepancy. If self-reports are accurate measurements of delinquency then why are black youths overrepresented in official tallies? Many scholars accounted for this inconsistency by arguing "selection bias" or "discrimination"— that the juvenile justice system differentially "selects out" or "discriminates against" lower class and black youth. Others pointed to the many methodological shortcomings of the self-report technique. The honesty of respondents and the ability to recall past events may cast doubt on the results obtained. There are also sampling problems in that relatively few self-report surveys have included race as a variable of contrast. Perhaps most important is the comparability of self-report and official crime counts since self-reports are weighted to rather trivial incidents such as fighting, drinking alcoholic beverages, smoking cigarettes, and the like. Thus, it has been argued that the two measurement sources are not comparable or that the results obtained from these two measures may not be so discrepant if one takes into consideration the "seriousness" question (Hindelang, et al., 1979; Elliot and Ageton, 1980). In sum, self-report surveys do reveal opposite findings with regard to race when compared to official statistics and, like official statistics, suffer from many unresolved methodological short-comings (McNeely and Pope, 1981).

Victimization Surveys

A third way of measuring crime developed in the mid 1960s and focused upon crime victims. During the 1970s these victimization surveys were collected on a national probability basis and within selected major met-ropolitan cities. Respondents were asked whether or not they had been the victim of a crime, the nature of the crime, the characteristics of offenders and whether or not the crime was reported to the police. Initial analyses of these data with regard to race revealed findings consistent with those found in official statistics—that blacks were overrepresented with regard to their population base in crimes of a personal nature. With regard to both offenders acting alone and in groups overrepresentation of non-whites in the offender population was found to exist across eight major cities (Hin-delang, 1976).

In a later study comparing the UCR and National Crime Panel (victim survey) estimates for race of arrestees and offenders in 1974 Hindelang (1978) reached similar conclusions. Blacks were found to be overrepresent-ed with respect to their population base in the common law personal crimes of rape, robbery, and aggravated and simple assault. These relation-ships held for those offenders under 18 years of age as well as those offenders over 18 years of age. As Hindelang (1978:101) observed:

> Thus, both among adults and juveniles, blacks are substantially overrepresented in relation to their representation in the general population regardless of whether the NCP data or the UCR data are used.

At first glance these results may seem to resolve the controversy regard-ing the findings of official statistics and self-report surveys but such a conclusion would be premature at best. Like both official statistics and self-report surveys, victimization surveys suffer from particular methodo-logical problems that may call into question categorical conclusions. As has been argued elsewhere, arrest statistics and self-report and victim surveys may not be congruent measures of the same phenomena and suffer from perceptual distortions that are likely to attenuate their findings (McNeely and Pope, 1980).

Overall, our review of trends and measurement issues in estimating black youth crime reveals a number of factors that must be taken into consideration before drawing any conclusions. Official arrest statistics do reveal that youthful crime generally, and specifically among blacks, is indeed a serious and increasing problem. It is these statistics that shape public perception regarding the crime problem and frequently lead to policy changes (Pope and McNeely, 1981). It is also true that these official statistics may not be an accurate representation of the crime problem. Moreover, self-report surveys have reached opposite conclusions while victim surveys have tended to support the official perception. It must be kept in mind that perceptual distortions plague all three measurement sources, all suffer from methodological shortcomings and thus may not be measuring the same phenomena. Also the degree to which selection bias permeates official statistics has not been ultimately resolved. Categorical conclusions will have to await further methodological refinement and more vigorous research designs dealing with the selection bias issue.

OFFICIAL PROCESSING OF BLACK YOUTH

Having reviewed trends and issues associated with the measurement of juvenile delinquency, our attention now turns toward the operation of the juvenile court system. Once juveniles have been identified as having violated a criminal law, or in many states, as having committed a so-called "status" offense (a non-criminal offense such as ungovernability, truancy, or runaway) then a variety of official decisions must be undertaken. Perhaps the most pivotal and fundamental initial decision is whether to refer the youth to the juvenile court. Here, the police, parents, and schools have an enormous amount of discretion in deciding whether to take action and the nature of that action. In some instances a juvenile's violation may be ignored (especially if it is considered non-serious and is the first offense) while in others it may be handled informally such as by providing professional counseling or by turning the case over to juvenile intake. If the case is brought to the attention of the juvenile authorities, then a variety of subsequent decisions begin to fall into place.

It must be determined, for example, whether or not the juvenile needs to be detained in a secure or non-secure facility and for how long. Some jurisdictions are more conscientious than others in providing criteria for reaching such a decision and establishing limits upon the length of confinement. Initial screening decisions frequently include deciding whether to close a case without action, handle it informally, or file a formal petition of delinquency. These decisions most often are made by probation officers who work for the juvenile court. If a formal petition is filed the case must eventually reach some final or ultimate disposition. In this instance the juvenile court in most jurisdictions has a variety of options, including closing the case, placing the juvenile on probation, or establishing wardship of the state which may result in placement in a shelter care or secure institutional facility. These decision points all involve a number of critical issues, including who is most likely to receive which alternative and under what circumstances. What factors, then, tend to influence the decision making at these various points?

A number of attempts have been made to examine the decision-making process in both the adult and juvenile justice systems. The results of these analyses do not lead to any ultimate conclusion regarding what factors are most important. Some argue that "achieved" characteristics or legal factors such as the nature of the offense, prior police or juvenile court contact, and the like, are most important criteria in reaching official decisions to arrest, prosecute, convict, and sanction. Others point to "ascribed" characteristics or extra-legal factors such as race, gender, appearance, or demeanor as most pronounced. Platt (1969), Martin (1970) and Schur (1973), for example, maintain that decisions within the juvenile justice system are frequently based on social attributes rather than legal criteria. As Schur notes:

> In our society, lower class children more than middle class ones, black children more than white ones, and boys more than girls, face high probabilities (i.e., run a special categorical risk in the actuarial sense) not only of engaging in rule violation in the first place, but also becoming enmeshed in official negative labeling processes (1973: 125-126).

Empirical support for this premise can be found in a study that reexamined 17 studies and considered the relationship between social class, race, and legal decision making in the juvenile justice system (Liska and Tausig, 1979). With regard to race, the authors found that while many of the reported findings resulted in non-significant racial differences, there was a strong amplification effect. Thus, a relatively heterogenous pre-arrest population quickly became transformed into a homogeneous non-white institutional population. Initial racial disparities become amplified at subsequent stages of juvenile processing. Feyerherm (1981), in examining case decisions focusing on juvenile status offenders, obtained similar results. In discussing those findings Feyerherm notes:

> Moreover, this amplification process, if it occurs at additional points in the processing of cases, would result in a situation in which the overall operation of the juvenile justice system would have the effect of introducing substantial biases in the treatment of classes of juveniles (especially minorities). However, an examination of biases at any single stage of the process would not reveal major evidence of biases. In short, while there was not evidence of blatant discrimination in these data, there is a suggestion of accumulations of discrimination, which collectively may have the same results (1981: 142-143).

Theoretical support can be found in both the conflict and labeling perspectives which stress that differential processing based on social characteristics is to be expected. Vold (1958), Turk (1966), Quinney (1970), and other conflict theorists argue that because of differences in the use of and access to power, minorities, the unemployed, and those from lower class positions in society are frequently treated more severely. Similarly, Becker (1963), Erickson (1962), Kitsuse (1962), and other labeling theorists argue that such groups are defined and stereotyped as criminal or delinquent because of the attributes they possess.

Existing research in both the adult and juvenile justice systems does not entirely support these allegations, however. Moreover, empirical research focusing on race differences in police, court, and correctional decision making have not yielded consistent findings. For example, with regard to sentence severity, studies by Johnson (1941), Garfinkel (1949), Bullock (1961), Foley and Rasche (1979), Meyers (1979), Farrell and Swigert (1978) Thomas and Cage (1977), and Uhlman (1979) found evidence of discriminatory treatment in that blacks were handled more severely than whites. Opposite conclusions were reached by Bensing and Schroeder (1960), Green (1961, 1964), Moore and Roesti (1980), Dison (1976), and Sutton (1978), who found no evidence of discriminatory treatment when comparing white and black offenders. While some of these discrepant findings may be accounted for by sampling and other methodological problems (Hagan, 1974; Hindelang, 1969; Pope, 1976; Cohen and Kluegel 1978), the lack of consistency in research findings and the increasing number of studies reporting race differences are cause for concern.

Police-Juvenile Encounters

Police, schools, and parents are the primary, although not the only, way in which youths are referred to the juvenile justice system. On the average, the major source of referrals to the juvenile court are the police. In one study of juvenile processing within ten California counties approximately 85 percent of all referrals to probation intake were from police agencies (Pope and Feyerherm, 1981). Most referrals by parents and school authorities generally occur as a result of "status" (non-criminal) offenses. These decisions to refer are highly discretionary especially in cases involving status offenses and those offenses of a less serious nature. There have been some attempts in recent years to identify and examine those factors that influence police decisions to arrest and refer; however, as in other areas of juvenile processing, these findings have been mixed.

In an early observational study of police-juvenile encounters Piliavin and Briar (1964) found that the police, in exercising their discretion, often responded to the demeanor of those youths they encountered. Youths who exhibited an uncooperative manner were more likely to be arrested, and black youth were proportionately more likely than white youth to be uncooperative—and thus to be arrested. Further, the police were found to focus their surveillance activity in areas with high black concentrations. It should be noted that these racial differences held only for crimes of a less serious nature. In a subsequent observational study of police-citizen encounters Black and Reiss (1970) found no evidence of race bias in the police handling of both adults and juveniles. Approximately 80 percent of those encounters observed were citizen initiated and, in the majority of instances, the police were most responsive to the wishes of the complainant. Initial race differences disappeared when the race of the complainant was taken into consideration—black complainants were more likely to request official action of some type. In those instances where there was no complainant, race differences were negligible.

In those studies utilizing official records the results are again inconsistent. Research by Goldman (1963), Ferdinand and Luchterhand (1970), Thornberry (1973, 1979) and Wolfgang, et al. (1972) indicate the possibility that in some jurisdictions the police are influenced by the race of the youth in making decisions. However, Terry (1967), Weiner and Willie (1971), Hohenstein (1969), McEachern and Bauzer (1967) could find no empirical evidence that such decisions were influenced by the race of the apprehended youth. In an interesting study of police arrest practices in a midwestern city, Hepburn (1977) concluded that police often arrested blacks on the basis of less evidence. Consequently, prosecutors were more likely to dismiss cases against black offenders because the evidence would not support the charges. These findings varied depending on the seriousness of the offense and racial composition of the population residing within the precinct area. Race differences were most likely to occur when the offense was of a less serious nature and the population composition was predominately black. In an examination of police post-arrest decisions to release burglary arrestees, Pope (1977) found race effects in the absence of legal factors such as prior record. For those offenders with no prior record, 91 percent of black arrestees were held for prosecution compared to 68 percent of all white arrestees (Pope, 1977:43). This relationship held for both adult and juvenile offenders.

The Decision to Detain

After the initial referral decision, a subsequent decision must be made as to whether a youth needs to be detained in a secure facility. In some jurisdictions it was not uncommon for youths to be detained for great lengths of time or up until the disposition of their cases. More recently, however, many jurisdictions have placed statutory limits on the length of confinement and mandate an attempt to find other ways for the youth to be handled, thus limiting the use of detention. It has often been observed that the effects of decision making are cumulative in that decisions made early on frequently affect those coming at later stages. Many observers have noted that those youths detained subsequent to arrest often face the most severe dispositions. This effect was illustrated in a study of the Massachusetts Department of Youth Services (DYS) which noted:

> The early detention decisions, which seem haphazard at best, serve to attach lasting labels to youths. These labels are regarded by persons in the corrections system as characteristics of the youth and are relied upon as the basis for making placement and treatment decisions. Not only does the fact of detention adversely affect future decisions, but also the place where one is detained. (Coates, et al., 1978).

According to the authors those detained in secure custody facilities were viewed as being more dangerous, more hardcore, more recidivistic when in fact, the data did not support this. Because they were viewed in this manner, however, they received the most severe dispositions. Thus, detention decisions can have an important impact on youth and are especially disturbing if such decisions are based on race.

In examining juvenile processing in a number of California counties, Pope and Feyerherm (1981) found that within the racial categories of black, Mexican-American, and white, those detained after arrest were most likely to have a formal petition filed. In a 1975 study of pre-hearing detention decisions Dungworth (1977) found that rates of detention were higher for non-whites compared to whites for those charged with status offenses. Similar results were obtained by Feyerherm (1981) who found that those charged with incorrigibility, truancy, and curfew violations were more likely to be detained than those charged with non-status offenses. Chused (1973) found that in two of the counties which he examined, blacks were more likely than whites to be detained even when controlling for prior record and seriousness of the offense. On the other hand, neither Sumner (1968) nor Cohen (1975) could find race differences in detention rates even when control variables were introduced.

Initial Screening Decisions

As noted above, initial screening decisions are frequently made by probation officers who decide whether to close the case, place the youth on informal probation, or file a formal delinquency petition. In some jurisdictions other options may be available but these are perhaps the three most common. Closed cases warrant no further action if, for example, the offense was not serious or the first one, or if the case is referred to another agency (welfare or health departments), or transferred outside the court's jurisdiction. Informal probation is often an agreement between parents and the probation officer in which the juvenile is placed under supervision but is not made a ward of the court. If a formal delinquency petition is filed, then the delinquency is officially adjudicated and may result in a variety of outcomes including commitment to a secure facility. Again, such decisions have very severe implications for these youth.

In examining these initial dispositions within selected California counties Feyerherm (1981) found that black youth were most likely to have a formal petition filed, followed by Mexican-American and white youth respectively. Further, substantial variations in the filing of a formal petition were found depending on the county in which the case was processed, ranging from a low of 22 percent to a high of 59 percent (Feyerherm, 1981:134). County variations were also found to exist by race, with blacks being treated more severely in some counties and less severely in others. In a similar study conducted by Pope and Feyerherm (1981) racial differences in the filing of a petition were evident. For example, in the case of status offenders, 50 percent of all black juveniles had a petition filed compared to 39 percent for white juveniles, and 43 percent for Mexican-Americans (Pope and Feyerherm, 1981:295). While race effects were found in these data, the direct effect of race was not pronounced. Nevertheless, various racial groups experienced different outcomes depending upon the source of referral, whether or not they were detained, and the type of referral offense. In another examination of differences between status and non-status offenders, Carter (1979) found race differences, with black youth being handled more severely. In an initial analysis of screening decisions in a major midwestern city, Moeller (1981) found that, for both males and females, non-whites were substantially more likely than whites to have a formal petition filed. Race differences in initial screening decisions were also found by Thornberry (1973,1979), Chused (1973) and Arnold (1971), depending upon the seriousness of the offense and number of prior offenses. However, with regard to intake decisions, Cohen and Klugel (1979), Terry (1967) and Thomas and Sieverdes (1975), found that differences between white and black youth were either minimal or non-existent.

Final Disposition

This represents the final stage in the progression of youths through the juvenile court system. Generally, three options are available: closing the case, placing the juvenile on probation (in some jurisdictions without wardship), or establishing formal supervision of the juvenile. In the last instance the youth remains under the authority of the court and can be handled in a variety of ways including placement in a shelter care facility or secure juvenile institution. Most often, juvenile court judges preside over a formal hearing at which the disposition of the case is determined. In some jurisdictions the juvenile has a right to a jury trial. Again, depending upon the jurisdiction and the nature of the case, the prosecuting attorney (and, correspondingly, defense attorney) may be involved in these proceedings. It should be kept in mind that the number of juvenile cases reaching final disposition is much smaller than those arrested by the police or processed through the initial intake. At the latter stage, a large number of cases are closed without further action or youths may be placed on informal probation. For the most part, only those cases for which a formal petition is filed go forward to a formal hearing and disposition. Also, for crimes of a relatively serious nature, the juvenile can be waived to the criminal court and handled as an adult. The final disposition is important as it can result in institutional confinement with all its attendant deprivations. Also, in many jurisdictions the youth can be confined until the age of his or her majority. It is at this later stage that race effects may be most pronounced in creating, as some authors have argued, a homogeneous black institutional population.

It has frequently been noted that both those committing the most serious offenses and the least serious (or non-criminal status offenses) are most likely to receive more severe final dispositions. In examining gender differences in the disposition of runaways, Mann (1979) found that black females were more severely sanctioned than black males. As she notes:

> . . . the present study found that black youths comprised the majority of runaways handled by the juvenile court observed. While the black female status offenders of this type were sanctioned more severely by the court than black males who had committed the same offense; contrarily, white boys who had left home without permission were more harshly treated than adolescent white females.

In another examination which included all status offenses, Feyerherm (1981) found that those most likely to receive formal supervision included females and non-whites (especially blacks). Also, there was substantial variation across county jurisdictions in the use of options available at final disposition. Datesman and Scarpitti (1977) found that females were treated more severely for status offenses than males but noted few racial differences, although there was some variation depending upon the degree of prior delinquent involvement. Thomas and Cage (1977) found that a number of extra-legal factors influenced the disposition of juvenile offenders leading them to conclude:

> Both blacks and school drop-outs are considerably more likely to face confinement for their offenses than whites and those still in school, regardless of the number of prior offenses. (1977:248).

Among those studies that did find racial differences at final disposition (blacks being treated more severely) included Thornberry (1973, 1979), Figuerra-McDonough (1979), Carter and Chelland (1979), Strasburg (1978), and Arnold (1971). The absence of race effects at final disposition were reported by Scarpitti and Stephenson (1971), Ferdinand and Luckterhand (1970), Schuster (1981), Cohen and Kluegel (1978), Carter (1979), Pawlak (1973), Horwitz and Waserman (1980), and Terry (1967). Again, as with our examination of other decision points in juvenile processing, the results are inconclusive with regard to race effects.

THE LEGACY OF JUVENILE JUSTICE

The legacy of the juvenile justice system began in 1899 in Illinois with the passage of the Juvenile Court Act, which created special court proceedings in the handling of juveniles. The official rationale for the juvenile court was the "protection of children"—to remove the stigma of "criminal" and to act in the best interests of youths. Major forces behind passage of the act, which quickly spread to other states, included humanitarian and religious concerns regarding the treatment of children. These concerns were philosophically derived from the concept of "parens patriae"—that the state functions as surrogate parents in acting on behalf of and in the best interest of juveniles. Children were not to be viewed as necessarily "bad, evil or wicked" but as somehow "sick, misguided or wrongful." They were not to be punished as adults fully responsible for their actions but rather were viewed as being in need of care and treatment. This was the "ideal." The development of the juvenile court was marked by informal procedures and lack of procedural safeguards in order to accomplish this "ideal" as quickly as possible.

Unfortunately, the ideal vision of the juvenile court did not necessarily measure up to its reality. Some scholars, for example, in reviewing the history of the juvenile court have noted that it resulted in no major innovations and functioned primarily to serve the middle class value system of the reformers (Platt, 1969; Fox 1970). In this sense, it was seen as a conservative movement designed, intentionally or not, to control and repress lower-class working people and their offspring. The "ideal" was also called into question in a series of Supreme Court decisions affecting juveniles that were decided in the late 1960s. Among these cases were included Kent v. United States, 383 U.S. 541 (1966), In re Gault, 875 S.Ct. 1428 (1966), and In re Winship, 90 S.Ct. 1068 (1969), all of which dealt with procedural safeguards. In perhaps the most famous of these cases, In re Gault, the Supreme Court held that juveniles facing possible deprivation of liberty have certain constitutional rights, among which include the right to be notified of the charges, to confront and cross-examine witnesses and the right to have counsel present. In reaching its decision, the Court reviewed the history of juvenile justice noting its humanitarian concerns and the goal of treatment and protection of youth. However, the Court also noted that juvenile offenders often faced the loss of their freedom for many years in secure confinement and that such decisions were often reached in an informal and perfunctory manner. As Justice Fortas stated:

> Ultimately, however, we confront the reality of that portion of the juvenile court process with which we deal in this case. A boy is charged with misconduct. The boy is committed to an institution where he may be restrained of liberty for years. It is of no constitutional consequence—and of limited practical meaning that the institution to which he is committed is called an Industrial School. The fact of the matter is that, however euphemistic the title, a "receiving home" or an "industrial school" for juveniles is an institution of confinement in which the child is incarcerated for a greater or lesser time. (Cited in Cohen, 1981:573.)

Thus, even under the guise of "treatment," both juveniles and adults can be made to suffer severe consequences.

The ideal is also to treat juvenile offenders equally with regard to social characteristics such as gender and race. However, a variety of studies focusing upon the juvenile court have shown that substantial differences in the treatment of status offenders often exist in that females are recipients of the most severe outcomes (Pope and Feyerherm, 1982; Sarri, 1978). Similarly, with regard to race, our review of the juvenile court system has shown that at some points in time and in some jurisdictions black youth are treated differently than white youth. As noted, these findings have not been consistent, in that some research shows no evidence of racial bias. Some of these inconsistent findings can be accounted for by sampling and other methodological problems but others cannot. Research is necessarily imperfect since it is virtually impossible to accurately measure all that one may want and research designs do differ with regard to methodological rigor. However, those findings which demonstrate that one's racial status affects juvenile court outcomes cannot be categorically ignored and dismissed.

CONCLUSION

This review has been necessarily brief and not exhaustive of all procedures and issues involved in the administration of juvenile justice. While we have examined police discretion in handling juveniles, we did not examine how parents and schools make similar decisions or, for that matter, private police agencies. For example, in a recent study examining decisions by store employees to refer those apprehended for shoplifting Lundman (1978) discovered that both adult and juvenile non-whites were most likely to be referred, again underscoring the importance of race. Similarly, custodial decisions have important implications for youth, such as the manner in which they are housed and when they are released. In a study of Camp Hill, a secure juvenile facility in Pennsylvania, Sprowls and Bullington (1977) found that, when contrasted with whites, blacks served much longer sentences. Similarly, Miller and Ohlin (1981), in examining juvenile corrections in Massachusetts, found that minority youth and those of lower socioeconomic status were overrepresented in secure care facilities. Discretion exercised at these points has a critical impact on delinquent youth and needs to be critically examined.

This chapter underscored a number of recurrent themes found in the juvenile justice literature. Police, parents, probation officers, judges, and other court functionaries have a tremendous amount of discretion in reaching a variety of decisions affecting juveniles. Such discretion is most likely to be used in those instances where the offense is of a less serious nature especially in cases of status offenders. That status offenders are frequently treated the same as or more harshly than those charged with the most severe infractions is indeed cause for concern. Although some jurisdictions have sought to remove status offenders from the purview of the juvenile court, in many places status offenders are held in detention and ultimately confined in secure facilities for offenses that would not be criminal had they been adults. Another important theme focuses on the dynamic nature of juvenile processing and the effects that early decisions have upon later ones. If these early decisions, such as detention, are made in a haphazard or discriminatory manner then later decisions are likely to amplify this effect. Finally, a number of studies reported here and elsewhere have noted the impact that organizational constraints may place on juvenile justice decision making (Pope, 1981). Cicourel (1968) and Emerson (1969), for example, have demonstrated the fact that internal organizational policies often play a major role with regard to juvenile processing decisions. In examining decisions regarding violent juvenile offenders in three metropolitan New York Counties, Strasburg (1979) found that dispositions varied greatly depending upon the county in which the youth was processed. Further, there was some indication that these organizational decisions varied depending upon the race of the offender. In summary, then, what ultimately happens to juvenile offenders may be a function of what one has done, who one is, and where one is processed.

References

Arnold, W.R. "Race and ethnicity relative to other factors in juvenile court dispositions." American Journal of Sociology 2:211-227, 1971.

Becker, Howard. The Outsiders. New York: Macmillan, 1963.

Bensing R.C. and Schroder O. Homicide in an Urban Community. Springfield, Ill: Charles C. Thomas, 1960.

Black, D. and Reiss A. "Police control of juveniles." American Sociological Review 35:63-77, 1970.

Bullock H. A. "Significance of the racial factor in the length of prison sentence." Journal of Criminal Law, Criminology and Police Science 52:411-417, 1961.

Burke, P. and Turk A. "Factors affecting post-arrest dispositions: a model for analysis." Social Problems 22:313-332, 1975.

Carter, T.J. "Juvenile court dispositions: a comparison of status and non-status offenders." Criminology 17(3):341-360, 1979.

Carter, T.J. and Chelland, D. "A neo-marxian critique: formulation and test of juvenile dispositions as a function of social class." Social Problems 27(1):96-108, 1979.

Chambliss, W. and Seidman, R. Law, Order and Power. Reading, Mass.: Addison-Wesley, 1971.

Chambliss, W. and Nagasawa, R.H. "On the validity of official statistics: a comparative study of white, black and japanese high school boys." Journal of Research in Crime and Delinquency, 1969.

Chused, R.H. "The juvenile court process: a study of three New Jersey Counties." Rutgers Law Review 26(2):488-589, 1973.

Cicourel, Aaron. The Social Organization of Juvenile Justice. New York: John Wiley, 1968.

Coates, R.D., Miller, A.D., and Ohlin, L.E. Diversity in a Youth Correctional System: Handling Delinquents in Massachusettes. Cambridge, Mass.: Ballinger, 1978.

Cohen, F. The Law of Deprivation of Liberty: A Study in Social Control. St. Paul, Minn.: West, 1981.

Cohen, L.E. "Pre-adjudicatory detention in three juvenile courts: an empirical analysis of the factors related to detention decision outcomes." Analytic Report SD-AR-8. Washington, D.C.,: U.S. Government Printing Office, 1975.

Cohen, L.E. and Kluegel, J.R. "Determinants of juvenile court dispositions: ascriptive and achieved factors in two metropolitan courts." American Sociological Review 43(2):162-176, 1978.

Cohen, L.E. and Kluegel, J.R. "Selecting delinquents for adjunction." Journal of Research in Crime and Delinquency 16(1):143-163, 1976.

Copeland, J.E., et al. "The plague of violent crime." Newsweek (March):46-54, 1981.

Datesman, S.K. and Scarpetti, F.R. "Unequal protection for males and females in the juvenile court," in Theodore N. Ferdinand (ed.) Juvenile Delinquency: Little Brother Grows Up. Beverly Hills, Ca.: Sage, 1977.

Dison, J.E. "An empirical examination of conflict theory: race and sentence length." Unpublished Ph.D. dissertation, North Texas State University, 1976.

Doleschal, E. and Wilkins, L. Criminal Statistics. Washington, D.C.: U.S. Government Printing Office, 1972.

Dungworth, T. "Discretion in the juvenile justice system: the impact of case characteristics on prehearing detention," in Theodore N. Ferdinand (ed.) Juvenile Delinquency: Little Brother Grows Up. Beverly Hills, Ca: Sage, 1977.

Elliot, D. and Ageton S.S. "Reconciling race and class differences in self-reported and official estimates of delinquency." American Sociological Review 45(1):95-110, 1980.

Emerson, R.M. Judging Delinquents: Context And Process In The Juvenile Court. Chicago, Ill.: Adline, 1969.

Erickson, J. "Notes on the sociology of deviance." Social Problems 9:307-314, 1962.

Farrell, R.A. and Swigert, V.L. "Legal disposition of inter-group and intra-group homicides." The Sociological Quarterly 19(4):565-576, 1978.

Figuerra-McDonough. "Processing juvenile delinquency in two cities." Journal of Research in Crime and Delinquency 16(1):114-142, 1979.

Ferdinand, T.N. and Luckterhand, E.G. "Inner-city youth, the police, the juvenile court and justice." Social Problems 17:510-527, 1970.

Feyerherm, W. "Juvenile court dispositions of status offenders: an analysis of case decisions," in R.L. McNeeley and Carl E. Pope (eds.) Race, Crime and Criminal Justice. Beverly Hills, Ca: Sage, 1981.

Foley, L. and Rasche, C.E. "The effect of race on sentence, actual time served and final dispositions of female offenders," in John A. Conley (ed.) Theory and Research in Criminal Justice: Current Perspectives. Cincinnati, Ohio: Anderson, 1979.

Fox, S.J. "Juvenile justice reform: an historical perspective." Stanford Law Review 22:1187, 1970.

Garfinkel, H. "Research notes on inter- and intra-racial homicides," Social Forces 27:369-381, 1949.

Gold, M. Delinquent Behavior in an American City. Belmont, Ca.: Brooks/Cole, 1970.

Goldman, N. The Differential Selection of Juvenile Offenders for Court Appearance. New York: National Council on Crime and Delinquency, 1963.

Gould, L.C. "Who defines delinquency: a comparison on self-reported and officially reported indices of delinquency for three racial groups." Social Problems 16:325-336, 1966.

Green, E. "Inter- and intra-racial crime relative to sentencing." Journal of Criminal Law, Criminology and Police Science 55:348-358, 1964.

Green, E. Judicial Attitudes in Sentencing. London: Macmillan, 1961.

Hagan, J. "Extra legal attributes and criminal sentencing: an assessment of a sociological viewpoint." Law and Society Review 8:357-383, 1974.

Hepburn, J.R. "Race and the decision to arrest: an analysis of warrants issued." Journal of Research in Crime and Delinquency 15:54-73, 1977.

Hindelang, M.J. "Race and involvement in common law personal crimes." American Sociological Review 43:93-109, 1978.

Hindelang, M.J. An Analysis of Victimization Survey Results from the Eight Impact Cities: Summary Report. Washington, D.C.: U.S. Government Printing Office, 1976.

Hindelang, M.J. "The uniform crime report revisited." Journal of Criminal Justice 2:1-18, 1974.

Hindelang, M.J. "Equality under the law." Journal of Criminal Law, Criminology and Police Science 60:306-313, 1969.

Hindelang, M.J., Gottfredson Michael R., and Flanagan, Timothy J. Sourcebook of Criminal Justice Statistics-1980. Washington, D.C.: U.S. Government Printing Office, 1981.

Hindelang, M.J. Hirschi, T. and Weis, J.G. "Correlates of delinquency: the illusion of discrepancy between self-report and official measures." American Sociological Review 44(6)-995-1014, 1979.

Hirschi, T. Causes of Delinquency. Berkeley: University of California Press, 1969.

Hohenstein, W.F. "Factors influencing the police disposition of juvenile offenders," in Thorsten Sellin and Marvin Wolfgang (eds.) Delinquency: Selected Studies. New York: John Wiley, 1969.

Horwitz, A. and Wasserman, M. "Some misleading conceptions in sentencing research: an example and a reformulation in the juvenile court." Criminology 18(3):411-424, 1980.

Johnson, G.B. "The negro and crime." Annals of the American Academy of Political and Social Science 271:93-104, 1941.

Kitsuse, J.E. "Societal reaction to deviant behavior: problems of theory and method." Social Problems 9:247-256, 1962.

Liska, A.E. and Tausig, M. "Theoretical implications of social class and racial differentials in legal decision making for juveniles." The Sociological Quarterly 20:197-208, 1979.

Lundman, R.J. "Shoplifting and police referral: a reexamination." Journal of Criminal Law and Criminology 69(3):395-401, 1978.

Mann, C.R. "The differential treatment between runaway boys and girls in juvenile court." Juvenile and Family Courts Journal 30(2):37-48, 1979.

Martin, J.J. Toward a Political Definition of Delinquency. Washington, D.C.: U.S. Government Printing Office, 1970.

Miller, A.D., and Ohlin, L.E. "The politics of secure care in youth correctional reform." Crime and Delinquency 27(4) 449-467, 1981.

McEachern, A.W. and Bauzer, R. "Factors related to disposition in juvenile police courts," in Malcolm W. Klein and Barbara G. Myerhoff (eds.) Juvenile Gangs in Context: Theory, Research and Action. Englewood Cliffs, N.J.: Prentice-Hall, 1967.

McNeely, R.L. and Pope, C.E. "Socioeconomic and racial issues in the measurement of criminal involvement," in R.L. McNeely and Carl E. Pope (eds.) Race, Crime and Criminal Justice. Beverly Hills, Ca: Sage, 1981.

McNeely, R.L. and Pope, C.E. "Racial issues in the measurement of criminal involvement." The Journal of African-Afro-American Affairs (Spring) 4:9-26, 1980.

McNeely, R.L. and Pope, C.E. "Race and involvement in common law personal crime: a response to Hindelang." The Review of Black Political Economy 8:405-410, 1978.

Meyers, M. "Official parties and official reactions: victims and the sentencing of criminal defendants." Sociological Quarterly 201:529-549, 1979.

Moeller, R. "Gender bias in juvenile court processing." Unpublished master's thesis, University of Wisconsin-Milwaukee, 1981.

Moore, L.A. and Roesti, P.M. "Race and two juvenile justice decision points: the filing of a petition and declaration of wardship." Paper presented at the annual meetings of the Midwest Sociological Association, Milwaukee, Wisconsin, 1980.

National Council on the Aging. The Myth and Reality of Aging in America. Washington, D.C.: U.S. Government Printing Office, 1975.

Pawlak, E.J. "Differential selection of juveniles for detention." Journal of Research in Crime and Delinquency (July) 152-165, 1973.

Piliavin, I. and Briar, S. "Police encounters with juveniles." American Journal of Sociology 70:200-214, 1964.

Platt, A. The Child Savers: The Invention of Delinquency. Chicago, Ill.: University of Chicago Press, 1969.

Pope, C.E. "Changing conventional systems: theoretical and analytic perspectives." Crime and Delinquency 27:127-134, 1981.

Pope, C.E. "Race and crime revisited." Crime and Delinquency 25:347-357, 1979.

Pope, C.E. "Post-arrest release decisions: an empirical examination of social and legal criteria." Journal of Research in Crime and Delinquency 15:35-53, 1977.

Pope, C.E. "The influence of social and legal factors in sentence dispositions: a preliminary analysis of offender based transaction statistics." Journal of Criminal Justice 4:203-221, 1976.

Pope, C.E. and Feyerherm, W.H. "Gender bias in juvenile court dispositions." Journal of Social Service Research (forthcoming).

Pope, C.E. and Feyerherm, W.H. "Race and juvenile court dispositions: an examination of initial screening decisions." Criminal Justice and Behavior 8(3):287-301, 1981.

Pope, C.E. and McNeely, R.L. "Race, crime and criminal justice: an overview," in R.L. McNeely and Carl E. Pope (eds.) Race, Crime and Criminal Justice. Beverly Hills, Ca.: Sage, 1981.

Quinney, R. The Social Reality of Crime. Boston, Mass.: Little Brown, 1970.

Sarri, R.C. "Status offenders: their fate in the juvenile justice system," in Richard Allinson (ed.) Status Offenders and the Juvenile Justice System: An Anthology. National Council on Crime and Delinquency, 1978.

Scarpetti, F.R. and Stephenson, R.M. "Juvenile court dispositions: factors in the decision-making process." Crime and Delinquency 17(2):142-151, 1971.

Schur, E.M. Radical Non-Intervention: Rethinking the Delinquency Problem. Englewood Cliffs, N.J.: Prentice-Hall, 1973.

Schuster, R.L. "Black and white violent delinquents: a longitudinal cohort study," in R.L.

McNeely and Carl E. Pope (eds.) Race, Crime and Criminal Justice. Beverly Hills, Ca.: Sage, 1981.

Skogan, W.G. "Crime in contemporary America," in Hugh D. Graham and Ted R. Gurr (eds.) Violence in America. Beverly Hills, Ca.: Sage, 1979.

Sprowls, J.T. and Bullington, B. "Removing juveniles from camp hill: a case study," in Theodore N. Ferdinand (ed.) Juvenile Delinquency: Little Brother Grows Up. Beverly Hills, Ca.: Sage, 1977.

Strasburg, P.A. Violent Delinquents. New York,: Monarch Press, 1978.

Sumner, H. Locking Them Up: A Study of Initial Juvenile Detention Decisions in Selected California Counties. National Council on Crime and Delinquency, 1968.

Sutton, L.P. Variations in Federal Criminal Sentences: A Statistical Assessment at the National Level. SD-AR-17 U.S. Department of Justice: U.S. Government Printing Office, 1978.

Swan, Alex T. "Juvenile delinquency, juvenile justice, and black youth," in Robert T. Woodson (ed.) Black Perspectives on Crime and the Criminal Justice System. Boston, Mass.: G.K. Hall, 1977.

Terry, R.M. "The screening of juvenile offenders." Journal of Criminal Law, Criminology and Police Science 58:173-181, 1967.

Thomas, C.C. and Cage, R.J. "The effect of social characteristics on juvenile court dispositions." Sociological Quarterly 18:237-252, 1977.

Thomas, C.A. and Sieverdes, C.M. "Juvenile court intake: an analysis of discretionary decision-making." Criminology 12(4):413-432, 1975.

Thornberry, T.P. "Sentencing disparities in the juvenile justice system." Journal of Criminal Law and Criminology 70(2):164-171, 1979.

Thornberry, T.P. "Race, socioeconomic status and sentencing in the juvenile justice system." Journal of Criminal Law and Criminology 64(1):90-98, 1973.

Turk, A. Criminality and the Legal Order. Skokie, Ill.: Rand McNally, 1966.

Uhlman, T.M. Racial Justice. Lexington, Mass.: Lexington, 1979.

Vold, G.B. Theoretical Criminology. New York: Oxford University Press, 1958.

Weiner, N.L. and Willie, C.V. "Decisions by Juvenile Officers." American Journal of Sociology 77(2):199-210, 1971.

Williams, J.R. and Gold, M. "From delinquent behavior to official delinquency." Social Problems (Fall) 209-228, 1972.

Wolfgang, M.E., Figlio, R.M., and Sellin, T., Delinquency in a Birth Cohort. Chicago, Ill.: University of Chicago Press, 1972.

Zeisel, H. "The Future of Law Enforcement Statistics—A Summary View. Federal Statistics: A Report of the President's Commission, Vol II. Washington, D.C.: U.S. Government Printing Office, 1971.

7

Women, Race, and Crime*

Vernetta D. Young

This article examines the interrelationships among women, race, and crime as they are purported to occur in the comprehensive discussion of female crime provided by Freda Adler in 1975. Adler's thesis was that patterns of female criminality differ because of differential opportunities historically available to offenders. The empirical assertions concerning the pattern of crime for black and white males and females are examined using victim survey data. It was concluded that the explanations for racial differences in female crime and delinquency advanced by Adler have little value since the empirical differences they purport to explain are not supported by the data.

The purpose of this chapter is to examine the interrelationships among women, race, and crime as they are purported to occur in the comprehensive discussion of female crime provided by Adler (1975). A central hypothesis advanced by Adler is that patterns of female criminality differ by race because of differential opportunities historically available to offenders.

Adler (1975) speculates that the current pattern of black female crime is indicative of the future pattern for white female criminals. She proposes that, since slavery, "sex-role convergence" has occurred among black males and black females to a far greater degree than among white males and white females. This has led, according to Adler, to a similarity, not only in the criminal behavior patterns of black males and black females but also in the patterns for black females and white males. Furthermore, with the emergence of the women's liberation movement, Adler suggests that there will be the same sex-role convergence among white males and white females resulting in similar patterns of criminal behavior.

In addition to Adler's general thesis, a number of more specific propositions relevant to the relations among sex, race, and crime were also advanced and merit empirical scrutiny:

(1) The pattern of criminal involvement for females differs by race

---

* *Criminology*, vol. 18, no. 1, May 1980, pp. 26-34. Reprinted with permission.

with black female offenders concentrated in crimes against persons and property and white female offenders involved in both "blue collar" crimes (vice, assault, robbery, and so on) and white collar crime.

(2) The pattern of criminal behavior of black females is closer to the pattern of white males than it is to that of white females.

(3) Black female criminality parallels the criminality of black males more closely than the criminality of white females does that of white males.

(4) The ratio of black to white female criminal involvement is much larger than the black to white male ratio.

This chapter will address the tenability of Adler's predicted relationships. Victim survey data will be used to address Adler's assertions concerning the pattern of crime for blacks and whites with a central focus on female criminality. Ideally, a test of Adler's theory would rely on longitudinal data, relating changes in patterns of female criminality to changes in sex-role convergence. However, at a minimum, the theory also demands that the postulated relationships among sex, race, and crime are empirically tested. The victim surveys, based on representative samples of households and commercial establishments, provide new data that permit an examination of characteristics of offenders and incidents that are independent of official statistics. Thus, for example, they provide information about the offenders in victimizations regardless of whether the event was reported to the police.

THE DATA

Under the auspices of the Law Enforcement Assistance Administration, the Bureau of the Census conducts the National Crime Survey. This series of victimization surveys, initiated in 1972, is composed of both a national panel survey and a number of city surveys. The data to be used in this article are derived from the city surveys. Between 1972 and 1975, 26 of the nation's largest cities were surveyed.[1] In each of the cities surveyed, a stratified probability sample of households was drawn and residents were asked to report personal and household victimizations suffered by household members age 12 or older during the 12 months preceding the interview. Only personal victimizations (i.e., rape, robbery, assault, and larceny from the person) will be studied here, as it is only in these face-to-face confrontations that the victim can report on the characteristics of the offender. Demographic information about the household and the respondent (age, race, sex, education, family income), a series of individual screen questions designed to discover whether any of the survey crimes had occurred during the preceding 12 months, and (when the preceding was answered affirmatively) a detailed incident report were the three major portions of the survey instrument for personal and household respondents.[2]

OFFENDER CHARACTERISTICS AND CRIME PATTERNS

Studies in the area of female crime and delinquency generally report consistent findings with respect to race and age. Black and other minority women and young women have been found to be disproportionately involved in crime and delinquency (Hendrix, 1972; Katzenelson, 1975). Similarly, the victim survey data indicate that female offenders were perceived to be black in 64% of the victimizations, white in 29%, other racial groups in 5%, and from more than one racial group in 2%.[3]

With regard to the age of the offender(s), however, in victimizations committed by only one offender (lone offender), persons 21 and over account for 67% of white female crime and 56% of black female crime. By contrast, for multiple female offenders[4] the 12-14- and the 15-17-year-old groups account for 69% (33% and 36%, respectively) of black female crime.

Finally, lone criminal offenders made up a larger proportion of white female criminality (79%) than they did of either black (61%) or other racial groups (64%). Conversely, black females (39%) and females from other racial groups (36%) were more likely to be involved in group offenses than were white females (21%).

PATTERN OF CRIME BY RACE OF OFFENDER(S)

One empirical finding Adler relied upon heavily in support of her etiological statements was:

> The figures nation-wide illustrate unequivocally that the black female's criminality exceeds that of the white female *by a much greater margin* than black males over white males [Adler, 1975: 139; italics added].

In the victim survey data, however, the ratio between the volume of crime for black males and white males was about 2 to 1 and this ratio held for black females and white females (69% to 31%).[5]

With respect to the pattern[6] of female crime by race, a number of studies indicate that the pattern differs for black and white females (Van der Hyde,

1970; Katzenelson, 1975). Furthermore, it has been reported that the pattern of crime for black females and black males is more alike than the pattern for white females and white males (Wolfgang, 1958; Adler, 1975). These hypotheses are testable with the victimization data. The data indicate that, contrary to the Adler's hypothesis, overall the patterns of criminal involvement in personal victimizations reported for lone female offenders by race were very similar across offense categories. Assault, simple and aggravated, comprised the bulk of offenses reported for both white and black female offenders.

The pattern for multiple female offenders is somewhat different. Black female offender groups differed substantially from white female offender groups in some specific offense categories. Assault (simple and aggravated) made up 72% of total victimizations by white offenders but only 44% of the total by black offenders. Theft (robbery and larceny with contact) accounted for 56% of the victimizations by black female offender groups but only about 28% of those by white female offender groups.

Briefly, these data indicate that the patterns of crime for lone black and white female offenders are very similar whereas those for multiple female offenders differ considerably by race. White female offender groups were more than two and one-half times more likely to be involved in assaultive offenses than in theft offenses, whereas black female offender groups were about as likely to be involved in assaultive as in theft offenses.

Adler's second hypothesis, that the pattern for black males and females is more alike than that for white males and females, is also testable. Simple and aggravated assault account for 75% of victimizations by lone white females and 71% of those by lone white males but 66% of victimizations by lone black females and only 40% of those by lone black males. Theft offenses (robbery and larceny with contact) accounted for 25% of all victimizations committed by lone white females, 24% of those by lone white males, 34% of those by lone black females, and 55% of those by lone black males. In multiple-offender victimizations, there is a difference of 21 percentage points in the contributions of assaultive offenses to total victimizations by black females (44%) and the contribution to total victimization by black males (23%). For white offenders, there is only a 13 percentage point difference by sex of the offender group. This same level of difference is apparent when looking at theft offenses. Thus, the pattern of crime is more similar for white males and females than for black males and females, thereby questioning (or failing to support) Adler's hypothesis.

Adler's final hypothesis is that the pattern of crime for black females is closer to the pattern of white males than it is to that of white females. The data indicate that the pattern for lone black females is very similar to that of both lone white female and lone white male offenders. In the case of multiple offenders, the pattern for multiple black female offenders is more similar to that of multiple white male offenders than it is to that of multiple white female offenders. Although the difference is very small, the pattern for multiple black female offenders is more similar to that of multiple black males than it is to multiple white males. Therefore, it seems more reasonable to conclude that the pattern of crime for black females is close to the pattern of crime for white male offenders in both lone and multiple victimizations and close to that of white female offenders in lone but not in multiple victimizations.

SUMMARY AND IMPLICATIONS

These data indicate that there is no simplistic answer to the question of whether female offenders differ by race. Adler (1975), in examining the relationship between race, sex, and involvement in crime, based her explanations of assumed differences in female criminality by race on assumptions about the historical impact of slavery on black women, on black men, and, generally, on the black family.

In this article, offender characteristics and crime patterns were examined using a previously unexplored data source—victimization surveys. Because these surveys are not dependent on official sources and include crimes not reported to the police, they are useful in assessing the empirical validity of some of Adler's hypotheses. First, Adler hypothesized that the ratio between the volume of crime for black females and white females would be greater than that for black males and white males. This hypothesis was not supported by the victim survey data. Second, Adler hypothesized that the patterns of criminal behavior for black males and black females were more alike than the patterns for white males and white females. The victim survey data indicated that the patterns of crime for black males and black females were less similar than those for white males and white females.

Finally, Adler hypothesized that the pattern of crime for black females was closer to the pattern of white males than it was to that of white females. This hypothesis was partially supported by the victim survey data. In multiple-offender victimizations, the pattern for crime for black females was closer to that of white males than to that of white females; however, in lone-offender victimizations, there was very little difference in the patterns of crime for the three groups.

Briefly, black and white female offenders were found to be similar in their pattern of involvement in personal victimizations. They differed mostly, however, in the group context of their victimizations which in turn accounted for differences in the age of the offender. Differences by race of the offender were apparently related to the type of offense and other offender characteristics.

There are two limitations of this study that should be noted. First, the offender characteristics reported here are based on victim's reports of perceived characteristics. The validity of these perceptions has not been carefully studied to date. Second, the range of offense behavior studied here is limited to interpersonal crimes of theft and violence. Excluded are organizational and white collar crimes and crimes against commercial establishments. Thus, these results cannot be seen as indicative of the validity of Adler's hypothesis with respect to these offenses. With these limitations in mind, overall Adler's hypothesis concerning the relationship between race, sex, and crime was not supported. Briefly, Adler's explanation of black female criminality rests heavily on her assumptions about the historical impact of slavery on the black family. According to Adler, as a consequence of the slave era there exists sex-role reversal among black males and black females. These circumstances are meant to explain why the pattern of black female criminality differs from that of the white female and why the pattern for black females is closer to the pattern of white males than it is to the pattern for white females. In addition, they are meant to explain why the pattern of criminal behavior for blacks by sex is more parallel than is the pattern for whites by sex. The implication from this study is that the explanations for racial differences in female crime and delinquency advanced by Adler (1975) have little value since the differences they purport to explain are not supported by the data.

This study indicates that the phenomenon of female crime and race is one of considerable complexity. Although a general description of the female offender and her victimization is relatively easy to deduce, there are, as this report has demonstrated, important relationships by race between offender characteristics that affect differences in the victimization interaction involving black and white female offenders.

Notes

[1] The following cities were surveyed: Atlanta, Baltimore, Cleveland, Dallas, Denver, Newark, Portland, St. Louis, Chicago, Detroit, Los Angeles, New York, Philadelphia, Boston, Buffalo, Cincinnati, Houston, Miami, Milwaukee, Minneapolis, New Orleans, Oakland, Pittsburgh, San Diego, San Francisco, and Washington, D.C.

[2] For a more comprehensive discussion of the data source, see Garofalo and Hindelang (1978).

[3] The 26 cities had a total female population of 9 million persons: 68% white, 29% black, and 2% other (figures do not equal 100% due to rounding).

4 Multiple-offender victimizations included only those same-sex and same-race offender groups.
5 Lone- and multiple-offender victimizations were combined to determine the ratios.
6 Pattern of crime in this context refers to the type of crime.

References

Adler, F. Sisters in Crime: The Rise of the New Female Criminal. New York: McGraw-Hill, 1975.

Garofalo, J. and M. J. Hindelang. An Introduction to the National Crime Survey. Analytic Report SD-VAD-4. Law Enforcement Assistance Administration, National Criminal Justice Information and Statistics Service. Washington, DC: Government Printing Office, 1978.

Hendrix, O. A Study in Neglect: A Report on Women Prisoners. Report submitted by Omar Hendrix, Ford Foundation Travel-Study Grants, 1972.

Katzenelson, S. "The female offender in Washington, D.C." Washington, DC: Institute of Law and Social Research, 1975.

Van Der Hyde, V. Study of Female Offenders. Olympia, WA. Office of Research, Division of Institutions, Department of Social and Health Services, 1970.

Wolfgang, M. E. Patterns in Criminal Homicide. Philadelphia: University of Pennsylvania Press, 1958.

8

Variations in Sex-Race-Age Specific Incidence Rates of Offending*

Michael J. Hindelang

In this important study, incidence rates—rates of offending in personal crimes (rape, robbery, assault, and personal larceny)—are studied using data from the National Crime Survey (NCS) for 1973-1977, conducted by the U. S. Bureau of the Census. The NCS data reveal that victims' reports of offenders' sex, race, and age are strongly related to incidence rates of offending. The highest incidence rate in personal crimes is for male, black, 18 to 20 year olds. Arrest data at the national level for robbery yield comparable results. Household crimes—burglary, household larceny, and vehicle theft—in which the victims saw and were able to report offenders' sex, race, and age constituted about 5 percent of all household crimes. The patterns in incidence rates of offending in these household crimes closely parallel those for personal crimes.

Until the self-report method of measuring illegal activities was used by Short and Nye (1957), most research into the factors associated with involvement in crime and deviance had relied exclusively on official arrest or offense data from the police or courts. This chapter examines a third source of data, victimization survey data, for information about variations in rates of offending across demographic subgroups.

Because Short and Nye's analysis indicated that class was related to official but not self-reported delinquency (for another interpretation see Hindelang, Hirschi, and Weis, 1979), both sociological research and theory have emphasized racial and class biases in criminal justice processing. From the point of view of sociologists interested primarily in etiology, the question becomes one of measurement error introduced into official data by inappropriate labeling of persons as "delinquent" or "criminal" due solely to discrimination—that is, when there is no behavioral justification for the

---

* *American Sociological Review,* vol. 46, 1981, pp. 461-474. Reprinted with permission.

label—and, conversely, the failure to label an offender because of his or her privileged status.

The available research suggests that "conduct" variables (such as involvement in a crime or the seriousness of an offense) account for far more of the variance in "labeling" than do "status" variables such as race (Tittle, 1975; see Gove, 1980 for an update). For example, Wolfgang, Figlio, and Sellin (1972: Table 13.5) present a table showing the effects of their social class indicator, race, and the Sellin-Wolfgang seriousness score, on the probability that the police would release or further process boys in their cohort. The data show that (holding the remaining variables constant) on the average, lower class subjects were very slightly (4%) more likely than higher class subjects to be further processed by the police and that nonwhites were on average about 14% more likely than whites to be further processed. However, the average effect of more versus less seriousness of the instant offense yields a difference of 45% in the likelihood of further processing, with race and class controlled. This suggests negligible class bias, some racial bias, and a large effect (in the expected direction) for the seriousness of the contact offense. Many other studies produce findings of this order, indicating that, overall, although official data have labeling errors based on unwarranted discrimination, conduct differences are the principal known determinants of the label (see generally Gove, 1980).

The accuracy of official data has also been assessed by comparing the results from official data to those from self-report studies. For example, in official data the black/white race difference in the incidence of crime and delinquency is generally large (particularly for Uniform Crime Report Index offenses), virtually irrespective of how "crime" or "delinquency" is defined (Wolfgang, et al., 1972; Webster, 1979). Unfortunately for those seeking compatibility, however, with few exceptions (e.g., Berger and Simon, 1974; Elliott and Ageton, 1980) self-report studies have found minimal differences, the mean black to white rate ratio being on the order of about 1.1:1 (e.g., Elliott and Voss, 1974; Williams and Gold, 1972; Gold, 1970; Hirschi, 1969; Epps, 1967). Although this lack of difference seems to call into question the validity of official data, self-report data, or both, there are many reasons why this conclusion may be premature. Most of the self-report studies published to date (e.g., Williams and Gold, 1972; Gold and Reimer, 1975) have had too few blacks to provide a meaningful test. In addition, omnibus or total scale scores may mask racial differences, because most self-report scales have been dominated by items that are of low seriousness and high frequency, and whites tend to report greater involvement in these events while blacks tend to report involvement in less frequent, more serious offenses (see Hindelang, Hirschi, and Weis, 1979). National victimization survey results, which focus on UCR index crimes (Webster, 1979), produce racial differences in offending that are compatible with official data (Hindelang, 1978) but are incompatible with the no-race-difference conclusion in most self-report studies. Evidence from a reverse record-check study of self-reported delinquency shows that the failure of black male offenders to report known official offenses is about three times as great as is the failure of white male offenders to report known official offenses (57% vs. 20% for serious offenses) (see Hindelang, Hirschi, and Weis, 1981). Thus, differential validity in itself may account for the failure of the self-report method to produce the racial differences expected on the basis of results from other sources (UCR arrest data and reports of victims in surveys).

One of the problems with using UCR arrest data to explore the rates of offending at the national level is the inability to construct such rates for specific population subgroups. Although the personal characteristics of arrestees are available by race and age group and by sex and age, they are not available by race and sex, nor by race, sex, and age group (this is with good reason: the data collection form used does not permit the latter two crosstabs). Furthermore, although the UCR shows total general population counts for jurisdictions reporting arrestee data, the general subpopulation details required to compute age-sex-and/or-race-specific rates of offending are not presented for the jurisdictions reporting.[1] But it is possible to circumvent these shortcomings, by studying data from the National Crime Survey.

THE PRESENT STUDY

The National Crime Survey (NCS) is a general population survey conducted by the Bureau of the Census under the specifications of the Bureau of Justice Statistics in the U. S. Department of Justice. This survey is a continuous panel survey in which nationally representative samples of households and persons are interviewed twice per year, at six month intervals throughout the year (i.e., January-June; February-July; etc.). In a six-month period, interviews are completed in about 65,000 households, in which all persons 12 years of age or older are eligible for interview (therefore, in a given six-month period more than 130,000 individuals in these 65,000 households would be interviewed). According to the NCS sponsor, "interviews were obtained in about 96% of all eligible housing units, and about 99% of the occupants of those households participating in the survey" (Law Enforcement Assistance Administration, 1976:4).

Respondents are personally interviewed and provide information about their background characteristics (such as age and education) as well as about victimizations that they (or the household) may have suffered during the previous six months. Of particular interest here are data on the personal crimes of rape, robbery, assault, and larceny; household data will be discussed briefly below. The incidents (if any) reported to interviewers are weighted according to the inverse of the probability that they would occur in the sample. For the crimes studied here, the incident weights vary from about 1,000 to 2,000. In the analysis and presentation of data these weights have been used to provide population estimates for the United States (see Law Enforcement Assistance Administration (LEAA, 1976) for more details on procedures and the NCS instruments). The data used in this paper are national data from the 1973 to 1977 period.

Because the National Crime Survey interviewers ask victims to report on the sex, age group, and race of the offender, and because the survey generates its own age-sex-race-specific counts on the general population, it can provide age-sex-race-specific estimates of rates of offending at the national level that UCR arrest data (as currently collected) cannot.

Interviewees who report having been victims of the crimes covered by the survey are asked a set of detailed questions regarding the event, including the characteristics of the offender(s) involved. Specifically, victims are asked the age group (under 12, 12-14, 15-17, 18-20, and 21+), sex, and race of the offender(s). For the purposes of the analyses reported here, three age groups (under 18, 18-20, and 21 or older) and two racial groups (white and black) are used. Offenders of "other" races are excluded: this eliminates about four percent of the offenders in personal crimes. The data tapes provided by the Census Bureau follow its convention of classifying persons of Spanish origin as white.

Because victimization survey data are generated independently of the criminal justice system, include relatively serious offenses, and are sufficiently numerous to provide reliable estimates of rates of offending for various demographic subgroups, the NCS data seem to be worth exploring. One limitation, however, is that it is not possible to tell the extent to which a small number of offenders account for a large proportion of offenses; i.e., the survey produces incidence rather than prevalence rates. Arrest data published annually in the Uniform Crime Reports share this limitation: it is not possible to ascertain the number of distinct offenders arrested in a given period. The survey data have sufficient compensating advantages to recommend their use for studying rates of offending.

The incidence rates of offending reported in this section are based on the victims' perceptions of the offenders' age group, sex, and race. These offending-rate data are designed to parallel arrest data as closely as possible. That is, given that the survey data are incapable of providing prevalence rates based on the number of distinct offenders involved in offenses suffered by different victims, incidence rates are used. The incidence rates of offending take into account the total number of offenders in each sex-race-age subgroup subject to arrest for the offense reported to survey interviewers. For example, if one victim reports having been victimized by one white, male adult and two white, female juveniles and another victim reports having been victimized by one black, female adult and one white, male adult, the sex-race-age subtotals for these victimizations would be two white, male adults, two white, female juveniles, and one black, female adult. This subtotaling process continues across all incidents reported to survey interviewers and results in a total number of offender-weighted offenses for each sex-race-age subgroup. Rather than simply cumulating the raw numbers of offenders in each subgroup, the incident weight—the inverse of the probability that an incident will be sampled—is cumulated for each sex-race-age subgroup. This is necessary because, owing to the complex design of the survey, not every incident has the same likelihood of appearing in the sample. The subgroup totals serve as the numerators for the rates of offending reported in the following tables;[2] the denominators are estimates of the number of persons in the general population (i.e., potential offenders) in each sex-race-age subgroup.[3] Incidence rates of offending are reported per 100,000 potential offenders, and they convey the number of offender-weighted incidents occurring for every 100,000 potential offenders with specific demographic characteristics; they reflect the incidence rate of offending in personal or household victimizations.[4]

Because the oldest offender age-category in the survey data is "21 or older," it is not possible to remove from the numerator of the adult rates of offending the small proportion of crimes committed by people over, for instance, forty years of age. The result is that the adult offending rate for persons between 21 and 40 years of age is underestimated; UCR arrest data show that over 90 percent of arrestees for the crimes with which we are concerned are under forty. Making estimates from UCR arrest data, we increase the estimates of the incidence rates of offending for adults 21 to 40 years of age by about 60 percent. As will be apparent in the figures presented below, however, even if the offending rates for the adults were doubled to compensate for this phenomenon, the general patterns in the data (i.e., the adult rate of offending being the lowest) within sex-race groups would be preserved.

PERSONAL CRIMES

In the 18 to 20 and 21 or older age groups in Figure 1, black males have the highest incidence rate of offending in personal crimes (rape, robbery, assault, and larceny from the person), white males the second highest rate, black females the third highest, and white females the lowest. The pattern is similar for the 12 to 17 age group except that black females have a rate of offending slightly in excess of the rate for white males. Among females, there is a sharp, consistent decline of more than 80 percent in the incidence rates of offending in personal crimes as age increases. Black females in each age group are about four to five times as likely as their white counterparts to offend in face-to-face personal crimes. Among males, the black to white ratio of incidence rates of offending is also about 5:1, but the peaks in the 18 to 20 age group are striking.

The pattern of offending in Figure 1 is paralleled by the patterns in Table 1, which show the incidence rate of offending in each of the personal crimes, by sex, race, and age of offender. In this connection, violent offenses are a simple sum of rapes, aggravated assaults, and simple assaults; theft offenses are a simple sum of robberies and larcenies. Again, the peak age for violent offenses is 18 to 20 for males, where the incidence rate of offending for black males is more than three times that for white males. The incidence rates for robbery and personal larceny are relatively low for white females, black females, and white males, while the incidence rates of offending for black males are extreme outliers, eleven to twenty times those of the next highest group.

My discussion has been focused on the relative differences rather than on the absolute level of incidence rates in the data. That males, youthful (18-20) offenders, and blacks have the highest rates of offending could have been anticipated on the basis of prior research using official data. What is surprising, however, is the exceedingly high incidence rate of offending in personal crimes among young, black males: 85,000 offender-weighted personal offenses per year for every 100,000 persons in this subgroup. One reason why this result is so striking may be a previous lack of information: in recent years although published UCR data have presented graphs of the age distributions of the general population, no data taking race, sex, and age group into account simultaneously have been presented (Kelley, 1977:171). Also, any rates derived from UCR data are based on arrests, but an arrest is unlikely if the offense is not reported to the police (about half of personal crimes reported to survey interviewers are not reported to the police). Even if reported, the crime must be "solved" before an arrest can be made. Each of these conditions, while perhaps not affecting the relative rates of offense significantly, reduces the absolute rates substantially.

It must be recalled that the rates of offending presented are not prevalence rates; there are an estimated 84,504 incidents committed by offenders in personal crimes—many of whom are duplicative—per 100,000 persons in this sex-race-age subgroup. Part of the problem may be that this high-rate group is the 18 to 20 year old age group, for whom victims' perceptions are probably more prone to error, due to the narrowness of the age category. This would suggest looking to the extreme age groups for greater stability in comparisons. But even among juveniles (12-17), an age category encompassing six rather than three years, and hence presumably less subject to error in victim perceptions, the incidence rate of offending for black males is 43,158 per 100,000, a very high annual rate, and one which is five times greater than that of their white male counterparts (7,974).

How can we determine whether these rates are on the order of magnitude that we would expect on the basis of other data? UCR national arrest data seem appropriate as a comparison source, especially the data on robbery.[5] One important question is to what extent the percent distribution of UCR robbery arrestees for a given year approximates that for NCS robbery offenders across age group and race. Because, with the exception of offenders' age, UCR data are more limited than NCS data in terms of demographic subgroups for which national data are available, the UCR data-presentation format will limit the comparisons that can be made. The data in Table 2 show, for age group and race, the percent distribution of all UCR 1976 robbery arrestees falling into each race and age group cell; comparable data are shown for NCS offender-weighted incidents. The two data sources are in close agreement regarding these percentages. For example, UCR arrest data and NCS offender data show that about one-fifth of the robberies were accounted for by black juveniles, and yet black juveniles constitute only 2 percent of the general population; this demographic subgroup, therefore, is represented among robbers at about 10 times their proportionate representation in the general population. When age group and sex are examined in a similar way, both the UCR and NCS data (not shown in tabular form) indicate that in 1976 about three out of ten robbery arrestees (UCR) or offenders (NCS) were males under 18 years of age. This is a substantial (4:1) overrepresentation of the proportion of 12 to 17 year old males in the general population.

The UCR and NCS data can be said to produce strikingly similar distributions for these variables, considered on the bivariate basis shown. Unfortunately, the UCR does not present the requisite trivariate age, sex, and race arrest data required to check further the NCS offending-rate results. However, by making an assumption we can estimate the trivariate distribution among UCR robbery arrestees by age group, sex, and race.

From UCR data on arrestee's age group, sex, and race (e.g., Kelley, 1977: Tables 32, 34, and 35) we can obtain at least a crude approximation of arrestee's trivariate age-group-sex-race distribution by assuming no correlation between demographic variables whose joint distributions are not published in the UCR (e.g., sex by race). Undoubtedly, this introduces some error, but because these estimates are for order-of-magnitude purposes, we need not be unduly concerned at this point. By way of illustration, UCR arrest data show that 93 percent of robbery arrestees are male, that 23 percent are 18 to 20 years of age, and that 60 percent are black. In Table 3, therefore, the percentage of all UCR arrestees estimated to be male, 18 to 20 years of age, and black is $93\% \times 23\% \times 60\% = 12.8\%$. Table 3 shows (Column A) the estimated UCR arrest percent distribution across all age-sex-race cells; also shown (Column B) is the percent distribution of NCS offender-weighted robbers. As was true at the bivariate level, the UCR and NCS data at the trivariate level are in general agreement. Both UCR and NCS percent distribution data indicate that white females and adults tend to be underrepresented among robbery offenders in comparison to the representation of these demographic subgroups in the general population.

Columns D and E index the overrepresentation of demographic subgroups for the UCR and NCS data, respectively. As was foreshadowed by the data in Columns A and B, the sources are again similar. Here, however, the ratio of the percent distribution in the offending populations to the percent distribution in the general population is a clear index of the extent of the overrepresentation of particular subgroups. Within Columns D and E, the index figures can be viewed in relation to each other. In both columns, for example, black males 18 to 20 years of age are overrepresented among robbery offenders at the rate of 29 or more to 1. At the other extreme, white females of all ages tend to be substantially underrepresented among offenders by either the UCR or NCS criterion.

If we assume that the victimization survey data provide our best estimate of the total number of offender-weighted personal robberies—primarily because the NCS data show that only half of these robberies become offenses known to the police and a relatively small percentage of those reported result in arrest (Webster, 1979)—we can use this base to convert the percentage figures shown in Columns A and B to offender-weighted rates of personal robbery victimizations for the UCR and NCS percentages, Columns F and G. To the extent that the respective percentages in Columns A and B are similar, so too are the corresponding rates of personal robbery offending. The level of rates in Columns F and G, however, are a function not only of the percentages shown in A and B, but also of the total number of offender-weighted robberies against which these percentages are applied. Using the NCS total number of offender-weighted personal robberies as the best available estimate of persons subject to arrest for committing personal robberies will not bias the resultant incidence rates of offending; it is, in effect, a linear transformation of the UCR and NCS percentages.

As expected in light of the data in Columns A through E, the incidence-rate data in Columns F and G are compatible with each other. The rates for black males in all age groups—particularly the two youngest groups—stand out from those of all other groups. This is true whether the UCR or the NCS criterion is used. For example, according to UCR-based estimates, black males 18 to 20 and juvenile black males have incidence rates of robbery offending per 100,000 of 25,263 and 15,615; the comparable rates in the NCS are larger for the youthful offenders and slightly smaller for juvenile offenders (31,362 per 100,000 and 15,116 per 100,000). The similarity in the rankings of rates is indicated by a Spearman rank-order correlation coefficient of .95.

In summary, the extreme incidence rates of robbery for black male youth are not caused primarily by the NCS count being greater than the UCR arrest count. Plotting Column D's values for white and black males will produce a graph very much like that shown in Figure 1.

HOUSEHOLD CRIMES

In addition to the personal crimes discussed above, the NCS collects data on crimes construed to affect the household—burglary, household larceny, and vehicle theft. These data are collected from the "household respondent," someone who is knowledgeable about the affairs of the household. Because of the nature of these crimes—typically the victim and the offender(s) do not come face to face—for most of them offender's characteristics are unknown. For a small minority of household crimes, however, the victim and offender do come into contact. In the 1973-1977 period, victims were able to report on offenders' characteristics in 6 percent of the burglaries and vehicle thefts and in 4 percent of the household larcenies. Because of the large number of household crimes occurring in this period, even these small proportions yield large numbers of events to analyze: 6,000 unweighted (sample) household crimes reported, 1,600 burglaries, 4,000 larcenies, and 300 vehicle thefts—or an estimated (weighted) 2 million burglaries, 5 million larcenies, and .4 million vehicle thefts. There is no a priori reason to believe that there are offender-linked characteristics associated with those household crimes that do (about 5 percent) or do not (about 95 percent) result in the victims' being able to report offenders' characteristics to the interviewer.[6] Because the clearance rate for these crimes in UCR data is so low—less than 20 percent (Kelley, 1977:161)—when the rate at which NCS incidents are reported to the police is taken into account [about 70 percent for vehicle theft, 50 percent for burglary, and 25 percent for household larceny, according to NCS figures (LEAA, 1976)], UCR arrest data also exclude the vast majority of offenders in these crimes. Therefore, NCS data may be superior to UCR arrest data for analysis of the characteristics of household-crime offenders because the NCS data are closer to the crime (Sellin, 1951) and subject to fewer filtering mechanisms than the UCR arrest data.

Figure 2 depicts very striking sex, race, and age group differences in incidence rates of offending for those household offenses in which victims reported offenders' demographic characteristics; these patterns mirror those shown for incidence rates of offending in personal crimes. When the individual household crimes are examined (data not presented) they show, for example, that the incidence rate of burglary offending for the black, male, 18-20 year old group (4,446) is more than 5 times the rate of the next closest white sex-age-group (white males, 12 to 17: 871 per 100,000). Again, among black males, the incidence rate of burglary offending shows a sharp rate increase from the juveniles (1,985) to the youthful offender group (4,446), which then falls sharply to the (still relatively quite high) incidence rate of more than (800) for black male adults. In the three age groups, the smallest black-white difference is 2:1 among juveniles and the largest is among adults (about 5:1). The other household crimes show similar patterns to that for burglary, and hence for the personal crimes examined above.

DATA LIMITATIONS

The NCS survey only includes data on "street" crime of the UCR index variety. The NCS is also known to undercount all offenses, particularly assault (LEAA, 1972) and to be subject to certain time-in-panel biases which reduce reported victimizations (Woltman and Bushery, 1977). Most important to this study is that the validity of results relies entirely on victims' perceptions of the characteristics of the offenders, and to the extent that these are inaccurate, the analysis must necessarily fall short. However, victims could (and sometimes did) answer that they "did not know," and these incidents were excluded from the analysis, which should have reduced biases in the data set.

While we would not expect the accuracy of victims' reports of the sex of the offender to be problematic, reports of the offender's race might well be. For example, persons of Spanish origin might be mistaken by some victims as black, but this would present difficulties in only some sections of the country. Age was expected to be the variable most difficult for victims to estimate, and so the NCS data were separated into three broad groups for the purpose of analysis and presentation; when age is used as a dichotomy (12-20 versus 21 or more) the results are not substantially affected, and when age is dichotomized the other way (12-18 versus 18 or more) the age effect diminishes but it is still pronounced.

In order to test the accuracy of victims' reports on offenders' characteristics, data available from a special study of rape in New York City were analyzed.[7] The study involved about 13,000 offenses for which data on suspects were collected; for most suspects (about 8,000), no arrest was made. For the 5,000 offenses in which an arrest was made, descriptions of the demographic characteristics of suspects reported to the police at the time of the offense were crosstabulated with the arrestees' characteristics. The age categories available from those data are under 14, 14 to 19, 20 to 24, 25 to 29, 30 to 34, 35 to 39, 40 to 45, 45 or more, and "don't know." Of the suspects reported to be under 14, 97 percent were found to be under 14 when an arrest was made. The following age groups estimated at the time of the offense yielded precisely the same age group at arrest: 14 to 19, 96%; 20 to 24, 89%; 25 to 29, 90%; 30 to 34, 90%; 35 to 39, 89%; 40 to 45, 91%; 45 or more, 96%. The offenders' age group reported on the offense form and the arrestees' age group yielded a Somers' d of .95. It is important to note that the agreement does not decline appreciably when only victims and offenders who were strangers are analyzed.

The race/ethnicity categories available in the New York data include persons of Spanish origin and hence are finer than the categories available for analysis in the NCS; they provide a more stringent test of victims' ability to report accurately on offenders' race.[8] The agreement between reports on the offender's race at the time the offense was reported and the race of the arrestee recorded on the arrest form was very high (lambda = .95). Among offenders reported to be white at the time of the offense, 96 percent were recorded as white on the arrest form. For blacks, the comparable figure is 99 percent, and for Hispanics, 98 percent. Of particular interest is the finding that only 1.6 percent of the Hispanic arrestees were erroneously reported to be black at the time of the offense (Hindelang and McDermott, 1981). These data suggest that, at least for this crime, victims are very accurate in their reports of offenders' age and race/ethnicity. But there are features to rape that may limit the generality of these findings, particularly the physical contact between the victim and the offender, which is sometimes of an extended nature in completed rapes, and the fact that the sex of the victim is virtually always female (99%). If we assume that attempted rapes are of a shorter duration than completed rapes, the former might be expected to produce less accurate offender data; however, the Somers' d value for offenders' age in attempted rapes as reported at the time of the offense and at the time of the arrest is .96, while the corresponding measure for race yields a lambda of .96, coefficients as high as in completed rapes. Despite the equality of the coefficients for attempted and completed rapes, these levels of accuracy should certainly be considered tentative until replicated with an independent data set.

DISCUSSION

The findings presented here in the form of incidence rates of offending parallel the findings in most sources of arrest data, despite sociologists' reluctance in recent decades to accept police and court data as evidence of involvement in crime. In addition, presenting the data in the form of the rates highlights most dramatically how closely both the crimes of adults and the crimes of juveniles are associated with the offenders' demographic characteristics. This is true not only for robbery, the "test" offense used in Table 3, but for all of the other personal and household offenses studied as well.

Very few data sets in the study of crime include information on adult offenders as well as juveniles, and certainly not of the average level of seriousness of the offenses reported to the NCS survey.[9] This lack of data, in combination with the fact that adolescent in-school populations are easier to study than general adult populations, has had the consequence that in sociology, etiological theories of juvenile delinquency are more common than etiological theories of adult crime. If we accept the NCS results at face value, they have important implications for sociological theory. The age, race, and sex variables account for an impressive percentage of the variability in incidence rates of offending. The lowest rate group, white, female adults, has an incidence rate of offending in personal crimes of less than 270, while the black, male, 18 to 20 year old group has an incidence rate of offending that is more than 300 times this rate. (If the smaller base of adults in the offending age range is used, this ratio drops to about 150.) The ratio between the incidence rates of white, male adults and 18-20 year old, black males is 22:1. The sorts of variables used by contemporary sociological theorists to explain involvement in criminal and delinquent behavior—social class, differential opportunity, stakes in conformity, maturational reform, educational aspirations, pluralistic ignorance, attachments, etc.—are rarely found in research to produce ratios in rates of offending between contrast groups (in which each contains a reasonable proportion of the sample) that exceed two or three to one (Williams and Gold, 1972; Gold and Reimer, 1975; Elliott and Ageton, 1980).

It is likely, of course, that the demographic variables studied here are, themselves, indicators of variables like these that are more likely to be found in sociological theories of etiology. For example, late adolescence (18-20), in the market place of employment, may be the time when the effects of differential opportunities are greatest and attachments to the school and family are the least; hence it is the peak age of offending among males. In this age group, blacks particularly may have lower stakes in conformity due to their historically high rate of unemployment and an average educational attainment level that is lower than that of whites; blacks correctly perceive that they have lower stakes in conforming to legal norms. The large sex difference may be due to the greater attachment of females than males to each other, to the school, to their families of origin, and later to their offspring. The much lower rate of offending for adults than for the two youngest age groups may be indicative of maturational reform. Unfortunately, the nature and pattern of demographic correlates of crime are often compatible with competing theories.

The question of what specific mechanisms link particular demographic variables to offensive behavior must be addressed by research beyond the scope of the NCS data. Regardless of what those speculations are, these data strongly support the importance of sex, race, and age in accounting for differences in rates of offending. The strength of these correlations with criminal behavior was anticipated from arrest data (e.g., Kelley, 1977: Tables 32, 34, 35). However, the general agreement between the UCR and NCS on offenders' sex, race, and age characteristics increases the probability that both are acceptably valid for the purposes of this paper, particularly because the NCS data are collected independently of the criminal justice system and hence are subject to very different distortions than arrest data.[10]

If sociological theorists of crime and delinquency were to use the "clues" provided by known correlates of criminal behavior—in this instance sex, race, and age group—as a basis for generating and modifying theory, theory and research might be able to advance more steadily. Sociological theorists must demonstrate their ability to accommodate these associations of demographic variables to incidence rates of offending in "street" crime before their theories are taken seriously. Theories that cannot should be discounted until they can.

Notes

[1] It is possible that the denominator for these rates is the same as for the United States as a whole, but this assumption may not be warranted for some subgroups.

[2] We excluded incidents in which the victim did not know whether there was one or more offender because in such cases the victim was not asked the sex, race, or age of the offender(s). Incidents involving multiple offenders of mixed sexes or races were excluded for the same reason. These exclusions constituted about 11% of total personal incidents. When offenders were of mixed ages, the age group of the oldest was arbitrarily used to prevent the loss of additional cases; treating mixed age-group offenders as all in the youngest age group resulted in only minor variations from the results obtained when the oldest age-group rule was used.

[3] Population bases shown in Appendix A are the estimated 1973-1977 aggregated counts in each subgroup. When these bases are divided into their corresponding 1973-1977 aggregated offender-weighted offenses, this division (times 100,000) yields the average annual rates of offending shown in the figures and tables reported here.

[4] In this paper, the general population base for the rate of juvenile offending is persons between 12 and 17 years of age. The victimization data show that fewer than one percent of the survey victimizations are committed by persons perceived by victims to have been

under 12 years of age. In light of this, and since general population estimates were not made for persons under 12 because they did not fall within the scope of the victimization survey, the base of the juvenile offending rate is simply the number of 12 to 17 year olds in the general population. That is, the numerators of rates of offending for 12 to 17 year olds include a small proportion of crimes for those under 12, whereas the denominators include only persons in the general population aged 12 to 17. Because of the small number of offenders under 12, this has a trivial effect on the rates of offending for this group.

5 The crime of rape is too rare statistically to use it. Historically, the NCS has had some difficulty measuring assault (LEAA, 1972) and the UCR larceny category includes arrests for many larcenies not in the scope of the NCS, particularly shoplifting. The NCS robbery data used in the comparison to the UCR exclude commercial robberies.

6 Household crimes in which the offender(s) were seen, as expected, were more likely to be reported to the police (e.g., burglary: 61% versus 50%) and less likely to result in something being stolen (all household crimes: 52% versus 79%).

7 The data were provided by Sergeant Dennis Butler of the New York City Police Department. We are grateful for his assistance.

8 As noted for race in the NCS, the Census Bureau's classification system counts Hispanic and Anglo offenders as white; therefore, even if their numbers had been sufficiently large, they could not have been treated separately in the analysis of offending rates.

9 Despite the fact that as a set the NCS data contain many serious victimizations in terms of harm to the victim—certainly events that have a median harm value in excess of national self-report surveys (e.g., Elliott and Ageton, 1980)—the NCS data also contain many reports of victimizations that would have to be characterized as minor. For example, of NCS victimizations categorized using the Sellin and Wolfgang (1964) system, Gottfredson and Hindelang (1979) found one-quarter resulting in no harm or minor harm (e.g., scrapes) to the victim. Thus, the NCS data cover a very wide range of seriousness, and yet as a set simply include more serious offenses, largely because of the huge number of personal interviews conducted each month.

10 Ecological-level comparisons of the UCR/NCS correlation for rates of crime found that the two sources are in general agreement for theft crimes, but that for some other crimes, particularly assault, the intercity correspondence across 26 cities is poor (Nelson, 1979). Although these assault findings suggest that caution is warranted, they do not necessarily say anything about the individual-level agreement between the two sources in, for example, offender characteristics. It is possible, in other words, for both sources to provide reasonably accurate data on offender characteristics and yet, for a variety of reasons, have uncorrelated intercity rates of offenses. In short, factors that vary from city to city and serve to over- or underestimate rates of crime as measured in either source do not necessarily distort characteristics of offenders as measured by the two methods. Likewise, on the national level, comparisons of UCR and NCS trends (Eck and Riccio, 1979) say little in themselves about the validity of correlates of offending on the individual level.

References

Berger, Alan S. and William Simon. "Black families and the Moynihan report: a research evaluation." Social Problems 22:146-61, 1974.

Eck, J. and Lucius Riccio. "Relationship between reported crime rates and victimization survey results." Journal of Criminal Justice 7:293-308, 1979.

Elliott, Delbert and Suzanne Ageton. "Reconciling differences in estimates of delinquency." American Sociological Review 45:95-110, 1980.

Elliott, Delbert S. and Harwin L. Voss. Delinquency and Dropout. Lexington, MA: D. C. Health.

Epps, E. G. "Socioeconomic status, race, level of aspiration, and juvenile delinquency: a limited empirical test of Merton's conception of deviation." Phylon 28:16-27, 1967.

Gold, Martin. Delinquent Behavior in an American City. Belmont, CA.: Brooks/Cole, 1970.

Gold, Martin and David J. Reimer. "Changing patterns of delinquent behavior among Americans 13 through 16 years old: 1967-1972." Crime and Delinquency Literature 7:483-517, 1975.

Gordon, Robert A. "Prevalence: the rare datum in delinquency measurement and its implications for the theory of delinquency." Pp. 201-89 in Malcolm Klein, ed., The Juvenile Justice System. Beverly Hills, CA: Sage Publications, 1976.

Gottfredson, Michael R. and Michael J. Hindelang. "A study of the behavior of law." American Sociological Review 44:1-28, 1979.

Gove, Walter. "Postscript to labelling and crime." Pp. 264-9 in Walter Gove, ed., The Labelling of Deviance, 2nd ed. Beverly Hills, CA: Sage Publications, 1980.

Hindelang, Michael J. "Race and involvement in common law personal crimes." American Sociological Review 43:93-109, 1978.

Hindelang, Michael J., Travis Hirschi, and Joseph G. Weis. "Correlates of delinquency: the illusion of discrepancy between self-report and official measures." American Sociological Review 44:955-1014, 1979.

————. Measuring Delinquency. Beverly Hills, CA: Sage Publications, 1981.

Hindelang, Michael J. and M. Joan McDermott. Juvenile Criminal Behavior: An Analysis of Rates and Victim Characteristics. Washington, D. C.: Government Printing Office, 1981.

Hirschi, Travis. Causes of Delinquency. Berkeley, CA: University of California Press, 1969.

Kelley, Clarence. Crime in the United States. Washington, D.C.: U. S. Government Printing Office, 1977.

Law Enforcement Assistance Administration. San Jose Methods Test of Crime Victims. Statistics Technical Report No. 1. Washington, D. C.: U. S. Government Printing Office, 1972.

————. Criminal Victimization in the United States. Washington, D. C.: U. S. Government Printing Office, 1976.

Nelson, James F. "Implications for the ecological study of crime: a research note." In W. H. Parsonage (ed.) Victimology. Beverly Hills, CA: Sage Publications, 1979.

Schmid, C. F. "Urban crime areas: part I." American Sociological Review 25:527-42, 1960a.

————. Urban crime areas: part II." American Sociological Review 25:655-78, 1960b.

Sellin, Thorsten. "The significance of records of crime." Law Quarterly Review 67:489-504, 1951.

Sellin, Thorsten and Marvin Wolfgang. The Measurement of Delinquency. New York: Wiley, 1964.

Shaw, Clifford R. and Henry D. McKay. Juvenile Delinquency and Urban Areas. Chicago: University of Chicago Press, 1942.

Short, James F. and F. Ivan Nye. "Reported behavior as a criterion of deviant behavior." Social Problems 5:207-13, 1957.

Tittle, Charles R. "Labelling and crime: an empirical evaluation." Pp. 241-70 in Walter Gove, ed., The Labelling of Deviance: Evaluating a Perspective, 2nd ed. Beverly Hills, CA: Sage Publications, 1975.

Webster, William H. Crime in the United States, 1978. Washington, D. C.: Government Printing Office, 1979.

Williams, Jay R. and Martin Gold. "From delinquent behavior to official delinquency." Social Problems 20:209-29, 1972.

Wolfgang, Marvin, Robert Figlio, and Thorsten Sellin. Delinquency in a Birth Cohort. Chicago: University of Chicago Press, 1972.

Woltman, Henry and John Bushery. "Update of the NCS panel bias study." Mimeographed. U. S. Bureau of the Census, Washington, D. C., 1977.

Figure 1   Estimated Annual Rates of Offending in Total Personal Crimes (per 100,000 Potential Offenders in Each Population Subgroup), NCS National Data, 1973-1977 Average

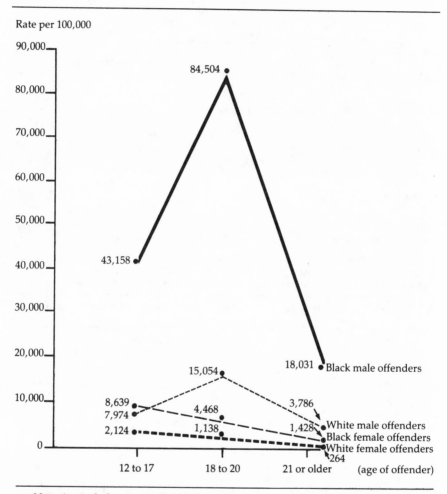

Note: Age includes perceived age of lone offender and perceived age of oldest member of an offending group.

Excluded are incidents (about 11% of the total) in which the victim did not know whether there was one or more than one offender and incidents involving offenders of mixed sexes or mixed races.

The numerator of the rates of offending 12 to 17 year olds includes incidents (about 1% of the total) in which the offender was perceived by the victim to be under 12 years of age. The denominator of the rate is the number of 12 to 17 year olds in the general population.

Table 1   **Estimated Annual Rates of Offending in Personal Crimes (per 100,000 Potential Offenders in Each Population Subgroup), NCS National Data, 1973-1977 Aggregate.**

Race, Sex and Age of Offender	Rape	Robbery	Aggravated Assault and Simple Assault	Personal Larceny	Violent	Theft	Total
White males:							
12 to 17[a]	77	1,203	6,436	259	6,513	1,462	7,974
18 to 20	291	2,245	12,144	374	12,435	2,619	15,054
21 or older	152	463	2,100	72	3,252	535	3,786
Black males:							
12 to 17[a]	403	16,663	21,619	4,473	22,022	21,136	43,158
18 to 20	1,624	35,030	39,990	7,860	41,614	42,890	84,504
21 or older	735	7,000	9,108	1,188	9,843	8,188	18,031
White females:							
12 to 17[a]	5	212	1,854	52	1,859	264	2,124
18 to 20	0	71	1,035	33	1,035	104	1,138
21 or older	0	33	219	11	219	44	264
Black females:							
12 to 17[a]	92	1,307	6,736	504	6,828	1,811	8,639
18 to 20	39	703	3,074	651	3,113	1,354	4,468
21 or older	7	164	1,120	138	1,127	302	1,428

Note: Age includes perceived age of lone and perceived age of oldest multiple offender.

Excluded are incidents (about 11 percent of the total) in which the victim did not know whether there was one or more than one offender, and incidents involving offenders of "mixed" sexes or "mixed" races.

[a] The numerator of the rates of offending for 12 to 17 year olds includes incidents (about 1 percent of the total) in which the offender was perceived by the victim to be under 12 years of age. The denominator of the rate is the number of 12 to 17 year olds in the general population.

Table 2   **Percent Distributions for Offender-Weighted Incidents in NCS Data and Arrests in UCR Data, for Personal Robbery, 1976 National Data.**

Age of Offender	Race of Offender		Total
	White	Black	
Under 18			
UCR	11[a]	20	31
	(9,728)	(17,929)	(27,657)
NCS	11[b]	19	30
	(176,901)	(297,972)	(474,873)
18 or older			
UCR	29	40	69
	(25,500)	(35,752)	61,252)
NCS	26	44	70
	(402,506)	(688,205)	(1,090,711)

Source: UCR data are Kelley, 1977:186, 187.

[a] Percent based on total number of UCR robbery arrests in 1976 as shown in Kelley, 1977:186, 187. "Other" races are excluded.

[b] Percent based on total estimated number of NCS offender-weighted robbery incidents. Excluded are incidents (about 8% of the total) in which the victim did not know whether there was one or more than one offender and incidents involving offenders of mixed races. Other races are also excluded.

Table 3   Comparison of NCS and UCR Offense Data for Personal Robbery, 1976 National Data.

Race, Sex and Age of Offender	A Estimated percent distribution of UCR robbery arrestees[a]	B Estimated percent distribution of NCS offender-weighted robbers[b]	C Estimated percent distribution of the general population[c]	D Ratio of UCR percent of arrestee population to percent of general population	E Ratio of NCS percent of robber population to percent of general population	F Estimated rate of robbery offending (per 100,000) based on UCR percents (Column A) times estimated NCS total of offender-weighted robbers divided by general population count for each subgroup	G Estimated rate of robbery offending (per 100,000) based on NCS percents (Column B) times estimated NCS total of offender-weighted robberies divided by general population count for each subgroup	H Ratio of estimated UCR rates (See Column F) to estimated NCS rates (See Column G)
White males:								
12 to 17	12.33	9.68	6.25	1.96	1.55	1,706	1,340	1.27
18 to 20	8.42	6.85	3.00	2.81	2.28	2,432	1,980	1.23
21 or older	16.00	17.81	33.57	.48	.53	413	459	.90
Black males:								
12 to 17	18.79	18.19	1.04	18.07	17.49	15,615	15,116	1.03
18 to 20	12.84	15.94	.44	29.18	36.23	25,263	31,358	.81
21 or older	24.39	26.38	3.57	6.83	7.39	5,919	6,400	.92
White females:								
12 to 17	.96	1.07	6.01	.16	.18	138	154	.90
18 to 20	.66	.34	3.10	.21	.11	184	95	1.94
21 or older	1.25	1.10	36.98	.03	.30	29	26	1.12
Black females:								
12 to 17	1.46	.74	1.05	1.39	.70	1,203	613	1.97
18 to 20	1.00	.74	.51	1.96	1.45	1,704	1,254	1.35
21 or older	1.90	1.16	4.48	.42	.26	367	225	1.63

[a] UCR data are from Kelley, 1977; Tables 32, 34, and 35. Trivariate distribution is estimated based on the data in Kelley (1977: Tables 32, 34 and 35) under the assumption that the demographic variables are uncorrelated with each other. Note "other" races are excluded.

[b] These data are taken from the NCS survey for 1976. Excluded are incidents (about 11 percent of the total) in which the victim did not know whether there was one or more than one offender and incidents involving offenders of "mixed" sexes or "mixed" races. Note "other" races are excluded.

[c] Estimates based on NCS data for 1976. Persons under 12 are ineligible to be interviewed and are excluded from the survey.

Figure 2   Estimated Annual Rates of Offending in Total Household Crimes in Which the Offender Was Seen (per 100,000 Potential Offenders in Each Population Subgroup), NCS National Data, 1973-1977 Average.

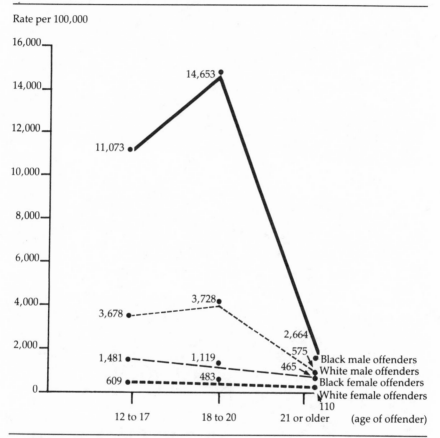

Rate per 100,000

Note: About 95% of household crimes, in which the offender was not seen, are excluded.

Age includes perceived age of lone offender and perceived age of oldest member of an offending group.

Excluded are incidents in which the victim did not know whether there was one or more than one offender and which involved offenders of mixed sexes or races.

The numerator of the rates of offending for 12 to 17 year olds includes incidents (about 1% of the total) in which the offender was perceived by the victim to be under 12 years of age. The denominator of the rate is the number of 12 to 17 year olds in the general population. See population base estimates in Appendix A.

9

The Criminal Justice System and Minorities—A Review of the Literature

Daniel Georges-Abeyie

The disproportionate manifestation of minority crime and criminal victimization is well documented in official government publications such as the FBI's annual Uniform Crime Report and the Justice Department's National Criminal Justice Information Service's yearly document entitled Criminal Victimization in the United States, as well as in numerous documents, annuals, and articles published in both the public as well as the private sector. What remains open to debate are the dynamics of the criminal victimization process, the extent of minority crime and criminal victimization, the accuracy of crime data, the interpretations of crime causation theories, explanations for racial and ethnic minority propensity for criminal activity and/or criminal victimization, the lack of minority group familiarity with the legal functioning and components of the criminal justice system as well as the lack of fairness in the processing of non-whites, and negative minority group perceptions of the criminal justice system. This chapter does not attempt a comprehensive review of the numerous topics just cited. Rather, it explores the dynamics and extent of minority crime and criminal victimization, racial bias in the criminal justice system, and minority perceptions and knowledge of the components and processing mechanisms of the American criminal justice system. This chapter will also provide a brief overview of the literature that attempts to document minority crime and criminal victimization and the intricacies of the criminal justice process as well as the nature and extent of negative perceptions held by racial and ethnic minorities in regard to the system itself.

MINORITY CRIME AND CRIMINAL VICTIMIZATION

There can be little doubt that racial and ethnic minorities perpetrate a disproportionate share of street crime, and that they are in turn disproportionately represented in the ranks of the criminally victimized, both as victims of crime and as victims of the criminal justice system. The extent of their crime perpetration and criminal victimization varies with the crime-specific category; that is, blacks and other minorities are likely perpetrators and victims of certain crimes such as criminal homicide, forcible rape, robbery, and assault as well as household burglaries and larcenies. They are not, however, likely perpetrators of sedition, espionage or white-collar crime nor victims of white-collar crimes. Nor are racial and ethnic minorities always disproportionately represented among the ranks of those who perpetrate what the FBI labels "Crime suggesting personal disorgani-zation," e.g., runaways, offenses against the family or children, certain forms of gambling, driving while intoxicated, drunkenness, the proprietors of commercialized vice or the frequenters of prostitutes.

Any number of theories and conjectures have been offered as explana-tions for minority predeliction toward criminality and crime victimization. There are those theories that offer analyses of subcultural and contra-cultural variants on lifestyle as crime causation explanations, such as Lynn A. Curtis' *Violence, Race and Culture* or Wolfgang and Ferracuti's *Subculture of Violence*.[1] Other theoreticians and theories offer what are essentially ecolog-ical (spatial) explanations, such as Keith Harries' *The Geography of Crime and Justice*,[2] Daniel E. Georges-Abeyie and Keith Harries' *Crime: A Spatial Perspective*,[3] and David Herbert's *The Geography of Urban Crime*,[4] or the many varied works of the Chicago School of Sociology.[5] Examples of other types of explanations include those that emphasize economic factors, often grouped under the titles of "radical," "Marxist," or "critical" criminology,[6] and those that provide a synthesis of the economic, ecological, and cultural theories.[7]

In evaluating the explanatory power of such theories, one must remain cognizant of the serious nature of those crime-specific categories in which blacks and other non-whites are not as disproportionately represented; that is, white-collar crime, crimes against the state, such as espionage, sedition, and subversion, as well as certain types of property crimes. These crimes result in millions, if not billions, of dollars of lost revenue that might be taxed and then redistributed in a manner beneficial to whites as well as blacks, the middle class as well as the working and lower classes.

Nonetheless, white-collar crime, certain crimes suggesting personal dis-organization, and crimes against the state do not appear to be dominant in the American public's consciousness. The American public appears to be obsessed with the unlikely possibility of its victimization in a street crime incident, and has altered aspects of its lifestyle out of fear. This is especial-ly noteworthy when the centrographic and intraracial nature of most street crime victimization is considered.[8]

One might contend that such a divergence in regard to the centralization and centrographic nature of crime on the one hand, and the pervasive nature of fear on the other, is the logical consequence of ethnic/racial residential and "social sphere" segregation in almost every aspect of American life, and the development of a mass media that is quick to capitalize on the public's receptivity to news stressing the sensational and the deviant. It is not unusual to find the first three or four pages of the local paper reporting some aspect of criminal violence, often of an interracial nature in which the victim is white and the offender or suspect is black or non-white.

Although minority crime and victimization is a very real and disturbing problem, it is neither omnipresent nor is it rampant throughout the country. For example, the *National Crime Survey Report: Criminal Victimization in the United States—1980* noted the following personal victim characteristics: (1) Victimization rates for personal crimes of violence (rape, robbery, and assault) were relatively higher for males, younger persons, blacks, the poor, and for those separated or divorced. For personal crimes of theft, males, young persons, whites, and the more affluent were the more likely victims; (2) blacks had a higher robbery rate than whites, but the apparent differences for the other two personal crimes of violence were not statistically significant (see Table 1); (3) the rate for violent crime was highest for black males, followed by that for white males (see Table 2); and (4) black males age 12 and over had a substantially higher rate than their white counterparts for crimes of violence; as a group, however, white males age 16 to 19 and 20 to 24 had substantially higher victimization rates than their black counterparts (see Table 3). The 1980 *National Crime Survey* also lists following household victim characteristics: (1) crimes against household property (burglary, larceny and motor vehicle theft) generally affected blacks, Hispanics, younger individuals, renters, and members of large households more than other persons; (2) for two forms of household burglary, blacks had a higher rate than whites; as a result, the overall rate for that crime was much higher among blacks (see Table 4); (3) for each of the three household crimes, white renters had a substantially higher rate than white homeowners; this pattern also held for blacks (see Table 5); (4) black homeowners recorded higher rates for burglary and motor vehicle theft than did white homeowners (see Table 5); (5) black renters had a higher burglary rate than white renters, but the opposite was true with respect to household larceny (see Table 5); and (6) burglary was more prevalent among black householders in central cities and suburbs than among their white counterparts (see Table 4).

Thus, criminal victimization data reveal the variegated nature of the victimization process in regard to race. That is, although whites are substantially represented in some personal and property victimization categories, such as rape, assault and crimes of theft, this is not the case in all categories. In fact, blacks, rather than whites, are the more likely victims of the dynamics of the criminal victimization process.

THE CRIMINAL JUSTICE SYSTEM: AN IDEAL TYPE CONSTRUCT

The American criminal justice system is extremely complex. There is little question why a process that involves such subprocesses as crime detection, arrest, prosecution, courts, and corrections remains a mystery to those so often caught in its web. In addition, the potential for miscarriages of justice to occur is furthered by human frailties that account for graft, corruption, incompetence, and ethnically and racially motivated actions. There are also those who contend that the system may be better suited for the maintenance of law and order than the assurance of justice for America's racial and ethnic minorities.[9] In fact, there are those who argue that the system was never intended to assure racial, economic, social, political, or legal justice; that standards for equal treatment for American racial and ethnic minorities are absent and that that absence is intentional.[10] Other jurists, criminal justice practitioners, and academics argue that intentional or not, the criminal justice process discriminates on the basis of race, ethnicity, class, and culture[11] and that this unequal treatment can be found throughout every stage of this system.[12]

There is no question that non-whites are both aware and resentful of the unequal application of the law and the resultant criminal justice process,[13] although it appears that whites have a more comprehensive understanding of the components and nuances of this system than do some of the ethnic and racial minorities.[14] It also appears that whites have a fuller knowledge of how to modify that system than do non-whites.[15]

THE AMERICAN CRIMINAL JUSTICE PROCESS: A LEGACY OF INJUSTICE

As was mentioned in the previous section, there is strong supportive evidence for the contention that the American criminal justice system does not function in a racially and ethnically blind manner, and that this shortcoming was intended from the inception of the system itself. Long, Long, Leon and Weston's fascinating account of racial and ethnic injustice, entitled *American Minorities: The Justice Issue* (1975), provides a comprehensive and scholarly documentation of America's legacy of racial and ethnic oppression—a legacy which includes Anglo-Saxon domination, the continuing struggle for civil rights, violent racial/ethnic confrontations, political trials, and discrimination in correctional systems—a legacy that calls for the creation of special standards for equal treatment of minorities and the need for new perspectives about criminal justice and minorities in such areas as minority representation in criminal justice agencies, police-ghetto relations, community responsibility in intergroup conflicts, free speech and a free press, and equal justice under the law. More specifically, Long, Long, Leon, and Weston (1975) along with Haywood Burns (1973) and Derrick Bell (1973) cite numerous laws and articles (within the Constitution of the United States) that made bondage for blacks a lifetime and hereditary condition that: (1) barred blacks from bringing lawsuits or testifying against white persons; (2) regulated the physical mobility of blacks; (3) denied blacks the ability to maintain a stable nuclear family relationship; (4) denied blacks freedom of press, speech, and assembly; (5) applied criminal sanctions for blacks according to a different and harsher standard than applied to whites; (6) accorded blacks a status of three-fifths of a person, for the purpose of white slave holder representation; (7) barred blacks from certain types of employment; (8) banned blacks from the borders of certain territories; (9) required segregated schools and public facilities; and (10) denied blacks the franchise.[16] In brief, racial discrimination and unequal treatment under the law was *law* in the United States.

One should not, however, assume that all discrimination within the American Criminal Justice System was intentional and thus legally sanctioned by the law or by the courts. Legally sanctioned discrimination was only the tip of the iceberg if credence is given to the works of such noted jurists and academics as Howard (1975), Bell (1973), Swett (1969), Wolfgang and Riedel (1973), Kuykendall (1970), Crockett (1972), Thornberry (1973), Somerville (1968). These works will be discussed briefly in the following sections.

BENIGN NEGLECT IN THE ENFORCEMENT OF EQUAL PROTECTION UNDER THE LAW?

Judge Joseph C. Howard is one among a number of distinguished black jurists who has argued that racial discrimination in criminal sentencing is rarely discussed in judicial circles or addressed by legal authorities, even though this discrimination is perceived in communities and is supported by statistics.[17] Howard believes that three negative concepts of blacks have grown out of the American social milieu and that these concepts may shade judicial thinking at the time of sentencing. The first is the "less-than-human" concept. This concept applies when certain people are perceived as being different from oneself both materially and psychologically, with different feelings and outlooks; as such, these individuals deserve less. The disproportionate use of the death penalty upon blacks is cited as an example of this.[18] Howard states that the second social concept that interferes with equitable sentencing is "that of belonging." This concept stresses that society will react with disparate treatment toward a group it feels does "not belong" because of perceived social or cultural differences. These perceptions are regarded as being uncritically examined and internalized.[19] The third social attitude that Howard cites as affecting equitable sentencing is "our penchant for punishing people whom we regard as a threat to the system . . . the so-called militant, power advocate, and political activist."[20] Minorities, especially blacks, disproportionately fall within these categories.

Judge Howard goes on to argue that we should expect the victims of a dual system of justice to adopt dual standards of morality, since—

. . . people who are subjected to values which make them valueless will create values of their own, and that people who find they cannot participate peaceably in the order of things will create disorder . . .[21]

There is empirical evidence to support Howard's thesis. One such study is that done by Howard himself entitled *The Administration of Rape Cases in the City of Baltimore and The State of Maryland* (1967). Numerous other classic studies, such as Wolfgang and Riedel's "Race, Judicial Discretion, and the Death Penalty" (1973) clearly document the imposition of more severe dispositions for minorities than for whites found guilty of similar crimes. For example, Wolfgang and Riedel have concluded that "racial variables are systematically and consistently related to the imposition of the death penalty."[22] Wolfgang and Riedel (1973) also noted that it is not the presence of the non-racial factor of contemporaneous offense that affects the decision to impose the death penalty more frequently on blacks. Rather, it is the racial factor of the relationship between the defendant and victim that results in the use of the death penalty, with the combination of black defendant and white victim receiving an overwhelmingly disparate proportion of the death sentences in their study.[23]

Judge George W. Crockett concurs with the conjectures made by Howard, Wolfgang and Riedel, and others that racism has been an integral part of American law. In fact, he states that it has been an integral part of American law since the first black indentured servants arrived in Virginia in 1619.[24] He concludes, as does Judge Howard, that a society's laws as well as a society's jurists can be no better than the society of which they are a part, and that a racist society creates racist laws and racist jurists whose "racism in the law today is camouflaged under such terms as administrative or judicial discretion."[25]

Other prominent lawyers such as Haywood Burns (1973) and Derrick Bell (1973) address themselves to the thesis that the criminal justice system is permeated by racism. Academics as well as jurists have noted that racial duality of the enforcement of law and subsequent sentencing. For example, Terence Thornberry's "Race, Socioeconomic Status and Sentencing in the Juvenile System" (1973) makes the following conclusions:

... [the] data reveal that blacks are treated more severely than whites throughout the juvenile system. At levels of the police and the juvenile court there are no deviations from this finding, even when the seriousness of the offense and the number of previous offenses are simultaneously held constant. At the level of the intake hearing this conclusion is generally supported.[26]

Bill Somerville's "Double Standards in Law Enforcement with Regard to Minority Status" (1968) is also supportive of the dual application model. More specifically, Somerville states that—

... the double standards expressed themselves in a generalized response to the Negro community by police aimed at the community's lowest denominator. All Negroes are seen as potential violators [and are thus subjected to police harassment associated with such stereotypic thinking].[27]

Leo Carroll and Margaret Mondrick (1976) acknowledge a series of studies that champion the widespread belief that blacks and other minorities are discriminated against by agents of the criminal justice system. They note the development in recent years of theories concerning the relation between law and social structure that incorporate this belief. Such proponents of these theories as Quinney, Turk, and Chambliss and Seidman see minorities as victims of the legal process because they are in conflict with dominant groups that use the law to protect and advance their own interests. These theories also stress the importance of labels, since minorities are unable to protect themselves against the imposition of criminal labels and are thus the objects of unfavorable stereotyping.[28]

While Carroll and Mondrick conclude that research evidence bearing upon the question of racial discrimination is inconclusive, they present their study of "Racial Bias in the Decision to Grant Parole" (1976) as evidence in support of their position. In this study they found that black and white prisoners had different criteria to meet in order to be paroled. Specifically, blacks had the additional requirement of participation in institutional treatment programs. The imposition of this additional criterion was seen as indirectly resulting in racial inequities. Black treatment participants who were paroled served a significantly longer portion of their sentence than did white participants. However, the few black prisoners who were paroled without participating in treatment programs served a shorter portion of their sentence than other prisoners. Carroll and Mondrick note that "these few black prisoners were older, more likely to be property offenders and had slightly more prior convictions than black treatment participants. These findings are interpreted as indicating a bias against social militancy."[29]

Edwin Hall and Albert Simkus' "Inequity in the Types of Sentences Received by Native Americans and Whites" (1975) concluded that native

Americans receive significantly more severe sentences than whites and that this difference in severity of sentence might in part be due to white society's negative labeling of native Americans, i.e., the drunken, wild, Indian stereotype.

Daniel Swett's study of "Culture Bias in the American Legal System" (1969) contends that a marked cultural difference exists between predominantly white police officers and judges, on the one hand, and the non-whites whom they process on the other hand. He concludes that these cultural differences result in a built-in bias against the culturally different.

Judges Howard and Crockett do not stand alone, then, in regard to their contention that the American criminal justice system is guilty of racial bias. It should also be noted that the views and studies discussed so far on criminal justice system bigotry have been substantially supported by important new studies, e.g., the 1981 Carl Pope and William H. Feyerherm study "Race and Juvenile Court Dispositions: An Examination of Initial Screening Decisions"; the 1983 Rand Corporation Study prepared by Joan Petersilia for the National Institute of Corrections and U.S. Department of Justice, entitled *Racial Disparities in the Criminal Justice System;* and the 1983 Samuel Gross and Robert Mauro study, entitled "The Race Factor in Death Sentences."

CLASSIC STUDIES REJECTING RACISM IN THE COURTS AND IN LAW ENFORCEMENT

Discretionary policies by the police and the courts have resulted in a dual system of American justice—a system that is at times more punitive when applied to blacks than to whites—in the application, for example, of severe judicial sanctions applied to incidents which involve a white victim and a black (or non-white) offender—while at other times this dual system of American justice appears to dispense more lenient sentences to non-whites who victimize non-whites. Nonetheless, a discussion of police and court discretion would not be complete without a section that highlights those studies which take the position that official tallies of arrests and processing procedures by the courts do not seem to be strongly biased by extralegal considerations such as race and ethnicity. Prominent social science researchers who represent this position include Hindelang (1969), Goldman (1963), McEachern and Bauzer (1967), Piliavin and Briar (1964), Terry (1967), Hohenstein (1969), Weiner and Willie (1971), and Arnold (1971). These researchers conclude that the gravity of the crime as well as the prior arrest record of the suspects are the principal factors in either determining a decision by the police to proceed with judicial action or the courts to impose a severe sentence. The following sections summarize a number of studies that review police discretion and reject the reactive measures position often cited by radical, Marxist, or critical criminologists.

Goldman's Research

Goldman's research (1963) is often cited as conclusive evidence that with juveniles the gravity of the crime is a principal factor in determining the decision by police to proceed with judicial action. His research and findings have not been reported, however, without severe criticism. For instance, Nettler (1978) notes that Goldman did not control for age and number of previous offenses in his analysis. This may be significant since the decision of the police to refer juveniles to court, while not influenced by sex, was influenced by age, with the older the offender the more probable a court referral. This may account for the differential disposition of older youths' cases.[30] Nettler makes a similar criticism of Goldman's analysis of ethnicity as a factor in court referral. Goldman found little difference in the disposition of the cases of black and white youths arrested for serious offenses, but he did find a statistically significant difference in the disposition of minor offenses. A black child arrested for a minor offense was found to be more likely to be taken to juvenile court than a white child. However, it is impossible to conclude that discrimination accounts for this difference because the number of previous offenses was not controlled for.[31]

McEachern and Bauzer's Research

By analyzing a random sample of records drawn from the juvenile index of the Los Angeles County Sheriff's Department and a substantial number of police contacts contained in the Santa Monica police records, McEachern and Bauzer (1964) attempted to isolate those factors that appeared relevant in the disposition of juvenile offenders by police. They determined that with the size of the samples used in a study such as theirs, almost everything seemed significantly related to whether or not a court petition was requested. Individual factors which were found to influence the police disposition include the youth's sex, age, number of previous offenses, whether or not he was on probation, the year in which he was born, and whether or not he came from an intact family. External factors that were found to have a significant influence were the type of offense, the police department, and the year in which the incident took place. Of particular interest is that one factor which was not found to be important was the child's ethnicity. It was found that "after apprehension by the police, there was no systematic or consistent difference in the proportion of blacks, Chicanos, or 'Anglos' referred to juvenile courts."[32]

Piliavin and Briar's Research

Nettler (1978) has pointed out that a deficiency of much of the research utilizing official statistics is that such research begins only after the police contact has been made and the judicial process initiated. Piliavin and Briar's study (1964), which entailed the observation of police in the field to assess the determinants of police decisions to initiate arrest and the role and operation of their discretion in this decision-making process, is presented by Nettler as an alternative investigative method. The issue which Piliavin and Briar focused on was whether police discretion in making the arrest decision was influenced by the characteristics of the youth or whether it was solely a function of what the youth had done.[33] The behavior of 30 policemen was observed and systematic data were collected on 66 encounters between police and juveniles. Major findings of their study, as reported by Nettler, show that for serious offenses the personal or social characteristics of the offender had a minimal affect on police discretion. However, these serious offenses, rape, arson, robbery, homicide, aggravated assault, grand larceny, and automobile theft, accounted for only about 10 percent of the encounters. The vast majority of the encounters involved minor offenses, and in these cases police discretion was found to be affected by a youth's personal and social characteristics. Those boys whose appearance and demeanor indicated "that they were 'tough guys' and disrespectful toward the police were more likely to be arrested than boys whose bearing in similar situations was judged less 'delinquent.' "[34] The conclusion reached is that for juveniles, and for most minor offenses, police patroling may be discriminatory and may lead to legal decisions based more on a youth's personal or social characteristics than on the offense committed.[35] Nettler does note that the generalizability of this study's findings to police-juvenile encounters in general is hampered by the particular characteristics of the group Piliavin and Briar studied. Their research was conducted on a juvenile bureau committed to a "delinquency prevention" program. Officers assigned to this bureau were selected "on the basis of their commitment to delinquency prevention and they performed essentially as patrol officers cruising assigned beats."[36]

Black and Reiss's Research

Black and Reiss's study of police-citizen encounters was conducted in selected precincts of Boston, Chicago, and Washington, D.C. during the summer of 1966. Trained observers provided detailed descriptions of the behavior of policemen and citizens in more than 5,000 encounters between the two groups.[37] These incidents were characterized as to type of mobilization (i.e., whether police attention to a situation was initiated by a call for service, by the officer himself where events occurred in his presence, or by requests for action from citizens in the field) and then tabulated by the race and social status of the citizens involved and by the gravity of the offense.[38]

The allegation that police respond to offenses and offenders in a prejudicial manner was not borne out in Black and Reiss's research. Outside of one qualification, no evidence was found of racial or class discrimination on the part of police officers in the many encounters between police and citizens that were observed. Police were actually found to be less brusque and hostile towards blacks than they were to whites, and also ridiculed them less.[39] The one qualification is that in response to felonies, though not for misdemeanors, police were found to show more concern when "white-collar" citizens rather than "blue-collar" citizens were the complainants. This concern was evidenced by police being more attentive when a white-collar citizen reported himself to have been victimized by a blue-collar citizen, and also by the fact that police did not investigate with this same vigilance when one blue-collar citizen reported himself to have been victimized by another blue-collar citizen. A result of this bias is a lower blue-collar arrest rate.[40]

Nettler also has presented the findings of another study done by Black and Reiss (1970) in which police encounters with juveniles only were examined for type of police mobilization and for the presence of discrimination as to handling by police. The findings from this study paralleled those of their earlier study in that the preponderance of contacts were initiated by citizen complaints and that no difference between types of mobilization as regards the race of the suspect was found.[41] Arrest rates did differ, however, if the contact was made with the complainant present. The police were typically found to comply with the desire of the complainant when the complainant explicitly expressed a preference for either leniency or an arrest. Part of the higher juvenile arrest rate for blacks is said to be accounted for by the fact that blacks were charged with more serious crimes than whites, and by the fact that blacks were more frequently in situations in which there were complainants who also were primarily black.[42]

Terry's Research

Terry (1967) examined over 9,000 offenses committed by juveniles in a midwestern American city over a five-year period. The focus of his inquiry was whether discriminatory treatment was present during the processing of juveniles by the police, the probation department, and the juvenile court.[43] Nettler has reported that Terry found, as did Black and Reiss, that the majority of offenses studied had been citizen initiated and not the result of police surveillance and, furthermore, that the treatment of offenders did not vary with sex, race, or socioeconomic status "when the gravity of their offenses and their records of previous offenses are considered."[44]

Hohenstein's Research

In order to ascertain those factors that influence police discretion, Hohenstein (1969) analyzed a ten percent sample of all serious offenses committed by juveniles in Philadelphia in 1960. Three major factors were found to influence police decisions: (1) the victim's attitude, (2) the juvenile's record, and (3) the gravity of the reported offense.[45] Of these three factors, the victim's attitude was especially important. Hohenstein found that if the victim did not want to prosecute the police tended to respond in the least serious fashion available, even when the crime was serious and the accused has a previous record. It was also found that when the gravity of the offense, the juvenile's record, and the victim's attitude were considered neither the race nor the age of the accused had a significant impact on the police decision.[46]

Hindelang's Research

In his study, "Equality Under the Law," Hindelang (1969) reviews and analyzes those empirical works that have addressed themselves to the question as to whether defendants receive differential judicial treatment as a function of their race.[47] In so doing, Hindelang attempts to reconcile the divergent findings of the studies reviewed by noting their findings in the light of temporal, geographical and methodological variability across studies. Nevertheless, Hindelang does not find credence in that position which states there has been a systematic bias in sentencing based upon race and ethnicity.

MINORITY KNOWLEDGE AND PERCEPTIONS OF THE CRIMINAL JUSTICE PROCESS

If the findings of the classic Williams and Hall study, "Knowledge of the Law in Texas: Socioeconomic and Ethnic Differences" (1972) is indicative of American minority group knowledge of specific laws and the legal process in general, then ignorance of the law is a serious problem within the minority community as is the inability to fully appreciate and utilize the law as a constructive social process. The Williams and Hall study addressed two basic hypotheses. The first concerns knowledge of the law. It is hypothesized that since many citizens are unaware of how the law may be used for their protection and to their advantage, the law may be a less effective social tool than it might be. This lack of knowledge is seen as a possible cause for negative attitudes toward the law and as a reason why individuals tolerate injustices—they are simply not aware that the law could protect their interests or that the law is different from practice.[48] The second hypothesis is that different groups in the population will differ in their knowledge of the law. Economic and ethnic groups were expected to have different levels of knowledge. It was anticipated that both knowledge and positive attitude toward the law would increase with economic status and majority group membership.[49] Poor groups, as compared to those more economically well-off, were given special interest since so many government programs had been developed to help them with their legal problems, and since they are often seen as being most vulnerable to illegal practices.

The Williams and Hall study uncovered a number of fascinating, but perplexing findings. Of particular interest is the fact that in the mid-'60s most respondents felt that the purpose of the law was "social order," a source of order, control, and regulation. Anglos were found to be more likely than non-Anglos (blacks and Chicanos) to mention social order as a purpose. Williams and Hall feel these results convey a picture of the law in the minds of these respondents as a coercive force to prevent regression from the status quo, rather than as a constructive force.[50]

These respondents perceived a purpose shockingly similar to that forwarded by Crockett (1972), Burns (1973), and Bell (1973). But perhaps, an even more startling finding was that Anglos mentioned civil rights and liberty as a purpose of the law more frequently than did non-Anglos.[51] Does this finding mean that minorities no longer expect the law to serve as a guardian of their civil rights? The Williams and Hall study also notes that a higher percentage of Anglos than non-Anglos mentioned the need for tackling more problems related to discrimination.[52]

Williams and Hall also found that most of the privileged groups (the high- and middle-income Anglos) expressed the least satisfaction with the laws as they were. In fact, over half of all individuals in the low income and minority groups expressed satisfaction with the laws "as they are" and very few who stated that they were not satisfied with the current state of the law were able to single out any particular dissatisfaction.

The Williams and Hall study also indicated that the majority of the minorities surveyed would not try to change laws if they did not like them, while the majority of the Anglos said that they would. Equally interesting was the finding that most Anglos dissatisfied with the law would contact public officials and organizations (a direct and immediate form of pressure) while the majority of the few non-Anglos who stated that they would attempt to change the law stated that they would engage in the franchise to bring about a change in the law. In brief, minorities would engage in an indirect and slow process of electing new officials, a process which would not guarantee a change in the law, while Anglos would put immediate pressure on their current elected officials to right what they perceived as injust legislation. Thus, in general, the Williams and Hall study (1972) found that low-income, non-Anglos groups in particular do not know how one goes about changing the laws. They also found that low-income minority groups were extremely ignorant of the law as it existed in Texas. This was evidenced by the fact that low-income minority group members gave accurate answers on only a little over one-third of the questions put to them that related to knowledge of the law.[53] Further evidence is the fact that many members of the ethnic and racial minority groups who were questioned thought that a law forbidding "open" housing existed. Unfortunately no new comprehensive study replicates the Williams and Hall study. Thus one can only speculate as to whether blacks and other non-whites have become more sophisticated in the 1980s in the perception of the intricacies of the criminal justice system as well as how to modify it and make it work more toward their perceived interest.

Minority groups generally have a negative view of the criminal justice system. It appears that minorities not only perceive the law enforcement process as inadequate, but also believe that it is performed in a basically hostile manner by non-black officers.

Furstenberg and Welford (1973) conclude in their study entitled "Calling the Police: The Evaluation of Police Service" that while the majority of citizens who call police for service are satisfied with the quality of service provided by the police, blacks are consistently more critical than whites of the quality of police service and have a generally lower opinion of the police than do whites. It is also of interest to note that black respondents in particular are unwilling to criticize police performance unless interviewed by civilians (as opposed to police officers), a finding which may add credence to the argument that non-whites, blacks in particular, view police officers as individuals to be feared and avoided.

Hahn's study, "Ghetto Assessments of Police Protection and Authority" (1971), pointedly reflects the perplexing dilemma of a desire for increased police protection among blacks along with the counter belief that the police function in a brutal and inadequate manner, to insure justice or domestic or neighborhood tranquility. Hahn feels that this dilemma may be the result of modern police practices such as "preventive patroling," which often lead to abrasive encounters between police and residents of high-crime areas and at the same time take police manpower from the investigation of the offenses that plague these areas.[54] Nonetheless, Hahn contends that although blacks have a negative perception of the law enforcement agents, blacks have not given up on the law enforcement process.

Jacob's study of law enforcement and justice in Milwaukee, entitled "Black and White Perceptions of Justice in the City" (1971) concurs with the basic findings of the studies and documents previously cited. He concludes that: (1) perceptions of policemen varied both within and between neighborhoods. Race, the quality of the respondent's experience with the police, and certain socio-economic characteristics were found to be associated with these variations; (2) perceptions of policemen were found to be closely associated with perceptions of judges. Jacob feels these perceptions can be generalized to reflect perceptions of the "injustice" system; and (3) there were considerable differences between expectations about policemen and perceptions of their actual behavior. These differences were found in every neighborhood, though the gap was particularly large and frequent in the black neighborhood. Jacob notes that expectations about policemen and judges were almost constant between neighborhoods, and believes the perception of injustice results primarily from perceptions of actual policemen and judges, which were found to be related primarily to race and experience, and less to socio-economic characteristics.[55]

The Smith and Hawkins study, "Victimization, Types of Citizen Police Contacts, and Attitudes Toward the Police" (1973) also concluded that the majority of citizens held positive views of the police. As expected, race was strongly related to attitudes about police fairness. The majority of non-whites held negative attitudes about police performance, while the large majority of whites held positive views. What was most interesting, but also most disturbing, were the findings that neither arrest nor victimization experiences significantly influenced the high level of negative feelings minority group members held about the police. Race was not found to be related to victimization within the past year and the proportion of respondents who reported past arrests was not felt to be particularly divergent for the two groups—20 percent of the non-whites reported having been arrested in the past compared to 14 percent of the whites.[56] It was also found that "[m]inority groups held low images of the police regardless of age."[57]

There appears to be a profound subcultural element to minority sentiments about police in the black ghetto, and this negative perception extends beyond the immediate stimulus response reaction of a "real" police-citizen contact (be it lawful and polite or brutish).

Each of these studies clearly documents either negative criminal justice agency contacts or attitude by the minority community, be these the result of perceived or real infractions in the criminal justice system: Berman, 1976; Zeitz, 1965; Kuykendall, 1970; Berleman, 1972; Davis, 1974; Kleinman and David, 1973; Boggs and Galliher, 1975; Bayley and Mendelson, 1969. One should be cognizant of the fact that much of the perceived bias noted by blacks has been supported by the work of such social scientists as Hepburn (1978), Goldman (1963), Schwartz (1967), and Wilson (1968). It should also be noted that some studies have shown that, contrary to expectation, black persons of higher social status hold even more unfavorable attitudes towards police than persons of lower status. Boggs and Galliher (1975) attribute this to the fact that both higher and low-status blacks have been found to have been subjected to discriminatory practices by police. The greater resentment higher-status blacks feel about these experiences is felt to lead to their more negative evaluations of police.[58]

One should be cognizant of the fact that there have been studies which forward the contention that, in general, citizens, while acknowledging that there is room for improvement in police-community relations, have been pleased with previous contact with police. According to these studies, the black community has been among those communities which have reviewed police service in the community as "good" or "very good" (i.e., for combined figures of almost 50 percent). The Knowles and Brewer study of "The Black Community: Attitudes Toward Community Problems, Crime and the Police" (1973) was among them. It is safe to conclude, however, that the findings of the Knowles and Brewer study (1973) as well as studies with similar conclusions are in the minority.

THE BLACK CRIMINOLOGIST

Criminology has remained a white social science, if the number of prominent black criminologists is used as an index to the discipline's multiracial nature. Charles Reasons, editor of *Race, Crime and Criminal Justice* (1972), and Robert Staples (1975) are two of the most prominent black academicians involved in the study of crime and criminals. Reasons' *Race, Crime and Criminal Justice* (1972) provides a comprehensive review of the literature on black crime causation, crime rates, minorities, the courts, and the police. Staples' "White Racism, Black Crime, and American Justice" (1975) applies the "colonial model" in an attempt to explain the relationship between race and crime. This theory notes that "law" has been formulated by white men to protect white interests and supress non-white people. This theory also notes that police are agents of white America and have been involved in numerous killings of blacks while being overly tolerant of illegal activities in black communities. It also notes the lax manner of police response to the call for help by black residents in black communities. Staple's theory also addresses discriminatory sentencing practices, racially biased juries, inadequate legal representation, the illegitimacy of black cultural values and linguistic barriers, and the need for black community control of black neighborhoods. Violence is seen by Staples as a means of breaking into the white controlled socioeconomic-political system; black crime is viewed by

Staples as structured by the black man's relationship to white socio-economic-political power and racial inequality.

Roy Austin, a black sociologist at Pennsylvania State University has investigated the relationship of race, father-absence, and female criminality (1978). Austin concluded that father absence had detrimental effects only on whites, especially girls.

Julius Debro, a black criminologist and administrator at Atlanta University, has investigated the role of the black offender as victim (1976). Debro has been concerned with whether discrimination exists within the criminal justice system at the federal level. He concludes that while discrimination does exist in sentencing within federal districts, it is much more subtle and covert than that which exists at the state or local level. He notes that the criminal justice system takes into account such legitimate factors as seriousness of the offense, prior arrest record and educational background at the time of sentencing, factors which work to the disadvantage of the minority offender.

Vernetta Young, criminologist at American University, has researched in the area of women, race, and crime (1978) noting the historical impact of slavery on the black family.

Daniel E. Georges-Abeyie, social urban geographer/social ecologist/criminologist, has explored the relationship of ethnic and racial heterogeneity, and black crime rates (1975) as well as criminal violence and the elderly (1977-78). Georges-Abeyie (1975, 1981) has noted the myopic vision of sociological and criminological theories and research which treats black ghetto and slum-ghettos as monolithic ethnic/racial entities (and thus blacks as one ethnic group). His research has also focused on the positive correlation between ethnic/racial heterogeneity and elevated black crime rates as well as the social-spatial dynamics of black crime perpetration.

Recent publications edited by black criminologists Jimmy Bell and Charles Owens (1977), and Robert Woodson (1977) offer valuable insights into black perspectives on crime, criminal justice and racism. Among black criminologists cited in these works are Benjamin Carmichael (Woodson, 1977), and Alex Swan (Woodson, 1977; Owens and Bell, 1977). Perhaps the most recent and comprehensive index to black criminological and criminal justice research is Scott Christianson's *Index to Minorities and Criminal Justice: 1981 Cumulative Edition.*

THE BLACK JURIST: JUDGES, STATES
ATTORNEYS, AND LAWYERS

Lawyers, black lawyers included, are probably viewed by many as the guardians of the status quo, since it is their function to argue the intricacies and nuances of the criminal justice system; judges are probably and frequently viewed as the ultimate arbiters of the final "correct" interpretation of the law. Nonetheless, the black jurist has been in the forefront of the battle for judicial equality for America's black citizenry. *From the Black Bar* (1976), edited by Gilbert Ware, offers uncompromised views of black jurists at odds with the racism of a judicial system which they are so much a part. This work documents the political nature of law and justice as applied to black people. Another noteworthy work by a prominent black jurist and professor is Derrick A. Bell Jr.'s *Race, Racism, and the Law.* This casebook reviews the development of racism in American law and the black man's struggle for full rights of citizenship as well as the right to education, decent housing, employment, and justice.

Criminology has remained a white social science. Nevertheless, more and more black jurists, criminal justicians, and academics are becoming involved in research that reveals the injustices blacks continue to suffer in their contacts with police, the courts, and prisons. Although most would agree that the criminal justice system, as a human process, is imperfect, few are willing to denounce the system as overtly racist, unconscionably subjective, or simply intentionally unfair when it comes to justice for blacks and other minorities. What is crucially in order, then, is black commitment to revealing the full extent of criminal justice injustice, the consequences of those injustices, and the necessity for radical changes in the system's treatment of minorities.

Notes

1 Lynn Curtis, *Violence, Race and Culture* (Lexington, Ma: Lexington-Heath Books, 1974); Marvin E. Wolfgang and Franco Ferracuti, *The Subculture of Violence: Towards an Integrated Theory in Criminology* (London: Tavistock, 1967).

2 Keith Harries, *The Geography of Crime and Justice* (New York: McGraw-Hill, 1974).

3 Daniel E. Georges-Abeyie and Keith Harries, *Crime: A Spatial Perspective* (New York: Columbia University Press, 1980).

4 David Herbert, *The Geography of Urban Crime* (New York: Longman Group, Ltd, 1982).

5 See, e.g., Clifford Shaw and Henry McKay, *Juvenile Delinquency and Urban Areas* (Chicago: University of Chicago Press, 1942).

6 William J. Chambliss and Robert B. Seidman, *Law, Order and Power* (Menlo Park, Ca:

Addison Wesley, 1971); Willem Adriaan Bonger, *Race and Crime.* Trans. Margaret Mathews Hordyk (Montclair, NJ: Patterson Smith, 1969).

[7] Richard Block, *Violent Crime* (Lexington, Ma: Lexington Heath Books, 1977); Michael J. Hindelang, Michael Gottfredson and James Garofalo, *Victims of Personal Crime: An Empirical Foundation for a Theory of Victimization* (Cambridge, Ma: Ballinger, 1978).

[8] Daniel E. Georges-Abeyie and Kirk Kirksey, "Violent Crime Perpetrated Against the Elderly in the City of Dallas." *Journal of Environmental Systems* 4(2) (1977-1978): 149-198; Lynn Curtis, *Criminal Violence* (Lexington, Ma: Lexington-Heath Books, 1974); Curtis, *Violence, Race.*

[9] Derrick A. Bell, "Racism in American Courts: Cause for Black Disruption or Despair?" *California Law Review* 61 (1973): 165-204;

[10] E. Long, J. Long, W. Leon, and P. Weston, *American Minorities: The Justice Issue* (Englewood Cliffs, NJ: Prentice-Hall, 1975); Haywood Burns, "Black People and the Tyranny of American Law," *Annals of the American Academy of Political and Social Science* (March, 1973): 156-166.

[11] Edwin L. Hall and Albert A. Simkus, "Inequity in the Types of Sentences Received by Native Americans and Whites," *Criminology* 13 (Aug. 1975): 119-219; John S. Goldkamp, "Minorities as Victims of Police Shootings: Interpretations of Racial Disproportionality and Police Use of Deadly Force," *Justice System Journal* 2(2) (Winter 1976):169-183; Bill Somerville, "Double Standards in Law Enforcement With Regard to Minority Status," *Issues in Criminology* (Fall, 1968): 35-43; Terence A. Thornberry, "Race, Socioeconomic Status and Sentencing in the Juvenile Justice System," *Journal of Criminal Law and Criminology* 64(1) (1973): 90-98; George W. Crockett, "Race and the Courts," in L. Brown, ed., *The Administration of Criminal Justice: A View from Black America* (Washington, D.C.: Institute of Urban Affairs and Research, Howard University, 1974); Marvin Wolfgang and Marc Riedel, "Race, Judicial Discretion, and the Death Penalty," *Annals of American Academy* (May, 1973): 119-133; Richard Block, "Why Notify the Police," *Criminology* (February, 1974):555-569; Furstenberg; Daniel H. Swett, "Cultural Bias in the American Legal System," *Law and Society Review* (August 1969):79-109; Bell, "Racism in American Courts"; Howard, "Racial Discrimination in Sentencing"; Leo Carroll and Margaret E. Mondrick, "Racial Bias in the Decision to Grant Parole," *Law and Society Review* 11(1) (Fall, 1976):93-107.

[12] Bell, "Racism in American Courts"; President's Commission on Law Enforcement and Administration of Justice (1967), *Task Force Report: The Police* (Washington, D.C.: U.S. Government Printing Office).

[13] Charles W. Thomas, R. J. Cage, and S. C. Foster, "Public Opinion in Criminal Law and Legal Sanctions: An Examination of Two Conceptual Models," *Journal of Criminal Law and Criminology* 67(1) (1976):110-116; Block, "Why Notify the Police"; Roger Woodbury, "Delinquents' Attitudes Towards the Juvenile Justice System," *Psychological Reports* 32 (1973):1119-1124; Lyle Knowles and Jesse Brewer, "The Black Community: Attitudes Toward Community Problems, Crime and the Police," *The Police Chief* (August, 1973):48-51; John A. Davis, "Justification for No Obligation: Views of Black Males Toward Crime and the Criminal Law," *Issues in Criminology* 9(2) (Fall, 1974)69-84; Sarah L. Boggs and John F. Galliher, "Evaluating the Police: A Comparison of Black Street and Household Respondents," *Social Problems* 22 (Fall, 1975):393-406; Paul E. Smith and Richard O. Hawkins, "Victimization, Types of Citizen-Police Contacts, and Attitudes Toward the Police," *Law and Society* (Fall, 1973):134-152; Frank F. Furstenberg and Charles F. Wellford, "Calling the Police: The Evaluation of Police Service," *Law and Society Review* (Spring, 1973):393-406; Leonard Zeitz, "Survey of Negro Attitudes Toward Law," *Rutgers Law Review* 19 (1965):288-303.

[14] Martha Williams and Jay Hall, "Knowledge of the Law in Texas: Socioeconomic and Ethnic Differences," *Law and Society Review* (Fall, 1972):199-210.

[15] Ibid.

[16] See also, A. Leon Higginbotham, Jr., *In the Matter of Color: Race and the American Legal Process: The Colonial Period* (New York: Oxford University Press, 1978).

17 Howard, "Racial Discrimination in Sentencing," *Judicature* 59(3) (October, 1975):121-124.

18 Ibid.

19 Ibid., p. 124.

20 Ibid.

21 Ibid., p. 121.

22 Wolfgang and Riedel, "Race, Judicial Discretion, Death Penalty," p. 120.

23 Ibid., pp. 129-132.

24 Crockett, "Commentary."

25 Ibid., p. 1136.

26 Thornberry, "Race, Socioeconomic Status, Sentencing," p. 95.

27 Somerville, "Double Standards," p. 40.

28 Carroll, "Racial Bias," p. 93.

29 Ibid.

30 Gwynn Nettler, *Explaining Crime* (New York: McGraw-Hill, 1978), p. 65.

31 Ibid.

32 Ibid.

33 Ibid., p. 66.

34 Ibid.

35 Ibid.

36 Ibid.

37 Ibid.

38 Ibid.

39 Ibid., pp. 66-68.

40 Ibid., p. 67.

41 Ibid., p. 68.

42 Ibid., p. 67-68.

43 Ibid., p. 68.

44 Ibid.

45 Ibid.

46 Ibid.

47 Michael J. Hindelang, "Equality Under the Law," *Journal of Criminal Law, Criminology and Police Science* 60 (September 1969):306-313.

48 Williams, "Knowledge of the Law," p. 100.

49 Ibid.

50 Ibid., pp. 108-109.

51 Ibid., p. 109.

52 Ibid.

53 Ibid., p. 113.

54 Harlan Hahn, "Ghetto Assessments of Police Protection and Authority," *Law and Society Review* 183 (November, 1971):183.

55 Herbert Jacob, "Black and White Perceptions of Justice in the City," *Law and Society Review* (August, 1971):87.

56 Smith, "Victimization," pp. 136-137.

57 Ibid., p. 146.

58 Boggs, "Evaluating the Police," pp. 394-395.

References

Arnold, William R. "Race and ethnicity relative to other factors in juvenile court dispositions." American Journal of Sociology 2 (1971):211-227.

Austin, Roy. "Race, father-absence, and female delinquency." Criminology 57 (1978):487-503.

Bayley, David and Harold Mendelsohn. Minorities and the Police. New York: Free Press, 1969.

Bell, Derrick A., Jr. "Racism in American courts: cause for black disruption or despair?" California Law Review 61 (1973):165-204.

Bell, Derrick A., Jr. Race, Racism and American Law. Boston: Little, Brown and Company, 1973.

Bell, Jimmy and Charles E. Owen (eds.). Blacks and Criminal Justice. Lexington, Ma: Lexington-Heath Books, 1977.

Berleman, William C. "Police and minority groups: the improvement of community relations." Crime and Delinquency, 18(2) (1972):160-167.

Berman, John J. "Parolees' perception of the justice system: black-white differences." Criminology 13 (February, 1976):507-520.

Black, Donald and Albert Reiss. "Police control of juveniles." American Sociological Review 35 (1970):63-77.

Block, Richard. "Public attitudes toward the police." Paper presented at the American Sociological Association Meeting, August, 1969.

Block, Richard. Violent Crime. Lexington, Ma: Lexington-Heath Books, 1977.

Block, Richard. "Why notify the police." Criminology, 11(4) (February, 1974):555-569.

Boggs, Sarah L. and John F. Galliher. "Evaluating the police: a comparison of black street and household respondents." Social Problems 22 (Fall, 1975):393-406.

Bonger, Willem Adrianna. Race and Crime. Montclair, NJ: Patterson Smith (1969). Translated by Margaret Mathews Hordyk.

Burns, Haywood. "Black people and the tyranny of American law." Annals of the American Academy of Political and Social Science 407 (May, 1973):156-166.

Carroll, Leo and Margaret E. Mondrick. "Racial bias in the decision to grant parole." Law and Society Review 11(1) (Fall, 1976):93-107.

Chambliss, William J. and Robert B. Seidman. Law, Order and Power. Menlo Park, Ca: Addison-Wesley, 1971.

Christianson, Scott and David Parry (eds.). Black Crime: An Annotated Bibliography. Albany, NY: Education Project in Criminal Justice, School of Criminal Justice, State University of New York (March, 1980).

Christianson, Scott (ed.). Index to Minorities and Criminal Justice. The Center on Minorities and Criminal Justice, School of Criminal Justice, State University of New York at Albany (1981).

Clark, Kenneth B. "Color, class, personality and juvenile justice." Journal of Negro Education 28(3) (1959):240-251.

Clinard, M. The Sociology of Deviant Behavior. New York: Holt, Rinehart and Winston (1963).

Crockett, George W. "Racism in the law." Science and Society 33(2) (Spring, 1969):223-230.

Crockett, G.W. "Racism in courts." Journal of Public Law 20(2) (1971):385.

Crockett, George W. "Commentary: black judges and the black judicial experience." Wayne Law Review 19 (1972):61-71.

Crockett, George W. "Race and the courts." In L. Brown (ed.), The Administration of Criminal Justice: A View from Black America. Washington, DC: Institute of Urban Affairs and Research. Howard University (1974):12-22.

Curtis, Lynn A. Criminal Violence. Lexington, Ma: Lexington-Heath Books, 1974.

_____. Violence, Race and Culture. Lexington, Ma: Lexington-Heath Books, 1975.

Davis, John A. "Justification for no obligation: views of black males toward crime and the criminal law." Issues in Criminology 9(2) (Fall, 1974):

Debro, Julius. "The black offender as victim." Afro-Americans: A Social Science Perspective. Washington, DC: University of America (1976):354-370.

Ennis, P.H. Criminal Victimization in the United States. President's Commission on Law Enforcement and the Administration of Justice. Washington, DC: U.S. Government Printing Office (1967).

Federal Bureau of Investigation. Crime in the United States: Uniform Crime Report. Washington, DC: U.S. Government Printing Office (annually).

Furstenberg, Frank F. and Charles F. Wellford. "Calling the police: the evaluation of police service." Law and Society Review 7 (Spring, 1973).

Georges-Abeyie, Daniel and Kirk Kirsey. "Violent crime perpetrated against the elderly in the city of Dallas, October 1974-September 1975." The Journal of Environmental Systems 4(2) (1977-1978):149-198.

Georges-Abeyie, Daniel and M.M. Zandi. "The study of bombings, incendiaries, and bomb threats in the city of Dallas for the Year 1975." Journal of Environmental Systems 8(1) (1978-1979):57-97.

Georges-Abeyie, Daniel. "The ecology of urban unrest: the cage of arson in Newark, New Jersey." Journal of Environmental Systems 5(3) (1975).

Georges-Abeyie, Daniel. "Toward the development of a realistic approach to the study of black crime." In Paul and Patricia Brantingham (eds.), Environmental Criminology. Beverly Hills, Ca: Sage Publications, Inc. (1981).

Georges-Abeyie, Daniel and Keith Harries (eds.). Crime: A Spatial Perspective. New York: Columbia University Press (1980).

Goldkamp, John S. "Minorities are victims of police shootings: interpretations of racial disproportionality and police use of deadly force." Justice System Journal 2(2) (Winter, 1976):169-183.

Goldman, Nathan. The Differential Selection of Juvenile Offenders for Court Appearance. New York: National Council on Crime and Delinquency (1963).

Gottfredson, Michael R., et al. (eds.). Sourcebook of Criminal Justice Statistics—1980. Washington, DC: U.S. Department of Justice, Law Enforcement Assistance Administration, Government Printing Office (1980).

Green, Edward. Judicial Attitudes in Sentencing. New York: St. Martin's Press (1961).

_____. "Inter- and Intra-racial crime relative to sentencing." Journal of Criminal Law, Criminology and Police Science 55 (September, 1964):348-358.

_____. "Race, social status and criminal arrest." American Sociological Review 35(3) (1970):476-490.

Gross, Samuel and Robert Mauro. "The race factor in death sentences." Unpublished manuscript, 1984.

Hahn, Harlan. "Ghetto assessments of police protection and authority." Law and Society Review 183 (November, 1971):183-193.

Harries, Keith. The Geography of Crime and Justice. New York: McGraw-Hill, 1974.

Hepburn, J.R. "Race and the decision to arrest: an analysis of warrants issued." Journal of Research in Crime and Delinquency 15(1) (1978):54-73.

Herbert, David. The Geography of Urban Crime. New York: Longman Group, Ltd. (1982).

Hindelang, Michael J. "Equality under the law." Journal of Criminal Law, Criminology and Police Science 60 (September, 1969):306-313.

Hindelang, Michael J., Michael Gottfredson, and James Garofalo. Victims of Personal Crime: An Empirical Foundation for a Theory of Victimization. Cambridge, Ma: Ballinger Publishing Co. (1978).

Hohenstein, "Factors influencing the police disposition of juvenile offenders." In Thorsten Sellin and Marvin Wolfgang (eds.), Delinquency: Selected Studies. New York: Wiley (1969).

Howard, Joseph C., Sr. The Administration of Rape Cases in the City of Baltimore and the State of Maryland. Baltimore: Monumental Bar Association (1967).

Howard, Joseph C., Sr. "Racial discrimination in sentencing," Judicature. 59(3) (October, 1975):121-124.

Jacob, Herbert. "Black and white perceptions of justice in the city." Law and Society Review (August, 1971):69-89.

Jordan, Vernon E. "The system propagates crimes." Crime and Delinquency 20 (July, 1974):233-240.

Kleinman, Paula H. and Deborah S. David. "Victimization and perception of crime in a ghetto community." Criminology 11(3) (November, 1973):307-343.

Knowles, Lyle and Jesse Brewer. "The black community: attitudes toward community problems, crime and the police." The Police Chief 40(8) (August, 1973):48-51.

Kuykendall, Jack L. "Police and minority groups: toward a theory of negative contacts." Police (September-October, 1970):47-55.

Lemmert, E. Social Pathology: A Systematic Approach to the Theory of Sociopathic Behavior. New York: McGraw-Hill (1951).

Long, E., J. Long, W. Leon, and P. Weston. American Minorities: The Justice Issue. Englewood Cliffs, NJ: Prentice Hall (1975).

Lundsgaarde, Henry P. "Racial and ethnic classifications: an appraisal of the role of anthropology in the lawmaking process." Houston Law Review 10 (March, 1973):641-654.

Martin, J. David and John P. McConnell. "Black militant ideology and the law." Criminology 10(1) (May, 1972):111-116.

McEachern and Bauzer. "Factors related to disposition in juvenile police contacts." In M. Klein and B. Myerhoff (eds.), Juvenile Gangs in Context. New York: Prentice-Hall (1964).

Mulvihill, D.J., et al. Crimes of Violence. A Staff Report submitted to the National Commission on the Causes and Prevention of Violence, Vol. 12. Washington, DC: U.S. Government Printing Office (1968).

National Criminal Justice Information and Statistics Service. Criminal Victimization in the United States—1975. Washington, DC: U.S. Government Printing Office (1978).

Nettler, Gwynn. Explaining Crime. New York: McGraw-Hill, 1978.

Newman, Donald J. Introduction to Criminal Justice (2nd ed.). Philadelphia: J.B. Lippincott Co (1978).

Petersilia, Joan. Racial Disparities in the Criminal Justice System. Santa Monica, Ca: Rand Corporation (1983).

Piliavin, Irving and Scott Briar. "Police encounters with juveniles," American Journal of Sociology 70 (September, 1964):206-214.

Pope, Carl E. and William H. Feyerherm. "Race and juvenile court dispositions: an examination of initial screening decisions." Criminal Justice and Behavior 8(3) (September, 1981).

President's Commission on Law Enforcement and Administration of Justice. The Challenge of Crime in a Free Society. Washington, DC: U.S. Government Printing Office (1967).

President's Commission on Law Enforcement and Administration of Justice. Task Force Report: The Police. Washington, DC: U.S. Government Printing Office (1967).

President's Commission on Law Enforcement and Administration of Justice. Task Force Report: Assessment of Crime. Washington, DC: U.S. Government Printing Office (1967).

Quinney, Richard. Criminology: Analysis and Critique of Crime in America. Boston: Little, Brown and Co. (1975).

Reasons, Charles and Jack Kuykendall (eds.). Race, Crime and Justice. Pacific Palisades, Ca: Goodyear, 1972.

Reckless, Walter. The Crime Problem. New York: Meredity (1961).

Sellin, T. and M. Wolfgang. The Measurement of Delinquency. New York: Wiley (1964).

Smith, Paul E. and Richard O. Hawkins. "Victimization, types of citizen-police contacts, and attitudes toward the police." Law and Society 8 (Fall, 1973):135-152.

Shannon, L.W. "Types and patterns of delinquency referral in a middle-sized city." British Journal of Criminology. Delinquency and Deviant Social Behavior 4(1) (1963):24-36.

Somerville, Bill. "Double Standards in Law Enforcement with Regard to Minority Status." Issues in Criminology (Fall, 1968):35-43.

Staples, Robert. "White racism, black crime, and American justice: an application of the colonial model to explain crime and race." Phylon 36 (March, 1975):14-22.

Sutherland, E. and D. Cressey. Principles of Criminology (6th ed.). Philadelphia: J.B. Lippincott Co. (1960).

Swett, Daniel H. "Cultural bias in the American legal system." Law and Society Review 4 (August, 1969):79-109.

Terry, R.M. "Discrimination in the handling of juvenile offenders by social control agencies." Journal of Research in Crime and Delinquency, 4(2) (1967):218-230.

Thomas, Charles W., R.J. Cage and S.C. Foster. "Public opinion in criminal law and legal sanctions: an examination of two conceptual models." Journal of Criminal Law and Criminology 67(1) (1976):110-116.

Thornberry, Terence P. "Race, socioeconomic status and sentencing in the juvenile justice system." Journal of Criminal Law and Criminology 64(1) (1973):90-98.

Turk, Austin. Criminality and Legal Order. Chicago: Rand McNally (1969).

Ware, Gilbert. From the Black Bar. New York: G.P. Putnam (1976).

Weiner, Normal L. and Charles V. Willie. "Decisions by juvenile officers." American Journal of Sociology 77(2) (1971):199-210.

Williams, Martha and Jay Hall. "Knowledge of the law in Texas: socioeconomic and ethnic differences." Law and Society Review 7 (Fall, 1972):99-118.

Wilson, James Q. Varieties of Police Behavior: The Management of Law and Order in Eight Communities. Cambridge, Ma: Harvard University Press (1968).

Wolfgang, Marvin E. and Franco Ferracuti. The Subculture of Violence: Towards an Integrated Theory in Criminology. London: Tavistock (1967).

Wolfgang, Marvin E., Robert M. Figlio, and Thorsten Sellin. Delinquency in a Birth Cohort. Chicago: University of Chicago Press (1972).

Wolfgang, Marvin E. and Marc Riedel. "Race, judicial discretion and the death penalty." Annals of the American Academy of Political and Social Science 407 (May, 1973):119-133.

Woodbury, Roger. "Delinquents' attitudes towards the juvenile justice system." Psychological Reports, 32 (1973):1119-1124.

Woodson, Robert L. Black perspectives on crime and the criminal justice system. Boston: G.K. Hall and Co. (1977).

Wright, Nathan, Jr. "A view from the bench." In Gilbert Ware, From the Black Bar. New York: G.P. Putnam (1976).

Yearwood, Homero. "Police and community relations." Issues in Criminology. 4(1) (1968):45-60.

Young, Vernetta. "Women, race and crime." Paper presented at the Academy of Criminal Justice Sciences Meeting, March 9, 1978, New Orleans, LA.

Zeitz, Leonard. "Survey of negro attitudes toward law." Rutgers Law Review 19 (1965):288-303.

Table 1   Personal Crimes, 1980: Victimization rates for persons age 12 and over, by type of crime and race of victims

(Rate per 1,000 population age 12 and over)

Type of crime	White (157,081,000)	Black (19,691,000)	Other (3,578,000)
Crimes of violence	32.2	40.2	36.8
Rape	0.9	1.1	1.0
Robbery	5.7	13.9	2.4
Robbery with injury	2.0	4.3	0.0
From serious assault	1.0	2.5	0.0
From minor assault	1.1	1.8	0.0
Robbery without injury	3.7	9.6	2.5
Assault	25.5	25.2	33.4
Aggravated assault	8.7	12.3	14.4
With injury	2.8	5.0	7.5
Attempted assault with weapon	5.9	7.3	6.9
Simple assault	16.9	12.9	19.0
With injury	4.7	3.8	5.6
Attempted assault without weapon	12.2	9.1	13.4
Crimes of theft	83.2	79.1	84.9
Personal larceny with contact	2.6	6.2	4.1
Purse snatching	0.9	2.8	1.1
Pocket picking	1.7	3.5	2.9
Personal larceny without contact	80.6	72.9	80.8

Note: Detail may not add to total shown because of rounding. Numbers in parentheses refer to population in the group.

Source: National Criminal Justice Information and Statistics Service, *Criminal Victimizations in the United States, 1980.* Government Printing Office, Washington, D.C., 1982, p. 25.

Table 2   Personal Crimes, 1980: Victimization rates for persons age 12 and over, by type of crime and sex and race of victims

(Rate per 1,000 population age 12 and over)

	Male		Female	
Type of crime	White (75,659,000)	Black (8,864,000)	White (31,421,000)	Black (10,827,000)
Crimes of violence	43.1	52.3	22.0	30.3
Rape	0.3	0.2	1.5	1.8
Robbery	7.8	20.6	3.8	8.5
Robbery with injury	2.5	6.3	1.6	2.6
Robbery without injury	5.3	14.2	2.2	5.9
Assault	35.0	31.6	16.7	20.0
Aggravated assault	13.2	18.4	4.5	7.3
Simple assault	21.8	13.2	12.3	12.6
Crimes of theft	88.5	87.2	78.4	72.5
Personal larceny with contact	1.9	3.9	3.2	8.2
Personal larceny without contact	86.6	83.3	75.1	64.3

Note: Detail may not add to total shown because of rounding. Numbers in parentheses refer to population in the group.

Source: National Criminal Justice Information and Statistics Service, *Criminal Victimization in the United States, 1980.* Government Printing Office, Washington, D.C., 1982, p. 25.

Table 3   Personal Crimes, 1980: Victimization rates for persons age 12 and over, by race, sex, and age of victims and type of crime

(Rate per 1,000 population in each age group)

Race, sex, and age	Crimes of violence	Crimes of theft
White		
Male		
12-15 (6,113,000)	64.6	128.3
16-19 (6,850,000)	93.3	136.0
20-24 (8,543,000)	92.5	147.8
25-34 (15,523,000)	48.8	106.3
35-49 (15,761,000)	24.7	70.3
50-64 (13,958,000)	14.4	49.8
65 and over (8,913,000)	9.7	29.5
Female		
12-15 (5,866,000)	32.0	116.8
16-19 (6,805,000)	45.6	123.3
20-24 (8,734,000)	46.0	129.9
25-34 (15,659,000)	28.0	90.4
35-49 (16,330,000)	16.5	77.9
50-64 (15,220,000)	8.9	49.7
65 and over (12,807,000)	3.8	21.6
Black		
Male		
12-15 (1,086,000)	75.7	99.0
16-19 (1,087,000)	77.7	99.4
20-24 (1,101,000)	82.8	146.3
25-34 (1,706,000)	55.7	116.1
35-49 (1,627,000)	31.6	63.3
50-64 (1,377,000)	25.8	49.0
65 and over (879,000)	27.1	31.6
Female		
12-15 (1,063,000)	30.6	95.3
16-19 (1,168,000)	61.2	76.1
20-24 (1,382,000)	51.7	107.8
25-34 (2,165,000)	41.1	99.3
35-49 (3,139,000)	21.3	70.7
50-64 (1,672,000)	6.9	35.2
65 and over (1,237,000)	5.2	16.4

Note: Numbers in parentheses refer to population in the group.

Source: National Criminal Justice Information and Statistics Service, *Criminal Victimization in the United States, 1980.* Government Printing Office, Washington, D.C., 1982, p. 27.

Table 4   Household Burglary, 1980: Victimization rates, by race of head of household, annual family income, and type of burglary

(Rate per 1,000 households)

Race and income	All burglaries	Forcible entry	Unlawful entry without force	Attempted forcible entry
White				
Less than $3,000 (3,517,000)	109.3	37.9	48.1	23.2
$3,000-$7,499 (11,350,000)	82.8	27.5	35.4	19.9
$7,500-$9,999 (5,092,000)	72.0	24.5	32.6	14.9
$10,000-$14,999 (11,575,000)	79.5	27.6	35.2	16.7
$15,000-$24,999 (17,983,000)	77.5	23.9	37.4	16.1
$25,000 or more (13,084,000)	84.8	27.2	41.6	16.0
Black				
Less than $3,000 (1,250,000)	118.4	47.9	35.9	34.6
$3,000-$7,499 (2,372,000)	130.4	68.0	36.0	26.4
$7,500-$9,999 (798,000)	105.3	49.1	36.3	19.9
$10,000-$14,999 (1,380,000)	101.1	39.8	32.1	29.1
$15,000-$24,999 (1,314,000)	106.5	50.8	28.6	27.2
$25,000 or more (606,000)	122.3	46.1	42.6	33.5

Note: Detail may not add to total shown because of rounding. Numbers in parentheses refer to households in group; excludes data on persons whose income level was not ascertained.

Source: National Criminal Justice Information and Statistics Service, *Criminal Victimization in the United States, 1980.* Government Printing Office, Washington, D.C., 1982, p. 39.

Table 5   Household Crimes, 1980: Victimization rates, by type of crime, form of tenure, and race of head of household

(Rate per 1,000 households)

Type of crime	Owned or being bought			Rented		
	All races (52,363,000)	White (47,759,000)	Black (3,936,000)	All races (28,614,000)	White (23,143,000)	Black (4,789,000)
Burglary	71.5	69.4	100.0	107.4	103.6	126.7
Forcible entry	24.5	22.6	48.4	39.3	35.8	56.4
Unlawful entry without force	32.5	32.8	28.8	44.3	45.4	39.3
Attempted forcible entry	14.6	14.0	22.7	23.7	22.4	31.1
Household larceny	112.9	111.6	124.0	151.6	153.4	141.6
Less than $50	55.8	57.1	38.3	71.0	74.5	55.5
$50 or more	42.9	41.2	61.7	63.5	62.9	64.1
Amount not available	5.9	5.5	11.5	6.2	5.7	9.0
Attempted larceny	8.2	7.8	12.6	10.8	10.3	13.0
Motor vehicle theft	13.7	12.6	26.8	22.3	21.9	23.8
Completed theft	9.6	8.8	19.4	14.5	14.6	13.9
Attempted theft	4.0	3.8	7.3	7.8	7.2	9.9

Note: Detail may not add to total shown because of rounding. Numbers in parentheses refer to households in group.
Source: National Criminal Justice Information and Statistics Service, *Criminal Victimization in the United States, 1980.* Government Printing Office, Washington, D.C., 1982, p. 41.

Table 6   **Household Crimes, 1980: Victimization rates, by type of locality of residence, race of head of household, and type of crime**

(Rate per 1,000 households)

Area and race	Burglary	Household larceny	Motor vehicle theft
All areas			
White (70,902,000)	80.5	125.2	15.6
Black (8,725,000)	114.7	133.6	25.1
Metropolitan areas			
Central cities			
White (18,638,000)	109.3	153.6	22.2
Black (5,129,000)	132.0	144.9	31.0
Outside central cities			
White (28,669,000)	79.5	131.0	17.7
Black (1,865,000)	99.3	137.7	27.1
Nonmetropolitan areas			
White (23,595,000)	59.1	95.8	8.0
Black (1,732,000)	79.8	95.9	5.7

Note: Numbers in parentheses refer to households in group.

Source: National Criminal Justice Information and Statistics Service, *Criminal Victimization in the United States, 1980.* Government Printing Office, Washington, D.C., 1982, p. 44.

PART 2

Blacks, Law Enforcement & the Courts

Introduction

That blacks are no strangers to law enforcement and the courts is beyond refute; one need but visit any police station or criminal court in any major American city with a moderate to large black population to see that this observation is true. What is at question, however, is the treatment these blacks, and other minorities, receive as they are processed through the system.

A related issue is how black criminal justice personnel work within the system; how are they viewed by the community they serve and by their white colleagues? Can racism within the ranks undermine the effectiveness and motivation of black officers? Alfred Dean, a black Director of Public Safety, Harrisburg, Pennsylvania, discusses black police officer-black community interaction and the sensitive issue of police brutality. Dean also points out the valuable sensitivity black officers bring to their jobs while experiencing racial discrimination, heightened stress, and a strong will to succeed in their vocation.

Pennsylvania State University sociologist Roy Austin examines the practice of discriminatory court processing of blacks which has resulted in harsher penalties than those received by whites and as more lenient penalties when blacks are the victims of crimes, especially if whites are the offenders. Professor Austin views this discriminatory processing as a corollary to white racism and economic deprivation—a two-prong reality which operates to keep racial minorities underrepresented on juries and weak clients in an adversary judicial system in which the quality of counsel and investigation is directly related to ones' ability to finance such input.

Judge George W. Crockett, Jr., former justice on Detroit's Recorders Court (criminal court) and current member of the U.S. House of Representatives, agrees with Professor Austin's assertion that racism pervades every area and facet of American life—the judicial process included. Judge Crockett also notes in "The Role of the Black Judge" that one's ability to pay, one's economic standing, definitely affects the quality of justice that person receives. It is crucial, according to Judge Crockett, that black judges be "psychologically black" (ethnically and racially identifying) on the bench.

Judge Crockett's perspective is also reflected in Judge Bruce McM. Wright's "A View from the Bench." This famous speech emphasizes the necessity for black judges to be sensitive to the black experience; such a sensitivity, according to Judge Wright, is essential to overcome inherent biases in the system and to respond in a manner that reflects a deep understanding of blacks and criminal behavior. It should be noted that Judge Wright, one of this country's most outspoken jurists, now sits on the Supreme Court of the City of New York after many years as a Criminal Court Judge in New York City.

Howard Stewart, a black Assistant District Attorney in Dauphin County, Harrisburg, Pennsylvania (the state capitol) regards fairness as the keystone to justice, and describes his efforts to achieve a balance of justice in the courtroom. Stewart's point of view represents a more conservative approach to the requirements of justice as they relate to minorities, sentencing, and equal treatment of white and black defendants.

Joan Petersilia, a Rand Corporation criminal justice researcher, raises the issue of racial differences in case processing, post-sentence treatment and offender behavior while noting racial similarities in crime commission rates and probability of arrest. Ms. Petersilia also offers implications for future criminal justice research and policy implications.

10

Black Police Officers: An Interview with Alfred W. Dean, Director of Public Safety, City of Harrisburg, Pennsylvania*

It is generally assumed that the increased hiring of black officers will alleviate police-community problems. Black officers in the city of Harrisburg, however, have been found guilty of a disproportionate percentage of citizen complaints against the local police. Negative or inappropriate value systems apparently transcend racial categories. It appears that some black officers in an attempt to be accepted by their white counterparts identify with racially insensitive white officers. Mr. Dean, one of the few black Directors of Public Safety in this country, touches on this problem as well as a number of other sensitive issues—educational levels, abuse of authority, and career advancement—that impact on black police officers and the community they serve.

Question: Have you found black police officers to be more or less effective in policing the minority community than white officers?

Answer: Many black police officers are very effective in policing the minority community, for obvious reasons. However, I have also found that some black police officers can aggravate already strained community relations. For example, presently in the city of Harrisburg, 17 percent of the police bureau is black; that 17 percent is responsible for 61 percent of all complaints against police officers. Clearly, the statistics indicate that in Harrisburg, some black police officers abuse their authority. I have found, since I've been here, that a disproportionate number of disciplinary problems are also associated with black officers. I am appalled by the fact that black police officers here cause many of our police-community problems. This is an important point, which is never discussed because of the assumption that more blacks on a police department equals better police-community relations. Obviously, given this department's statistics, that premise is not always valid.

What we need are individuals with proper attitudes. I think attitude transcends racial or ethnic group identification. I have found that many

---

* Interview conducted by Daniel Georges-Abeyie on December 7, 1983.

blacks, as well as non-black police officers, do not have the appropriate attitudes for their work.

Question: Why do you think black officers would encounter more problems with the community than other officers?

Answer: One of my pet theories is that some black officers want to identify with non-sensitive majority officers. Therefore, sometimes black police officers identify with their peer group at the expense of the black community. This theory appears to be particularly applicable to the situation in Harrisburg. Blacks and whites in this area who join the police bureau generally have education levels which preclude significant contact with sociological/economic groups different from their own, so they tend to be very limited and parochial in terms of their contact with and understanding of other groups. Additionally, many Harrisburg non-minority police officers come from or presently reside in rural areas, not Harrisburg. Therefore, when they come to work in Harrisburg, which is basically a metropolitan area with diverse social and ethnic groups, with no experience in terms of dealing with cultural diversity, they reject what seems foreign and out of their realm of experience.

Question: Where do most of the black officers in Harrisburg come from? Are they predominately local?

Answer: Most of the black officers do not live in the city of Harrisburg. However, with few exceptions, they are originally from Harrisburg.

Question: In many books on police-community relations or blacks and policing, it is noted that black officers frequently have more training or more education than the white officer and that they generally have a negative view of their white colleagues which creates tension. These books state that black officers use policing as a vertical mobility reality, whereas white officers move into the officer area because it is the only job available. There are two questions: One is whether you think this is accurate in the case of Harrisburg or departments you're familiar with? The second is how do white officers view black officers who have had more educational preparation for policing?

Answer: In Philadelphia, where I spent nineteen years as a police officer, black police officers who initially joined the police department didn't have higher educational levels, not initially. However, blacks who joined the police department tended to be highly motivated. As an example, when I joined the police department I had finished only about four or five college courses. However, during my tenure I completed a masters degree program. This was the case for many black officers, but I think there is now a larger proportion of black police officers who have college degrees when they enter the profession. When I was an officer blacks with college degrees usually would not join a police department. As you know, blacks have an historical disdain for police. There are two significant reasons, then, that blacks take jobs as police officers: (1) they need work and (2) it is a means of economic and social mobility. It is not always because they have a high regard for the police profession. This assumption may not be valid in Harrisburg, though. Here, police officers' educational levels, black and non-black, tend to range from a high school education to some college. However, blacks in this area generally have less than a high school education and those who become police officers identify with non-black police officers because they have many of the same values and are limited in terms of understanding cultural differences. In other words, many black police officers in this area are insensitive to the people in the community because they don't understand the black community's problems any better than non-black police officers. By contrast, in Philadelphia black officers are better educated and tend to be more community minded. But, Philadelphia is now experiencing problems recruiting minority officers. Many applicants are not high school graduates. Many have not had military training, which is necessary to understand the military/police model. During the 1960s, blacks who applied for a position with the Philadelphia Police Department were, in fact, better qualified overall than those applying today. When I joined the Department in 1962 there were no federal assistance programs. No agency tutored applicants for the entrance examination. Then, applicants were personally responsible for discovering application prerequisites and meeting job requirements. Applicants who successfully passed the entrance examination did so completely on their own initiative. Beyond that, officers individually overcame the racism and inequities inherent in the organization. I believe that in the main, blacks are still not highly educated when they join police departments. Those who acquire a higher education do so because of personal motivation. Many blacks do take advantage of educational opportunities when they join police departments, which often leads them to outside enterprises if, for some reason, they do not advance vertically within the department. For example, two or three police officers I have known for years are very successful businessmen. Early in their careers, they recognized that they had little mobility in the department, so they placed their emphasis outside.

Question: What are some of the structural problems with mobility for blacks in police departments?

Answer: The most profound problem is racism.

Question: What are some of the other specific forms racism takes within the department?

Answer: Sometimes in the ability to get a good assignment. For instance, a few minority police officers are assigned to acceptable positions. On the other hand, minorities are often used exclusively in certain types of assignments. These details (narcotics, prostitution, and vice details, for example) are for the most part more dangerous and require considerably more decision-making ability than other more routine assignments. Unfortunately, then, with this type of assignment structure, non-blacks are gaining more experience in the skills that are required for successful job mobility. Consequently, I view this "horizontal assignment" of black police officers as a form of racism. Another manifestation is the application of discipline. Often blacks are disproportionately disciplined in relation to non-blacks. This is clearly identified in relation to the number of disciplinary actions and the severity of penalties broken down by race.

Question: Many law enforcement people say that black officers and white officers view policing from different perspectives. They say in some major cities black officers, at least the black officers' associations, talk about keeping the peace. Whereas, white officers and white associations talk about maintaining and enforcing the law. Do you agree with this analysis?

Answer: Yes. There is a distinctly different philosophy between those points of view. From my experience as a member of the Executive Board of the Guardian Civic League, which is a branch of the National Black Police Association Chapter in Philadelphia, I recognized that our organization was primarily concerned with order maintenance—keeping the peace as well as maintaining the law. That orientation embraces the problem of crime control, but does not see crime control as the sole purpose of policing. Obviously, if the organizational perspective is exclusively law enforcement, the service-related aspect of police service suffers. Persons involved in law enforcement must always remember that for the most part police work is service related. Therefore, police officers who view their responsibility as primarily, "catching criminals" fall short of the true purpose of the police profession—service to the community.

Question: I want to ask about the social integration in police departments. One thing you frequently hear when talking with New York City police officers is the diversity and extent of ethnic/racial divisions within the police force. You would find that very few Transit Authority policemen, housing policemen, or city police who were black had close white friends in the police department. Black officers often say that there are subtle as well as some overt forms of racism when it comes to integration within the force. Did you experience this in Philadelphia?

Answer: Yes and no. Some strong interpersonal relationships do develop that transcend racial considerations. However, when functioning within a community that is basically heterogenous, exclusive association with one group may cause problems. As a police officer, it is extremely important to understand the idiosyncracies of different groups.

Question: Let me ask you a question about affirmative action. You have mentioned 17 percent of the force approximately is black, that approximately 61 percent of the proven complaints have been made against black officers. Do you think affirmative action has failed, or do you feel that overall it has been a success?

Answer: Affirmative action, in many instances, has failed to identify individuals compatible to law enforcement. While it is true that affirmative action has increased the aggregate number of minorities entering law enforcement, it has not increased minority mobility. My personal thinking is that recruiting should not be done exclusively in disorganized sections of cities, in areas which have traditionally had poor mobility levels for minorities, but from institutions of higher learning where minority individuals have proven testing and academic skills along with demonstrated motivation. This process will identify those individuals with the capabilities required for successful advancement.

Question: Let me ask you one final question. If you were to direct a course for officers coming into the force and this course was to be concerned with relationships between officers, black and white, and relationships between the officer and the black community, what types of things would you include in the course?

Answer: Basically, the course would identify the diverse needs of the community as well as the structural needs of the police organization. Specifically, the composition of the community and the differences between community groups would be focused on. Also, police attitudinal training, comprehensive understanding of the basic tools of law enforcement, criminal law, human behavior and human relations would be emphatically stressed.

11

The Court and Sentencing of Black Offenders

Roy L. Austin

It is the frequent allegation of discrimination against blacks that best justifies a separate study of black experiences with the judicial system. This discussion, however, is not intended specifically as a collection of evidence on the unequal treatment of black people in the American judicial system. Instead, the chapter provides a survey of the judicial process; the officials who determine the severity of sentences; the purpose of sentencing; the factors that affect sentence variation, and recent thinking on the best means to achieve an equitable system of justice.

INFLUENTIAL OFFICIALS

Once you move beyond arrest and the selection of the initial charges, legislators, prosecutors, judges and parole board members must determine what sentence should be served by an offender. Of these officials, the prosecutor, or district attorney, has the primary determining role. The defense attorney and the jury also influence the disposition of the accused.

The Legislature

Cases are supposed to be decided and sentences imposed on the guilty in accord with the Constitution and the laws of the nation. Laws usually indicate appropriate sanctions to be used against those who violate the laws. Thus, the lawmaking body or legislature plays an important role in determining sentence severity. In the United States, the custom has been for the legislature to set maximum penalties for particular violations leaving the discretion of the actual sentence in a specific instance in the hands of other actors. In such a system, the judge is able to place an offender on probation for a crime carrying a maximum penalty of many years.

The Prosecutor

Before a criminal reaches the judge, the prosecutor usually has the legal authority to drop all charges, to determine the offenses with which a person will be charged, and to reduce charges and recommend a lenient sentence in exchange for a guilty plea.

At the federal level, the prosecutor is appointed by the President. At other governmental levels, this official is most likely to be elected locally. The office is highly political not only because of the manner in which it is attained but also because incumbents often use it as a stepping stone to more desirable political positions or to the bench (Newman, 1974:599).

Prosecutors find guilty pleas highly desirable because trials greatly increase their workload and that of judges, police officers, and others. Partly on the basis of findings by Newman (1956), Blumberg (1967), and Chambliss and Seidman (1971) estimate that "at least *ninety percent of all criminal prosecutions result in guilty pleas,* most of them after negotiations between the accused (or his counsel) and the prosecuting attorney." They also regard the guilty plea as psychologically satisfying to law enforcement officials. Police officers feel that their suspicions were not wrongly placed, prosecutors obtain a feeling of competence, and judges have little fear that their decision will be overturned since sentences are ordinarily not appealable. Correctional authorities, too, supposedly enjoy some psychological advantage from the guilty plea because they believe that an acknowledgment of guilt may be a prerequisite for rehabilitation.

The Judge

In the criminal justice process, the role of the judge "is the least questioned and the most respected of all the participants" (Lefcourt, 1974:259). During a trial, the judge must enforce procedural rules, determine admissible evidence, and then decide the sentence for defendants found guilty. In addition, in non-jury trials the judge determines guilt or innocence; in jury trials, the judge advises the jury on points of law. A judge is also the administrator of a complex and often busy agency.

In general, judges at the state and local levels are elected while those at the federal level are appointed. There are also states that use a system of appointment for a limited period of time followed later by a popular referendum. Election may be by the people or the legislature (South Carolina); and candidates run on partisan, (Pennsylvania) or non-partisan (Minnesota) tickets (U.S. Department of Justice, 1981). In the non-partisan election, candidates get on the ballot by obtaining a required number of signatures of voters on a petition.

Appointment of federal judges is the responsibility of the President, but the appointee must obtain Senate confirmation. Senators do also provide the President with the names of persons they consider to be qualified for judgeships; and since the latter part of the Truman Administration, the American Bar Association's Committee on Federal Judiciary has played a role in the appointive process by investigating and rating prospective nominees.

There is an agreement that the expected impartiality of a judge may be compromised by both the elective and the appointive processes. But there is some sentiment favoring appointment because the chief executive is more likely than the populace to have access to information on a candidate's qualifications. Also, it is claimed that "in a free society, the people —at least in theory—are always in a position to hold [the executive] accountable" (Abraham, 1975:32).

The combination of appointment and popular vote is best exemplified by the "Missouri Plan" which was first used in Missouri in 1940. Abraham (1975:35) describes the plan as follows:

> [N]onpartisan nominating boards known as the Missouri Appellate Commission, operating on different court levels, select three candidates for every vacant judgeship. For the Supreme Court and the appellate courts, the commission consists of the Chief Justice of the State Supreme Court, and Chairman; three lawyers, elected by the state bar, one from each of the three courts of appeals; and three citizens not members of the bar, appointed by the Governor, again on the basis of one from each of the three appellate districts . . . The members of all these nonsalaried commissions are designated for staggered six-year terms of office with changes taking effect in alternate years. Since the governor has a four year term and cannot succeed himself, it is thus impossible for him to appoint all of the lay members. To ensure an additional degree of impartiality, commissioners are permitted to hold neither public office nor an official position in a political party.

The candidate which the governor appoints from the three nominees must run unopposed in a nonpartisan election after sitting on the bench for one year. A favorable vote by the electorate gives the judge a six or twelve year term depending on the level of the court. The number of judges retained by the voters, 178 of 179 between 1940 and 1970, suggests that the plan yields acceptable judges. Adoption of the plan by 10 states leaves the same impression.

Defense Counsel

There are states that have recognized for a long time the desirability of having a criminal defendant represented by counsel. A defense attorney was provided for in Pennsylvania law as early as 1701 (Perry, 1969). However, it was not until the U.S. Supreme Court decision in *Gideon v.*

Wainwright (372 U.S. 335, 1963) upheld the constitutional right to counsel for indigent defendants that the right applied nationwide. Even then the right held only for trials in which there was the possibility of a "substantial prison sentence," interpreted to mean felonies and serious misdemeanors. Subsequently, the right was extended to cover petty misdemeanors (*Argersinger v. Hamlin,* 404 U.S. 25, 1972) and to guilty plea proceedings.

For the poor, defense counsel usually takes the form of a public defender or the assignment by the court of a lawyer from a bar association list. Strengths and weaknesses have been noted for both methods (Newman, 1974). It is claimed that the public defender's office does not get the better lawyers; but proponents of the system say that a lawyer from the public defender's office is more likely to be experienced in criminal trials than a randomly assigned lawyer. And, given an estimate of only six percent of practicing attorneys being criminal lawyers (*Washington Post,* February 23, 1973), a real problem of uneven representation seems likely under random assignment. But the weak legal representation of the poor is caused by more than incompetence of counsel. Further, even some persons who engage a private attorney may receive less than adequate representation if they cannot afford the exorbitant fees an attorney commands for a great demand on his time. Both the private attorney in this situation and the public defender are inclined toward plea bargaining because it maximizes their rewards.

Unfortunately, while the guilty plea may be organizationally advantageous in lessening the workload of judges, prosecutors, and defense counsel, it may be disadvantageous for the defendant. According to Chambliss and Seidman (1971), private attorneys who frequent the courts know that cooperation with the prosecutor and the court staff will be rewarded with favors that make them more attractive to clients. The public defender learns that cooperation increases the efficiency of his office and the probability of a favorable evaluation from his superiors. Therefore, many attorneys, instead of adopting the adversary role, traditionally associated in legal circles and by the laymen with the defense attorney, aim to be reasonable to the extent of trading wins in cases on occasions.

The corruption of the ideal adversary role of the defense counsel is clearly delineated in Sudnow's (1965) report of his observations in a public defender's office in California:

> Both P.D. and D.A. are concerned to obtain a guilty plea wherever possible and therefore avoid a trial. At the same time, each party is concerned that the defendant "receive his due." The reduction of offense X to Y must be of such a character that the new sentence will depart from the anticipated sentence for the original charge to such a degree that the defendant is likely to plead guilty to the new charge and, at the same time, not so great that the defendant does not "get his due."

The P.D.'s activity is seldom geared to securing acquittals for clients. He and the D.A., as co-workers in the same courts, take it for granted that the persons who come before the courts are guilty of crimes and are to be treated accordingly.

. . . the way defendants are "represented" (the station manning rather than assignment of counselor to clients), the way trials are conducted, the way interviews are held and the penal code employed—all of the P.D.'s work is premised on the supposition that people charged with crimes—have commited crimes.

The impression that the defense attorney is coopted by the court and fails to use all his resources in the interest of his client is also portrayed in Blumberg's (1967) reported observations of "many years of legal practice in the criminal courts of a large metropolitan area." He maintains that the criminal lawyer seeks diligently to limit the scope and duration of a case and often seeks the aid of the accused's relatives to achieve this goal. Also, contrary to what may be popularly believed, he found that the defense attorney was far more likely than any other person to be the first to suggest a guilty plea. And the suggestion of a guilty plea on first contact with a client was most likely to be made by a court assigned lawyer, with the legal-aid lawyer next most likely and the private lawyer least likely. Blumberg interprets these and other findings as evidence of the willingness of defense counsel to bow to the demands of the court for maximum production. Like Sudnow (1965), he believes that the defense counsel cooperates because of selfish concerns such as career advancement and the maximization of his financial rewards.

The Jury

The American judicial system makes use of grand juries and trial juries. The grand jury does not decide guilt or innocence but examines the evidence presented by the prosecutor's office to determine whether a criminal trial should be held. The trial jury, on the other hand, returns a verdict on the guilt or innocence of an accused.

In America, a grand jury inquiry is constitutionally required at the federal level for capital and other serious offenses. Also, the Sixth and Seventh Amendments to the Constitution make a trial jury mandatory in all federal criminal cases and in civil cases where the amount at issue exceeds 20 dollars. At the state level, there is no requirement for a grand jury although some states do resort to its use especially in cases involving corruption among public officials.

There is also no explicit requirement that trial juries be used at the state level. However, a 1968 Supreme Court ruling made this a right at the state level while in 1970 the Court exempted crimes classified as misdemeanors with penalties of less than six months imprisonment. In those cases where the grand jury is not employed, the prosecutor draws up a document called an information containing the charges and the evidence bearing on the charges. This document is presented before a court of original jurisdiction to be examined for "probable cause," unless the state allows the defendant to waive this hearing (Newman, 1974).

Since the enactment of the Jury Selection and Service Act in 1968, federal juries are selected by lot from voter registration lists by the jury clerk. The "key man" system which was widely used before that year continues to be used in many jurisdictions below the federal level. Under this system, the jury clerk selects a panel of jurors from a list of names supplied by prominent citizens (Abraham, 1975).

Both the "key man" and voter registration systems of selection are likely to leave racial and ethnic minorities underrepresented on juries either because members of these groups are not registered to vote or because they are excluded from "key man" lists. Indeed, two California judges have admitted to practices that kept Mexican-Americans off juries. One claimed that the only Mexican-Americans he knew were his gardener and garbageman. The other selected most of his nominees from the membership of a tennis club but indicated that Pancho Gonzalez and Pancho Segura were members of the club (Civil Rights Digest, 1969).

It is unlikely that judges are unaware that systematic exclusion of members of a racial or ethnic group from a jury is a violation of the due process and equal protection clauses of the Fourteenth Amendment. But they may have been comforted by rulings of the U.S. Supreme Court in 1948 such as *Moore v. New York* (333 U.S. 565) that these clauses of the Fourteenth Amendment did not require "that a jury must represent all sections of society (Abraham, 1975). However, a more recent Supreme Court ruling (*Peters v. Kiff*, 407 U.S., 493, 1972) has held that the systematic exclusion of blacks from a jury may have an impact on a trial that cannot be ascertained— "and that consequently any indictment or conviction returned by such tribunals must be set aside."

It is not only at the earlier stages of selection that minority group members are excluded from juries. Peremptory challenges which require no stated reasons are used to remove minorities from trial juries in which minorities are defendants (Long et al., 1975:132). Unlike challenges for cause, there is a limit to the number of peremptory challenges allowed. But given the small number of minorities likely to be selected, only a few challenges are required to have an all-white jury. Abraham (1975:117) indicates that three peremptory challenges are normal in federal trial courts but cites one trial in which the prosecutor was permitted eight, and mentions that in Pennsylvania the defense and prosecution are each usually allowed 20 in murder cases.

Pressures within the jury room also seem weighted toward an outcome unfavorable to minority defendants, if it is assumed that middle- and upper-class persons in the proprietor and clerical occupational categories are more likely to be of a law and order disposition than groups of lower status. The research of Strodtbeck et al. (1957) showed that the higher status categories named were more dominant in jury discussion and had more influence on the selection of a chairperson than skilled workers and manual workers. This influence has consequences not only for a finding of guilt or innocence but also in some instances for the severity of the sanctions imposed. The jury in some jurisdictions has sentencing authority in all serious crimes, and in states which used capital punishment the final decision to impose the death penalty often rested with the jury (Newman, 1974).

PURPOSE OF THE SENTENCE

When legal authorities respond to crime with a sentence the offender usually suffers some sort of deprivation that is likely to be regarded as punishment. Some deprivations, such as a small fine or a required monthly visit with a probation officer, may not be severe. Others, such as an extended period of imprisonment or the loss of a limb or one's life, are more severe. Whatever the severity, the reasons that have been advanced for the imposition of these deprivations may be classified either as retributive or as utilitarian. The utilitarian category may be further divided into rehabilitation or reformation, specific deterrence, general deterrence, and incapacitation.

The retributivist doctrine has also been called vengeance, retaliation, atonement, and reprobation. The nonutilitarian label given this doctrine is justified by pointing to the apparent claims of its proponents that under certain circumstances the "infliction of suffering is a good thing in itself" (Quinton, 1972:6). For example, Kant (1887:194) held that "Juridicial punishment can never be administered merely as a means for promoting another good, either with regard to the criminal himself or to civil society, but must be imposed only because the individual on whom it is inflicted has committed a crime. For one man ought never to be dealt with merely as a means subservient to the purpose of another . . . ." Other ideas usually associated with the retributivist view are that "the function of punishment is the negation or annulment of evil or wrongdoing, that punishment must fit the crime (the lex talionis), and that offenders have a right to punishment. . . ." (Quinton, 1972:7).

The utilitarian view of punishment stresses the importance of inflicting suffering on a wrongdoer only if the suffering will benefit that person or some other person or group. Thus punishment is justified if it will change an evil person into a consciously good one (rehabilitation or reformation); if the person punished refrains from further wrongdoing to avoid punishment (specific deterrence); if the punishment of one person causes others to refrain from wrongdoing lest they too be punished (general deterrence); if the ability of the wrongdoer to engage in further wrongful acts is restricted by external constraints or terminated by death (incapacitation).

Does punishment have any of the effects that utilitarians require for its justification? Unquestionably, there are incapacitative effects, for if a person is incarcerated his/her ability to harm others is essentially limited to persons present at the place of incarceration. Also, execution will effectively bring an end to an offender's anti-social activities. Nevertheless, there are questions about incapacitation such as its cost to the community that must be raised; but these and other questions about punishment are beyond the scope of this chapter.

FACTORS AFFECTING VARIATION IN SENTENCE

Severity is the critical dimension that differentiates between sentences, and there seems to be agreement that the nature of the offense should influence this aspect of sentencing. Also, the characteristics of the situation in which the offense takes place receives much support today as a justifiable determinant of sentence severity, but this has not always been so. More controversial as determinants of sentence severity are the nature of court processing and characteristics of the offender other than psychological disability. Indeed, offender characteristics such as race and class are not likely to be acknowledged by court officials as influencing sentencing—but the belief that they do has encouraged much research. The relationship between offender characteristics and sentence severity is of particular interest since our focus is on the black lawbreaker, a member of a racial group subjected to humiliating and disabling discrimination in many institutional areas.

Offense Characteristics and Sentencing

The first edition of Caesare Beccaria's *On Crimes and Punishments* appeared in 1764. The book certainly did not represent the first proposal that punishments should be in accord with the seriousness of crimes, but it quickly influenced such a move in Europe, despite being placed on the index by the Church of Rome in 1766 and condemned for extremely rationalistic presuppositions (Beccaria, 1963:xi).

Beccaria argued that "for a punishment to attain its end, the evil which it inflicts has only to exceed the advantage derivable from the crime"

(1963:43). He believed that punishments which are too severe only encourage serious crimes, so that the most heinous crimes were to be found in countries notorious for the severity of their penalties. Further, he claimed that people hesitate to apply penalties they consider too severe and therefore allow crimes to be committed with impunity, a situation that causes an increase in crimes.

The certainty of punishment was regarded by Beccaria as an important part of making the penalty exceed the advantages of criminality. So important was certainty that he saw clemency and pardon as undermining the deterrent effect of punishment. This may be one reason he condemned the tendency of judges to be harsher with persons of low status and recommended elimination of judicial discretion. He desired laws so clear and precise that the "judge's duty is merely to ascertain the fact" (1963:21). Beccaria held that the seriousness of a crime should be determined by the harm done to society (1963:64), not by the extent of sinfulness, or the importance of the victim, or the intention of the offender, and he believed that all crimes, "even those of a private nature," injure society. The most serious crimes for him were those that directly destroy society or its representative. Treason was given as an example. The next most serious crimes were those which threaten the security of a citizen's life, goods, or honor. The least serious crimes were those which are proscribed or prescribed for the public good.

The name and ideas of Beccaria have become most closely associated with the pre-scientific system of "administrative and legal criminology" (Vold, 1958:32) known as the classical school. The influence of this school of thought on European law is seen in the French Code of 1971. The Code removed judicial discretion by arranging crimes on a scale with suitable penalties attached to each crime by statute. Unfortunately, the strict application of the principle of equal punishment for the same crime overlooked the differences between "the insane and the sane, the minor and the adult, the idiot and the person of normal intelligence. . . . There could be no statement for extenuating circumstances, no added penalty for the heinousness of the way in which a particular crime was committed" (Gillin, 1945:229).

Although the French Codes of 1810 and 1819 restored some discretion to judges there was "still no room for consideration of subjective intent" (Vold, 1958:24). This inflexibility was attacked by the neo-classical school who, like the classical thinkers, believed that people were reasonable beings, free to choose their actions, therefore are responsible for those actions and can be controlled by fear of punishment (Vold, 1958:25). However, the neo-classical thinkers felt that the freedom of people to choose was not absolute since it could be affected by mental and physical ailments and the amount of forethought. They also believed that the physical and mental conditions of the individual were valid reasons for modifying the severity of the sentence. That is, these circumstances should mitigate the severity of punishments because in their presence the individual was only partially responsible for his/her acts. In addition, they wanted the acceptance of expert testimony on the question of diminished responsibility.

The influence of neo-classical thought on criminal law in the United States should be obvious to anyone who is even vaguely familiar with this body of law. In particular, the acceptance of mitigating circumstances is quite clear. So too is the use of expert testimony. However, there have been efforts in recent years to create "a system in which punishment depends much more importantly than at present on the seriousness of the particular offense" (Zimring, 1981:327) that are reminders of Beccaria's attitude towards discretion in the criminal law. Zimring (1981:327) has noted that at least six books published between 1974 and 1976 had "proposed ending the arenas of discretion in the system." But these works represented a turnabout from the "broad discretion" allowed in the 1870 Statement of Principles by the National Congress Penitentiary and Reformatory Discipline, Maryland's 1951 Defective Delinquent Law, and the Model Penal Code produced during the 1950s and early 1960s (Gross and von Hirsch, 1981:47).

Discretion was at its utmost in the indeterminate sentences which was to be "limited only by satisfactory proof of reformation" that was recommended in the 1870 Declaration of Principles; and this unlimited discretion made sense to those who believed that the sentence could serve to rehabilitate the offender. By the early 1960s, it is deterrence that was used by the drafters of the Model Penal Code to justify the discretion they provided the court in setting the minimum sentence. The maximum was to be set by statute. In 1976, the Twentieth Century Fund Task Force stated that the discretion of the sentencing judge and the parole board had to be limited but that a totally inflexible system was undesirable. The Task Force claimed that its recommendations would leave judges and parole authorities "some degree of *guided* discretion" (emphasis added). However, the specificity with which this group expects the legislature to set sentences really leaves the judge and the parole board with little to do other than "ascertain the fact" as Beccaria recommended.

In the recommendations of the Task Force, the legislature is expected to set a "presumptive sentence" which indicates the punishment for each crime before any consideration of aggravating and/or mitigating factors. The legislature also specifies percentage increases for multiple offending and for an excess of aggravating over mitigating factors. Similarly, a specific percentage decrease is provided for instances where mitigating factors exceed aggravating ones; and a formula based on the time in prison during which no infraction occurs is used for calculating good time off. In addition, the legislature is expected to "define specific aggravating and mitigating factors" and to determine whether guilty pleas and cooperation with the authorities should influence sentencing.

The basis of the proposals of the Task Force was the belief that punishment for criminality had become a haphazard affair. Sentencing had lost its deterrent effect because there was little certainty to it, although, according to the Task Force, the deterrent effect of certain punishment had been demonstrated.

There are persons like Morris (1981:264), however, who favor a system of sentencing based primarily on retribution and see recent recommendations by von Hirsch and others as having the same basis. This willingness to justify punishment by pointing to effects that have no social benefits suggests that the American people are seen as ready to accept this kind of justification.

Like any set of recommendations, even those that deal with more tractable issues, weaknesses in the Task Force proposals have been pointed out. For example, Zimring (1981:331) notes the recommendation of a "presumptive sentence" for rape with bodily harm that is one year greater than that for intentional killing. Furthermore, he is concerned about the ease with which legislatures can increase the severity of "presumptive sentences" and thereby undermine the best sentencing system our present knowledge allows. But the most important question he raises is whether we have "the ability to comprehensively define in advance those elements of an offense that should be considered in fixing a criminal sentence" (1981:331).

Studies of the factors influencing sentencing show that there is agreement that type of offense *should* be one factor. Thus, 15 of 20 studies of the influence of "extra-length attributes" on judicial disposition examined by Hagan (1974) incorporated controls for type of offense, a "legal factor"; and Chiricos and Waldo (1977:759) examined sentencing disparities within offense categories in order to control for seriousness of offense, "another significant variable." But the extent to which the type of offense does influence variation in sentencing is often unobtainable because of the methodology employed in studies. However, some indication is given by Cohen and Kluegel (1978) whose study of juvenile dispositions included the variables of race, parental income, present activity (working and/or in school versus idle), offense type, prior record, court (Denver compared to Memphis), and severity of dispositions. They reported that "the two variables with the strongest net impact on the severity of disposition accorded are offense type and prior record" (1978:168). The same conclusion is reached by Gottfredson (1981). The second of these variables is discussed in the next section.

Offender Characteristics and Sentencing

There seems to be agreement that prior record is one of those legal attributes which, like offense type, *should* influence the severity of the sentence. Six of the 20 studies evaluated by Hagan (1974) used prior record as a control while trying to determine the importance of extralegal attributes. More recent studies of the influence of extralegal factors (Chiricos and Waldo, 1975; Cohen and Kluegel, 1978) also control for prior record. In addition, von Hirsch (1981:244) believes that prior record should be taken into account in assessing seriousness and that the use of the seriousness of an offense to determine the severity of punishment "is a requirement of justice." Norval Morris (1981:258) has stated that the principle of just desert prohibits the imposition of a sanction "greater than that which is 'deserved' by the last crime, or series of crimes, for which the offender is being sentenced." However, his discussion of extended sentences for the repetitively violent suggests that other principles such as incapacitation of the dangerous many be called upon to justify the use of prior record in determining sentence severity.

The other variables that will be discussed in this section are race and class, often referred to in the literature as extra-legal attributes. Unlike offense type and prior record, race and class are not likely to be defended as variables that should influence the severity of punishment. But many respected social scientists believe that the blindfold often falls from the eyes of justice and results in harsher penalties for all lower class persons and especially members of disadvantaged minority groups.

Race

In 1857, legal discrimination against black people in America was supported by the Supreme Court in the Dred Scott decision. The opinion of the Court which was delivered by Chief Justice Taney was that black people were not entitled to "the rights and privileges and immunities" guaranteed to citizens by the Constitution. The Thirteenth Amendment which proscribed slavery in the United States, the Fourteenth Amendment granting "equal protection of the laws" to all persons residing in the United States, and the 1875 Civil Rights Act should all have made discrimination against blacks illegal. But the highest court in America continued to uphold discrimination against blacks. For example, the 1896 *Plessy v. Ferguson* decision upheld segregation in public transportation provided that facilities were equal. This separate but equal principle was extended to other areas by later decisions of lower federal courts and was not rejected until 1954 by *Brown v. Board of Education.*

Individual cases of unjust sentencing of black people charged with crimes are unlikely to be regarded as convincing evidence of discrimination against blacks in sentencing. But the statistics on sentencing that are used to determine whether there is discrimination in sentencing are made up of individual cases. Therefore, it should be instructive to recount a case mentioned by Haywood Burns (1976:27):

> I think a good example of what I am talking about is the experience of a young brother, Lee Otis Johnson, whose alleged crime was the giving of a marijuana joint to an undercover agent, but whose real crime was that he was a SNCC worker, that he was a political activist and a threat to the Texas Establishment. Upon conviction of this charge, this political man was given thirty years in prison. This kind of situation is repeated throughout the country, where a person may be charged with one thing of which he or she may well be innocent, and upon conviction be sentenced for another because of who he or she is.

There are a number of empirical studies which suggest that Otis Johnson's case is not an isolated event and that black people are more likely than whites to receive the kind of severe punishment that he was accorded. But empirical evidence has also been used to reject the claim that discrimination in sentencing against minorities is a regular feature of American courts.

Several of the studies of discrimination in sentencing are concerned with the question of whether severity depends not solely on the race of the offender but on the offender-victim racial combination. The hypothesis tested is that the order of severity of treatment, from most to least severe, is black offender/white victim (BW), white offender/white victim (WW), black offender/black victim (BB), and white offender/black victim (WB). The rationale for this order is that the white power structure cannot let a black person get away with harming a white person; but whites are not about to be overly concerned if a black person hurts another black (Johnson, 1941). Also, when a white harms a white, the law has to be upheld but there is not the same threat to the power structure as in the BW combination; and when a white harms a black, there are likely to be extenuating circumstances such as a black "sassing" a white person or "looking at" a white woman.

Johnson's (1941) analysis of court statistics on murder indictments in North Carolina, Georgia, and Virginia between 1930 and 1940 supported his hypothesis. When severity of disposition is judged by percent convicted, percent receiving death sentences, and sentence length the most severe treatment was received by the BW combination, followed in order by WW, BB, and WB. The results of this study are supported by Garfinkel's (1949) findings for homicide in North Carolina covering 1930 to 1940. Garfinkel shows that reductions in the Grand Jury charges by the prosecuting attorney was in the predicted order with the BW combination least likely to show a reduction from first degree murder; and dispositions for those charged with first degree murder and those convicted of first and second degree murder are also as predicted. For example, of those charged with first degree murder, the death sentence was imposed on 36 percent of the BW combination but 10.9 percent, 4.0 percent and .0 percent of the WW, BB and WB combinations, respectively. Life imprisonment followed the same order, the percentages being 9.7, 3.0, 0.3 and .0. On the other hand, acquitals were most likely for the WW combination (27.7 percent) and least likely for the BW combination (14.6 percent).

A somewhat more recent study of a capital offense (rape) by Wolfgang and Reidel (1973) reports findings that agree with Johnson's and Garfinkel's for BW versus other combinations. A statistically significant relationship between race and type of sentence (death versus other) was also reported. The data analysed for this study cover the years 1945-65 and were obtained from seven states where executions for rape had occurred during these years: Alabama, Arkansas, Florida, Georgia, Louisiana, South Carolina, and Tennessee.

In order to determine whether other variables might account for the apparent racial bias, Wolfgang and Reidel examined 29 variables indicating offender characteristics, nature of the relations between the offender and the victim, circumstances of the offense and circumstances of the trial for associations with sentencing and race. Contemporaneous offense (whether another offense was committed at the same time as the rape) was significantly related to both variables; but further analysis showed that within the group with a contemporaneous offense as well as within the group without a contemporaneous offense the offender-victim combination was significantly related to imposition of the death penalty. More specifically, 39 percent of the black defendants with white victims in each group received the death penalty but only 3 percent (contemporaneous offense) and 2 percent (no contemporaneous offense) of other combinations.

Bullock's (1961) study in 1958 of inmates in the Texas State Prison in Huntsville yields findings consistent with Johnson, Garfinkel and Wolfgang/Riedel, if his interpretation is granted. He found that blacks from small cities were significantly more likely to receive longer sentences for burglary than whites; but for murder, whites received more severe sentences. He argues that his findings reflect the interracial character of burglary and the intraracial character of murder. Therefore, the offender/victim racial combination hypothesis may be supported by his results; but there is no direct empirical evidence for this interpretation. However, Bullock's study suggests that discrimination against blacks in sentencing is not limited to capital offenses but extends to the crime of burglary. This conclusion appears to hold even if prior record is taken into account. The data showed no significant difference in sentence received by those with less than two previous convictions and those with two or more, although the Texas Penal Code stipulated the maximum sentence rather than the minimum for a second felony and a life sentence for a third.

In a number of respects, one of the more important studies of unequal sentencing based on race is that of Green (1964). This study provides information on a non-Southern city (Philadelphia) for non-capital offenses (robbery and burglary). Further, the data were collected too early to have been affected by the 1960s fight for equal treatment by blacks. Yet, Green (1964:356) concluded that "the evidence does not support the hypothesis that the court differentiates the seriousness of crimes according to the race of the offender relative to the race of the victim—certainly not, as between Negro interracial and white intraracial offenders." And three reviewers of racial inequality in sentencing decisions (Hindelang, 1969; Hagan, 1974; Kleck, 1981) draw similar conclusions from Green's data. Hindelang states that "Green's analysis strongly argues that the variation in sentencing according to the racial composition of the offender-victim dyad exists as the result of legally relevant differences among the dyads, rather than as a result of racial discrimination on behalf of the court" (1969:312). Hagan says that the interracial hypothesis receives little support from Green's data. However, Green's data do *not* in fact reject the interracial hypothesis (Austin, 1982).

Green provides only a summary statement for his Table 6 on burglary that ignores the detailed information that must have been sought when he controlled for selected variables. Careful examination of the table shows that BW sentences exceed WW sentences in seven of nine available comparisons. In seven of nine instances BW cases also receive harsher sentences than BB cases. These and other comparisons (Austin, 1982) show that harsher sentences are likely where offenders are black and victims are white, and greater leniency occurs when the victim is black.

For robbery, Green presents a table similar to his table for burglary. Unfortunately, the absence of cases in some cells and only a single case in others allow little confidence in any interpretation of these findings. Still the tendency is toward bias against black offenders and victims, when proper detailed comparisons are made (Austin, 1982).

Correct interpretation of Green's data allows a set of conclusions that differ from four drawn by Hindelang (1969). It is not true that support for discrimination in sentencing against blacks comes only from southern data. It is also not correct to claim that evidence of discrimination disappeared in studies exercising more careful controls for relevant non-racial variables. On this question of the results of controls, it would be noted that Hagan's (1974) reanalysis of studies of non-capital cases leads to the same conclusion. For two of three studies, simultaneous controls for type of offense and prior record left statistically significant relationships where offenders had previous convictions. Also contradicting Hindelang's conclusions is the existence of evidence of discrimination after the 1954 *Brown v. Board of Education* Supreme Court decision and for both capital and non-capital offenses.

Do more recent studies also show discrimination against blacks in sentencing? The claims of two research reports (Cohen and Kluegel, 1978; McCarthy et al., 1979) suggest that there was no discrimination during the years in the 1970s in those places covered by their data. Thus, for Denver and Memphis in 1972, Cohen and Kluegel (1978:162) state in their abstract that "little support is found for the argument that race or social class bias directly affects the dispositions in [juvenile courts]. And for the state of New Jersey between October 1976 and September 1977, McCarthy et al. (1979:35) summarize their findings as follows:

> . . . racially different but otherwise similar offenders sentenced for similar offenses receive similar sentences in New Jersey. That is, when statistically accounting (controlling for) for the effects of key factors relating to the natures of the offender and the offense, the data do not support the contention that minority race offenders receive more severe sentences than similar white offenders. While blacks and to a lesser extent, Hispanics, receive on average more and longer jail sentences than whites, these groups also show equally sharp differences in factors which influence sentences.

One of the major differences between these two studies conducted in the 1970s and the earlier studies is that the more recent studies controlled more variables regarded as relevant to sentencing. For instance, Cohen and Kluegel (1976) controlled for "Present Activity" (working and/or in school versus neither working nor in school) which they indicate had not been previously studied. McCarthy et al. (1979) controlled for a similar variable ("Employ") as well as for drug dependence, whether activities after arrest are constructive, whether private counsel is retained, whether the offender seems remorseful or contrite, and many other variables absent from previous studies.

There is a form of the racial bias proposition that controlling for these variables does not reject, even if direct racial effects and interaction effects of race are not significant. Cohen and Kluegel (1976:172) note that race may be indirectly related to disposition because members of one racial group are more likely to be labeled as crime prone if they are less likely to be gainfully employed. A similar labeling argument may be made for the likelihood of being remorseful and for post-arrest activities.

The data in both studies show some evidence of indirect racial bias through labeling. Cohen and Kluegel's (1976:172-173) analysis of this question seems to confirm the existence of this form of bias, although they say that the interpretation is not unequivocal. Non-whites in their study were more likely to be idle and to have a prior record, the category with the most severe disposition. McCarthy et al. paid no attention to indirect or interaction effects but some of the associations reported are consistent with the labeling hypothesis. For instance, employment is significantly related to the decision to imprison a robbery offender; 57 percent of whites versus 38 percent of blacks are favorably situated with respect to employment. Likewise 21 percent of whites versus 13 percent of blacks are remorseful and 39 percent of the whites versus 26 percent of the blacks show constructive post-arrest activities. Remorse was found to be significantly related to imprisonment for robbery offenders while those with constructive post-arrest activities were less likely to be placed in state prison (most severe placement).

In addition, there are methodological reasons why the results of Cohen and Kluegel (1976) cannot be accepted as rejecting an interaction effect involving race and a legal factor on sentencing. Cohen and Kluegel (1976:-172) acknowledge that this is one form in which racial bias may be present, but their analysis could have masked an interaction between race and referral source (police versus other agency) that had earlier been reported by Cohen (1975:48) for the Memphis data (56 percent of the non-whites and 28 percent of the whites referred by the police received more severe dispositions).

The earlier study by Cohen also reported an interaction between race and present activity for the juvenile court in Montgomery County, Pennsylvania. The data for this county, which showed the strongest association between race and disposition (Tau = .15 versus .08 for Memphis and .07 for Denver), are excluded from the later study; the Memphis data are combined in the later study with the Denver data for which the disposition was earlier favorable to non-whites after controls were effected (Cohen, 1975: Table 20, p. 42). That is, separate analyses of the Montgomery County and Memphis data, even using the log-linear analysis procedure employed in the later study could have yielded conclusions opposed to those reported for the combined Denver/Memphis data or for Denver alone.

However, it remains unclear whether the Denver data will reject the racial bias hypothesis when blacks and whites are compared. In Denver, 71.5 percent of whites, 66 percent of Hispanics and 57.1 percent of blacks received the least severe disposition (unofficial adjustment). The most severe disposition (incarceration) was received by 2.6 percent of whites, 2.4 percent of Hispanics, and 4.6 percent of blacks (Cohen, 1975:25). Even with this knowledge, multivariate analyses were performed by Cohen (1975) and Cohen and Kluegel (1978) on a dichotomous race variable that combined blacks and Hispanics together as non-whites.

Three methodological problems make the rejection of the racial bias hypothesis by McCarthy et al. (1979) also unacceptable. First, these researchers pay no attention to interactions between race and legal factors.

Secondly, although 128 tests of the hypothesis were conducted, only in one instance were blacks separated from other minorities; this occurred for an offense (robbery) for which incarceration rates suggest that blacks were treated more leniently than other minorities. In all other instances, blacks were combined with other minorities who often seemed to receive less severe dispositions. Thirdly, the researchers pay no attention to the likelihood that their regression analyses may have shown no significant association between race and disposition once other variables were controlled because of interdependence within the independent variables. Further, as the number of independent variables increases harmful interdependence (multicollinearity) becomes more likely (Farrar and Glamber, 1967:94). Therefore, any effort to control all relevant variables in examining the racial bias in sentencing hypothesis must be sensitive to the complexities in interpretation introduced by multicollinearity. The New Jersey data analysed by McCarthy et al. (1979) show associations between race and so many other independent variables that no confidence can be placed in the rejection of the hypothesis until some analysis of multicollinearity is conducted.

There are, in any event, some studies that report finding evidence of racial bias in sentencing in the 1970s. Thompson and Zingraff's (1981) data showed discrimination against blacks in 1977, although there was none in 1969 or 1973. There is the suggestion that a relaxation of vigilance and/or deteriorating economic conditions can cause a resurgence of discrimination in sentencing. In addition, Jankovic (1978:13) claims that in California data for 1969-1974 "whites are more likely to get milder sentences and less likely to be incarcerated than non-whites" for a second drunk-driving offense. Hispanics form an overwhelming majority of the non-whites shown in one of his tables. Furthermore, there is evidence of harsher penalties against blacks in Pennsylvania court data for 1977 (Kempf, 1982).

There is a relatively recent study by Kleck (1981) that seems to reject the hypothesis of racial discrimination in sentencing. This study is likely to be influential because of its publication in the highly respected *American Sociological Review* and its impressive coverage of the literature on the topic of interest (over 100 citations). However, careful reading of the article shows the author really indirectly admitting the existence of evidence of discrimination but claiming, like Hindelang, that it is "*almost* limited to the South" (emphasis added). Another indirect admission of discrimination is found in his statement that the evidence is *largely* contrary to the hypothesis that racial discrimination in sentencing in non-capital cases is *general* or *widespread* (emphasis added).

In addition, when errors in Kleck's analysis are removed, the evidence shows discrimination to be more widespread than he allows (Austin, 1982). For example, he claims that for capital punishment only two non-southern studies show racial discrimination while five show no discrimination. But three of the studies he regards as showing no discrimination (Bedau, 1964; Wolf, 1964; Bedau, 1965) show some evidence of discrimination against blacks when the data are properly analysed. In addition, Kleck is one of those researchers who accepted the erroneous conclusions of Green (1964) that were earlier discussed.

The empirical evidence clearly suggests disparities in sentencing that place black people at a disadvantage. A dramatic depiction of this situation may be found in a statement by Joseph Howard, a black associate judge of the Supreme Bench of the city of Baltimore:

> My study of *The Administration of Rape Cases in the City of Baltimore and the State of Maryland* (1968) revealed that all of the 55 death penalties issued for rape in that state were for attacks upon white women; only five of the 55 were white men. Even though black women were raped more than ten times as often as white women, never in the history of Maryland had any man been executed for raping a black woman (1975:123).

The careful social scientist regards such statements as only the beginning of any effort to determine whether there is racial discrimination in sentencing. For instance, Green (1964:348) believes that the differences reflect "legally significant differences between whites and racial minorities in patterns of criminal behavior." He argues that an assault of a black against another black is least severely punished because it is usually impulsive, and low in repetition and malicious intent. On the other hand, the extreme severity meted out to black offenders with white victims is due to the more aggravated nature of the offense. However, when Green's findings are correctly interpreted, his arguments are not supported. Also, more recent efforts (Kleck, 1981; Cohen and Kluegel, 1978; McCarthy, et al., 1979) claiming that the effect of race disappears when legally relevant variables are controlled are not convincing. In sum, the bulk of the research evidence has failed to show that differential sentencing by race of offender and victim may be explained in terms other than discrimination against blacks.

There are those who will not be surprised at the failure of research to reject the racial discrimination hypothesis. Such people are likely to agree with associate Judge Howard (1975:122) that judges are "like other human beings," tending to relate to the familiar and to fear that which is foreign. He also holds that "the social climate at a given time or place contributes considerably to a judge's attitude, orientation, and action base, which in turn is translated into judicial behavior." In Howard's view, then, the racial climate of the community will influence sentencing decisions.

There is an alternative image of the judge in a racist environment that is stated by Green (1964:357):

> The view that the prevailing racial biases of the community automaticaly infect the decisions of criminal court judges fails to consider that persons differ in their susceptibility to prejudice depending upon the character of their involvement in the community structure. . . . The presiding judge by virtue of the technical requirements of the law, his professional training, and his oath of office is, of all public officials, one of the least likely to bow to local custom or prejudice when it opposes the American creed.

After the vigorous defense of the integrity of judges, Green admits that "there are judges of lesser commitment to this ideal" (1964:357). It should also be noted that in a racially divided community some judges may obtain their position precisely because they do not subscribe to the ideal of racial equality. If they wish to continue in office, it is necessary to demonstrate allegiance to community norms—even those which may be contrary to the American creed.

Class

Even in courts where racial bias does not exist, black people may find themselves at a disadvantage because of the disproportionate representation of blacks at lower levels of the class structure. This conclusion will find support in the claims of conflict criminologists such as Chambliss who has provided the following argument:

> The lower-class person is (1) more likely to be scrutinized and therefore more likely to be observed in violation of the law, (2) more likely to be arrested if discovered under suspicious circumstances, (3) more likely to spend the time between arrest and trial in jail, (4) more likely to come to trial, (5) more likely to be found guilty, and (6) if found guilty, more likely to receive harsh punishment than his middle or upper-class counterpart (1969:86).

However, the empirical evidence on the punishment claim, which is our primary concern, is no less controversial than that on race and sentencing. Hagan (1974) has reanalysed the findings of six studies published before 1970 to determine the statistical significance of the findings and the strength of associations and after controlling for type of offense and prior record. For non-capital cases both before and after controlling for type of offense, the punishment of lower class persons was significantly greater than the punishment of those higher in class. When prior record was controlled in the single instance where this was possible (federal larceny case in Nagel's 1969 study), the relationship was no longer significant.

In capital offenses, Hagan again reports significant differences that favor higher classes. In Judson et al.'s (1969) study the results remained statistically significant after controls for prior record were introduced. Judson et al. (1969) reported that upon conviction for first degree murder 42.1 percent of the blue-collar defendants as opposed to 4.8 percent of the white-collar defendants were sentenced to death.

Studies not covered in Hagan's evaluation show no more agreement than those that he covered. Terry (1967) reports little or no relationship between social class and severity of disposition (institutionalization versus probation) for delinquents in an unnamed Midwestern state. Willick et al., (1975) report the same for felonious homosexuality in California. And Chiricos and Waldo (1975) examined 17 different criminal offenses for all felons received in the prisons of Florida (June 1, 1969 to May 30, 1970), North Carolina (January 1, 1969 to April 30, 1970), and South Carolina (January 1, 1969 to June 30, 1971). They controlled for prior record, race, age and county of sentencing but found only one of 185 zero-order correlation coefficients statistically significant and in the direction predicted by the conflict hypothesis. There were 10 statistically significant correlations favoring a hypothesis of more severe punishment for those of higher social status.

Confidence in the Chiricos and Waldo study has been undermined by several critical comments. Greenburg (1977) has pointed to the need to take account of the social status of the victim, a procedure that proved important in several studies of racial bias in sentencing and in a study of homicide sentences. Swigert (1975) found sentences to be higher when the victim was of higher socioeconomic status. Another serious problem in the study is the limitation of punishment severity to differences in the length of sentence. It may be plausibly argued that a more important distinction for the question of interest is that between incarceration and a milder sanction such as probation or a fine (Greenberg, 1977; Jankovic, 1978). Also, it has been asked whether the restricted representation of upper status persons in a population of felons allows a proper test of the conflict hypothesis (Hopkins, 1977; Reasons, 1977; Jankovic, 1978). This hypothesis predicts differences in punishment between classes while a population of felons might allow determination of only within-class differences.

Studies not evaluated by Hagan (1974) that claim support for the conflict hypothesis of class bias include those of Thornberry (1973) and Jankovic (1978). Thornberry examined data on a cohort of 3,475 boys born in 1945 and residing in Philadelphia at least between their tenth and seventeenth birthdays and who had been recorded as delinquent by the police at least once. He reports that the more severe sentence of institutionalization (rather than probation) was received by 39.5 percent of the boys from lower status census tracts and by 28.6 percent of the boys from higher status tracts. The greater likelihood that the boys from lower status tracts would receive the harsher sentence remained when the seriousness of the offense and prior record was controlled.

Jankovic's (1978) research involved 2,250 persons sentenced in the criminal courts of a California county from January 1969 to December 1974. The offenses covered are drunken driving, narcotics violation, public drunkeness, burglary and robbery. One set of results shows that 18 of 20 product-moment correlation coefficients have a direction favorable to the hypothesis of class bias. These results were obtained by correlating the offenses separately and collectively with three separate measures of class. Nine of the 18 coefficients are significant while none of the two unfavorable to the hypothesis of bias is significant. These results contrast with Chiricos and Waldo's (1975) findings of a preponderence of coefficients which rejected the hypothesis of class bias and no significant coefficients favorable to class bias. Jankovic believes that the different results in the two studies are due in part to the greater variation in his severity of sentence measure which ranged from small fines to lengthy imprisonment.

To summarize, there is empirical evidence favorable to the hypothesis of class bias in sentencing even when the seriousness of the offense and prior record is controlled (Judson et al., 1969; Thornberry, 1973). There is also evidence favorable to the hypothesis in studies that have not controlled for prior record and where offense seriousness is controlled only in the sense of examining different offenses separately (Forslund, 1969; Jankovic, 1978). Even if one were to ignore the methodological weaknesses that are regarded as invalidating Chiricos and Waldo's (1975) conclusions, this finding of no bias in this study holds only for the three states in which it was conducted and for the years covered by the data. But Jankovic's data are for essentially the same years, the early 1970s. Therefore, it cannot be said that discrimination against persons of lower status might have disappeared by this time, and whether discrimination was absent in the three states covered by Chiricos and Waldo is uncertain given the methodological problems in the study.

CONCLUSION

Sentencing is a rather late phase in the criminal justice process. Had it been shown that there was no bias against disadvantaged minorities and lower class individuals in sentencing, one still could not absolve the criminal justice system of practicing such bias. In any event, it would be difficult to convince disadvantaged minorities that the kind of injustice visited upon the Scottsboro boys (Symons, 1966) is an isolated event in America. Although the only evidence against the nine black youths came from the two white alleged rape victims and their four white male companions, all except one of two 13-year-olds were sentenced to death. At a second trial one of the alleged victims said that she had laid the charge of rape against the boys only to escape a charge of vagrancy herself. Still, the black youths remained incarcerated until they were in their thirties. The oldest at the time of the alleged offense in 1931 was 21.

In contrast to the treatment of the black youths in the Scottsboro case, is the acquittal in 1955 of two white men charged with the murder of a 14-year-old black youth, Emmett Till, in Mississippi (Shostak, 1974-75). The two white men had abducted Emmett from his home at gun-point for supposedly asking the wife of one of them for a date and embracing her. The badly mauled body of Emmett was found in the Tallahatchie river a few days later with a bullet hole in the right ear. A black youth testified at the trial that he had seen Emmett in the back of one of the white accused's truck, had heard someone being beaten in a barn where the truck had stopped, and noticed that the back of the truck was covered with a tarpaulin when it subsequently left. It took the jury only a bit more than an hour to return a verdict of not guilty.

It may be that such blatant miscarriages of justice are unlikely to occur in America in the 1980s. But as long as minorities continue to be under-represented as police officers, prosecutors, defense attorneys judges, and jurors it will be difficult for the criminal justice system to escape charges of discrimination against minorities at all levels. There is no reason why people who suffer discrimination in other areas of the society should regard those who guard the gates of justice as exceptional and therefore unlikely to practice discrimination. Unfortunately, limited opportunities because of discrimination in the general society will continue to prevent many minorities from qualifying for the important criminal justice positions—and those who qualify will find that discrimination and methods of selection will still operate against them.

What is presently called determinate sentencing was recommended earlier by Beccaria as a means of reducing disparity in sentencing. But unlike Beccaria, many advocates of determinate sentences today also seek harsher penalties; and, in states such as California, determinate sentencing statutes do include stiffer penalties (Gettinger, 1979). Also, in California, the expected decrease in prison violence had not occurred two years after the introduction of determinate sentencing; and it was estimated that the increase in inmates due to longer sentences would cost the state an additional 22 million dollars annually (Gettinger, 1979).

The black community will undoubtedly be pleased with any reduction in racial disparity in sentencing. However, the large disproportion of blacks in the prison population means that stiffer sentences will affect the black community disproportionately. Many black families will be deprived of the presence of a member for a longer period of time. Should determinate sentences have a deterrent effect as some expect, then there will be a positive effect for blacks. But it is greater certainty of punishment rather than increased severity that is believed to deter. Further, it may be argued that a more desirable outcome is likely if money is spent on social programs directed at groups with a high likelihood of criminality than on increasing prison space. Of course, determinate sentencing does not logically include longer sentences. That harsher penalties have accompanied new sentencing statutes may be in part another reflection of the racial difference between lawmakers and lawbreakers and the racial prejudice that exists in America.

References

Abraham, Henry J. The Judicial Process. NY: Oxford University Press, 1975.

Austin, Roy L. "Unconvincing rejections of the hypothesis of racial discrimination in sentencing." Unpublished manuscript, Pennsylvania State University, 1982.

Beccaria, Caesare. On Crimes and Punishments, trans. Henry Paolucci. NY: Bobbs-Merrill, 1963.

Bedau, Hugo Adam. "Death sentences in New Jersey." Rutgers Law Review 19:155, 1964.

_____, "Capital punishment in Oregon 1903-1964." Oregon Law Review 45:1-39, 1965.

Blumberg, Abraham S. "The practice of law as a confidence game: organizational co-optation of a profession." Law and Society Review 1(2):15-19, 1967.

Bullock, Henry Allen. "Significance of the racial factor in the length of prison sentences." The Journal of Criminal Law, Criminology and Police Science 52:411-417, 1961.

Burns, Haywood. "Political Uses of the Law," in Gilbert Ware, ed., From the Black Bar, NY: G.P. Putnam's Sons, 1976. Published originally in Howard Law Journal (17)4:1973.

Chambliss, William J. Crime and the Legal Process. NY: McGraw-Hill, 1969.

Chambliss, William J. and Robert B. Seidman. Law, Order, and Power. Reading, MA: Addison-Wesley, 1971.

Chiricos, Theodore G. and Gordon P. Waldo. "Socioeconomic status and criminal sentencing: an empirical assessment of a conflict proposition." American Sociological Review 40(6):753-772, 1975.

Cohen, Lawrence E. Delinquency Dispositions: An Empirical Analysis of Processing Decisions in Three Juvenile Courts. Washington, D.C.: U.S. Government Printing Office, 1975.

_____ and James R. Kluegel. "Determinants of juvenile court dispositions." American Sociological Review 43(2):162-176, 1978.

Comment. "Jury duty: California." Civil Rights Digest 2:31-33, 1969.

Farrar, Donald E. and Robert R. Glauber. "Multicollinearity in regression analysis: the problem revisted." The Review of Economics and Statistics (49) 1:92-107, 1967.

Forslund, Morris A. "Age, occupation and conviction rates of white and Negro males: a case study." Rocky Mountain Social Science Journal, 6:141, 1969.

Garfinkel, Harold. "Research note on inter- and intra-racial homicides." Social Forces 14(4):369-381, 1949.

Gettinger, Stephen. "Tinkering with determinate sentencing." Corrections Magazine 3:54-55, 1979.

Gillin, John L. Criminology and Penology. NY: Appleton-Century-Crofts, 1945.

Gottfredson, Don. "Sentencing guidelines," in Hyman Gross and Andrew von Hirsch, eds., Sentencing. NY: Oxford University Press, 1981.

Green, Edward. "Inter- and intra-racial crime relative to sentencing." Journal of Criminal Law, Criminology and Police Science 551(3):348-358, 1964.

Greenberg, David F. "Socioeconomic status and criminal sentences: is there an association?" American Sociological Review, (42):174-75, 1977.

Gross, Hyman and Andrew von Hirsch, eds. Sentencing. NY: Oxford University Press, 1981.

Hagan, John. "Extra-legal attributes and criminal sentencing: an assessment of a sociological viewpoint." Law and Society Review (8):357-383, 1974.

Hindelang, Michael J. "Equality under the law." Journal of Criminal Law, Criminology and Police Science 60(3):306-313, 1969.

Hopkins, Andrew. "Is there a class bias in criminal sentencing?" American Sociological Review 42(1):176-177, 1977.

Howard, Joseph C. "Racial discrimination in sentencing." Judicature 59(3):121-125, 1975.

Jankovic, Ivan. "Social class and sentencing." Crime and Social Justice 10:9-16, 1978. (Fall-Winter):9-16.

Johnson, Guy. "The Negro and crime." Annals of the American Academy of Political and Social Science, 217:93-104, 1941.

Judson, Charles J., et al. "A study of the California penalty jury in first-degree murder cases." Stanford Law Review 21:1297-1331, 1969.

Kalvan, Harry, Jr. and Hans Zeisel. The American Jury. Boston: Little, Brown and Co., 1966.

Kant, I. The Philosophy of Law, Part II. Trans. W. Hastie. Edinburgh: T.T. Clark, 1887.

Kempf, Kimberly. Racial Discrimination Sentencing: An Assessment of the Situation in Pennsylvania. Master's Thesis, Pennsylvania State University, University Park, PA, 1982.

Kleck, Gary. "Racial discrimination in criminal sentencing: a critical evaluation of the evidence with additional evidence on the death penalty." American Sociological Review 46:783-805, 1981.

Lefcourt, Robert. "Law against the people," in Richard Quinney, ed., Criminal Justice in America: A Critical Understanding. Boston: Little, Brown and Co., 1974.

Long, Elton; James Long, Wilmer Leon, and Paul B. Weston. American Minorities: The Justice Issue. Englewood Cliffs, NJ: Prentice-Hall, 1975.

Morris, Norval. "Punishment, desert and rehabilitation," in Hyman Gross and Andrew von Hirsch, eds., Sentencing. NY: Oxford University Press, 1981.

McCarthy, John P. Jr., Neil Sheflin, and Joseph Barraw. Report of the Sentencing Guidelines Project to the Administrative Director of the Courts on the Relationship between Race and Sentencing. New Jersey: Administrative Office of the Courts Sentencing Guideline Project, 1979.

Nagel, Stuart. The Legal Process from a Behavioral Perspective. Homewood, IL: Dorsey Press, 1969.

Newman, Donald J. "Role and process in the criminal court," in Daniel Glaser, ed., Handbook of Criminology. Chicago: Rand McNally, 1974.

_____, "Pleading guilty for consideration: a study of bargain justice." Journal of Criminal Law, Criminology and Police Science 46, 1956.

Perry, Richard L., ed. Sources of Our Liberties. NY: Associated College Presses, 1969.

Quinton, A.M. "On punishment," in Gertrude Ezosky, ed., Philosophical Perspectives on Punishment. Albany, NY: State University of New York Press, 1972.

Reasons, Charles. "On methodology, theory and ideology." American Sociological Review, 42(1):177-181, 1977.

Sellin, Thorsten. The Penalty of Death. Beverly Hills, CA: Sage Publications, 1980.

Shostak, David A. "Crosby Smith: forgotten witness to a Mississippi nightmare." Negro History Bulletin 38(1):320-325, 1975.

Strodtbeck, Fred, R.M. James, and J.C. Hawkins. "Social status and jury deliberations." American Sociological Review, 22:713-719, 1957.

Sudnow, David. "Normal crimes: sociological features of the penal code." Social Problems 12:255-276, 1965.

Swigert, Victoria Lynn. Criminal Homicide: A Socio-Legal Analysis. Unpublished Ph.D. dissertation. State University of New York, Albany, 1975.

Symons, Julian. A Pictorial History of Crime. NY: Crown Publishers, 1966.

Terry, R.M. "Discrimination in the handling of juvenile offenders by social control agencies." Journal of Research in Crime and Delinquency, 4:218-230, 1967.

Thompson, Randall J. and Matthew J. Zingraff. "Detecting sentencing disparity: some problems and evidence." American Journal of Sociology 86(4):869-880, 1981.

Thornberry, T.P. "Race, socioeconomic status and sentencing in the juvenile justice system." Journal of Criminal Law and Criminology, 64:90-98, 1973.

U.S. Department of Justice. State Court Organization. Washington, D.C.: U.S. Government Printing Office, 1980.

Vold, George B. Theoretical Criminology. NY: Oxford University Press, 1958.

von Hirsch, Andrew. "Doing justice: the principle of commensurate deserts," in Hyman Gross and Andrew von Hirsch, eds., Sentencing. NY: Oxford University Press, 1981.

Willick, Daniel H., Gretchen Gehlker, and Anita McFarland Watts. "Social class as a factor affecting judicial disposition: defendants charged with criminal homosexual acts." Criminology 13(1):57-77, 1975.

Wolf, Edwin D. "Abstract of analysis of jury sentencing in capital cases: New Jersey: 1937-1961." Rutgers Law Review, 19:56-64, 1964.

Wolfgang, Marvin and Marc Riedel. "Race, judicial discretion, and the death penalty." Annals of the American Academy of Political and Social Science 407:119-133, 1973.

Zimring, Franklin E. "Making the punishment fit the crime: a consumer's guide to sentencing reform," in Hyman Gross and Andrew von Hirsch, eds., Sentencing. NY: Oxford University Press, 1981.

12

The Role of the Black Judge*

George W. Crockett, Jr.

The next two chapters represent two classic speeches made by two black jurists over a decade ago. Each presentation is a poignant statement of the extraordinary responsibility black judges have in eradicating racial discrimination in the courtroom. Both recognize racism as the single most damaging reality of the criminal justice system—a reality that is responsible for the disrespect, distrust, and fear that black people hold for the law. In this chapter, Judge Crockett maintains that the Bill of Rights clearly applies to all Americans, including blacks. But, according to his argument, concepts of democracy in the criminal process have never been realized. Specifically, the concept of fairness has been seriously demeaned and undermined by the racial discrimination that is practiced by the courts. The black judge's role, the focus of Judge Crockett's speech, is to be active in research and to work toward remedying those flaws in the system that have led to serious injustices for blacks who come into contact with the law.

The late President Roosevelt once remarked, in reference to the Daughters of the American Revolution, that there are so many people who are willing to die for the Constitution but so few are willing to read it; and that perhaps explains, more than anything else, why one judge who decided to do the unusual thing of applying the Constitution[1] suddenly receives the acclaim that you have given me today, following my introduction. It is a measure of the extent to which we have drifted away from basic constitutional rights and liberties in this country. I want, then, preliminarily, to look back to the Constitution to remind you that our Constitution, unlike the constitution of many other countries, is a product of our national experiences and when I say our, I am referring to the founders of our country and I emphasize *our* because when Chrispus Attucks fell on the common in Boston, he made this country mine as well as anyone else's. It's our country, it's our founders, it's our Constitution. The people who

---

* This speech is printed with the permission of both Judge Crockett and the Judicial Council. Parts of this speech were taken by the author from materials published in George Crockett, "Reflections of a Jurist on Civil Disobedience," *The American Scholar* 40(4): 584-591, 1971, and have been printed with the permission of that publication.

wrote that Constitution were searching for a new kind of democracy and they thought that one of the chief attributes of that democracy was the right of the people to get a fair trial whenever they were accused of crime. When the original draft of the Constitution was submitted to the Thirteen Colonies, they refused to adopt it unless and until the Bill of Rights was added. Now, if you review that Bill of Rights, you will be surprised to find out how many of those articles relate to this concept of fairness in the criminal process. The fourth amendment preserves to the people the right to be secure in their person and property from unreasonable search. The fifth amendment provides that no one shall be required to incriminate himself and the sixth amendment guarantees that no one shall be convicted unless he is confronted by his accuser, given the opportunity to cross examine his accuser, and provided with counsel for his defense. And finally, the eighth amendment provides that everyone shall be entitled to reasonable bail and shall be protected from cruel and unusual punishment. When you consider these amendments and the restrictions which they place upon criminal trials, you realize just how much our founders believed that democracy depended upon the fairness of the criminal process. I want, then, to talk to you generally about why some of these concepts of democracy in the criminal process have failed and continue to fail.

Crimes generally are committed by poor people. People whose families live below the poverty level, $3000 a year. Now only 12 per cent of our white families fall into that category while 40 per cent of our non-whites are designated as poor. There are many more white persons arrested each year than blacks, but there are many more blacks brought to court and convicted, particularly in our metropolitan areas than whites. My court, the Detroit Recorder's Court, serves as an example of what I am talking about. We have jurisdiction over every crime committed within the city of Detroit, whether it's walking against a red light or whether it's first degree murder—it comes up for trial in the recorder's court. Our court is the most integrated court in the entire state of Michigan. We have thirteen judges and of those thirteen judges, five are black. It's integrated for the very simple reason that it is elected by the people of Detroit and the black people of the city of Detroit today are approaching 50 per cent. But on the other hand, all crimes committed in Wayne County, outside the city of Detroit, are tried by the Circuit Court of Wayne County. That court is elected on a county-wide basis and of the twenty-eight circuit court judges there is only one black judge. Now those who are displeased with black judges in Michigan have a very subtle way of taking care of the situation and so there is pending in our legislature today a proposal to promote Judge Crockett and all of the other recorder's court judges and make them circuit court judges. Notwithstanding, we already receive the same salaries that the circuit court judges receive and we have just as much authority within our geographic limits as a circuit court judge has. So why this sudden interest in making me a circuit court judge? It's very simple: I would then have to run on a county-wide basis, and as a result, the most highly integrated court in Michigan would cease to be a highly integrated court.

But the point that I started off to make is that approximately 85 per cent of all defendants that come to recorder's court are black people, which illustrates the percentages that I just pointed out to you. Of that 85 per cent, at least 65 per cent are indigents for whom counsel has to be appointed and later on we will touch on the kind of representation that they receive from such counsel. The President's Commission on Law Enforcement and the Administration of Justice as well as the report of the National Advisory Commission on Civil Disorders and all of the official and unofficial groups and studies who have spoken on the subject have pointed up the urgent need for improving our courts and for upgrading the quality of justice in metropolitan areas. The National Advisory Commission on Civil Disorders, after examining the operation of criminal courts during the summer's disorders of 1967, had this to say:

> Some of our courts, moreover, have lost the confidence of the poor, the belief is pervasive among ghetto residents that lower courts in our urban communities dispense an assembly line justice; that from arrest to sentencing, the poor uneducated are denied equal justice with the affluent and that procedures such as bail and fines have been perverted to perpetuate class inequities.[2]

Then this report continues with the following indictment of the legal profession: "This prevalence of assembly justice is evidence that in many localities the bar has not met its leadership responsibilities."[3] Some of you perhaps noticed a few weeks ago in the magazine section of the *New York Times* an article by Federal Judge J. Skelley Wright from the District of Columbia on how our courts have failed the poor. The word "blacks" should have been substituted for the word poor and the article would have been much closer to the truth. The white poor have a chance of getting help from the bar association or from a legal aid clinic, even from a sympathetic judge who has not forgotten that his parents or his grandparents were once poor or of foreign ancestry. But in a society whose courts and lawyers and law enforcement officers are still predominantly white, the black defendant is not likely to encounter such good fortune. Why? Are we all this callous about justice for the poor in our midst—is it really true that we are without funds for more judges, for more policemen, for more court facilities, for more probation officers, for more and improved correctional and rehabilitation facilities? Not long ago I made a public statement following the New Bethel incident in Detroit,[4] in which I said that the causes of crime are steeped in racism, racism in our courts, in our jails, in our streets, and in our hearts. Shortly after I made that statement, a fellow member of our judiciary asked me if I was really serious, did I really believe that there was racism in our courts? When I answered with an unqualified "yes," my fellow jurist showed his pain and his disbelief—he showed the shock— shock that I, a judge, could be so disloyal to the judicial club as to come right out and say, "yes," there is racism in our courts. The trouble is, all of us who work in and around the courts know that racism is always present, but some of us prefer not to recognize this so we pretend it does not exist, and then there are others among us who become so callous that we are no longer even conscious of its existence. And so we talk about the courts failing the poor when what we really mean is that there is no equal justice for black people in our criminal courts today, and what's more, there never has been. And this is the shame of our whole judicial system. That in a country whose temple of justice is emblazoned with the motto "Equal Justice in the Law," the quantity and quality of justice is in direct proportion to the size of one's pocketbook and the color of one's skin. And this is so, not because written law says it shall be so, rather it is so because our judges, by their rulings, make it so.

In the past fifteen years, since the decision in *Brown v. Board of Education*,[5] the United States Supreme Court and a Democratic Congress have moved with courage and determination to wipe out all state and federal statutes which sanction racial discrimination. And in addition to that, the Warren Supreme Court has given us a national code of procedure which outlaws detestable police practices in the areas of arrest and detention, in the areas of search and seizure, in the areas of voluntary confessions and in the area of giving people effective assistance of counsel and reasonable bail. All of this has been done within the past 15 years. But the Warren Supreme Court has endured severe criticism from presidential candidates down to the cops on the beat, and it has endured this criticism because it has thus dared to standardize criminal procedure in the interest of bringing about that fairness in American democracy the founders of this country ordained in their Bill of Rights. Now, could it be that the intensity of this criticism against the Supreme Court is occasioned by the fact that the chief beneficiary of this return to constitutional principles happens to be black folk? The housing for prisoners, for example, in our metropolitan centers is horrible. The complete inadequacy of our correctional facilities, our rehabilitation facilities, and our probation facilities is notorious. Our juvenile detention accommodations are a national disgrace. Could it be that nothing is done about these conditions because they affect, in the main, black people? A rich white man is not likely to be arrested without a warrant, nor is he likely to be arrested in the dead of night. Actually, the federal court rules in the United States District Court in Detroit (the criminal court that tries most of the white collar crimes) contain a provision prohibiting the serving of an arrest warrant at night without a special order from the judge, and since in most cases, the defendants over there are white, it sort of gives your white defendants a little bit of immunity from being picked up at night when there is no judge available. In the case of a poor and/or black man, the arresting officer not only will neglect to obtain a warrant, more than likely he will deliberately wait until the regular court hours are over before making the arrest so that he can conveniently say there is no judge to whom he can take the arrestee to have him released on bond. And this well known course of racist conduct is known to every judge and every prosecutor, but it is almost never challenged by a prosecutor or by a judge. When a rich white man is arrested he will be given his *Miranda* warnings to keep silent, he will be accorded his *Escobedo* right to telephone and consult his attorney, and he will either be taken promptly before a magistrate, have reasonable bail fixed; or he will be left alone and unmolested in his cell until a magistrate is available. But, if he is poor and/or black, he is more than likely to be insulted, handcuffed, beaten, kicked, placed in a vermin-infested police station lockup, kept incommunicado and subjected to endless interrogation in an effort to force a confession, or some damaging admissions—and only after the effects of this treatment have subsided will he then be brought before a magistrate who will then fix his bail at a figure three to ten times this black man's annual income. This course of racist conduct also is well known in every criminal court but is almost never challenged by a prosecutor or a judge.

Now, at the trial and in the crucial pre-trial stages, the rich white man will have the best legal talent available, reinforced by an investigative team that will rival that of the prosecutor. And he will thus be able to avail himself of each of the many safeguards that the law in its wisdom has provided to insure a fair trial and to protect the innocent. But the poor and/or black man, lacking money for lawyer fees, will be assigned either a young and inexperienced attorney or an old and disillusioned one.

Is it any wonder, then, that in most cases, the accused poor and/or black man would rather plead guilty to a reduced charge than run the risk of a conviction of a greater charge initially lodged against him? Every prosecutor knows this, every judge knows it also, but changing this system means basically providing more money, more judges, more court personnel. It means improving the quality of criminal justice for poor and/or black people; and the establishment has neither the inclination to do this nor the financial ability to bring this about so long as we continue to spend billions for armament wasted in Viet Nam and more billions to subsidize the militarism in Germany and still more billions to stifle democratic freedoms in Africa and South America. This, then, is why racism remains embedded in our legal system. To change this, to cleanse the system, means upgrading the lives of the poor, the blacks, the underprivileged in our society—and doing this at the expense of the rich, the white, the well-to-do. This the establishment is not ready to do.

The late Will Rogers used to say that the people of Kansas will vote dry as long as they can stagger to the polls. If he were around today, I suspect he would note that white Americans are prepared to do anything to win the war against crime, except pay for it. Not the least reason for coming out against coddling criminals and for stiffer sentences for the adoption of stop and frisk laws, for law enforcement being given permission to tap your telephone and to eavesdrop on your private conversations. Not the least reason for coming out for these so-called remedies is that the proponents feel that such measures won't require an increase in taxes, it won't materially improve the lot of the poor, it won't disturb the class relationships in our society and it won't interfere with their war profits. Now no other professional group bears a responsibility as great as that of the legal profession, both lawyers and judges, for ridding our law and our body of the cancerous growth of racism. We lawyers and we judges were and are the architects of the legal system of this nation—it is we who have written the constitutional guarantees of due process and equal protection of the laws and we have claimed for ourselves the ultimate prerogative of interpreting those constitutions and those laws. It is we who appoint or are appointed as police commissioners in charge of executing the criminal law; it is we who man the prosecutor's staff and the public defender's staff; we select the jury commissioners who in turn impanel a jury, and of course, we are the judges. The job, then, is a job for us to do.

There are a few hopeful signs—the appointment of a black Solicitor General or a black United States Supreme Court Justice is a hopeful sign; a couple of United States District Attorneys and fifteen out of more than 300 federal judges helps a little; as does the existence of about sixty-five black judges in state courts of record throughout the United States. But none of these legal positions are in the deep South where the bulk of the black people live, where a black judge can spell the difference between justice and injustice, and where the mere presence of a black judge would give concrete meaning to our national ideal of equal justice and would serve as a stimulus to Negro youth. I think, though, that the most hopeful sign is the growing political potential of the black vote and the increase in the number of black judges. And this brings me back to putting aside the prepared text and telling you a few things, a few conclusions that I think you are entitled to draw as a result of what happened in Detroit. I think there are three significant lessons for you here in Baltimore and for Negroes and the friends of Negroes in other metropolitan areas to draw from the Detroit action.

The first is that we who believe in democracy, we who believe in the Constitution, have been brain-washed. We have allowed ourselves to sit by and watch the erosion of constitutional rights and liberties for so long that to most of us, the violation of the law is the law. We have gone along believing now for years that police officers have the right to arrest anyone, put them in jail, and then investigate and find out whether or not the arrest was lawful in the first place. And as a result when one judge decides there is no such right, that when the Constitution provided that the writ of habeas corpus should never be suspended except in cases of war when the public welfare is threatened, when one judge decided to go back to horn-book law, the whole senate of one of our largest states grinds to a standstill while it adopts a resolution calling for an investigation of that judge. That's just how far our constitutional liberties have eroded in this country. It's time for us to take a lesson from Detroit and do something about it.

The second lesson you are entitled to draw from that experience is that the prompt and fair enforcement of the law can and will prevent urban racial explosions. People riot because they have no faith in your promises; they have no faith that they are going to get justice; they feel that they've reached the end of the rope; that the law is no longer relevant to them and therefore they just take the law into their own hands.

In 1967, 90 per cent of the people arrested in Detroit were black people. They were charged with violating the curfew—a criminal offense that is punishable as a misdemeanor, with imprisonment for ninety days and/or a fine of $100. But the prosecutor made a recommendation to our court that was followed by all of our judges (with one exception), which was that the minimum bail be fixed for everyone at $10,000.00. Now, how many Negroes have ever even heard of $10,000.00? And so the jails were over-crowded and the newspapers stated publicly that the reason for fixing the high bail was to "keep those people off the streets," and so the frustration fed the flames, and what could have been settled as an everyday racial disturbance had the law been applied, was magnified into a conflagration that all of us are ashamed of today.

A lesson from Detroit is one that was recently drawn by our new Detroit Commission, a commission headed up by Mr. Henry Ford, Mr. Townsend of Chrysler, and all of the big investors in Detroit. I don't want to sound egotistical, but I think the greatest compliment that has been paid to me is when that committee stated in writing, in a brief which they recently issued that but for the prompt action of Judge Crockett, we might have had a repetition of the summer of 1967. Apply the law promptly, equally and fairly and the people will have confidence and riots will cease.

Now the third lesson I think you have to draw from the Detroit experience is that there is a special role for black judges. I tell people and I repeat today that the most powerful public officials in America are not your legislators; with all due respect to your mayor, it's not your mayors; it's not your governors; it's your judges, and the establishment knows that and that's why the establishment wants to control the manner in which judges are selected. To the extent that you can limit or make it virtually impossible to get black judges who identify with the problems of black people you continue to control black people—it's as simple as that.

In my state, of course, we elect judges. We have a constitutional provision, and recently, we went so far as to not even let the governor pick someone to fill a vacancy; we said go and get one of the old retired judges. However, we went a little too far because we didn't have enough retired judges to fill the vacancy. So we amended the constitution and now we can appoint a judge to fill a vacancy but only until the next election comes up. We don't like to believe that judges should be put up in some ivory tower. The function of a judge is to identify with the people. As Socrates said, the judge's role is not just to decide, it is also to teach—to teach the people what the law is—to teach them a way of their rights; that's why a selection of judges should be a process in which the man and woman on the street, participate. Now, what significance does that have for black judges? I think a black judge, by nature, in this historical period has got to be a reformist— he cannot be a member of the club. The whole purpose for selecting him is that the people are dissatisfied with the status quo and they may want him to shake it up, and his role is to shake it up.

Now, a black judge has another role to perform. We who are products of the American common law are always extolling the virtues of a common law system and its ability to adapt to the growing needs of the people. In the past, white judges have really made the common law adaptable to what they conceive to be the desires of the American people. We black judges have to take a page from that book. If the common law is so adaptable, let's get down to books and find the remedies, and apply them to the old evils that have plagued the poor and the underprivileged in our society for so long. The answers are there. The special role of the black judge is to see what justice requires and then go to the books and get the remedies to apply to it. Most people assume that the law is something that is clear cut, it's written out, it's black and white; it's not so. Most of the law is a matter of discretion. What is discretion? Discretion is whatever the judge thinks it is as long as he can give a sound reason for it. A judge is a product of his own experiences, of his own history, of the people from whom he came. So a black judge's exercise of discretion is not going to necessarily be the same as that of a white judge. But as long as it is reason, and the law as made by precedents established by white people, that discretion stands. That's the big record that is available.

In Detroit, we have a serious problem with police brutality—we've got some policemen in Detroit who don't care what heads they beat—black as well as white—it just so happens they end up beating more black heads than they do white. Now, to say that under those circumstances you can bring suit for damages, well any lawyer in here knows what normally happens in that case; to say that you can get the prosecutor to indict that man for assault and battery or for assault with intent to do bodily harm, you know how frequently that happens. To say he can be brought before the police trial board, well, we have that in Detroit. The public never knows what happens before the police trial board—all they know is that he was either reprimanded or nothing whatever happened. Somehow this whole thing has got to be brought out into the open so that the people themselves can decide whether or not there is any truth to these repeated charges of police brutality. But how do you bring it out into the open— that's what bothered me—something had to be done about it. Well, I finally decided that one way to bring it out was to use discretion. Now— how is judicial discretion to be used? Well, once a man is convicted the law leaves it up to the judge to decide what shall be done about him. The judge could put him on probation or the judge could send him to prison for a certain number of years. It's up to the judge; as long as the judge acts within the confines of those statutory limitations, he's right and nothing can be done about it. I see that the consternation all over Detroit has made the front pages of my hometown paper, in Jacksonville, Florida, when I simply announced that when and if I was satisfied that the police had taken it upon themselves to charge a man, arrest a man, try him, convict him and then punish him, I am not going to be disposed to send that man to prison. The police will not get the vicarious pleasure that they anticipate over having beaten the accused half to death, then having a black judge send him off to prison. So, last week, and maybe this news hasn't reached here yet, I had such a case and it's interesting what happens in a case like that. Lawyers actually go out and find the witnesses on the street who saw the beating. And here is a man who's beaten so that both of his eyes are closed up while he is handcuffed and then brought into the police station, taken in the garage and beaten again until the officer in charge comes out and to all his little braves says, "I think that's enough now, take him to the hospital." And so I didn't send him to prison. Now my chief justice disagrees with me—he thinks we should leave such matters to the ordinary, so I don't know whether I'll be sustained, but one thing is certain; a lot of people are going to start thinking about devising new remedies to take care of old ills and I hope a lot of Negro judges will start doing that.

Now, there is one final role that I think the black judge could play—he is a symbol of all that we hold dear in this country—he is a symbol of American democracy. In my courtroom, teachers frequently bring their little youngsters, and my bailiffs have standing orders that when the students come in, clear the front row, this court belongs to them. At least one judge is going to bridge the generation gap. Occasionally if I am trying a case without a jury, I'll pick out twelve of those bright-eyed youngsters, put them in the jury box, have the bailiff give them a piece of paper, will go on with the trial and I will render the decision. Then while I am waiting for the next case, I'll talk with my young friends to see what's their reaction to it. In this situation, they are not afraid of courts, they are not afraid of judges, they are not afraid of policemen, they feel that this institution belongs to them, they are a part of it. What really does me good is when I see the little black boy or girl with his little eyes dancing, looking up at me with my black robe on and then see him nudge his little white friend—I know what he's saying. And that I think, my friends, is perhaps the highest role the black judge plays—in being a symbol of law and order with justice insofar as the poor and underprivileged in our society are concerned.

13

A View from the Bench

Bruce McM. Wright

Presented here is Judge Wright's famous address to the Metropolitan Applied Research Center in New York City, which was given in April 1974. The points made in this speech, as those made by Judge Crockett in Chapter 12, apply as forcefully to today's black and Hispanic defendant in court as it did to those who faced the bench a decade ago. The recommendations made by Judge Wright are also equally applicable to contemporary black judges. Judge Wright sees an end to the inequities in the system only when judges are specially trained in ethnic sensitivity to become fully aware of institutional racism, when black people are familiarized with the law and the responsibilities of the bench, and when prison conditions are humanized. Judge Wright's most fervent message in this address is that black judges must practice a radical form of criminology if they seek to eliminate discrimination practiced under the guise of justice.

There are some sensitive people who believe that the criminal justice system, so far as the poor are concerned, is more criminal than just.

Many believe that it is not that the blacks and Puerto Ricans in Eastern urban areas are more criminal than others, but that they simply get caught more often because the police spend a great deal more time giving them close attention.

Ask any sensitive leftist, and he will tell you that the terms "law and order," "strict construction," "preventive detention," and "crime in the streets" are all racist code terms, meaning that the niggers and the spics are getting out of hand with an arrogance of knives, guns, cudgels, and lye.

Speak to any Black Panther or surviving veteran of the Black Liberation Army, and you will be told that the police and the FBI pick on anyone who fits the visual profile of a militant, a young lord, or a bad nigger.

The intellectual leftists, brooding in their beards and moods of discontent, will tell you that the Nixon rhetoric on law and order, coupled with his Southern strategy, is nothing but the mirror image of Adolf Hitler, speaking in 1932.

This is not as farfetched as it might seem. Nixon, after all, did many things in the name of national security. Hitler did say, in 1932, that the republic was in danger from within and without. "We need law and order!" he said. "Without law and order, our nation cannot survive."

Early in 1973, the President submitted to Congress his Criminal Law Reform Bill. He said, on that occasion, that there must be "punishment without pity."

There have always been some indications not only that punishment was without pity, but that the entire criminal justice system was without any compassionate understanding of cause and dealt rather impatiently with effect.

The great and tragic emphasis in our courts today is a judicial numbers game. The judges, for the most part, sit in the arraignment parts like Bill Baird puppets, where, for purposes of setting bail, too many judges allow the words of the district attorney to be strings activating their response.

Example: Last August, a sixteen-year-old Puerto Rican youth was arrested and charged with participating in a holdup. Held in exorbitant bail, he was placed in jail at Rikers Island. There was no time for investigation. The next day he committed suicide. Then the investigation began. It was the after-death discovery that the young lad spoke no English, that he had been in New York but two or three months, and that he had not participated in the holdup at all.

The presumption at his arraignment was that he was guilty.

Do the police really single out the black militant, the man with the afro, exploiting his nonknowledge of Africa and wearing a ferocious afro to prove it? Or are the blacks, longing for the perished glory of crumbled civilizations and mighty chiefs, simply paranoid?

Let's see, P. Jay Sidney, the actor, says that any black man in America who is not paranoid must be sick.

Example: On March 8 of 1974, William B. Saxbe and the FBI revealed that for the last four years, there had been an intensive campaign to harass and disrupt black militant organizations and their leaders. One way in which they did this was the making of repeated arrests of the same people, just to make certain they were off the streets and would finally face bail they could never post.

Most of the poor in our urban situation, are either black or Puerto Rican. In an example of the genetic dirty joke, some Puerto Ricans are not only poor, but black as well.

For many years, every Puerto Rican arrested was automatically described as white on his arrest record, no matter what his pigmentation. For some months in 1970 and 1971 I was assigned to Brooklyn. In case after case, I heard police testify as follows: "I observed the male white Puerto Rican perpetrator," etc. and, without exception, the "male white Puerto Rican perpetrator" sat there before me cleverly masked in a black skin.

After I had carefully dismissed each of the cases by reason of a mistake in identification, I was excommunicated from Brooklyn by District Attorney Eugene Gold, thereby suggesting rather strongly a nasty political taint to the virtue of our lady of justice and the assignment of judges.

The supervising judge in Brooklyn has been heard to certify that edict of banishment and exile by saying that so long as he remains in power, I will never sit in Brooklyn again.

When I faced the czar of all judges in New York City, Mr. Justice David Ross, and foolishly complained about politics making it possible for the district attorneys to shop for judges who would be more responsive to their thinking, as opposed to judges stupid enough to try to think on their own, I was met with a bitter tirade from the justice worthy of a Marine sergeant screaming at a treacherous private.

Thereafter I dealt with his lordship only in writing. In this entirely one-way correspondence, I have yet to have a response.

But back to other examples. The men who run our criminal justice system will know more about this symposium and my naming of names than any of you will remember. They will probably know by tomorrow and have a letter-perfect transcript.

Under our system of jurisprudence, one who is charged with crime is presumed to be innocent until proved guilty beyond a reasonable doubt. What a lovely and crucial fiction! All of us, I am certain, would wish to be presumed innocent, if indicted, as opposed to being presumed guilty, when arrested.

If presumed innocent, then one has the benefit of being paroled, instead of facing bail the size of the national debt. One needs to be free and out of jail in order to line up his witnesses, confer with his attorney, visit the scene of the alleged crime, and prepare a proper defense.

When Burton Roberts was the district attorney for the Bronx, he spoke to me on the question of bail and the presumption of innocence. And this is what he said: "The presumption is no more than a rule of evidence which begins to operate only at the time the trial begins."

Well, the reason for so many riots and dissatisfaction in the Tombs has been that it is so full of blacks and Puerto Ricans who have not been convicted and are simply awaiting trial. They are there because some judge has presumed them guilty and they cannot afford the bail then set.

What happens to presumption?

Apparently, the judges are of the Roberts mind on it. The logic of the Roberts Rule, then, is that when you are arrested, you are presumed guilty and even if it takes two years before your trial is reached, you are still presumed guilty until the trial begins. Then, miracle of judicial miracles, you are presumed innocent as the trial begins, with you still in custody.

This rule has the same quality of logic—ethnic logic, that is—as that expressed by a Housing Authority commissioner some years ago. As I rode up Lenox Avenue one day, I was astonished and unbelieving. I saw a housing project under construction named for Stephen Foster, the all-American composer who celebrated the happiness of the darkies as slaves. I feared that the next project, there in Harlem, would be the Old-Folks-at-Home Project.

An angry letter from me to the Housing Authority resulted in a reference by the chairman to the man who had named the project. He happened to be the only black member of the authority. I transferred my surprise and wonder to him. He replied as follows:

> Dear Sir: I do not generally answer the letters of cranks. But obviously, you do not know that the songs of Stephen Foster prepared the North for the migration of the Negroes from the South.

I asked what they did for those who remained there, thus managing to get no answers to two questions.

I mention these things only to demonstrate how many people there are in government in positions of power who arbitrarily determine the shape of fate.

The same Burton Roberts who would delay the presumption of innocence is now a State Supreme Court justice and able to enforce his odd theories of justice.

Those of us who know him are not surprised by the prince of the law and the decibels of his ambition.

In 1969, referring to the South Bronx as the "Jungle" and as "Fort Apache," he allowed himself to be quoted in the pages of *New York* magazine, referring to the blacks as *schvartzes,* the Yiddish term for nigger. At the same time, the article described him as rolling his eyes and using a darky accent, a minstrel in white face.

In 1972, just before becoming a Supreme Court justice, Roberts commented on an arrest of two campaign workers for allegedly drawing weapons on the opposition. The New York *Times* report on August 18, 1972, is quoted as follows: "Jesting about the incident, Mr. Roberts remarked: 'That's the way they run elections in the Bronx. What do you think this is, civilization?' "

We may assume that an uncivilized electorate made him first a district attorney and then a Supreme Court justice.

For years people have said that the judges, generally a white and middle-class census of legally created gods, have been hostile to the poor. Is this again the paranoia of the poor, or is it the general rule, showing like a white slip beneath the black robes of the bench?

On December 20, 1970, some federally funded antipoverty law groups revealed that they had filed complaints against several judges, documenting judicial intemperance and prejudice against the poor, coupled with outright hostility. Nothing more has been heard or published on this subject.

It is worth noting, however, that the antipoverty lawyers claimed that the judges favored Establishment individuals—that is, those who most resembled the judges themselves. The judges were, it was said, executing unwritten custom and enforcing rudeness, malice, and prejudice.

And then, late in 1973, a committee of judges themselves issued a printed and bound report in which the justice system was called a failure. The report suggested that the police are more diligent in apprehending blacks than whites. One example of discrimination was underscored, and this should be a warning to all of us who are black parents. It said that the charge most often leveled against a white male in a stolen car case is "unauthorized use of a vehicle." But, "virtually all black males [are] charged with grand larceny, auto."

Unauthorized use is merely a misdemeanor. Grand larceny is a felony.

This is what is called the Dred Scott Syndrome among the judges—not by the judges, of course. Students of the theory of blacks as three-fifths-of-a-man in our constitutional history will remember that Chief Justice Roger Brooke Taney laid down the rule that no Negro had any rights which any white man was bound to respect. Taney was a Roman Catholic zealot, whose devout Christianity nevertheless allowed him to be a slave-owner. It is not known whether the judges today who execute his 1857 theory are slaveowners.

In the summer of 1972 it was revealed that in Villavicencio, Colombia, everybody killed Indians. It was sport. One Colombian, charged with that offense, said, "From childhood, I have been told that everyone kills Indians." Another, amazed that he was charged, said, "All I did was kill the little Indian girl and finish off two who were more dead than alive anyway." Another said, "For me, Indians are animals, like deer. Since way back, Indian hunting has been common practice in these parts."

Translate this into "kill me softly," and you have the Indian scene of South America transferred to the inner cities of America.

An exaggeration? Not really.

Omar Hendrix, in 1972, a member of the city's Correction Department staff, wrote a one-page essay called "Visitations." In horror-stricken nostalgia, he recalled his youth in rural Georgia. Sometimes, he said, on Sundays, the family would visit some of the kinfolk confined to a prison camp. One had been said to have "kilt a nigger." The visit was a picnic affair. After lunch, two white prisoners went off to the Negro section of the jail and brought back two black prisoners. Then the white prisoners encircled the blacks and ordered them to "fight for us." This, Hendrix said, was an old ritual—that is, black men forced to fight for the pleasure of whites.

There is still the mixture as before, with a difference now: We pay the blacks to fight for the whites. . . .

If we live in an atmosphere heavy with built-in discrimination and historical insults, there is little reason to believe that the justice system, which selects most of its judges and district attorneys from the whites who live with the tradition of white supremacy, should be any different on the bench from what they are in private life.

Prisoners, in this respect, are little different from the white judges (and some black ones). A white prisoner who is a bigot seldom emerges from prison transformed into a flaming integrationist. In 1972 there were several stabbings in the New Jersey State Prison at Trenton. An investigation revealed that there was a war between the black and white prisoners. It seems that the whites controlled the drug traffic in the prison and were charging the blacks twice as much for a sale of dope as the white prisoners were charged.

Thus, another mirror image inside the walls of what occurs outside.

I have long urged the abolition of all prisons as they are now constituted. This is not to say that there are nothing but angels out in the streets. Far from it. But the people who really need to be kept in durance vile are not that numerous. And the only reason for prisons and their inhumanity is to avoid and ignore rehabilitation and to encourage recidivism.

Just last month a Congressional subcommittee which has been studying the nation's prison system said that if only the public knew the truth about our prisons, it would demand instant reform.

Shortly after the Attica rebellion I heard a black voice wail over the radio station WBAI, say that he was a survivor, and then, on the question of rehabilitation, asked: "How the hell we gonna be rehabilitated when we ain't never been habilitated in the first place?"

We tend to think of our court system as being pretty much that gloomy and filthy pile of cement known as the Tombs and 100 Centre Street. But the plot against justice infects that lovely granite and marble architecture known as the Federal Courthouse as well.

In a fraud case, involving illegal trading in stock, through numbered Swiss bank accounts, to the tune of $20,000,000, the rich defendant was represented in court by a former federal judge.

The defendant and his firm had received illegal profits of some $225,000, and besides, the defendant had perjured himself during the grand jury investigation. He was fined $30,000, received a suspended jail term, and was placed on probation.

One week later, the same judge had before him an unemployed Negro shipping clerk. The Negro was married, with two children and a prior record of one robbery. He was charged with stealing a television set worth $100 from an interstate shipment. He received one year in jail.

The *New York Times,* in describing this gross disparity in meting out justice by Judge Irving Ben Cooper, noted that the discrimination exhibited was not simply a personal quirk of Judge Cooper, but was a distortion of justice common to his fellow judges.

One needs no help from the lens at Palomar to see the gross distinctions too often made between the wealthy defendant and the poor one.

Wonder still fills the sense and sensibility of many of us who recall the grand manner in which Spiro Agnew arrived at court to say he had no defense to a felony charge. Although the then Attorney General read off a long catalogue of offenses which could have been proved against Agnew, he was allowed to say he had no defense to only one.

He came to court in an expensive suit, in a chauffeured limousine, and with Secret Service bodyguards. He left with what was tantamount to a light rap on his wrist and a fine which was but a tiny fraction of the sum he had embezzled through the years, without paying any taxes on. He left court in the same way he arrived.

But every morning and night black paddy wagons with barred windows arrive at the Criminal Courthouse in Manhattan, to discharge its herd of two-legged beasts, all chained and shackled together as they are hurried into the pens, to await the awful wrath of a harried judge, who will set bail for them and detain them for the crime of being poor, as well as the other crime they must face.

It is a curious experience to see and hear the police in their testimony. The police academy turns out a plastic pattern of the same man with a different name. If all Negroes are said, with false allegiance to a native stereotype, to look alike, it may be said, with more accuracy, that all police sound alike. Invariably, they will say that they "observed the perpetrator," doing whatever the story calls for him having seen.

No cases of streaking have come before me yet, so I can only imagine how they would describe such a "perpetrator." The latter-day annals do, however, report the case of two students from the mainland arrested in San Juan for streaking. Their case was dismissed for insufficient evidence.

The police also generally testify with a masked face—that is, no emotion is tolerated to show through. This serves to camouflage the ancient enmity between the police and the blacks in New York. It began a long time ago and may be roughly dated from the so-called Negro plot of 1741, in New York City. The so-called plot was pretty much the fabrication of an Irish serving girl anxious to win freedom from her indenture and a reward of 100 pounds, then a great fortune.

She invented a story about an interracial plot to burn a local fort and make one plotter king and the Negro New York's governor. Both the police and the militia then began to round up the city's Negroes, whether free, enslaved, or indentured. Most were examined in the most cursory manner, and then justice was speedy. They were ordered lashed to a stake and burned. And they were, by the hundreds.

A report of that fearful era which rivals anything Salem had to offer, says that:

> As every attorney in the city was actively associated with the prosecution, the poor Negroes had no lawyers to defend them. William Smith, in conducting the prosecution, made an impassioned speech on the ingratitude of the Negroes, and expatiated on the kindness and tenderness with which they had always been treated. The Negroes died in agony. The crowd returned home well satisfied.

This early precedent for lynching, as all of you know, later spread to the barbaric South. In any case, it laid a local foundation for treating the lower orders.

The Irish Potato Famine of the 1800's resulted in large numbers of the Irish coming to New York. When they arrived, they were treated as white niggers and barred from many public places and restricted in the kinds of employment available. They competed for the meanest work with the city's Negroes, and there was great enmity between the niggers, white and black.

The unemployed Irish bully boys, traveling the streets in packs, used to beat up the local police officers. They were appalled to see, walking the city's streets, police dressed as English bobbies. This inflamed the traditional hate between the Irish and the symbol of English authority and persecution.

The bully boys would invariably attack and beat up the police. The head of the police then allowed his officers to serve on duty in ordinary street clothes, wearing a simple star to identify their status. Not fooled by such nonsense, the bully boys continued to beat them up, calling them, derisively, "coppers" from the circumstance of the copper stars they wore. This was later shortened to just "cops," a term which remains to this day.

In desperation, the first metropolitan police commissioner dragooned the bully boys onto the force, thus beginning the continuing tradition and saga of the Irish Mafia on the police force of the city, as well as in Boston. This then gave the Irish armed allies in their combat against the Black Nigger competition for jobs, while leaving some vacancies for the Negroes in night soil chores—the cleaning of backhouses.

It is almost as though the police remember the former competition and their ancestors' designation as white niggers. The getting even process is dramatized daily and nightly in our courts. The police seem to have adopted the antebellum view of Negroes as the "Drones and Pests of Society" and fair prey to the human hunt, or the not-quite-human hunt.

Many blacks, while they may be unaware of any historical basis for police attitudes, are aware of the plain enmity of the police.

No close reading of the draft riots of 1863 is necessary for the blacks to appreciate animosity. It was then that the Irish demonstrated their intention not to go off and fight for the niggers in the Civil War. Then the great poverty sore on the body politic, the Irish themselves, were caught up in poverty and resentment. They had no $300 to purchase freedom from military service, and many set a precedent for the Catonsville raid upon draft records and their destruction. This uprising included the destruction of the colored orphan home here in New York and the killing of some of its helpless infants.

Some among us have attributed our addiction to "black English" to our bitter rejection of social authority—"that is, prestige of public administrators and police." Dr. Clark may recognize the last quotation as an excerpt from his little pamphlet *The Zoot Effect in Personality: A Race Riot Participant.*

It was a reprint from the *Journal of Abnormal and Social Psychology*, issued in 1945, dealing with the 1943 Harlem riot. His coauthor, nearly thirty years ago, was one James Barker, a name not now known to me.

With the proliferation of so-called black studies, to be distinguished from a brown study, blacks are learning more and more about their urban ordeal. I am persuaded that a good deal of their enmity toward the police is reinforced by knowledge of the social isolation of blacks in our society. What Dr. Clark refers to as the zoot personality is perhaps an off-shoot of the chronic humiliation and discrimination against the black skin.

The killing of police officers by some blacks, including some black officers, is evidence that those blacks who cooperate with authority by joining it are lumped with white authority. The police, of course, in avenging their dead must do so with an even hand and include even black officers among their martyrs.

Discussions by the police of black militance is always accompanied by descriptions which give great force to the costumes adopted by so many blacks. Therefore, the ferocious afro, the wearing of beads, teeth, fetish necklaces and the like always define a militant black radical. It is of no matter that these outer camouflages for the black ego and devotion to retrospective glory are no more than a ghetto fashion. These are the stigmata of the enemy to the police.

And even worse, the judges themselves regard such men as dangerous to the commonwealth. If a black man is lucky enough to have made bail or be paroled while his case pends, his luck may end when his case is called and he summons up his compensatory arrogance and bops up to the bench with what the judge interprets as black insolence.

In a study of juries and judges in criminal cases, it was discovered that both jurors and judges bring to the courtroom their personal bias and prejudices. One juror interviewed said: "Niggers have to be taught to behave. I felt that if he hadn't done [what he was accused of], he'd done something else probably even worse and that he should be put out of the way for a good long while."

Another study reveals that there is a subtle interreaction between judgments reached on the basis of poverty and those reached on the basis of racial bias. The trouble is that most of the defendants in criminal proceedings are both poor and black, and without confessions from interviewed jurors and judges, it is difficult to know when there is a basic discrimination against one because of his poverty or because of his race or because of both.

There is little doubt that one is often penalized under our system for being poor. The favorite outcry of the white man who has avoided the relief rolls is that "we were immigrants, too, and we did it, so why can't the colored people be like us." There is little consideration given to the manner of the black immigrant's arrival on these shores or the black codes which regulated him after the fashion of an electronically controlled and obeisant robot.

While there is a glorious rhetoric concerning every man's entitlement to counsel of his choice, the government makes very little effort to ensure that the poor have experienced and competent counsel.

While district attorneys are selected with some care to their scholarship, their competence and energy to translate both into successful prosecutions, the legal aid attorney is often employed because he could not get work elsewhere or because, emotionally, his heart is in the right place. So it becomes an uneven battle from the beginning.

Too many judges look with contempt upon the efforts of the attorney assigned to the poor, and that attitude is often communicated to the jurors.

Too often, the public in its snobbery of social distance from the criminal courts, unless they have been ripped off or are jurors, has neglected a secret society which has decimated black reputations and lives. One should not assume that all is well, simply because the pillars of the Temple of Justice, in their imitation of Greek architecture, seem to suggest confidence and a clean ethnic.

All of us should pay closer attention to the palaces of justice. If it is true that black men can be expected to be arrested at least once before reaching the age of twenty-five, that ruthless average may reach out for our sons and daughters. I have opened my court to the public and daily have students sitting with me on the bench so they can see the practical side of perjury, lies, cheating, and honest errors.

Some of my learned brothers have deplored this practice and treat me as though I am [*sic*] a fraternity brother who has advertised the secret society's afterdark practices. They suggest that the presence of strangers on the bench presumes to diminish the judge's power, his discretion, and his prestige.

What they really mean is that it may be publicized what goes on in their Greek revival temples of heedless discretion. One judge said to me that if any community groups came down to spy on him, he would have them thrown out. It is only judicial paranoia which can justify the term "spy" simply because a citizen may wish to discover what happens in the courts which their taxes support.

One of Roberta Flack's managers was in a motor accident last winter and had a fractured arm in a cast for some time. While recuperating, he and a companion went into a Yonkers' liquor store. The owner, seeing two black men enter, one with his arm inside his coat, supported by a sling, immediately pressed an emergency button which told the police that there was a robbery in progress.

The police arrived, roughed up the Flack manager, refractured his arm, and arrested both men, charging them with robbery. Miss Flack, matching action to her sense of outrage, chartered buses and loaded them with black citizens to fill the courtroom for the trial. With such an angry and curious census present for the judge to see, he was transformed into a twentieth-century John Brown. He not only acquitted the defendants, but castigated the police for shabby and discriminatory overzealousness. Yonkers and the police are now being sued for the conduct of the gung-ho police.

Until black citizens fill up courtrooms and look closely at the bench and its conduct, that public institution will remain secret in its work and assume that blacks like to be discriminated against in the courts. There will be the additional assumption, as well, that the black public approves the manner of selecting judges.

That "manner," so far, has neglected thousands of qualities which one might wish to see in a judge. Theoretically, a judge is supposed to be endowed with wisdom, learning, impartiality, and the basics of fairness. He is supposed to be emotionally stable, not troubled by psychological disorders, patient, kind, thoughtful, and courteous.

Even as Diogenes searched in vain for an honest man, his philosophical descendants today might well be hard put to discover such a person on the bench. And now, with urban America's problems being almost synonymous with inner-city problems, the blacks should be even more fascinated by the judicial process.

Why are there no more judges?

Why, among, the 100 judges of the Criminal Court in this city, are there only 10 or so who are black, while the defendants who parade before the bench are 85 to 90 percent black?

Why are there only two Puerto Rican judges on that bench?

Why is the court administrator's office all white?

Is this because the whites know all about black rage, black criminal neuroses?

Is it because a white man, Jack Greenberg, is our NAACP Legal Defense Fund leader that we support the theory that a white will have to lift our veil of ignorance and judge us for our black sins?

Is it because so many of us are middle class?

Why is it that black judges become so enthralled by the black robe that they believe that everyone in the courtroom stands because [they enter]?

Why do black judges become distant and superior gods after they ascend the bench?

Why do black judges become autistic on the great debates which derive from the Constitution and stand mute?

Is it because they are happy, satisfied, smug, too upper middle class to identify with those who have not made it?

With preventive detention practiced every day in their courts, by the imposition of bail on the poor which rivals the national debt, why do black judges not cry out and say something?

With professors and researchers writing about racism in the courts and the corruption of justice, why do black judges refuse to rock the boat and demand changes?

Perhaps an excerpt from *Mrs. Wallop,* the Peter DeVries book, may shed some light on this dark judicial diffidence. Examining the American Negro, Mr. DeVries notes that they have progressed from sharecroppers to shareholders. He notes that many of them now have summer homes in Spook (I mean Oak) Bluffs, cottages at Sag Harbour, and sleek yachts in various marinas.

He concludes that the next book written about the suburbanization of the American Negro will have to be entitled *Uncle Tom's Cabin Cruiser.*

One of my fringe benefits from making such remarks is that my learned brothers on the bench do not speak to me.

However, I do have some suggestions for improving the judges on the bench, which will endear me to them even more.

In certain countries in Europe and Egypt, judges are selected from among the most brilliant and promising of the law students. During the last year of their law studies these students are allowed to opt for the profession of judging. They then receive special training for that lofty ideal. American law schools should adopt a similar policy.

Then judges in the urban areas could be trained in ethnic sensitivity, basic psychology of the poor, black history in the United States, to permit some knowledge of black heroes and the reason why there are such and institutional racism in the United States. All of this would be in addition to De Tocqueville and Myrdal. They would then have to become familiar with race, crime, and justice, and the Negro in court, all included in the President's Crime Commission Task Force Report in 1967.

There would be courses in the importance of regarding defendants as individuals and human beings, as opposed to faceless ones to be hurried along through the system.

Topping all of this off would be a period of in-depth exposure to a period of psychoanalysis, to determine whether or not the candidate really possessed the emotional stability and strength to sit in judgment of other humans.

Every graduate of a law school who passes his bar examination in New York must first pass a Committee on Character and Fitness before being admitted to practice. Are character and fitness to be of no consequence when a man aspires to that high honor of the law, the bench?

There is too much cronyism in selecting judges these days. It's the old buddy-buddy politics-as-usual thing. Many judges are selected from a clubhouse where they have distinguished themselves by kissing the behind of the district leader or kingmaker. They are safe designees because they have made no waves and have led a career devoid of merit. They have remained neuter, subservient to power and wholly without imagination. They are no threat to anyone.

When I was sent to the committees by Mayor Lindsay for them to see if I was fit for the bench, the prestige committees looked at my résumé, saw that I had been associated with a Wall Street law firm, and immediately said that I was overqualified for the Criminal Court bench. No one said a word about the fact that I had never had a criminal case in my life.

When I mentioned my utter lack of experience in criminal law, Mayor Lindsay said that was all to the good because a "fresh" approach was needed at court. Several months later he was heard to say that he never meant quite fresh, and I was accused on television of "judicial insensitivity." This is proof certain that I needed the very instruction I have outlined as necessary for judges.

While I always advocate the abolition of prisons as they [are] now run and operated, I realize that this suggestion, in a time of law and order, may result in my confinement to Bellevue. Therefore, I have an alternative suggestion. While we do have prisons, there should be an upgrading of prison personnel. For the most part, our state prisons are located in rural hinterlands. They are filled with urban rejects. Both prisoners and their keepers are strangers to each other, neither knowing very much about the other and each suspecting the worst.

Prisons should be closer to the urban areas which feed them, so that the urban experience is not wholly unknown to the keepers. They should be more open and available to the visits of family and friends. The prisons are now dehumanizing institutions in which the prisoners brood about new crimes and getting even with the society which put them there. They are breeding grounds for a cycle of revenge which produces endless recidivism. . . .

The view from the bench, then, is a sad excitement. One sees the walking dead, hapless in their terminal disease of life. I owe it to my selected profession and the honor of judging, to continue to point out my club's imperfections, in the hope that the attention of the public will be aroused enough to bring about the drastic changes so much needed, if the people are to have a calm confidence in both judges and what they do.

If we do not have radical criminology from the black judges, they can never justify their existence as judges. If we allow our judges, especially our black ones, to be called "your honor," simply because they don the black robe of their high office, then we deserve what we get as the end product. And, if we wish our black judges to be indistinguishable from the white ones, then there is no point in having black ones.

In this season of impeachment rumors in the highest places and fearing that one day soon my head may be upon a platter, I end this reading.

14

A Black District Attorney's View of Criminal Court: An Interview with Mr. Howard Stewart, Assistant District Attorney, Dauphin County, Pennsylvania*

Mr. Stewart's experience as a black assistant district attorney is explored. The impact of being a black state's attorney is discussed in terms of defendants' perceptions and judicial sentencing. The significance of race and economic status to the courtroom process is also examined, with an emphasis on bail decisions. Observations on the unique problems encountered by blacks in law schools conclude the interview.

Question: What is the extent of your experience as a practicing State's Attorney?

Answer: Despite the fact that my experience is limited to 19 months, the amount of actual experience in terms of handling cases, and I mean major cases—felony cases, murder cases—is quite extensive. As an example, I would say that in my 19 months here I've probably tried at least 25 jury trials and I can't even begin to tell you the number of trials to a judge or bench trials that I've tried. By contrast, a D.A. I know in Philadelphia, after four years in the district attorney's office, had tried 13 jury trial cases and of that 13, I believe, he was about to try his second felony trial. So even though Dauphin County is a rather small county, because the crime rate here is the highest in the state, I think my 19 months has given me a considerable amount of experience.

Question: How does the fact that you are a black assistant district attorney affect the cases you litigate?

Answer: One thing I would say is that my race has, in many cases, worked to my advantage. For example, a large number of the defendants here in Dauphin County are black. But I would like to think that I am straight down the line no matter what the race of the defendant is. When I go to the bar before the judge and ask for a maximum sentence for a black

* Interview conducted by Daniel Georges-Abeyie on December 14, 1983.

219

defendant who has been convicted of armed robbery, I have no qualms if the objective facts of the case call for such a sentence. I have a great amount of success with sentences in this county, which means that I've received extremely good sentences when I've asked for them—robbery cases in particular. But what I think being black has done for me, and perhaps the citizens of Dauphin County, is that, in an indirect sense, I have been able to bring pressure on judges to be fair in their sentencing. For example, I argue a robbery case involving a black defendant and, given the facts, recommend the maximum sentence; the judge agrees. A term or month later I argue the same offense before the same judge, but this time the defendant is white. Can the judge, (who may have, in my opinion, a tendency to be more lenient toward white defendants) given the same offense and similar circumstances, ignore my recommendation for the maximum sentence and give the white defendant a lighter sentence? It's not likely, unless the judge is heedless of the types of censure such inconsistent, seemingly racially motivated decisions could elicit. Summing this all up, I've had success in having whites and blacks treated pretty much the same. Generally, I think that my being black doesn't have any real effect on my job, or in relation to how defendants view me, but I do think that it puts pressure on the judge to be fair.

Question: Are blacks treated differently than white defendants in Dauphin County?

Answer: Generally speaking, I would say that blacks seem to receive stiffer sentences. This is a general observation, however. Sentences are supposed to be individualized, and I can't say that every black first offender receives some kind of jail sentence and every white offender does not—that's simply not the case. But my basic feeling is that blacks do tend to receive harsher sentences.

Question: From your observations, do you think that some judges' decisions may be influenced by interracial factors that are tied to cases involving violent acts?

Answer: Yes. Take rape cases, for example. When a white woman is raped by a black man the chances of conviction are greater than if a white individual were the defendant. This is a well-known reality, and is supported by statistics. In the case of murder where the victim is a white woman who is the girlfriend of a black defendant, chances are that's murder three; and if you don't watch out, you may get voluntary manslaughter out of that—I don't care if the defendant poisoned her. So, when the crime is particularly violent, I think the race factor does play an important role.

Question: Have you encountered any unique problems being a black district attorney?

Answer: I am treated a little differently, especially in terms of the sentencing process as I mentioned earlier. This has been noticed by the other attorneys in my office. Also, we have a special career criminal unit here in Harrisburg that argues to get stiffer sentences for repeat offenders. Quite frankly, I generally seem to have better success at sentencing than this unit. I attribute this success to the pressure that my being black puts on the judge in terms of equitable sentencing. A minor problem I've encountered is the accusation that I strike blacks off juries, but that is simply unfounded. I am also concerned about my reputation in the black community because I think that people who are not crime victims and do not have contact with the courts tend to think I might be a bit arrogant because of the authority I have. Finally, I am more-or-less known as the *black* attorney, and that offends me. That is, people are more aware of me as the black district attorney instead of just being a D.A., but other than that I feel comfortable around the courthouse.

Question: Do you think there is a black perspective in terms of prosecuting, as Milton Allen, a Baltimore district attorney, contends? That is, Mr. Allen maintains that a black judge should be consciously and psychologically black on the bench. This doesn't mean that he should bend the law, but that he should be aware of the many types of problems that black defendants may have. Do you agree?

Answer: Yes. We have a black judge in Dauphin County, Clarence C. Morrison. He does seem to be much more fair than some other judges in seeing that minority members are treated equitably in court. For example, Judge Morrison recently heard a case involving a few upper-class defendants who had been convicted of some sort of larceny from businesses they were involved in. These men probably had two or three of the more well-known and costly attorneys in town come in and plead their case on a first offense basis. Usually in a case of theft on a first offense, depending upon how much is involved, you can have your case disposed of through an ARD program, which is probation. But in regard to this case, the judge, without hesitation, decided that these men violated a sacred trust of sorts and sentenced them to a state institution—which in my opinion was more than justified. That day closed with the judge putting on probation a Spanish defendant who obviously didn't have any money who had also made a theft, but it was a theft from a supermarket or something like that. I feel confident in saying that had that been another courtroom in all likelihood those white defendants at the beginning of the day would probably have been put on probation, and that Spanish shoplifter, who did have a prior record I believe, would probably have gotten time in a county jail.

Question: Many commentators contend that extra-legal considerations such as economic class and race bear heavily on the quality of justice an individual receives. Do you agree that the use of excessive bail has resulted in the imprisonment of large numbers of blacks and others incarcerated without trial in the county jails and prisons? Do you agree, in other words, with Judge Bruce Wright, a judge on the supreme bench in New York City, that jails have become debtors prisons and that minorities are disproportionately sent to these jails?

Answer: I've just been assigned the bail program here in the office, which means I set bail for people who are picked up off the street. I'll be quite honest with you. I don't care what the race of the individual is, I'm pretty hard on setting bail. That is, normally I am placed in the situation of setting bail for someone who has failed to show for court. I don't set bail on the first instance. So normally we're talking about a situation where an individual been given a court date and has failed to show. He's been running around for maybe eight or nine months and has not bothered to contact the DA's office to tell us about an address change or whatever—minor offenses for the most part. But it is my position that the administration of justice cannot be taken so lightly by the defendant. I realize the fifth amendment doesn't require the defendant to implicate himself in a crime. But I don't think it allows him to roam the streets free when as part of his bail he's required to give us notice of his address. I don't think bails are set that high in this county because someone is black. I certainly don't. I can't tell you the race of the last eight people whose bail I've set. But I can tell you that I've probably been very hard on those last eight people. But again, it is only because they've failed to show and the purpose of bail is to assure that you show at your next hearing and sometimes setting bail at $2,000 for one man is prohibitive. He's not going to make it. You just know he's not going to make it. We have a bail program where we have a gentleman at the prison who monitors the prison population and as that population fills he then goes through the people who are there and finds people who are not regarded as high risk releases—someone who writes bad checks for instance, an individual who has written a bad check may find himself in jail because I've set his bail at $2,000 and will not let him out on his own recognizance. He must post 10 percent of that bail. Within a month or two, if the prison population fills, I may be faced with a request by this gentleman who controls the population to now make that $2,000 ROR. ROR doesn't require him to post any percentage and would thus permit him to leave the prison. He, having been in jail for maybe two to three months, perhaps I'd be more than willing to make it ROR, but I would initially ask for some kind of posting of bail. Thus, I would agree to some extent that an individual's economic status can affect the meting of justice. Let me add, though, that I don't think the issue is strictly whether you do or do not have money. That is, what the money does do for you is to allow an attorney to better prepare your case. Most of the minorities that come into Dauphin County are represented by public defenders. A public defender may have five, six, or seven different cases to prepare for a given court term. He cannot give equal attention to each of those cases, so they have to be prioritized. He'll probably give more attention to the cases that will go to the jury. A defendant who is going to come in and plead guilty will probably receive the least amount of attention. He may not even be interviewed by the public defender until the day he comes in to plea. The problem is that you need your lawyer to be as prepared in a guilty plead as you do in a trial by jury because you're going to admit your guilt and essentially throw yourself on the mercy of the court. A person with money can hire a private attorney and depending on the amount of money he is willing to spend, make that attorney spend so many number of hours preparing his case. So if a defendant is wealthy and he is going to come in and plead guilty to something, he can afford to have a lawyer explore his background, explore other alternatives to incarceration and then present them to a judge. For example, the person may have an alcohol problem. His attorney can afford to go and have a doctor examine the individual and come in and tell us that he really is an alcoholic; this takes money because doctors aren't going to come over here for nothing to tell us that the defendant has an alcohol problem. Those kind of things have to be taken into consideration in sentencing. It's not that minority people don't have the same types of problems, it's just that the person who is asked to speak on their behalf is not paid the fees necessary to do a lot of outside research or investigation. So in that sense, whether you're guilty or not, if you have the money you can get a well-stated case. And there is no question that a well-stated case may make the difference between a life sentence on a first-degree murder and a ten-year sentence on a manslaughter conviction. I think that's where money makes a difference.

Question: If you were dean of a law school and you had power to change the structure of the law program, would you incorporate any courses that dealt with blacks or minorities?

Answer: I think I would strive instead to include more minority people in the program. That would seem to be a more effective approach than simply offering courses dealing with minorities and have only minorities take the courses, which is what I generally believes happens. My experience as the only black law student in the program leads me to think that an active program to encourage minorities to apply is *the* way to open a career in law for these people and to sensitize the legal professional to the diverse cultures that comprise society.

15

Racial Disparities in the Criminal Justice System: Executive Summary of Rand Institute Study, 1983*

Joan Petersilia

Over the last three decades, social science researchers have repeatedly addressed the possibility of racial discrimination in the criminal justice system, but it remains an open question. Because of problems with data and methodology, no study has established definitively that the system does or does not discriminate against racial minorities.

This two-year study approached the issue by comparing the treatment of white and minority offenders at key decision points in the system, from arrest through release from custody, and by investigating possible racial differences in criminal behavior that might influence that treatment. It attempted to overcome the material and methodological limitations of earlier research in two ways: (1) By using both official records and information from a large sample of prison inmates about aspects of their background and criminal behavior; and (2) by using multiple regression techniques when possible to analyze the resulting data, techniques that allow the analyst to control for other factors besides race that might affect the system's handling of minority offenders.

The study was supported by the National Institute of Corrections, Bureau of Prisons, U.S. Department of Justice. The report should be of interest to criminal justice researchers who are investigating the system's operations, and to policymakers who are looking for mechanisms that will ensure equal treatment for offenders, regardless of race.

*Prepared under Grant No. EB-2 from the National Institute of Corrections, Bureau of Prisons, U.S. Department of Justice, June 1983. Because the study deals with a complex and sensitive issue, the report describes the data, methodology, and findings in considerable, technical detail. To accommodate readers who are more concerned with policy than with research, the following is the Executive Summary of the study's conclusions and policy implications. Reprinted with permission.

I. INTRODUCTION AND SUMMARY

Critics of the criminal justice system view the arrest and imprisonment rates for blacks and other minorities as evidence of racial discrimination. Although the laws governing the system contain no racial bias, these critics claim that where the system allows discretion to criminal justice officials in handling offenders, discrimination can, and often does, enter in. They argue that blacks, for example, who make up 12 percent of the national population, could not possibly commit 48 percent of the crime—but that is exactly what their arrest and imprisonment rates imply. Defenders of the system argue that the statistics do not lie, and that the system does not discriminate but simply reacts to the prevalence of crime in the black community.

Statistics on street crime lend support to this argument. An astonishing 51 percent of black males living in large cities are arrested at least once for an index crime during their lives, compared with only 14 percent of white males.[1] Fully 18 percent of black males serve time, either as juveniles or adults, compared with 3 percent of white males (Greenfeld, 1981). Blacks are also disproportionately victimized by crime: Murder is the leading cause of death for young black males, and is also high for young black females.

Crime, then, is a fact of life in the ghetto. Blacks and other minorities must deal with crime and the criminal justice system much more than whites. Moreover, as crime rates continue to rise, the nation's overcrowded prisons find their economic and operational problems compounded by racial problems. In many prisons, racial gangs maneuver for dominance and victimize racial minorities—and whites are often a minority. These conditions have given rise to the question of racial discrimination; to address it, our study pursued three objectives:

(1) To discover whether there is any evidence that the criminal justice system systematically treats minorities differently from whites;
(2) If there is such evidence, to see whether that treatment represents discrimination or is simply a reaction to the amount of crime committed by minorities; and
(3) To discuss the policy implications for correcting any bias.

METHODOLOGY AND DATA

Social science researchers have been addressing the question of discrimination in the system for more than thirty years, but have failed to reach consensus on almost every point. Studies have offered evidence both for and against racial bias in arrest rates, prosecution, conviction, sentencing, corrections, and parole. There are many reasons for these contradictions. Some studies have data bases too small to permit any generalization. Others have failed to control for enough (or any) of the other factors that might account for apparent racial discrimination. Most studies have looked at only one or two levels of the system. And no studies have examined criminals' pre-arrest contact with the system—a point at which many believe the greatest racial differences in treatment exist.

We attempted to overcome those shortcomings by using data from official records and prisoner self-reports, by examining the evidence for discrimination throughout the criminal justice system, and by controlling for the major variables that might create the appearance of discrimination. Whenever the data were sufficient to do so, we used multiple regression analyses of system decisions and criminal behavior to control for the most obvious variables. In the comparisons, then, the offenders were somewhat "interchangeable" except for race.

The study data came from two sources: the California Offender-Based Transaction Statistics (OBTS) for 1980, and the Rand Inmate Survey (RIS). The OBTS is a computerized information system maintained by the California Bureau of Criminal Statistics that tracks the processing of offenders from arrest to sentencing. The RIS consists of data obtained from self-reports of approximately 1400 male prison inmates in California, Michigan, and Texas.

MAJOR FINDINGS

We found some racial differences in both criminal behavior and the treatment of offenders in the states involved. (See Table S.1.)

Racial Differences in Case Processing

Although the case processing system generally treated offenders similarly, we found racial differences at two key points: Minority suspects were more likely than whites to be released after arrest; however, after a felony conviction, minority offenders were more likely than whites to be given longer sentences and to be put in prison instead of jail.

Racial Differences in Post-Sentencing Treatment

In considering participation in treatment and work programs and the reasons inmates gave for not participating, we found no statistically significant differences that implied discrimination against minorities in corrections. However, in looking at length of sentence served, we found significant racial differences in California and Texas, but none in Michigan. These findings held even when we controlled for other major factors that might affect release decisions. In California prisons, blacks and Hispanics serve longer sentences than whites—largely, however, because of racial differences in court-imposed sentences. In Texas, minorities also serve longer sentences—appreciably longer than their court-imposed minimum terms. In Michigan the reverse is true. There, blacks enter prison with longer sentences than whites, but serve roughly the same time.

Racial Similarities in Crime Commission Rates and Probability of Arrest

The high post-arrest release rates for minorities do not indicate that police overarrest minorities *in proportion to the kind and amount of crime they actually commit.* We found that annualized crime commission rates were much the same among white and minority criminals. Moreover, there are no consistent, statistically significant, racial differences in the probability of arrest, given that an offender has committed a crime.

Racial Differences in Offender Behavior

There are some evident racial differences in criminal motivation, weapons use, and prison behavior, but most are not statistically significant. Blacks rated economic distress higher than other motivations, but not significantly more so than other groups. Whites rated hedonistic motives for crime significantly higher than blacks or Hispanics. In weapons use, there were only two significant findings. Hispanics were much more likely than the other groups to use knives, and black burglars were less likely to be armed. Racial differences were strongest in prison behavior. In Texas, blacks had a higher rate of infractions; in California, whites did.

CONCLUSIONS

These findings raise some important questions and identify some patterns that, together with other research, suggest tentative conclusions.

Disparities in Release Rates

Because we found that minorities do not have a higher probability of arrest, the release rates might be explained by evidentiary problems. Prior research indicates that prosecutors do have greater problems making minority cases "stick" because victims often have difficulty identifying minority suspects. Moreover, minority victims and witnesses often refuse or fail to cooperate after an arrest is made. Some racial differences in release rates may also result from the fact that police more often arrest white suspects than minority suspects "on warrant." Since the evidentiary criteria for issuing warrants approximate those for filing charges, it seems reasonable that fewer whites than minorities would be released without charges.

Disparities in Sentencing and Time Served

Controlling for the other major factors that might influence sentencing and time served, we found that minorities receive harsher sentences and serve longer in prison—other things being equal. However, racial differences in plea bargaining and jury trials may explain some of the difference in length and type of sentence. Plea bargaining resolves a higher percentage of felony cases involving white defendants, whereas jury trials resolve a higher percentage of cases involving minorities. Although plea bargaining ensures conviction, it also virtually guarantees a reduced charge or a lighter sentence, or both; conviction by a jury usually results in more severe sentencing.

Differences in sentencing and time served may also reflect the kinds of information that judges and parole boards use to make their decisions. Research has found that in 80 percent of cases, judges follow the sentencing recommendation made in the probation officer's pre-sentence investigation report (PSR). Moreover, in many states, the PSR becomes the heart of the parole board's case-summary file. These reports are usually very comprehensive "portraits" of offenders, containing personal and socioeconomic information, as well as any details the probation officer can get on their criminal habits and attitudes. This information can be, and evidently is, assessed for indicators of recidivism—that is, traits related to the probability that a released offender will return to crime. Blacks and Hispanics may have more such traits than whites (e.g., past unemployment).

The relation between court-imposed sentence and length of time served supports these conjectures. Minorities *received* longer minimum sentences than whites in all three states. However, that sentence had varying effects on time finally *served.* In California, racial differences in sentences served corresponded roughly to the differences in court-imposed sentences. In Texas, time served was appreciably longer for minorities than for whites— and appreciably longer than the court-imposed sentence. In Michigan, the reverse was true: There, blacks received longer court-imposed sentences than whites, but served roughly the same time.

California has a determinate sentencing policy, which explains the relation of sentence imposed to sentence served there. But the contrast be-tween Texas and Michigan can perhaps be explained by parole practices. Texas has a highly individualized process that incorporates the full range of an inmate's criminal history and personal and socioeconomic character-istics. In contrast, Michigan has adopted a risk-assessment formula for parole decisions that relies primarily on indicators of personal culpability such as juvenile record, violence of conviction crime, and prison behavior. This practice evidently avoids racial disparities in time served—and may overcome the racial disparity in court-imposed sentences.

Nevertheless, overcoming racial disparities in time served is not the definitive objective of parole boards. Their primary responsibility is to decide whether releasing an inmate will endanger society. By ignoring socioeconomic and other extralegal indicators of recidivism, they may reduce racial disparities in parole decisions, but they may do so at the expense of putting probable recidivists back on the street.

Indicators of Recidivism

If recidivism indicators are valid and explain racial disparities in sentencing and time served, the system is not discriminating. It is simply reflecting the larger racial problems of society, and it can do little about the overre-presentation of minorities in prison. However, the RIS data and some other research contain suggestions that the recidivism indicators may not be so "racially neutral" after all.

Minorities are overrepresented in the criminal population, relative to their proportion of the national population. However, they do constitute roughly half the criminal population. Thus, within that population, their characteristics should have no more effect on empirically derived indica-tors of recidivism than the characteristics of white recidivists—unless minorities have higher crime commission rates. We have found, however, that minorities and whites have similar crime commission rates, and other research has established that whites and minorities have approximately the same probability of recidivism. It is apparent that some indicators of recidivism overlap with race in ways that deserve investigation.

IMPLICATIONS FOR FUTURE RESEARCH AND POLICY

These findings and conclusions suggest some important research needs and policy initiatives. Among the research priorities are:

- Documenting the reasons for post-arrest/pre-filing release rates and controlling for race of the offender and type of arrest;

- Analyzing post-arrest problems with witnesses to discover whether and how the race of the suspect and/or of the witness affects cooperation;
- Determining the relation of plea bargaining and jury trials to race, and why minority defendants are less likely to plea-bargain;
- Establishing the reasons why minorities receive and serve longer sentences, paying particular attention to effects that length of court-imposed sentences, gang-related activities in prison, and prison infractions have on time served.

Although these and other issues deserve research attention, we believe that understanding why recidivism indicators more often work against minorities has a particularly high priority. The system is moving to heavier reliance on these indicators precisely to render sentencing and parole decisions more objective. Paradoxically, just the opposite may result if, as we suspect, some of these indicators overlap with race in ways largely unrelated to recidivism.

Definitive policy recommendations will not be possible until some of these research tasks are completed, but three interim policy initiatives may be useful:

- Police and prosecutors should take into account the obstacles to filing charges after minority arrests, particularly the problems with witnesses, and try to find ways of ensuring that pre-arrest identifications will hold firm.
- Plea bargaining needs close monitoring, perhaps by a single deputy, for indications that minority defendants are consistently offered less attractive bargains than whites.
- Until the quality and predictive weight of recidivism indicators can be tested, probation officers, judges, and parole boards should give more weight to indicators of personal culpability than to indicators based on group classifications, such as education and family status.

Although this study shows that minorities are treated differently at a few points in the criminal justice system, it has not found evidence that this results from widespread and consistent racial prejudice in the system. Racial disparities seem to have developed because procedures were adopted without systematic attempts to find out whether they might affect different races differently. Consequently, future research and policy should be concerned with looking behind the scenes at the key actors in the system and their decisionmaking process, primarily at the kind of information they use, how valid it is, and whether its use affects particular racial groups unfairly.

II. BACKGROUND, DATA, AND METHODOLOGY

BACKGROUND

The criminal justice system allows policemen, prosecutors, judges, and parole boards a great deal of discretion in handling most criminal cases. The resulting statistics on minorities in prison have convinced many people that this discretion leads to discrimination. Figure S.1 provides a provocative insight into this issue. Looking at the four top crimes, we find little disparity between the percentage of blacks arrested and the percentage serving prison terms for the crime. These figures suggest that between arrest and sentencing, at any rate, the criminal justice system is simply reacting to the relative number of blacks in the arrest population; however, these violent crimes allow agents of the system less discretion in handling or sentencing. When the crime is murder, forcible rape, robbery, or aggravated assault, a judge has less latitude in deciding about probation or sentence length, or whether the sentence will be served in jail or prison—no matter what color a man is.

Disparity crops up when we move down to lesser crimes. The most striking example is larceny: Blacks account for only 30 percent of the arrest population, but for 51 percent of those serving time for larceny. Why the disparity? One explanation may be that judges can exercise more discretion in dealing with offenders convicted of lesser crimes. If so, the numbers lend some credibility to the charge that discretion leads to discrimination.

Social science researchers have repeatedly addressed this issue, but for every study that finds discrimination, another refutes it. The reasons are various: limited data bases, inability to examine pre-arrest and post-sentencing experiences of offenders, and failure to control for other significant variables.

METHODOLOGY AND STUDY DATA

As described in Sec. I under "Methodology and Data," this study had the advantage of two rich data bases: the OBTS (Offender-Based Transaction Statistics) in California for 1980, and correctional records of prisoners who participated in the RIS (Rand Inmate Survey), which was also the source of the self-reports. This information allowed us to analyze offender behavior and system decisionmaking from crime commission through release from prison.

The OBTS is a computerized information system maintained by the California Bureau of Criminal Statistics. It tracks offenders from point of entry into the criminal justice system to the point of sentencing (or presentencing release). The data cover dispositions that occur in a given year resulting from adult felony arrests made in that year or previous years. Once an offender enters the system, a number of social and legal variables are recorded: sex, race, age, prior record, criminal status, and the original arrest offense. The OBTS also records the date of arrest and offense, conviction offense, date and point of disposition, type of proceeding, type of final sentence, and length of prison sentence.

With the OBTS data, the study could not only track racial differences in case disposition from arrest to sentencing, but could also control for factors such as type of crime and prior record. Both of these factors are essential in understanding whether severity of sentence in *average* statistics indicates racial discrimination.

The RIS consists of data obtained from a self-administered questionnaire completed by approximately 1380 male prison inmates in California, Michigan, and Texas in 1978. Together, these three states house 22 percent of the national population of state prisons. In each state, the survey procedures produced a sample of inmates whose characteristics approximated the statewide intake of male prisoners. The self-reports elicited information about inmates' crimes, arrests, criminal motivations, drug and alcohol use, prior criminal record, prison experience, and the like.

Because self-reports inevitably raise questions about the respondents' veracity, the survey was constructed to allow for both internal and external checks on validity. The questionnaire included pairs of questions, widely separated, that asked for essentially the same information about crimes the respondents had committed and about other topics. This made it possible to check for internal quality (inconsistency, omission, and confusion). Over 83 percent of the respondents filled out the questionnaire accurately, completely, and consistently. The responses were not anonymous, and the official records served not only as part of the analysis but also as an external check on the validity of the self-reports. Although the external check revealed more inconsistencies than the internal check, 59 percent of the respondents had an external error rate of less than 20 percent. However, for most disparities, the records were as questionable as the respondents' veracity. Records are often missing or incomplete, through no fault of the prisoners.

The cross-checking capability also permitted comparisons between inmate characteristics and the quality of the self-reports. One might suspect that some types of people would be less truthful than others. However, an earlier Rand study using the same data found that, with minor exceptions, such individual characteristics as conviction crime, self-image, activity in fraud or "illegal cons," and sociodemographic characteristics, were unrelated to the quality and validity of the response. It also showed no racial differences in validity based on external checks. However, the self-reports of black respondents had lower internal quality than whites' or Hispanics' reports, primarily because of inconsistency and confusion rather than omissions (Chaiken and Chaiken, 1982).

The RIS data permitted us to examine racial differences in crime commission rates—as opposed to arrest rates—and the probability of arrest. This information gave the study a considerable edge over much prior research because it provided a standard for assessing charges that minorities are overarrested. It also enabled us to examine questions of discrimination in corrections and length of sentence served, and of racial differences in crime motivation, weapon use, and in-prison behavior.

III. MAJOR FINDINGS

As Table S.1 indicated, we found some racial differences in the criminal justice system's *handling* of offenders, but few statistically significant racial differences in *criminal behavior.* However, strong trends in some of the data raise important issues for policy and future research.

CASE PROCESSING: ARREST THROUGH SENTENCING

Each year, more than 1.5 million adults in the United States enter the felony disposition process. This process, beginning with an arrest and ending with release or sentencing, is the heart of the criminal justice system. Although a great many people enter the process, very few remain at the end: About 30 percent are dismissed before the preliminary hearing; less than half of those who go to court are convicted; and less than 5 percent of those convicted are sentenced to prison (Greenwood, 1982).

Analysis of the OBTS Data

As for racial differences in the disposition process, the OBTS data revealed an interesting pattern in California. As Table S.2 shows, at the front end of the process, the system seems to treat white offenders more severely and minority offenders more "leniently"; at the back end, the reverse is true.

White suspects are somewhat more likely than minority suspects to be arrested on warrant, and considerably less likely to be released without charges. Whites are also more likely than blacks or Hispanics to have felony charges filed. However, a greater percentage of whites arrested on felony charges are subsequently charged with misdemeanors, while blacks and Hispanics are less likely to have the seriousness of their cases thus reduced.

Once charged, offenders of all races have about the same chance of being convicted of a felony, but white defendants are more likely than minorities to be convicted by plea bargain. In contrast, minority defendants are more likely than whites to have their felony cases tried by jury. Although plea bargaining, by definition, ensures conviction, it also ensures a reduced charge or a lighter sentence, or both. Moreover, prior research indicates that defendants receive harsher sentences after convictions by juries. These differences may contribute to the racial difference in sentencing. The study found that after a misdemeanor conviction, white defendants had a greater chance than minority defendants of getting probation instead of jail. After a felony conviction, minority defendants were somewhat more likely to get prison instead of jail sentences.

These aggregate findings treat all felonies as if they were the same. If minority defendants had committed more serious felony offenses and had more serious prior records, we would expect their treatment to be more severe. Actually, minorities in the 1980 OBTS did have more serious prior records; a greater proportion of them had been charged with violent crime; and a greater number were on probation or parole. However, by controlling for these factors using multiple regression techniques, we determined that the racial differences in post-arrest and sentencing treatment still held.[2] White arrestees were more likely than minorities to be officially charged following arrest. Black arrestees were more likely to have their cases dismissed by either police or prosecutor. After charges were filed, the conviction rates were similar across the races, but 4 percent more black defendants than whites or Hispanics were sentenced to prison.

Analysis of Court-Imposed Sentence Using RIS Data

Although the scope of our study and our data did not permit us to analyze case processing in all three of the RIS states, it did allow us to compare data on length of court-imposed sentences. And we preferred to use data that would yield findings on possible racial disparities in three states rather than only one. Regression analyses for each state revealed that minorities do receive longer sentences. Controlling for defendant's age, conviction crime, and prior record, we found that minority status alone accounted for 1 to 7 additional months in court-imposed sentences—relative to sentences imposed on white defendants.

CORRECTIONS AND LENGTH OF SENTENCE SERVED

From arrest to sentencing, the system duly records most major decisions involving offenders. Consequently, it is rather easy to see racial differences in handling. However, once a person is sentenced to prison, he is potentially subject to a range of decisions that are not systematically recorded. Prison guards and staff make decisions that strongly influence the quality of an offender's time in prison, and parole boards and other corrections officials decide how long that time lasts. The possibility of discrimination enters into all these decisions, but length of time served is the only one certain to be recorded. In other words, corrections is a closed world in which discrimination could flourish.

That charge has frequently been brought against the system, and the steady increase of prison racial problems makes it imperative to examine the treatment that different races receive in prison and at parole. We examined prison treatment and length of sentence served using the RIS and the official records of our sample, where available. Our analysis revealed some racial differences for participation in work and treatment programs, but they were largely determined by the prisoners, not by guards or staff.

To create a larger framework for assessing possible discrimination, the study established criteria for identifying inmates who needed education, vocational training, and alcohol and drug treatment programs. We then compared the percentage who had need with the percentage that participated for each racial group.

Although there were no significant racial differences in the overall rate of program participation, there were some differences in participation, relative to need. In all three states, participation matched need most closely for education. In all three states, a greater percentage of minorities than of whites were identified as having high need for education. However, in Texas, blacks received significantly less education treatment. Moreover in two of the study states, blacks had a significantly higher need for vocational training than whites or Hispanics, but did not have significantly higher participation rates. Compared with the other racial groups, blacks who needed alcohol treatment had a significantly lower participation rate.

Nevertheless, the reasons respondents gave for *not participating* suggested that minorities were discriminating against the programs, not vice versa. Prisoners most often said they were "too busy" or "didn't need" to participate; few said that they did not participate because staff discouraged them. The findings for work assignments were similar.

We found, however, that although minorities received roughly equal treatment in prison, race consistently made a difference when it came time for release. In Texas, blacks and Hispanics consistently served longer time than whites—and the disparity was appreciably larger than the disparity in court-imposed sentences. In California, blacks served slightly longer sentences, but the disparity largely reflected the original sentencing differences. In Michigan, the parole process evidently worked in favor of blacks.

Although their court-imposed sentences were considerably longer than those of whites, they did not actually serve longer (see Table S.3).

CRIME COMMISSION RATES AND PROBABILITY OF ARREST

To estimate whether minorities are overarrested, *relative to the number of crimes they actually commit,* analysts need comparable "pre-arrest" information—variety of crimes committed, incidence of crime or crime commission rates, and the probability of arrest—for white and minority arrestees. Although official records provide information on the crimes for which offenders are arrested and convicted, they provide no information on how many other crimes and types of crimes these people commit. To overcome this problem, we used data from the RIS on the actual types and number of crimes that offenders reported committing in the 15-month period preceding their current imprisonment. Inmates also reported on the number of arrests for each kind of crime they had committed during the same period. Using this information, we estimated each offender's annualized crime rate. Our purpose was to estimate separately the range of crime types in the different racial groups, the crime-commission rates for individuals in those groups, and then to estimate the probability that a single crime would result in arrest for members of that group. We found strong evidence that *in proportion to the kind and amount of crime they commit,* minorities are not being overarrested.[3]

There are racial differences in the range of crime *types* committed:

- More Hispanics reported committing personal crimes—both personal robberies and aggravated assault.
- More whites and Hispanics reported involvement in both drug dealing and burglary.
- Significantly more whites committed forgery and credit card and auto thefts.

We found few consistent, statistically significant, differences in *crime commission rates* among the racial groups. However, there were differences in rates for two particular crimes.

- Blacks reported committing fewer burglaries than whites or Hispanics.
- Hispanics reported fewer frauds and swindles than whites or blacks.
- Black and white offenders reported almost identical rates of robberies, grand larcenies, and auto thefts.

● Black and white offenders were involved in more drug deals than Hispanics, but the differences were not statistically significant.

That last finding illustrates the difference between range of criminality and incidence of crime. The findings on range indicate that more Hispanics than blacks reported being involved in at least one drug deal. However, the annualized crime rates, which represent incidence, indicate that once involved in drug dealing, blacks committed more of it than Hispanics did.

Even though minorities are not overarrested relative to the number of crimes they commit, it is still possible that they have a higher *probability* than whites of being arrested for those crimes. Critics of the system have argued that this explains why blacks are "overrepresented" in the arrest and prison populations. We found, however, that the probability of being arrested for a crime is extremely low regardless of race. For example, only 6 percent of the burglaries, 21 percent of the business robberies, 5 percent of the forgeries, and less than 1 percent of the drug sales reported by these offenders resulted in arrest. This finding held for all racial groups. We found no statistically significant racial differences in arrest probability for the crimes we studied with the exception of personal robbery. For personal robbery, blacks and Hispanics did report suffering more arrests relative to the number of crimes they committed.

MOTIVATION, WEAPON USE, AND PRISON BEHAVIOR

Motivation, weapon use, and prison behavior seem likely to influence the impression a prisoner makes on probation officers, judges, and parole boards. Using RIS data, we examined these characteristics for racial differences that might help explain the differences we observed in sentencing and time served. The statistically significant differences were few and not very helpful in explaining those decisions.

All three racial groups rated economic distress as the primary motive for committing crime, with "high times" second, and "temper" third. However, there was only one statistically significant difference in motivation: Whites rated "high times" much higher than blacks and Hispanics did. Nevertheless, there were some other, suggestive, differences. Blacks rated economic distress considerably higher than high times, while whites rated it only slightly higher. This suggests that socioeconomic conditions among blacks may be more consistently related to crime than they are among whites. That comes as no particular surprise; but if probation officers, judges, and parole boards see unemployment as an indicator of recidivism —rather than as a mitigating circumstance in crime—blacks or any unemployed offenders are likely to receive harsher sentences and serve longer.

In weapons use, the data revealed a few clear racial differences, but if those differences influence sentencing or parole decisions, they do so inconsistently. Hispanics are more likely than whites to be sent to prison and to stay there longer, and Hispanics show a statistically significant preference for using knives in all crimes. Moreover, they indicated a greater tendency to seriously injure their victims. In contrast, the proportion of blacks in prison for burglary is considerably higher than the proportion of blacks arrested for that crime (see Fig. S.1). Yet, in our sample, blacks were the least likely to be armed during burglaries. Indeed, they were less likely than whites to use guns and less likely than Hispanics to use knives. If these differences indicate that blacks are less violent and, perhaps, less "professional" than the other groups, probation officers and judges apparently do not recognize it. Our findings on prison violence raise similarly conflicting suggestions.

The percentage of inmates with behavioral infractions differs markedly across states—significantly for five of the seven infraction types we studied. We therefore examined each state separately. Racial differences were pronounced for prison behavior. However, in all three states, age was most strongly, and negatively, correlated with higher infractions. Younger prisoners in all three states got into the most trouble. After age came race, but not consistently for all states. In California, white inmates had the highest infraction rate; in Texas, blacks did. The high-rate infractors had the following profiles:

- California: a young white inmate who has had limited exposure to treatment programs, and who currently has no prison work assignment.
- Michigan: A young inmate serving for nonviolent crime.
- Texas: A young black inmate with few serious convictions, who has had limited exposure to treatment programs and currently has no prison work assignment.

Racial differences in prison behavior had no apparent relation to length of sentence served. In California, whites have significantly higher infraction rates than blacks. In Texas, the reverse is true. Yet, in both states, blacks serve longer sentences. (In Michigan, where there were no statistically significant racial differences in prison behavior, race also had no bearing on length of time served.)

Having looked at the criminal justice system's treatment of offenders and at offenders' behavior, we have still been unable to account for racial differences in post-arrest release rates, in sentencing, and in some portion of time served. Section IV presents some conclusions drawn from our findings and from other research that may explain these differences.

IV. CONCLUSIONS OF THE STUDY

We again advise the reader that, whenever the data were sufficient to do so, our analyses of system decisions and criminal behavior controlled for the most obvious variables that could reasonably account for apparent racial differences. In these comparisons, then, our offenders are rather "interchangeable" except for race. We also want to stress again that both our findings and our conclusions reflect data from only three states. Further, our self-report data come from prisoners, and conclusions drawn from those data are not applicable to the criminal population at large.

EXPLAINING DISPARITIES IN CASE PROCESSING AND TIME SERVED

At most major decision points, the criminal justice system does not discriminate against minorities. However, race does affect post-arrest release, length and type of sentence imposed, and length of sentence served.

Our analysis of the RIS data found that minorities are not overrepresented in the arrest population, *relative to the number of crimes they actually commit,* nor are they more likely than whites to be arrested for those crimes. Nevertheless, the OBTS analysis raised a question that the study could not answer: If blacks and Hispanics are not being overarrested, why are police and prosecutors so much more likely to let them go without filing charges? One possibility is that the police more often arrest minorities on "probable-cause" evidence that subsequently fails to meet the filing standard of "evidence beyond a reasonable doubt."

Prior research may shed some light on this phenomenon. Earlier studies have shown that arrests depend heavily on witnesses' or victims' identifying or carefully describing the suspect (Greenwood, Petersilia, Chaiken, 1978). Prosecutors may have a more difficult time making cases against minorities "beyond a reasonable doubt" because of problems with victim and witness identifications. Frequently, witnesses or victims who were supportive at the arrest stage become less cooperative as the case proceeds:

- White witnesses and victims appear to have a harder time making positive identifications of minority suspects than of white suspects.
- Crimes against minority victims are most often committed by minority suspects, often acquaintances. After the arrest, victims frequently refuse to prosecute, withdraw the identification, or refuse to testify.
- Witnesses also become uncooperative if they have been intimidat-

ed or feel threatened by the defendant or by aspects of the criminal justice system.

● A major factor distinguishing cooperative from uncooperative witnesses is simple confusion about where they are supposed to appear or about what they are supposed to do when they get there.

In addition to "evidentiary" problems, the study found another racial difference in case processing that may help explain a small proportion of the high release rates for minorities. A slightly higher percentage of white suspects than blacks were arrested with a warrant in the study period. Because the criteria for issuing warrants are essentially the same as the criteria for filing criminal charges, cases involving warrants would be less likely to develop evidentiary problems after arrest. However, there is only a 3 percentage point difference between whites and minorities for warrant arrests.

Nevertheless, this difference raises a provocative question: Why are the police apparently more hesitant to arrest white than minority suspects without a warrant? From the release rates, it appears that the police and prosecutors have a harder time making a "filable" case against minorities. Yet, by getting warrants more often to arrest whites, the police implicitly indicate that the reverse is true. Or, they may assume that minority suspects are less likely than white suspects to make false arrest charges or other kinds of trouble if a case is not filed.

Whatever their reasons, the racial differences in warrant arrests and release rates suggest that the police operate on different assumptions about minorities than about whites when they make arrests. Other study findings tend to reinforce the suggestion that the system regards minorities differently. Controlling for the factors most likely to influence sentencing and parole decisions, the analysis still found that blacks and Hispanics are less likely to be given probation, more likely to receive *prison* sentences, more likely to receive longer sentences, and more likely to serve longer time.

As Fig. S.1 showed, for very serious crimes, blacks are represented about equally in the arrest and prison populations. In other words, the prevalence of these crimes among blacks primarily dictates their numbers in the prison population. However, as we move to property crimes, the disparity between blacks' proportions of the arrest and prison populations widens considerably. This disparity suggests that probation officers, judges, and parole boards are exercising discretion in sentencing and/or release decisions in ways that result in *de facto* discrimination against blacks. The same is true for Hispanics, who serve even longer time than blacks.

Possibly, the racial differences in type and length of sentence imposed reflect racial differences in plea bargaining and jury trials. Fully 92 percent of white defendants were convicted by plea bargaining, compared with 85 percent for blacks and 87 percent for Hispanics. Those numbers imply the percentage that engaged in plea bargaining—since, by nature, plea bargaining virtually ensures conviction. However, it also virtually guarantees a reduced charge and/or lighter sentencing. Defendants who go to trial generally receive harsher sentences, and our study found that only 7 percent of whites prosecuted in Superior Court were tried by jury, compared with 12 percent for blacks and 11 percent for Hispanics.

However, even if these mechanisms did account for the apparent racial differences in sentencing, the implication of bias simply shifts to another node in the system. Why should minorities plea bargain less and go to jury trial more than whites? If the differences represent defendants' attitudes and decisions, then the system is not actively responsible for this racial difference. If these differences reflect decisions by prosecutors or decisions by default, then the issue of bias returns. And it may reflect the kind of differences that are implied by the prefiling release rates for minorities.

The suggestion that the system regards whites and minorities differently may enter into sentencing in another way. Judges may hesitate to send white defendants to prison for two reasons. First, research indicates that in prisons where whites are the minority, they are often victimized by the dominant racial group, whether black or Hispanic. (In most states, blacks now outnumber whites in the prison population.) Second, judges may regard whites as better candidates for rehabilitation.

Research on sentence patterns supports the implication that the system "values" whites more than it does minorities. For example, Zimring, Eigen, and O'Malley (1976) found that blacks who kill whites receive life imprisonment or the death sentence more than twice as often as when they kill blacks. Other research has tended to bear out this relationship for other crimes as well: Defendants get harsher sentences if the victim is white than if he is black.

INFORMATION USED IN SENTENCING AND PAROLE

Putting aside the ambiguity of findings about post-arrest release, the study found strong racial differences only in length and type of sentence imposed and length of time served. If there is discrimination in the system, it is inconsistent. Minorities are no more likely than whites to be arrested or convicted of crimes nor to be treated differently by corrections. Yet, they are given longer, harsher sentences at conviction, and wind up serving longer terms than whites in two of our study states. It may be possible to explain these inconsistencies by considering who makes decisions at key points in the system and what kinds of information they use to make those decisions.

As the accused moves through the system, more information about him is attached to his folder and that information is weighted differentially. Police and prosecutors are primarily concerned with "just deserts." Their legal mission is to ensure that criminals are convicted. They concentrate on the information they need to make arrest and conviction stick— primarily information about the crime and about the offender's prior record—according to strict legal rules. Judges also consider the nature of the crime and prior record in weighing just deserts, but they are further concerned with the defendant's potential for rehabilitation or recidivism. In other words, will returning him to society through probation or a lighter sentence endanger society? In deciding on probation, jail, or prison for an offender, they consider his conviction crime, prior record, *and* his personal and socioeconomic characteristics.

To provide the latter material, probation officers in most counties prepare a presentence investigation report (PSR), which contains a sentence recommendation. Probation officers are more concerned with analyzing and understanding the person and his situation, and they tend to deemphasize the legal technicalities necessary to assess guilt and convictability. The PSR describes the subject's family background, marital status, education and employment history, past encounters with the law, gang affiliation, drug and alcohol use, etc. In most states, it is the key document in sentencing and parole decisions. Its recommendations are generally followed by the sentencing judge, and its characterization of the defendant becomes the core of the parole board's case-summary file.

The influence of the PSR may help explain the racial differences in sentencing and time served: Minorities often do not show up well in PSR indicators of recidivism, such as family instability and unemployment. As a result, probation officers, judges, and parole boards are often impelled to identify minorities as higher risks.

These conjectures are supported by the comparison between length of sentence imposed and time served. In California, determinate sentencing practices make length of time served depend primarily on length of sentence imposed. Thus, racial differences in time served there, especially for Hispanics, reflect racial disparities in sentencing. Minority defendants also receive longer sentences than whites in Texas, and parole decisions there lengthen those sentences even more, relative to time served by whites. In Michigan, we found a reverse effect. Blacks received sentences 7.2 months longer than white defendants, but they served roughly equal time.

This contrast can perhaps be explained by the parole practices in Texas and Michigan. Texas has a very individualized, highly discretionary, parole process that incorporates the full range of an inmate's criminal history and personal and socioeconomic characteristics. Since 1976, Michigan parole decisions have been based almost exclusively on legal indicators of personal culpability, e.g., juvenile record, violence of conviction crime, and prison behavior. Evidently, this practice not only overcomes racial disparities in time served, but also even overcomes racial disparities in sentencing. Nevertheless, overcoming racial disparities in sentencing is not the primary, nor perhaps the proper, concern of parole boards. Their major responsibility is to decide whether an inmate can safely be returned to society. By putting aside the socioeconomic and other extra-legal indicators of recidivism, they may be setting potential recidivists loose.

ASSESSING THE INDICATORS OF RECIDIVISM

If the indicators of recidivism are valid, the criminal justice system is not discriminating against minorities in its sentencing and parole decisions; it is simply reflecting the larger racial problems of society. However, our research suggests that the indicators may be less objective (and certainly less "race-neutral") than past research and practice have indicated.

The overrepresentation of minorities in aggregate arrest statistics has tended to obscure the fact that the criminal justice system and criminal justice research are, nevertheless, dealing with a criminal population that is half white and half minority. Unless minorities in *that* population have had higher recidivism rates than whites, there is no reason why minorities should consistently be seen as presenting a higher risk of recidivism. There is clearly a much higher *prevalence* of crime within the minority portion of the national population—that prevalence largely accounts for their equal representation with whites in the criminal population. But there is no evidence that they have a higher recidivism rate.

The RIS data indicate that, once involved in crime, whites and minorities in the sample had virtually the same annual crime commission rates. This accords with Blumstein and Graddy's (1981) finding that the recidivism rate for index offenses is approximately 0.85 *for both whites and non-whites.* Thus, the data suggest that large racial differences in aggregate arrest rates must be attributed primarily to differences in *ever becoming involved in crime at all* and not to different patterns among those who do participate.

Under these circumstances, any empirically derived indicators of recidivism should target a roughly equal number of whites and minorities. The reason this does not happen may be the relative sizes and diversity of the base populations. The black portion of the criminal population draws from a population base that is much smaller and more homogeneous, socioeconomically and culturally. That is, black criminals are more likely than their white counterparts to have common socioeconomic and cultural characteristics. The white half of the criminal population comes from a vastly larger, more heterogeneous base. Individuals in it are motivated variously, and come from many different cultural, ethnic, and economic backgrounds. Consequently, the characteristics associated with "black criminality" are more consistent, more visible, and more "countable" than those associated with white criminality. Moreover, because *prevalence* of crime is so much higher than incidence of crime (or recidivism) among minorities, characteristics associated with prevalence of crime among blacks (e.g., unemployment, family instability) may overwhelm indicators of prevalence for the entire criminal population. They may also mask indicators of recidivism common to both blacks and whites.

The findings on criminal motivation and economic need lend support to this hypothesis. Blacks rated economic distress much higher than "high times" and very much higher than "temper" as their motive for committing crime. They also rated it more highly than either whites or Hispanics did. Moreover, the black inmates were consistently identified as economically distressed by the study's criteria for economic need. These findings imply that socioeconomic characteristics are more consistent and more consistently related to crime among blacks than they are among whites. Considering that blacks make up approximately half of the criminal population, their characteristics may have the same effect on indicators of prevalence and recidivism that the extremely high crime rates of a few individuals have on average crime rates.

This is a real vicious circle: As long as the "black experience" conduces to crime, blacks will be identified as potential recidivists, will serve prison terms instead of jail terms, will serve longer time, and will thus be identified as more serious criminals.

V. IMPLICATIONS FOR FUTURE RESEARCH AND POLICY

These findings and conclusions raise some compelling issues for criminal justice research and policy. The first priority for both will be to examine the indicators used in sentencing and parole decisions.

QUESTIONS FOR FUTURE RESEARCH

Assessing the Indicators of Recidivism

The criminal justice system is moving toward greater use of prediction tables that measure an offender's risk of recidivism. These tables are based on the actuarially determined risk associated with factors such as prior record, employment, and education. This "categoric risk" technique does not assume that the facts of each case are unique. Rather, it assumes that the risk of recidivism is distributed fairly uniformly among groups of individuals who share certain characteristics.

According to some experts, adopting this more objective technique reduces racial disparities because it severely limits discretion and because the indicators are racially neutral. However, as we argued in Sec. IV, these indicators may appear racially neutral, but in practice they may overlap with racial status. Using factors that correlate highly with race will have the same effect as using race itself as an indicator.

We need to reexamine the statistical methods and the evidence used to develop these risk prediction schemes. The minority half of the criminal population probably has more characteristics in common, especially socio-economic characteristics, than does the white half. Consequently, these characteristics may statistically overwhelm others that might indicate the risk of recidivism more precisely for both whites and blacks. Analysts will need a methodology that permits them to control for homogeneity in the minority (largely black) half of the criminal population.

If different recidivism indicators can be isolated using that methodology, researchers will then have to determine whether the resulting sentencing standards still lead to harsher treatment for minorities. Assuming that we want a system that can discriminate between high and low probability of recidivism, we also need some standard of judicial review that balances the state's interest in accurate identification of recidivists against the imperative that group classifications should not be implicit race classifications.

For each indicator that has racial links, we need to ask: How much predictive efficiency would the state lose by omitting this indicator from its sentencing standards? Thus framed, the question is not whether prediction tables could (or should) be used, but to what extent the state should sacrifice a degree of predictive efficiency to racial equity. Obviously, characteristics showing personal culpability (for example, prior convictions) should always be seen as acceptable factors for assessing risk. Even if minorities have a disproportionate number of them, these characteristics indicate individual, not group, status.

Post-Arrest Release Rates and Evidentiary Problems

Racial differences in post-arrest release rates should be explored. The RIS data show that the police are not simply overarresting minorities, relative to the crimes they commit, and then having to let them go. However, our findings do not discount the charge that the police arrest minorities on weaker evidence. Nevertheless, previous research suggests that the bulk of cases dismissed before filing involved uncooperative victims, and other research has suggested that minority cases more often have problems with victims and witnesses. Future research could inquire why so many victims become uncooperative, whether the reasons differ in minority cases, and how often either the suspect or the criminal justice system itself intimidates victims or witnesses.

Racial Differences in Plea Bargaining and Sentence Severity

This study did not control for plea bargaining in analyzing racial differences in sentence severity. If future research establishes that plea bargaining contributes to those differences, the next important research task would be to discover why minority defendants are less likely than whites to plea bargain and more likely to have jury trials. Do prosecutors consistently offer less attractive plea bargains to minority defendants, or do minority defendants simply insist more on jury trials?

Effect of Prisons' Racial Mix on Sentencing

If judges are increasingly reluctant to send white offenders to prisons where blacks and Hispanics outnumber them, racial differences in sentence severity will widen, and the disproportion of minorities in prison will grow. This sensitive issue will not be easy to resolve empirically. The first task would be to establish that judges are indeed influenced by reports that white prisoners are often victimized. The second task would be to establish whether these reports are valid; if they are, the criminal justice system will face harder issues than sentencing practices. Among the most serious might be pressure for segregated facilities.

How Prison-Gang Membership Affects Length of Sentence Served

We need to understand how gang-related activities affect length of sentence served and participation in prison treatment and work programs. In California, one out of every seven prisoners is currently held in administrative segregation, most of them for gang-related activities, and a greater proportion of the black and Hispanic inmates admit to gang membership. A greater proportion of minorities may be in segregation because of gang affiliation, and inmates in segregation may have restricted access to prison treatment and work programs. Since program participation affects release decisions, gang affiliation may contribute significantly to racial differences in time served.

The Prison Environment's Influence on In-Prison Behavior

Some inmates, predicted to be high infractors, exhibited rather exemplary behavior. To what extent can their good behavior be attributed to characteristics of the institution, e.g., specify security measures, inmate-to-staff ratio, recreational facilities, the total size of the institution, housing arrangements, and so forth?

The Connection Between Prison Violence and Idleness

Prison administrators face both rising violence and shrinking budgets. Research can help them cope by finding out more about the relationship between idleness and prison violence and identifying the kinds of inmates whose participation in programs will bring about the greatest reduction in violence.

POLICY RECOMMENDATIONS

Definitive policy recommendations must await findings from some of these research studies, but we can recommend some interim policy initiatives.

(1) *Police and prosecutors need to be more aware of the difficulty of getting adequate evidence with which to convict minority suspects.* The high release rates for minorities suggest that minority suspects are not as likely as whites to be identified from lineups or elsewhere, and that victims or key witnesses in minority cases often prove uncooperative after the arrest has taken place. Police and prosecutors may need to work harder at securing the trust and cooperation of minority victims and witnesses.

(2) *The plea bargaining process needs to be closely monitored for any indications that minorities are offered less attractive plea bargains than those offered to whites.* One way to assure greater uniformity is to have a single deputy review all the plea negotiations. Moreover, minorities' unfamiliarity with and distrust of the system may cause them to insist on a trial. If so, they should be informed that sentences resulting from jury trials are generally more severe.

(3) *Judges and probation officers must begin to distinguish between information concerning the defendant's personal culpability and information that reflects his social status.* The latter information may not be as racially neutral or objective as previous research has indicated. Until the indicators of recidivism have been reanalyzed, we recommend that officials weight the criminal's characteristics more heavily than socioeconomic indicators in sentencing and parole decisions.

(4) *To reduce prison violence, prison administrators should allocate work and treatment*

programs, particularly prison jobs, to younger inmates, who are responsible for most prison violence.

(5) Finally, *we recommend another look at rehabilitation.* It is perhaps unfashionable to talk about rehabilitation when prison administrators are faced with shrinking budgets, increased population, and more fractious inmates. In this context, most administrators have been forced to assign low priorities to treatment programs. Although rehabilitation programs have not yet lived up to expectations, the implications of this trend are troubling. The RIS data indicated that most inmates do not get the treatment that they need. Two-thirds of the inmates who were chronically unemployed preceding their imprisonment failed to participate in vocational training programs. Two-thirds of those with alcohol problems did not receive alcohol treatment. And about 95 percent of those with drug problems did not get drug treatment in Texas and California.[4] Most inmates reported that they failed to participate in programs because they "didn't have time" or "didn't need" them. Drug treatment was the exception. About one-third of the inmates who needed drug treatment said they were not in drug programs because no programs were available. This is especially distressing, because over half of those who did participate in a drug program believed it had benefitted them and that it had reduced their likelihood of returning to crime after release.

Like other public institutions, the criminal justice system faces growing economic restrictions. It has had to make hard choices among policies, programs, and research priorities. However, we believe that there could be no more important priority for policy and research than attempting to identify those aspects of the system that permit harsher treatment of minorities.

This study leaves us with guarded optimism concerning the system and the personnel who operate it. We did not find widespread, conscious prejudice against certain racial groups. Instead, what racial disparities we found seem to be due to the system's adopting procedures without analyzing their possible effects on different racial groups. Criminal justice research and policy now need to look behind the scenes. They need to focus on the key actors and their decisionmaking: what information they use, how accurate it is, and whether its imposition affects particular racial groups unfairly.

Notes

[1] Blumstein and Graddy, 1981. Index offenses are murder, rape, robbery, assault, burglary, larceny/theft, auto theft, and arson.

2 Previous research using the OBTS file has shown significant differences in the processing of defendants from different counties and arrested for different crimes. Consequently, for the regression analysis, we wanted a sample from the same county and charged with the same crime. We were able to obtain a large homogeneous sample (n=6652) by selecting defendants who were charged with robbery in Los Angeles County in 1980.

3 The RIS has certain limitations as a means of calculating crime rates and of detecting racial differences in these rates. All the respondents were in prison and the sample was chosen to represent each state's male prison population. Therefore, it is not appropriate to view these crime rates as applicable to offenders in the community. They refer only to a cohort of incoming prisoners in the states chosen for this study. Selection effects and other factors cause these rates to be substantially higher than those for "typical" offenders (Rolph, Chaiken, and Houchens, 1981).

4 In Michigan about half of the drug-dependent inmates received treatment.

References

Blumstein, Alfred, and Elizabeth Graddy. "Prevalence and recidivism in index arrests: a feedback model approach." Law and Society Review 16(2), 1982.

Chaiken, Jan, and Marcia Chaiken. Varieties of Criminal Behavior. Rand Corporation, R-2814-NIJ, 1982.

Greenfeld, Lawrence, A. "Measuring the application and use of punishment." (draft). National Institute of Justice, Washington, D.C., November 1981.

Greenwood, Peter W. "The violent offender in the criminal justice system." In Marvin E. Wolfgang and Neil Alan Weinter, eds., Criminal Violence. Beverly Hills, CA: Sage Publications, 1982.

_____, Jan. M. Chaiken, and Joan Petersilia. The Criminal Investigation Process. Lexington, MA: D.C. Heath, 1977.

Rolph, John E., Jan M. Chaiken, and Robert Houchens. Methods for Estimating Crime Rates of Individuals. Rand Corporation, R-2730-NIJ, March 1981.

Zimring, Franklin E., Joel Eigen, and Sheila O'Malley. "Punishing homicide in Philadelphia: perspectives on the death penalty." The University of Chicago Law Review 43(2), Winter, 1976.

Table S.1   Summary of Study Findings

Element Studied	Evidence of Racial Differences[a]
Offender Behavior	
Preference for different crime types	+
Volume of crime committed	0
Crime motivation	+ +
Type of weapon preferred and extent of its use	+ +
Victim injury	+
Need for drug and alcohol treatment	0
Need for vocational training and education	+
Assessments of prison program effects	0
Arrest	
Probability of suffering arrest	0
Whether arrested on warrant or probable cause*	+
Probability of having case forwarded to prosecutor*	+
Prosecution and Sentencing	
Whether case is officially filed*	+
Type of charges filed*	0
Reasons for nonprosecution*	+
Whether the case is settled by plea bargaining*	+
Probability of conviction*	0
Type of crime convicted of*	0
Type of sentence imposed*	+ +
Length of sentence imposed	+
Corrections	
Type of programs participated in	0
Reasons for not participating in programs	0
Probability of having a work assignment	0
Length of sentence served	+ +
Extent and type of prison infractions	+ +

Sources: The OBTS for starred (*) items; the RIS for all others.

[a] 0 = none; + = suggestive trend; + + = statistically significant.

Fig. S.1   Black Percentage of Arrests and of Prison Population

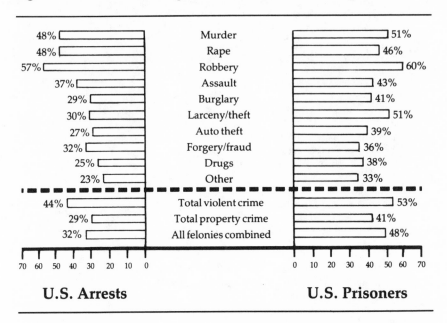

U.S. Arrests		U.S. Prisoners
48%	Murder	51%
48%	Rape	46%
57%	Robbery	60%
37%	Assault	43%
29%	Burglary	41%
30%	Larceny/theft	51%
27%	Auto theft	39%
32%	Forgery/fraud	36%
25%	Drugs	38%
23%	Other	33%
44%	Total violent crime	53%
29%	Total property crime	41%
32%	All felonies combined	48%

70 60 50 40 30 20 10 0   0 10 20 30 40 50 60 70

U.S. Arrests   **U.S. Prisoners**

Table S.2   Racial Differences in Case Processing

Stage	Percentage at Each Stage[a]		
	White	Black	Hispanic
Arrested "on warrant"	9	6	6
Arrested "on view"	91	94	94
Released without charges	20	32	27
Felony charges filed	38	35	35
Misdemeanor charges filed	41	33	37
Felony convictions	20	20	19
Convicted by plea bargain	92	85	87
Tried by jury	7	12	11
Sentenced to probation	21	15	12
Sentenced to prison	6	8	7

[a] *Source:* OBTS data for 1980.

Table S.3   Additional Months Imposed and Served for Minorities

State	Court-imposed sentence	Time Served
California		
Blacks	+1.4 months	+2.4 months*
Hispanics	+6.5 months*	+5.0 months*
Michigan		
Blacks	+7.2 months*	1.7 months
Hispanics	(small sample)	(small sample)
Texas		
Blacks	+3.7 months	+7.7 months*
Hispanics	+2.0 months	+8.1 months*

*Statistically significant.

PART 3

Blacks in Prison

Introduction

Tales of harsh and brutal imprisonment are legend. One need but read any one of a score of prisoner writs, autobiographies, or mass media exposes to be confronted with the realities of prison brutality. What is beyond question, though, is the disproportionate incarceration of blacks. Under jurisdiction of state and federal correctional authorities in 1981, for example, there were 168,129 black prisoners out of a total prisoner population of 368,772 (U.S. Department of Justice, Bureau of Justice Statistics, 1983:-18). A disproportionate incarceration rate also exists for residents of private juvenile custody facilities and inmates in local jails (Flanagan, Alstyne, Gottfredson, 1982:458, 462-465) as well as state and federal correctional facilities. And a perusal of *Capital Punishment 1981* (U.S. Department of Justice, 1981) dramatically documents the disproportionate percentage of blacks as persons sentenced to death between 1968-1981—a six percentage point increase over 1980. This document also notes that between 1930-1980 the majority of persons actually executed were black (54 percent) while 45 percent of the executed were white. But perhaps the most disturbing statement of "justice" in America was that of the 455 persons executed for rape between 1930-1980, almost 90 percent were black.

Part 3 documents the extensive incarceration of blacks in American prisons, which is increasing in terms of rate as well as absolute number—facts poignantly noted in Scott Christianson's "Our Black Prisons." Lynne Goodstein and Doris Layton MacKenzie's "Racial Differences in Adjustment Patterns of Prison Inmates—Prisonization, Conflict, Stress, and Control" points to the existence of two different worlds for black and white inmates in the same facility. They see the incoming black resident as more opposed to authority than whites, yet involved in fewer inmate-to-inmate conflicts. Goodstein and MacKenzie also demonstrate that blacks often encounter discriminatory treatment from the prison staff.

Illinois penologist Arthur Black concludes in "The Role of Education in the Prison and the Black Inmate" that rehabilitation is impossible for many black inmates since they have never been "habilitated," or integrated into the dominant culture's normative structure. Black also states that the educational process in prison can be very valuable to the black inmate as a means of self-improvement and success orientation, since the educational process often introduces the inmate to the majority value system while providing him with valuable skills and techniques that may increase his employability upon release from prison.

New York State Bureau of Program Development and Planning criminologists Sherwood Zimmerman and Bruce C. Frederick conclude in Chapter 19 that the empirical analysis of racial discrimination in criminal justice decisionmaking is complex, and such research often ignores the many less visible decisions in which discrimination might operate, such as the harassment of minorities by system personnel, job assignments, and indifference to cultural needs. Their study does present conclusive evidence, however, that there is a prima facie case that race plays an important role in sentencing defendants from the suburban and upstate regions of New York.

References

Flanagan, Timothy, David J. van Astyne and Michael Gottfredson. Sourcebook of Criminal Justice Statistics. Washington, D.C.: U.S. Government Printing Office, 1982, 458, 462-465.

Petersilia, Joan. Racial Disparities in the Criminal Justice System. Santa Monica, CA: Rand Corporation, June 1983.

U.S. Department of Justice, Bureau of Justice Statistics. Prisoners in State and Federal Institutions on December 31, 1981: National Prisoner Statistics Bulletin. Washington, D.C.: U.S. Government Printing Office, 1983, 18.

U.S. Department of Justice. Capital Punishment 1980. Washington, D.C.: U.S. Government Printing Office, 1982.

16

Our Black Prisons*

Scott Christianson

Americans have long taken it for granted that blacks and other minorities are highly overrepresented in prisons. However, the actual extent of that overrepresentation, the reasons for it, and its social, political, economic, and legal implications have remained neglected. A recent study reveals a nationwide pattern of vastly disproportionate incarceration rates for blacks and whites, and comparison with earlier surveys indicates that the problem has grown worse, not better, as greater attention purportedly has been paid to affirmative action. There is an urgent and long overdue need for social scientists, lawyers, criminal justice officials, and concerned citizens to join in confronting these issues. Notwithstanding some fundamental differences between imprisonment and capital punishment, many of the constitutional issues that have been raised for the death penalty can and should be applied to the more pervasive problem of invidious racial discrimination in the imprisonment of black males.

Everyone knows that blacks and other minorities are disproportionately represented in prison, but do we realize the real extent of that imbalance, its causes, and its effect on society?

As all of us are painfully aware, since the early 1970s expansion has been the dominant trend in correction. From December 31, 1971, to December 31, 1978, the population of state prisons in the United States rose from 177,113 to a record high of 276,799, an increase of 64 percent.[1] From 1973-79, the median rate of incarceration for the fifty states and the District of Columbia increased from about 75 persons per 100,000 to about 112.[2] This growth has also been evident in the greatest prison-building program in American history, with 907 federal, state, and local institutions, having a total estimated capacity of 199,238 beds, presently listed as proposed or under construction.[3]

These developments are all the more striking when one considers that they have occurred amidst a campaign promoting so-called alternatives to

---

* Originally published in *Crime and Delinquency*, vol. 27, no. 3, July 1981. Reprinted with permission.

incarceration, at a time when virtually everyone has agreed that imprisonment has failed to achieve its old stated goal of rehabilitation.

Many people may be unaware, however, that not only has the prison system gotten bigger, but it also has gotten blacker. Analysis of national prison statistics for 1973 and 1979 reveals that the number of blacks in state correctional institutions increased from about 83,000 to about 132,-000, and that the black share of the state prison population rose from about 46.4 percent to 47.8 percent.[4] Considering that blacks account for a minority of the total United States population—an estimated 11.5 percent in 1976[5]—this overrepresentation is very striking, indeed. Whereas the incarceration rate for whites increased from about 46.3 per 100,000 to about 65.1 from 1973 to 1979, the black incarceration rate rose from about 368 to 544.1 per 100,000 during that period.[6]

The gravity of the problem is compounded by the fact that these upsurges, both in the overall use of imprisonment and in racial disproportionality, have been close to nationwide. Rather than being concentrated in a particular region or a few states, overrepresentation of blacks in prison is pervasive throughout the United States.

In 1973 and 1979, for example, strong racial disproportionality was found in every region (see Table 1). In 1973 the white incarceration rates ranged from a low of 23.1 in the Northeast to a high of 66.6 in the South, while the black rates ranged from 340.3 in the Northeast to 452.5 in the West. Six years later the white rates had climbed to levels ranging from 36.7 in the Northeast to 100.5 in the South, but the black rates were up to 484.1 in the Northeast and 580.4 in the North Central States.[7]

For several years, the federal government's National Prisoner Statistics series has indicated significant regional differences in the use of incarceration, such as the fact that the South accounts for about one-third of the total United States population but nearly one-half of all state prisoners. When the results of the surveys for 1973 are ranked according to race by jurisdiction, they indicate that the white incarceration rates for the fifty states and the District of Columbia ranged from 19.5 in Hawaii to 110.8 in North Carolina, with a majority of jurisdictions reporting a rate of 42.4 or more. By 1979 these figures had risen to between 28.0 per 100,000 in Hawaii and 191.7 in North Carolina. Both surveys reported six of the top ten jurisdictions in the imprisonment of whites as located in the South.

Perhaps contrary to expectation, this pattern did not apply to the imprisonment of blacks. In 1973, for example, the black rates ranged from 39.9 per 100,000 persons in New Hampshire to 825.3 in Iowa, with a majority of jurisdictions reporting a rate of 366.9 or more. In 1979 they ranged from 50.0 in North Dakota to 1,341.8 in Washington, with a median rate of 600.0. In both years, only one of the top ten jurisdictions was located in the South.

Comparison of the data for 1973 and 1979 reveals some disturbing trends:

Incarceration rates for both races increased substantially in every region, the white rate going up by 40.6 percent and the black rate by 47.9 percent.

Disparities between rates of imprisonment for blacks and whites also went up significantly. In 1973 the difference between the rates was 321.7 for the entire United States—quite a substantial gap. Yet in 1979 the difference amounted to 479.0 persons per 100,000, an increase in disparity of 157.3 in only six years.

The widening gap between blacks and whites was almost nationwide, with forty-seven of fifty-one jurisdictions reporting an increase in disparity (see Table 2). (Only Colorado, Alabama, Indiana, and North Dakota registered decreases.)

THE PROBLEM IS ACTUALLY MUCH WORSE

Such statistics only begin to convey the nature and scope of the problem. When one considers that about 96 percent of all prisoners in state correctional institutions are males, even though males comprise only about 48.5 of the United States general population, the question of disproportionality takes on additional meaning.

In 1978, for example—the most recent year for which comprehensive prisoner statistics by race and sex are available—black males accounted for only 5.4 percent of the general population. Yet a staggering 45.7 percent of the prisoners were black males.[8]

By region, the imprisonment rates for black males that year ranged from 1,031.7 in the Northeast and 1,032.7 in the West to 1,108 in the South and 1,192.4 in the North Central region. At the end of 1978, the rate of imprisonment of black males nationwide was approximately 1.1 per 100 black men.

Ranked by jurisdiction, the 1978 incarceration rates for black males show three states (Washington, Arizona, and Alaska) with a shocking one of every fifty in prison; and several other jurisdictions were close behind (see Table 3).

The nature of these so-called rates of incarceration makes interpretation difficult, to be sure. After all, they are based on the number of prisoners in custody on a particular date (usually December 31), and thus simply reflect rates of commitment to prison. Since long-term prisoners (blacks more often than whites) are counted year after year, the rates cited actually reflect as well the length of time served in prison. To that extent, incarceration rates also reflect the jurisdictions' sentencing and release policies.

Even when we take into account that many inmates are repeat offenders and prisoners serving long terms of incarceration, it is obvious the percentage of black males who are imprisoned at some point in their lives is much greater than the percentage of white men imprisoned. Specific figures, from cohort studies or otherwise, are not available. However, there can be no doubt that a significant portion of black males—and very probably an even larger percentage of urban black males—are imprisoned at one time or another in their lives.

These figures only suggest the extraordinary impact of imprisonment upon the black community. This being so, it is all the more puzzling that no one has studied that impact in detail.

A RECORD OF NEGLECT

Historians and sociologists still write in great volumes about the legacy of slavery, an institution that was officially abolished over a century ago— some of them arguing, for example, for or against Daniel Patrick Moynihan's controversial thesis that enslavement wrecked the structure of black families and left a "tangle of pathology" that has persisted well into the twentieth century.[9] Many writers of various colors and persuasions have depicted welfare programs as a modern equivalent of slavery (or Reconstruction). Yet, surprisingly, no one has examined imprisonment in similar terms.

"Benign" or otherwise, this neglect represents an astonishing admission on the part of the intellectual community and society as a whole. Is there no one willing to confront this hideous reality? How many black Americans have a husband, son, brother, cousin, nephew, lover, friend, or neighbor behind bars? What effect does that experience have on the black family, the black community, the black individual, and the white?

This inattention seems even more striking when we recall that it was only a decade ago that the black prisoner was one of the most powerful symbols on the American political scene. Malcolm X, Eldridge Cleaver, George Jackson, and Angela Davis rattled the society to its foundations with their disturbing observations, Malcolm X going so far as to state, "That's what America means: prison."[10] In Soledad Brother, readers were told, "Black men born in the U.S. and fortunate to live past the age of eighteen are conditioned to accept the inevitability of prison. For most of us, it simply looms as the next phase in a sequence of humiliations."[11] A few months later, Attica exploded.[12]

Today there are no such voices being heard, and sometimes it seems that black prisoners have been abandoned in their cages by almost everyone, including most blacks. The old visions of "rehabilitation" have drowned under a wave of pragmatism that has killed any pretense of justification for reform. Most of the bright-eyed reformers have either burned out or succumbed to the sedatives of job security. Intended reforms, such as the abolition of parole, tend to have backfired, and hoped-for alternatives have turned out to be supplements to the traditional system, with "new" criteria that still serve to restrict clientele to those close in image to the program designers. The public wastes little sympathy on prisoners, particularly black prisoners.

The Legacy of Slavery

The usual response to statistics showing racially disproportionate incarceration rates is a very simple one. More blacks are sent to prison, we are told, because they commit more crimes than whites. Blacks receive longer sentences because their crimes are more serious or because they have heavier prior records. Black prisoners serve more time because they have committed more infractions inside the institution or because their lack of job qualification makes them unsuitable for release.

This line has become more sophisticated over the years, but essentially it has remained the same from one generation to the next. Positivist criminologists now refrain from describing themselves as such, and no one would ever explicitly state that black people are "born criminals" or suggest that their criminality is attributable to "degraded character" or other such "racial deficiencies." Officials who administer the criminal justice system have been cautioned by counsel not to admit that they are stopping suspects or excluding jurors simply because those persons happen to be black.[13]

The new style may be more subtle, but it produces the same result. The message is that blacks, because of the criminal acts they have committed, somehow deserve to be imprisoned more than whites.

These arguments are by no means persuasive, however. Dozens—perhaps hundreds—of studies suggest that racial discrimination in the criminal justice process is a significant factor in determining racially disproportionate rates of incarceration.[14] Indeed, the relationship between crime and incarceration rates is a matter of much dispute. William Nagel, writing in these pages a few years ago, found no significant correlation between a state's crime rate and the percentage of nonwhites in the population, or between its crime rate and incarceration rate. However, he did find, and subsequent tests by a competent (albeit blood-related) methodologist confirmed, a very strong positive correlation between a state's racial composition and its incarceration rate.[15] James Garofalo has reported finding a correlation between racial composition and rate of imprisonment that was too strong to be accounted for by indirect relationships (i.e., by types of crimes committed).[16] Richard Quinney and others have raised

serious questions about the definitional biases of white-dominated legislatures.[17] Obviously, space constraints prevent a recounting of the litany
against the criminal justice system and society at large in this regard. Yet
the debate over race and crime is sure to continue to occupy the attention
of criminologists for years to come.

Students of the matter might do well to consider for a moment the
historical record. David Brion Davis, the Pulitzer Prize-winning historian,
recently observed that "[w]e seldom think of black slavery as a penal
institution. Yet throughout history enslavement has been used as a form
of punishment, while some penal systems have acquired many of the
characteristics of chattel slavery."[18] Davis reminds us that for centuries,
slavery was regarded as a form of punishment for original sin. Some
European apologists insisted that the Atlantic slave trade performed a
beneficial service by rescuing many African heathens from savagery, and
American plantation owners defended their system as a Biblically inspired
instrument of rehabilitation.[19]

Thorsten Sellin has examined the links between slavery and imprisonment from antiquity to modern times, but his work scarcely scratches the
surface with regard to the American experience.[20] Lest we forget, it was
as prisoners—slaves—that African men, women, and children were trans-
ported to the Caribbean and America; and the majority of blacks continued
to live and die in a state of bondage until emancipation during the nineteenth century. The state prison as we know it arose in part as a replace-
ment for slavery, in order to control newly freed blacks.[21]

When Alexis de Tocqueville toured the United States, gathering material for what would later become *Democracy in America,* his official mission was
actually to study America's developing industrial penal system.[22] Tocqueville's and Gustave de Beaumont's impressions were published in 1833 as
the classic report *On the Penitentiary System in the United States and Its Application
in France,* in which they observed that the great majority of black persons
residing in the American South were kept as slaves, while "in those states
in which there exists one Negro to thirty whites, the prisons contain one
Negro to four white persons."[23] Numerous reports since the early nineteenth century have documented heavy overrepresentation of blacks in
American prisons.[24]

LEGAL IMPLICATIONS

Racially disproportionate rates of incarcerations have been part of criminal
justice in this country for more than a century, and the high rate of
imprisonment for blacks has surely had tremendous social and political
implications. As Tocqueville himself put it, "Scarcely any political ques-

tion arises in the United States that is not resolved, sooner or later, into a judicial question."[25] In the case of slavery, it took as long as 200 years for the courts to find the practice illegal. Sooner or later, judges will have to confront the unconstitutionality of racially disproportionate incarceration rates.

The recent experience of constitutional attacks on the death penalty offers many valuable lessons in this regard. By the early 1970s, social scientists and members of the bar were working closely in mounting challenges to the imposition of capital punishment. One of the important issues addressed was the strong overrepresentation of blacks among those sentenced to death and executed by state governments.[26] The result has been a series of Supreme Court decisions, some successful and some not, in which alleged racial discrimination has been scrutinized.[27]

Notwithstanding fundamental differences between capital punishment and imprisonment, it would seem that many of the constitutional issues that have been raised for the death penalty can and should be applied to other forms of punishment, including incarceration. Comparable data are available, which depict a similar racial imbalance. Unlike death sentence statistics, the statistics for incarceration show a pattern of racial discrimination that is nationwide, that apparently is not concentrated in the South. Also, as we have seen, this imbalance appears to be growing more pronounced.[28]

In order for such an effort to be successful, social scientists, lawyers, and members of the black community need to collaborate in a new and massive undertaking, involving intensive research and litigation.

Satisfactory judicial response is by no means assured. With many years of similar efforts in fighting the death penalty, Hugo A. Bedau expressed disappointment a few years ago over the way the Supreme Court had reacted, or failed to react, to social science research on capital punishment. This neglect, he cautioned, was particularly evident in the decision of *Gregg v. Georgia,* even though Chief Justice Burger had complained only a few years before about the "paucity" of evidence on such questions.[29] Rather than heed the findings of the social scientists, the Court went on to devise "remedies," such as guided discretion, which had already been shown to be ineffective in reducing racial disproportionality in capital sentencing.[30]

And yet, the nation and its highest court must be made to confront the nature of imprisonment in America. Until that happens, to paraphrase Thoreau, none of us can be free.

Notes

1 The primary source of United States prison statistics is the series of the National Prisoner Statistics special reports, *Prisoners in State and Federal Institutions,* published by the United States Department of Justice, Law Enforcement Assistance Administration, National Criminal Justice Information and Statistics Service.

2 Scott Christianson and Richard Dehais, *The Black Incarceration Rate in the United States: A Nationwide Problem* (Albany, N.Y.: Training Program in Criminal Justice Education, Graduate School of Criminal Justice, State University of New York, August 1980).

3 *Jericho* (Newsletter of the National Moratorium on Prison Construction, 324 C. St., S.E., Washington, D.C. 20003), Spring 1980, p. 12.

4 Christianson and Dehais, *Black Incarceration Rate,* pp. 9, 19, 43, 51.

5 Ibid., p. 31.

6 Ibid., pp. 10, 19.

7 Ibid. The regional breakdowns are as follows: Northeast includes Maine, New Hampshire, Vermont, Massachusetts, Rhode Island, Connecticut, New York, New Jersey, Pennsylvania; North Central is Ohio, Indiana, Illinois, Michigan, Wisconsin, Minnesota, Iowa, Missouri, North Dakota, South Dakota, Nebraska, Kansas; South is Delaware, Maryland, District of Columbia, Virginia, North Carolina, South Carolina, Georgia, Florida, Kentucky, Tennessee, Alabama, Mississippi, Arkansas, Louisiana, Oklahoma, Texas; West is Montana, Idaho, Wyoming, Colorado, New Mexico, Arizona, Utah, Nevada, Washington, Oregon, California, Alaska, Hawaii.

8 Ibid., p. 31. See Department of Justice, *Prisoners in State and Federal Institutions on December 31, 1978,* National Prisoner Statistics Bulletin No. SD-NPS-PSF-6 (Washington, D.C.: Govt. Printing Office, 1980).

9 See Daniel Patrick Moynihan, *The Negro Family in America: The Case for National Action* (Washington, D.C.: Office of Policy Planning and Research, Department of Labor, 1965); Herbert G. Gutman, *The Black Family in Slavery & Freedom, 1750-1925* (New York: Pantheon, 1976).

10 El-Haj Malik Shabazz (Malcolm X), quoted in Haywood Burns, "The Black Prisoner as Victim," *Black Law Journal,* Summer 1971, p. 120.

11 George Jackson, *Soledad Brother: The Prison Letters of George Jackson* (New York: Bantam, 1970), p. 9.

12 For two contrasting views by participants, see Richard X. Clark, *The Brothers of Attica* (New York: Links Books, 1973); and Russell G. Oswald, *Attica—My Story* (Garden City, N.Y.: Doubleday, 1972). Clark was a young Muslim prisoner, Oswald was corrections commissioner.

13 The literature on race and crime is reviewed in Carl E. Pope, "Race and Crime Revisited," *Crime & Delinquency,* July 1979, pp. 347-57; and in Scott Christianson and David Parry, *Black Crime: An Annotated Bibliography,* Education Project Monograph (Albany, N.Y.: Graduate School of Criminal Justice, State University of New York, March 1980). For commentary, see Charles E. Reasons, "Race, Crime and the Criminologist," in *The Criminologist: Crime and the Criminal,* Charles E. Reasons, ed. (Pacific Palisades, Calif.: Goodyear, 1974), pp. 89-97; Robert L. Woodson, ed., *Black Perspectives on Crime and the Criminal Justice System* (Boston: G. K. Hall, 1977); Charles E. Silberman, *Criminal Violence, Criminal Justice* (New York: Random House, 1978); Robert Staples, "White Racism, Black Crime, and American Justice: An Application of the Colonial Model to Explain Crime and Race," *Phylon,* March 1975, pp. 14-22.

14 See, for example, on arrest decisions: Irving Piliavin and Scott Briar, "Police Encounters with Juveniles," *American Journal of Sociology,* September 1964, pp. 206-14; William M. Kephart, "The Negro Offender: An Urban Research Project," *American Journal of Sociology,* July 1954, pp. 46-50; Guy B. Johnson, "The Negro and Crime," *Annals of the American Academy of Political and*

Social Science, September 1941, pp. 93-104; Thorsten Sellin, "The Negro Criminal: A Statistical Note," *Annals of the American Academy of Political and Social Science,* vol. 140 (1928), pp. 52-64. On bail, jury selection, and sentencing, see, for example: Jules B. Gerard and T. Rankin Terry, Jr., "Discrimination against Negroes in the Administration of Criminal Law in Missouri," *Washington University Law Quarterly,* 1970, pp. 415-38; Bernice Just, "Bail and Pre-Trial Detention in the District of Columbia: An Empirical Analysis," *Howard Law Journal,* vol. 17 (1973), pp. 844-57; Howard L. Alker, Carl Hosticka, and Michael Mitchell, "Jury Selection as a Biased Social Process," *Law and Society Review,* Fall 1976, pp. 9-41; Notes, "Voir Dire: The Due Process Clause of the Fourteenth Amendment Does Not Require That Prospective Jurors Be Questioned as to Possible Racial Prejudice When the Defendant Is Black unless Special Circumstances Are Present," *American Journal of Criminal Law,* vol. 4, issue 2 (1975-76), pp. 180-93; J. M. Gaba, "Voir Dire of Jurors: Constitutional Limits to the Right of Inquiry into Prejudice," *University of Colorado Law Review,* vol. 48 (1977), pp. 525-45; Stevens H. Clarke and Gary G. Koch, "The Influence of Income and Other Factors on Whether Criminal Defendants Go to Prison," *Law and Society Review,* Fall 1976, pp. 57-92; James Drew, "Judicial Discretion and the Sentencing Process," *Howard Law Journal,* vol. 17 (1973), pp. 859-64. On alternatives to incarceration and on parole, see, for example: David M. Petersen and Paul C. Friday, "Early Release from Incarceration: Race as a Factor in the Use of 'Shock Probation,'" *Journal of Criminal Law and Criminology,* March 1975, pp. 79-87; A. R. Smith, "Black Perspective on Pretrial Diversion," *Urban League Review,* Fall 1975, pp. 25-28; John J. Berman, "Parolees' Perceptions of the Justice System: Black-White Differences," *Criminology,* February 1976, pp. 507-20; Leo Carroll and Margaret E. Mondrick, "Racial Bias in the Decision to Grant Parole," *Law and Society Review,* Fall 1976, pp. 93-107.

[15] See William G. Nagel, "On Behalf of a Moratorium on Prison Construction," *Crime & Delinquency,* April 1977, pp. 154-72. His findings were subjected to statistical tests by his son, Jack, who published his conclusions in *Crime and Incarcerations: A Reanalysis* (Philadelphia: School of Public and Urban Policy, University of Pennsylvania, 1977).

[16] See James Garofalo, "Social Structure and Rates of Imprisonment: A Research Note" (Paper presented at the annual meeting of the Academy of Criminal Justice Sciences, Cincinnati, Mar. 15, 1979).

[17] See, for example, Richard Quinney, *The Social Reality of Crime* (Boston: Little, Brown, 1970).

[18] David Brion Davis, "The Crime of Reform," review of David J. Rothman, *Conscience and Convenience: The Asylum and Its Alternatives in Progressive America, New York Review of Books,* June 26, 1980, p. 14. See also David Brion Davis, *The Problem of Slavery in Western Culture* (Ithaca, N.Y.: Cornell University Press, 1965); David Brion Davis, *The Problem of Slavery in the Age of Revolution* (Ithaca, N.Y.: Cornell University Press, 1975).

[19] Ibid. See also Winthrop D. Jordan, *White over Black: American Attitudes toward the Negro, 1550-1812* (Chapel Hill: University of North Carolina Press, 1968).

[20] See Thorsten Sellin, *Slavery and the Penal System* (New York: Elsevier, 1976). For a review, see Scott Christianson, "Slavery and the Penal System," *Criminal Law Bulletin,* March-April 1977, pp. 168-70.

[21] The state of New York, for example, legislated both the emancipation of slaves and the creation of the first state prison on the same date in 1796.

[22] See George W. Pierson, *Tocqueville in America* (Garden City, N.Y.: Doubleday, 1959).

[23] Gustave de Beaumont and Alexis de Tocqueville, *On the Penitentiary System in the United States and Its Application in France,* Francis Lieber, trans. (Philadelphia: Carey, Lea & Blanchard, 1833), p. 93. This important study is available in a paperback edition from Southern Illinois University Press in Carbondale, with an introduction by Thorsten Sellin.

[24] See, for example, William Crawford, *Report on the Penitentiaries of the United States* (1835; rep. ed., Montclair, N.J.: Patterson Smith, 1969); Frederick L. Hoffman, *Race Traits and Tendencies*

of the American Negro (New York: Macmillan, 1896); William T. Root, Jr., *A Psychological and Educational Survey of 1916 Prisoners in the Western Penitentiary of Pennsylvania* (Pittsburgh: Board of Trustees of the Western Penitentiary, 1927); Sellin, "Negro Criminal," *Annals;* Leon F. Litwack, *North of Slavery: The Negro in the Free States, 1790-1860* (Chicago: University of Chicago Press, 1961); Hans von Hentig, "The Criminality of the Negro," *Journal of Criminal Law and Criminology,* January-February 1940, pp. 662-80; Edward Byron Reuter, *The American Race Problem,* rev. ed. (New York: Thomas Y. Crowell, 1927); Margaret Cahalan, "Trends in Incarceration in the United States since 1880," *Crime & Delinquency,* January 1979, pp. 9-41; Frank M. Dunbaugh, "Racially Disproportionate Rates of Incarceration in the United States, *Prison Law Monitor,* vol. 1, no. 9 (1979), pp. 1-4.

   25 Quoted in *Democracy in America,* vol. 1, Phillips Bradley, ed. (New York: Vintage, 1945), p. 290.

   26 See, for example, Frank E. Hartung, "Trends in the Use of Capital Punishment," *Annals of the American Academy of Political and Social Science,* vol. 284 (1952), pp. 8-19; Charles S. Magnum, *The Legal Status of the Negro* (Chapel Hill: University of North Carolina Press, 1940); Elmer H. Johnson, "Selective Factors in Capital Punishment," *Social Forces,* vol. 36 (1957), pp. 165-69; Marvin E. Wolfgang, Arlene Kelly, and Hans C. Nolde, "Comparison of the Executed and the Commuted among Admissions to Death Row," *Journal of Criminal Law, Criminology and Police Science,* September 1962, pp. 301-11; Hugo Adam Bedau, "Death Sentences in New Jersey, 1907-1960," *Rutgers Law Review,* Fall 1964, pp. 1-64; Rupert C. Koeninger, "Capital Punishment in Texas, 1924-1958," *Crime and Delinquency,* January 1969, pp. 132-41; Thorsten Sellin, *The Death Penalty* (New York: Harper & Row, 1967); Hugo Adam Bedau, ed., *The Death Penalty in America* (New York: Anchor, 1967).

   27 The most famous was Furman v. Georgia, 408 U.S. 238 (1972). Some other important cases have been Gregg v. Georgia, 428 U.S. 153 (1976); Woodson v. North Carolina, 428 U.S. 280 (1976); Profitt v. Florida, 428 U.S. 267 (1976); Jurek v. Texas, 428 U.S. 267 (1976); Roberts v. Louisiana, 428 U.S. 325 (1976); and Coker v. Georgia, 433 U.S. 584 (1977). For an interesting behind-the-scenes account of the development of the constitutional attack, see Michael Meltsner, "Litigating against the Death Penalty," *Yale Law Journal,* May 1973, pp. 1111-39.

   28 See the author's inquiries into this legal dimension, "Legal Implications of Racially Disproportionate Incarceration Rates," *Criminal Law Bulletin,* January-February 1980, pp. 59-63; "Racial Discrimination and Prison Confinement," *Criminal Law Bulletin,* November-December 1980, pp. 616-21.

   29 Hugo Adam Bedau, "New Life for the Death Penalty," *Nation,* vol. 223 (1976), p. 147. This disappointment is echoed by Professor Marvin Wolfgang in "The Death Penalty: Social Philosophy and Social Science Research," *Criminal Law Bulletin,* January-February 1978, pp. 18-33.

   30 Marc Riedel, "Discrimination in the Imposition of the Death Penalty: A Comparison of the Characteristics of Offenders Sentenced Pre-Furman and Post-Furman," *Temple Law Quarterly,* vol. 49, no. 2 (1976), pp. 261-87, pointed out, in fact, that the Court's remedies were proving counterproductive. However, his research was ignored, just as the Justices in *Gregg, Profit,* and *Jurek* ignored the social science research published since *Furman.*

Table 1   Incarceration Rates in the United States by Region and Race, 1973 and 1979[a]

	1973			1979		
	White	*Black*	*All Races*	*White*	*Black*	*All Races*
Northeast	23.1	340.3	60.5	36.7	484.1	88.7
North Central	35.1	365.3	64.9	59.5	580.4	108.5
South	66.6	367.0	131.5	100.5	558.1	194.9
West	65.0	452.5	86.1	61.6	497.5	106.5
United States	46.3	368.0	88.0	65.1	544.1	106.5

[a] Prisoners in state correctional facilities, per 100,000 civilian population.

Table 2   Jurisdictions Ranked by Change in Disparity between Black and White Incarceration Rates, 1973-79

1.	Idaho	850.4	27.	Tennessee	146.7
2.	South Dakota	657.6	28.	North Carolina	120.2
3.	Washington	611.2	29.	Illinois	118.9
4.	Delaware	598.4	30.	Rhode Island	117.2
5.	Nevada	569.0	31.	New Hampshire	106.9
6.	District of Columbia	471.2	32.	Missouri	94.6
7.	Connecticut	469.0	33.	Maryland	92.5
8.	West Virginia	456.4	34.	New Jersey	91.6
9.	Vermont	429.7	35.	Arkansas	89.8
10.	New Mexico	424.1	36.	Massachusetts	84.9
11.	Oregon	401.9	37.	Mississippi	83.2
12.	Arizona	400.0	38.	Alaska	74.5
13.	Wisconsin	393.5	39.	Georgia	58.2
14.	Michigan	344.9	40.	Wyoming	42.7
15.	Iowa	311.0	41.	Montana	33.6
16.	Ohio	283.1	42.	Oklahoma	32.8
17.	Utah	263.8	43.	Pennsylvania	27.5
18.	Virginia	246.9	44.	Nebraska	22.8
19.	Hawaii	229.0	45.	California	11.3
20.	Texas	222.8	46.	Kentucky	3.6
21.	Maine	215.9	47.	Minnesota	0.2
22.	Louisiana	190.2	48.	Colorado	−6.1
23.	Florida	184.9	49.	Alabama	−18.4
24.	Kansas	155.7	50.	Indiana	−19.7
25.	South Carolina	155.2	51.	North Dakota	−77.2
26.	New York	148.9			

Table 3   Incareration Rates per 100,000 for Black Males, 1978

1. Washington	2408.6	27. Minnesota	1114.8
2. Arizona	2210.3	28. Massachusetts	1107.7
3. Alaska	2200.0	29. New York	1076.5
4. Iowa	1972.2	30. Georgia	1039.7
5. Nevada	1963.2	31. New Jersey	1006.3
6. Delaware	1961.1	32. South Dakota[a]	1006.0
7. Nebraska	1834.8	33. Missouri	1002.9
8. Utah	1775.0	34. Louisana	975.0
9. Michigan	1734.7	35. South Carolina	954.5
10. Wisconsin	1734.2	36. Pennsylvania	879.2
11. New Mexico	1720.0	37. California	870.1
12. Florida	1577.0	38. Tennessee	845.7
13. Oregon	1520.0	39. Indiana	819.0
14. Maryland	1509.8	40. Illinois	810.3
15. Texas	1438.9	41. Maine	800.0
16. Ohio	1399.6	42. Arkansas	736.7
17. Connecticut	1378.6	43. Alabama	661.6
18. Oklahoma	1372.3	44. Kentucky	644.2
19. Idaho[a]	1301.7	45. New Hampshire	600.0
20. Rhode Island	1266.7	46. Montana	500.0
21. North Carolina	1246.5	47. Mississippi	463.8
22. Virginia	1233.1	48. North Dakota	400.0
23. Colorado	1211.4	49. Hawaii	350.0
24. Kansas	1208.2	50. Vermont[a]	225.7
25. West Virginia	1200.0	51. Wyoming	0.0
26. District of Columbia	1118.0		

[a]No estimates for the number of black males in the civilian population of these states were available for 1976. Therefore, these rates were computed from 1970 census figures. In all other cases, the source for general population statistics was Bureau of the Census, "Demographic, Social and Economic Profile of States: Spring 1976," *Current Population Reports* (Washington, D.C.: Govt. Printing Office, 1979), Series P-20, No. 334, pp. 10-18.

17

Racial Differences in Adjustment Patterns of Prison Inmates—Prisonization, Conflict, Stress, and Control

Lynne Goodstein and Doris Layton MacKenzie

This exploratory study of race and inmate adjustment to prison demonstrates that the experience of imprisonment differs for blacks and whites. Coming from an urban background and having been exposed to discriminatory treatment prior to incarceration, blacks enter prison with a stance in opposition to authority, while whites, with more diverse backgrounds, develop anti-authoritarian attitudes as a result of their exposure to prison life. In addition, perhaps because of their integration into an informal support network, it appears that blacks perceive less of a need than whites to present themselves assertively to other inmates; hence blacks become involved in fewer inmate conflicts. On the other hand, blacks may encounter some degree of discriminatory treatment by prison staff, a possible explanation for blacks' higher levels of conflict with guards and reduced control over legitimate events in the prison. Some of the findings presented in this chapter, particularly those that deal with inmate aggression, stress, and control, provide an intriguing counterpoint to the formulations described in earlier theories which characterize black prisoners as better prepared for prison life, more aggressive and more powerful.

EMERGING INTEREST IN RACIAL DIFFERENCES IN ADJUSTMENT TO PRISON

The informal social organization of the prison has been a topic of extensive study since Clemmer's *The Prison Community* was published in 1940. Literally hundreds of studies focusing on the means by which inmates adjust to prison life (c.f. Schrag, 1954; McCorkle and Korn, 1954; Morris and Morris, 1963; Glaser, 1964; Thomas, 1970; Thomas and Foster, 1972; Hepburn and Stratton, 1977; Akers, Hayner and Gruninger, 1977; Alpert, 1978), the informal social roles they take on (c.f. Schrag, 1961; Sykes, 1956, 1966; Sykes and Messinger, 1960; Irwin and Cressey, 1962; Garabedian, 1963),

271

and their patterns of change during their prison careers (c.f. Wheeler, 1961; Atchley and McCabe, 1968; Wellford, 1967; Faine, 1973; Thomas and Foster, 1972; Thomas, 1973, 1973a), have been published over the past half century.

A striking aspect of these studies is their avoidance of the role that race plays in inmate adjustment. For the most part, investigators of the social organization of the prison conceptualize its social structure as being divided into two camps, represented by the informal inmate subculture and the formal culture of prison staff and administration. According to this conceptual framework, all prison inmates form a cohesive, united front in opposition to the authority exercised by correctional staff members. Prisoners are characterized as conforming to an "inmate code" which emphasizes the following normative standards: refusing to report rule violations or deviant behavior committed by other inmates to the authorities, rejecting the value of treatment and work programs, and maintaining strong interpersonal associations with other inmates (Wellford, 1967). While acknowledging that inmates would subscribe to the inmate code to greater or lesser degrees depending upon background (c.f. Wellford, 1967; Irwin and Cressey, 1962) or institutional (Berk, 1966), factors, most researchers through the 1950s and 1960s appear to have accepted the validity of a single normative system for prisoners.

It was not until the 1970s and early 1980s, with the publication of several articles and a book by Jacobs (1974, 1976, 1977), and volumes authored by Carroll (1974), Johnson (1976) and Irwin (1980), that race in prison became a central focus of inquiry. These authors contend that the characterization of the inmate subculture as unidimensional presents a simplistic and largely inaccurate view of actual conditions within most correctional institutions. An inmate's self identification as a member of a racial group, the attitudes and values associated with that group, and one's affiliation with other racial group members while in prison must be considered if one wishes to understand fully the parameters governing prisoner adjustment. As Jacobs (1976) states:

> New analyses of prison organization must shake loose from the "total institution" model of imprisonment with its emphasis on individual and small group reaction to material and psychological deprivations. . . The old picture of the prison as an inclusive, normative and moral community toward which the individual had to take a stance is no longer accurate. The prison is now a conflict ridden setting where major battles are fought by intermediate level inmate groups rather than staff and inmates. . . Perhaps the prison community is more fruitfully viewed as an arena where competing groups seek at each other's expense larger memberships and greater power (p. 476).

The importance of focusing on race and its relationship to prisoner adjustment is underscored by two developments in recent years. First, relative to the population at large, a disproportionate number of minority group members, especially blacks, populate our prisons (Christianson, 1981; Owens, 1981; Reasons, 1974). Moreover, this rate has increased in some parts of the country, notably the northern and western regions, from the time of the early investigations of prison communities to the early 1970s (Irwin, 1977). The result of this disproportionately large representation of minorities in our prison populations is that in many of our institutions, racial minorities constitute the actual numerical majority, or at the very least, comprise a significantly larger component of the inmate population than the relative strength of minorities outside of prison.

The second recent development making race an important variable is the increasing visibility of informally organized groups based upon ethnic group identification. These groups, whether political, e.g., the Black Panthers; religious, e.g., Muslims; or social (gang-related), e.g., the Aryan Brotherhood and Mexican Mafia, in nature, emphasize distinctions based upon racial and ethnic identification and encourage intra-group affiliation among inmates (Jacobs, 1974; 1976).

A third dynamic emphasizing the importance of race and ethnicity is the importation of preprison cultural and social experiences into the prisoner social world (Irwin and Cressey, 1962; Irwin, 1977; 1980; Johnson, 1976). Researchers of prison social organization generally recognize that a major factor determining one's mode of adjustment to prison life is the set of personal characteristics and experiences one brings into prison. Johnson (1976) illustrates the necessity of distinguishing between various cultural groups in his attempt to analyze the qualities of psychological breakdowns in prison. The importance of culture, however, is not limited to an analysis of inmates with coping difficulties. That inmates from different cultural groups approach confinement with different frames of reference, and that confinement is a "qualitatively different experience" for inmates as a function of their cultural identification (Johnson, 1976), are realities that most likely apply to most incarcerated individuals. Moreover, within racial groups, one's specific subcultural affiliation, e.g., the tribe of a native American, place of origin of a black, etc., may strongly influence the quality of one's prison experience. The present paper is an attempt to uncover and investigate the ways in which race impacts upon inmate adjustment to prison. The authors focus the analyses on self report questionnaire data obtained from adult male prisoners in five correctional institutions in four states in an attempt to determine whether racial groups can be distinguished on the following variables: background characteristics, interpersonal conflicts, stress and anxiety, prisonization attitudes, and event control.

Before presenting the findings, it is necessary to review what is known in the literature about racial differences in inmate adjustment to prison. With a few exceptions (c.f. Johnson, 1976; Davidson, 1974), the majority of research on race in prison has centered around black/white differences. Since the data only allow for these comparisons to be made, the literature review is restricted to these groups as well.

ETHNIC/RACIAL DIFFERENCES—A BRIEF LITERATURE REVIEW

In recent years, a number of distinctions have been made in conceptualizing patterns of adjustment of blacks and whites in imprisonment. These distinctions generally fall into the following categories: (a) experience of ethnic/racial group solidarity; (b) expression of power and violence; (c) experience of stress; and (d) development of prisonized attitudes. These aspects of prisoner adjustment and the relevant data to support black/white differences will be discussed in turn.

Ethnic/Racial Group Solidarity

Identification with other inmates from similar cultural and racial backgrounds appears to be of high importance for black inmates in the contemporary prison. Indeed, Carroll (1974:91) asserts that "racial identification is the primary axis of life for most black inmates." In contrast, the white prisoner, called the "odd man out" by Johnson (1976), is considerably less likely to view himself as part of a larger social group. Rather, the social organization of white prisoners has been described as "splintered . . . into small cliques with diverse orientations, . . . an aggregation of individuals having little loyalty beyond their immediate associates and exhibiting diverse behavioral orientations" (Carroll, 1974:89).

The fact that blacks and whites appear to be dissimilar with respect to in-group identification has been attributed to several factors. First, as Johnson suggests, a major contributor to blacks' high degree of solidarity is their shared cultural background. A large proportion of black prisoners come from the ghettoes of the inner city (Fagan and Lira, 1978), which stress "survival, toughness, and resiliance" (Johnson, 1976). Whites, on the other hand, do not share a similar cultural or ethnic orientation. They may identify themselves with different types of reference groups, relating, for example, to their ethnic heritage (Italians, Poles, etc.), current activities ("bikers," "dopers"), or hometown (urban, rural) (see Irwin, 1980, for discussion of inmate reference groups). This heterogenity is reflected in their more diverse points of origin prior to prison life, many having come from rural and suburban as well as urban areas (Fagan and Lira, 1978).

Social class identification may also be somewhat more varied among white inmates than blacks because whites are faced less often with occupational instability, and when unemployment does occur, it is more transitory (Johnson, 1976). Greater employment opportunities for whites outside of prison allow for the possibility that there will be more diversity of socioeconomic status among white prisoners, because it is logical that some would have availed themselves of these opportunities while others would not. Blacks' narrower range of choices for employment outside may contribute to more similar social status backgrounds among black inmates, giving them yet another aspect of shared experience.

The fact that whites are not united by a homogenous background is aptly described by Roberg and Webb (1981). They state:

> Whites show more variation in social experience than do other ethnic groups in prison. Whites do not come from a common culture or subculture with shared meanings and symbols. Differences in social class and preprison experience form barriers to group formation. The lower middle-class white may snub the lower-class white. Urban whites may consider rural whites crude and stupid. Many whites may consider themselves noncriminal and normal, and perceive most others as deviants, perverts, and generally undesirable. This perspective promotes isolation and impedes group formation (p. 136).

In addition to shared preprison cultural and social class backgrounds, black prisoners have been characterized as more uniformly committed to membership in larger scale social, political, and religious groups within the prison context. Political movements for black nationalism, significant forces outside of prison in the 1960s and 1970s, met with strong confirmation among prison inmates through their commitment to complementary groups based within the prison walls. Despite some public interest in prison reform during this period, it has been argued that white prisoners did not recieve the external validation necessary to perceive themselves as part of a larger social movement to the same extent as blacks (Reasons, 1974; Irwin, 1980; Jacobs, 1976).

A third factor identified as contributing to a higher level of black in-group identification is the shared experience of racism and discrimination, both prior to and after entrance to prison. Blacks, "cast in the role of the victim, sealed off from conventional society" (Johnson, 1976:17), are not only aware that they are treated differentially in the outside society as a result of their race, but also know that other blacks share the same fate (Grier and Cobbs, 1968). Research has also demonstrated that blacks perceive their treatment by the criminal justice system to be more arbitrary and less fair than that received by whites (Johnson, 1976; Berman, 1976), a perception that has been empirically substantiated on numerous occassions (c.f. Wolfgang and Cohen, 1970; Thornberry, 1973; 1979; "Blacks and the Law," 1973; Uhlman, 1979). In addition, within the prison itself there is some evidence that black prisoners view themselves as discriminated against by correctional officers and as targets of racism by other (white) prisoners. Carroll (1974) found that blacks were disproportionately reported for disciplinary infractions, especially of a more serious nature. Moreover, he observed that correctional officers manifested a pattern of closer surveillance and control of black as opposed to white inmates. Held, Levine, and Swartz (1979) found similar results in their study of interpersonal aspects of dangerousness. While blacks did not see themselves as more aggressive than whites, guards rated blacks as more aggressive. In addition, blacks were written up for significantly more misconducts, particularly for those rule infractions which allowed guards to exercise the most personal discretion. These results suggest that rule enforcement in correctional institutions is governed by "the guards' own fears and biases rather than any greater degree of so called 'dangerous' behavior on the part of blacks as compared with whites" (Held, et al., 1979:52).

Expression of Power and Violence

Recent studies of prison social organization identify blacks as the dominant inmate group. In their study of juvenile institutions, Bartollas, Miller, and Dinitz (1976) characterized blacks as having more control and influence in day-to-day affairs of the institution than other inmate ethnic/racial groups. According to the authors, black inmates were in a position to make decisions concerning the use of communal resources whereas whites were not. For example, blacks could control the music played, the television programs watched, the kinds of food eaten, the style of clothing worn, and the language employed. Their interviews with white inmates provide a picture of blacks as dominating the inmate social structure:

> Blacks have more control in the jails than the whites do. They call it the revolution, and they kind of press down on it, too. They turn the whites into punks. You don't see any black punks around.

> Blacks are in control in here because of the black-dominated community. All blacks here try to be bad and stuff and show their masculinity. They always use the cop-out that they come from the ghetto and that they are better with their hands. I've only seen a very few blacks in the whole institution take whites for what they are and give them respect. They won't smoke after us; why should we smoke after them? The blacks want to bring slavery back to us now. They want to run everything. They always have to be first in line. They always have to be first to get their food. This ain't no good. They always try to take the white guys' goods they get from visitors. It just ain't no good.

> Blacks feel that they can exploit whites without being exploited because they use the old thing that they were slaves and the white dudes always picked on them. Like, in the detention home and any place I ever went, a black dude would get up and sucker

punch a white dude and when the boss comes down, they'd say, "Man, he was messing with me because I'm black; he called me a 'nigger' and things like that (p. 60).

This conceptualization of blacks as dominant is also reflected in recent research on inmate victimization. Blacks are most often characterized as the aggressors and white as victims in conflicts with other inmates. Fuller and Orsagh (1977), in their study of assault within the North Carolina prison system, found white victimization rates to be higher than black victimization rates due to the fact that blacks were more likely to victimize whites than vice versa. The relationship between race and victimization has been shown to be particularly strong when the type of violence perpetrated is sexual. Homosexual rapes have been found to be predominantly interracial in nature, with whites the most likely victims. For example, in his study of prison sexual violence, Lockwood (1980) found that about half of the whites in his sample of New York State prison inmates (71 percent in the youth prison) were targets of sexual aggression compared to about one-fifth of the blacks. Conversely, blacks were disproportionately represented among the aggressors in sexually violent incidents. Others have found similar patterns of sexual victimization (Davis, 1968; Bartollas et al., 1976; Carroll, 1974; Scacco, 1975).

Several explanations have been proposed for the differential rates of aggression perpetrated by blacks and whites in prison. Lockwood (1980:-105) states, ". . . it is not black culture that is behind prison sexual aggression; rather, it is a criminal, male, youthful, black subculture of violence." He relates prison sexual violence by blacks to a generalized orientation toward violent behavior that is reinforced by subcultural norms (Wolfgang and Ferracuti, 1967). Supporting this position is the fact that those inmates identified as sexual aggressors in his study were also involved in higher levels of non-sexual violent behavior both prior to and after entry to prison (Lockwood, 1980).

Others claim that black on white sexual violence is rooted in the social caste system favoring white domination and oppression of blacks throughout American history. Essentially, interracial prison violence is viewed as "an act of revenge . . . a retaliation in kind for the violent attacks of white males against black people" (Carroll, 1974:185). Scacco (1975) and Davis (1968) also identify black rage at the injustices perpetrated on blacks by whites and the desire of black prisoners to "get even" as a motivating force behind interracial prison violence.

Stress and Coping in Prison

In comparison to blacks, white prisoners have been described as suffering from greater difficulties in their attempts to cope with imprisonment

(Johnson, 1976; Fagan and Lira, 1978; Oldroyd and Howell, 1977).[1] Johnson (1976) has found that the rate of psychological breakdown of white prisoners is significantly higher than that of blacks, with whites particularly susceptible to crises of self mutilation and attempted suicide. In addition, in their study of youthful male offenders incarcerated in a medium custody Federal prison, Fagan and Lira (1978) concluded that in comparison with black inmates, whites reported significantly higher levels of general mood disturbance, more depression, and higher levels of tension-anxiety. White inmates also reported themselves as more confused and bewildered and as experiencing greater fatigue-inertia than blacks. These results were corroborated in a study of adult male inmates at the Utah State Prison, which found that blacks reported themselves as less depressed than whites (Oldroyd and Howell, 1977). Moreover, in a study by Edinger, Bailey, and Lira (1977) using an interpersonal approach gradient, white inmates demonstrated more discomfort when interacting with blacks than did blacks when interacting with inmates of either ethnic group.

Explanations for the greater problems encountered by white inmates in coping with imprisonment have been advanced by a number of authors. Some contend that the relative, and in some cases absolute, numerical dominance of blacks within the prison context creates a perception of threat and alienation among whites (Fagan and Lira, 1978). Additionally, the lower degree of in-group affiliation and solidarity among whites may make it more difficult for them to develop an adequate informal social support network to mediate against stress and anxiety. The fact that whites are less likely to enter prison with the acquaintanceship of former street associates has also been identified as a factor in making prison life more stressful (Fagan and Lira, 1978). In addition, as Johnson (1976) suggests, prison seems to be a more alien environment for white inmates, whose background experiences were more sheltered and whose values are at odds with dominant values shared by many prisoners. According to Johnson (1976), many whites react to their imprisonment as an indication that they have failed to maintain their commitments as father, worker, or husband, and this perspective may have adverse impacts on their sense of psychological well-being.

Finally, a major source of stress for white inmates has been described as their fear of physical threat and victimization. As discussed earlier, whites are disproportionately the victims of physical aggression, although as Toch (1976) and Lockwood (1980) made clear, the rates of actual assault are probably much lower than those imagined by many newly admitted white inmates and outsiders as well. Nevertheless, with limited information about prison life, white inmates may fear pressures and threats from other inmates—for sex, for material possessions, for social deference—and may also feel they possess inadequate knowledge of strategies for responding to these threats. These fears may produce extreme stress.

Racial Differences in Inmate Attitudes

Relatively little research focusing on racial differences in inmate attitudes toward prison has been performed. To some extent, this situation reflects the dominant theme in this line of research—an explanation of the concept of prisonization (Clemmer, 1940; see Thomas and Peterson, 1977, for a thorough discussion of this body of literature). Possibly because prisonization was defined as the adoption of attitudes supportive of a cohesive, oppositional inmate social structure, distinctions among various inmate subcultures have been largely ignored.

Two prisonization studies have yielded significant relationships between race and prisonization. Alpert (1979) conducted a short-term longitudinal study of a voluntary sample of adult inmates incarcerated in the Washington State system. He found that upon entrance to prison, blacks were more highly prisonized than whites. However, after six months of incarceration, whites had become significantly more prisonized than they were at entry, while blacks' degree of prisonization did not change. Hence, after serving only six months in prison, whites appeared to have adopted attitudes in opposition to institutional goals which blacks had espoused at their point of entry.

Similar findings were uncovered in a cross-sectional study of North Carolina female prisoners conducted by Jensen and Jones (1976). They found that blacks' degree of subscription to the inmate code remained constant over the early, middle, and late phases of incarceration. In contrast, white prisoners manifested the traditional U shape pattern of prison socialization, first demonstrated by Wheeler (1961) and later by Tittle (1972). That is, subscription to the inmate code was significantly higher during the middle phase of incarceration than during the early or late phases. In addition, it was found that for inmates incarcerated for serious offenses, thus presumably more committed to a criminalistic orientation, prisonization levels remained constant throughout all phases of inmate careers.

These findings suggest that race/ethnicity constitutes a variable with significant impact on the development and manifestation of prisonized attitudes. Noteworthy is the fact that blacks appear to retain the same level of prisonization throughout their careers while whites' degree of prisonization appears to be dependent upon their exposure to the inmate subculture and phase of prison career. Several explanations have been proposed to account for this interaction. First, as discussed previously, preprison culture experiences vary widely between blacks and whites. As Johnson

(1976) suggests, the values and norms of ghetto life are more consistent with the prevailing value structure among prison inmates. Hence, many blacks may be better prepared for prison and may "import" attitudes from the outside that are consistent with those held by many prison inmates. Second, as the targets of racism and discrimination prior to incarceration, blacks may be predisposed to enter prison with attitudes that are in opposition to the prison and its goals. In contrast, whites may enter prison with the intention of conforming to the norms espoused by prison staff and only learn over time of the social distance that exists between inmates and staff. Finally, as Jensen and Jones (1976) suggest, there may be differences between blacks and whites in the deprivational nature of the prison experience, such that the prison experience may be less depriving for blacks than whites.

RESEARCH QUESTIONS

Differential patterns of institutional adjustment for black and white prisoners have been proposed by a number of observers of the prison informal social organization. While there have been several quantitative studies of prisoner adjustment as a function of race (Fagan and Lira, 1978; Jensen and Jones, 1976; Fuller and Orsagh, 1977; Held, et al., 1979), much of the material upon which distinctions between blacks and whites are made has been largely derived from qualitative research methods (Irwin, 1977; 1980; Carroll, 1974; Jacobs, 1976; Bartollas, et al., 1976). The present study attempts to substantiate these observations and to further explore racial differences in inmate adjustment to prison through analyses of data from a large-scale multi-prison study of inmate adjustment.

The literature reviewed above suggests that blacks would be expected to behave more violently, be written up for more institutional rule violations, exert more control in prison, experience less psychological stress, and consistently maintain attitudes which are in opposition to institutional staff and administration. Conversely white inmates would be expected to be more fearful of violence, be involved to a lesser extent in rule violations, experience more stress, and perceive themselves less in control.

It is worthwhile noting, however, that these hypothesized racial distinctions are thought to be attributible to two factors: (1) structural differences in the experiences of blacks and whites, specifically cultural and socioeconomic characteristics and (2) the extent and nature of one's contact with the criminal justice system. For example, Johnson (1976) suggests that white prisoners are more likely to be middle class (or at least have middle-class aspirations) than black prisoners. Moreover, he suggests, and Fagan and Lira (1978) confirm, that whites are less likely than blacks to come from urban areas; hence they may be less "street wise." It would be important to control for these variables in the analyses to determine whether black/white distinctions in inmate adjustment can be attributed to differential pre-prison experiences.

In addition, several studies have demonstrated the importance of past experience with incarceration in determining one's current pattern of prison adjustment (Wheeler, 1961; Tittle, 1972; Glaser, 1964; Alpert, 1979). Since evidence exists that blacks may be treated more harshly by the criminal justice system ("Blacks and the Law," 1973; Uhlman, 1979), it is conceivable that racial differences in inmate adjustment may be attributable to the fact that blacks have had more extensive prison careers (both in terms of sentence lengths and number of times incarcerated) than have whites. Hence, it would be useful to control for amount of time served and number of prior incarcerations, as well as age[2] in analyses of racial differences in inmate adjustment.

If simple differences between black and white prisoners are eliminated after the above-mentioned control variables are introduced, and there are no interactions between race and the control variables, it may be inferred that racial differences in inmate adjustment to prison stem from differential experiences, either prior to prison or prison-related. For instance, although overall blacks may be more prisonized than whites, these attitudes may be characteristic of unemployed, urban men regardless of ethnic background. Therefore, controlling for these factors may result in eliminating racial differences, suggesting that whites and blacks with the same prior experiences express a similar degree of prisonization. On the other hand, if ethnic/racial differences are evident after these controls are introduced, or if there are interactions between race/ethnicity and the control variables, a different inference must be made.

Let us take each possibility in turn. First if interaction effects between control variables and ethnicity are found, this would suggest that the process leading to, for example, prisonized attitudes would be different for blacks than for whites. Second, controlling for sociocultural and prison experience variables may also result in racial differences in attitudes or responses to incarceration that were not evident when these variables were not controlled. Should this occur, it would suggest that blacks and whites with similar backgrounds respond differently to incarceration. In this case, the variance due to these control variables must be removed from the analyses for the racial differences to appear. Finally, if no interactions are found, but differences between blacks and whites remain even after controls are introduced, it must be inferred that some other variable or variables aside from culture/socioeconomic status and prison experience, are responsible for these racial differences.

METHOD

Research Settings

Inmates incarcerated in five prisons located in four states participated in the study. The five prisons were: Somers, Connecticut; Stillwater, Minnesota; Algoa, Missouri and Stateville and Logan, Illinois. All are large institutions of medium, maximum or mixed (medium and maximum) security levels for adult male offenders. Somers (population 1300), Stillwater (population 1150), and Logan (population 825) are mixed security level institutions.[3] Stateville (population 2150) is a maximum security institution. Algoa (population 700) is a medium-level institution for young adult offenders.

Sample Selection

Systematic random samples of inmates in the five prisons were contacted and asked to fill out a questionnaire. In all, a total of 3050 names were drawn and 1774 inmates (58.2 percent) consented to participate.[4] Eight-hundred forty-two reported their race as white, 776 reported black and 156 indicated some other race. The latter group (e.g., others) were deleted, leaving a total of 1618 inmates in the sample.[5]

Procedure

Inmates chosen as part of the sample were asked to attend questionnaire sessions in groups of approximately thirty. After the research was verbally described, a written explanation of the study, a consent form and a questionnaire were distributed to each inmate. It took approximately one hour to complete and each man received $1.50 for coming to the questionnaire session even if the questionnaire was not completed.[6]

INSTRUMENTS

Adjustment to Prison Variables

Situational stress was measured with anxiety and depression scales. Anxiety was measured using the State version of the State-Trait anxiety scale (Spielberger, Gorsuch and Lushene, 1970), a 20-item self-report summated rating scale with four response choices ("not at all" to "very much so"). Inmates were asked to circle the number that "best describes how you generally feel as a prisoner living in prison." A high score indicates a high level of anxiety.

A five-item Likert-type scale measuring depression was developed to focus on worrying, unhappiness, and lethargy (coefficient alpha = 0.78).[7] Instructions and response choices were identical to those of the anxiety scale. A high score was indicative of a high level of depression (see Appendix).

Conflict with other prisoners was measured with a six-item Guttman type scale written so that from item one to six progressively more severe conflict was indicated (Shoemaker and Hillery, 1980). For instance, item one refers to a disagreement whereas item six refers to a situation in which weapons were used. There were six response categories for each statement ranging from never to daily (coefficient alpha = 0.85). Inmates were asked to indicate how often they had "been involved with another prisoner in these situations during the past three months." Low summated scores indicate little conflict with others while high scores indicate frequent and severe conflicts.

A second conflict scale was identical to the Conflict with Prisoners Scale except the respondent was asked to fill out the items in terms of situations involving himself and guards in the institution (coefficient alpha = 0.84). Other than these instructions, the statements, responses and scoring were identical to the Conflict with Prisoners Scale.

Attitudes towards the institution, interactions with staff and other inmates, and radicalism were measured using five different five-point summated Likert scales. These scales were created from a large pool of items included in the questionnaire. Examinations of factor analyses and correlations indicated four separate scales: Staff Identification, Fearfulness, Radicalism and Assertive Interactions (see Appendix). The fifth scale was Thomas and Foster's (1972) eight-item Prisonization Scale. This scale reflects general attitudes of opposition to staff and institutional goals.

The degree to which the inmate felt it was appropriate to interact with staff was measured with a seven-item Staff Identification Scale (coefficient alpha = 0.71). High scores on this scale reflect the attitude that the staff are helpful, supportive, and more similar to the respondent than are many of the inmates.

A four-item Fearfulness Scale measured the amount of fear the inmate felt while in prison (coefficient alpha = 0.65). A high score indicated the inmate feared being victim of a physical attack.

The Radicalism scale, with six-items (coefficient alpha = 0.70), measured the degree to which inmates believe that society is unjust and forces people into crime and that inequity is the major reason the individual is in prison. It also measured the belief that as representatives of society, the prison staff is not to be trusted or blindly obeyed.

The Assertive Interactions scale is characterized by items relating to interpersonal relationships (coefficient alpha = 0.73). Those who scored high on this scale indicated a belief in the need to fight or stand up for one's beliefs to protect one's interests and to not be pushed around by others. In addition, those high on this scale indicated that inmates should not inform on others and not trust the prison staff.

The degree of choice or control in the prison environment was measured using a Likert-type Event Control scale (coefficient alpha = 0.77) (see Appendix). The summated scale, made up of six items with responses ranging from one (definitely yes) to five (definitely no), determined the degree to which inmates felt that if they desired, they could bring about specific events. Inmates were asked, for example, if they could get to see a counselor quickly, get a job change, and get their clothes pressed well.

Background Variables

Self-report information was collected on three characteristics expected to be related to cultural/socioeconomic background: educational attainment, employment history, and size of city or town lived in before arrest. Previous commitment to prosocial activities was classified from employment history into three levels: (1) full-time involvement in work or school, (2) part-time commitment to either work or school, and (3) no commitment to either work or school. There were six response categories for size of city or town, from large city (over 200,000) to small town or in the country.

Items referring to the extent and nature of the respondent's experience with the criminal justice system were: age, number of prior felony convictions, and date of entry to prison. Time served during present incarceration was calculated from the date of entry to prison and classified in a logarithmic-type scale emphasizing the early periods of incarceration: (1) less than 3 months, (2) 3+ to 6 months, (3) 6+ to 12 months, (4) 12+ to 24 months, (5) 24+ to 60 months, and (6) over 60 months. Prior convictions were classified into 0, 1, and 2 or more prior convictions.

RESULTS

Black and white inmates who completed the questionnaire were compared on background variables, attitudes, stress, and event control (Tables 1 and 2).[8] As shown in Table 1 illustrating the background variables, the inmates did not differ in age, education, or prior convictions. On the average, the inmates were approximately 28 years old, and had completed grade 11 in school. A little less than one-half had no previous felony convictions (42.0 percent), 26 percent had one, and 32.0 percent had two or more previous convictions. Blacks and whites did differ in time served, prosocial activities, and size of home city or town. The average member of both groups had served between one and two years in prison on the present sentence. However, blacks had served slightly more time than whites. While the majority of both groups had a full-time commitment to work or school, proportionately fewer blacks than whites were involved in full-time work and proportionately more blacks worked part time or were unemployed. The largest difference between the groups on background variables was the size of the city or town they lived in before arrest. The vast majority of blacks came from large (73.6 percent) or medium (10.1 percent) sized cities. Few blacks came from towns (2.0 percent) or rural areas (2.0 percent). In contrast, proportionately fewer whites came from large (27.8 percent) or medium (16.7 percent) sized cities and more came from towns (11.1 percent) or rural areas (17.3 percent).

Comparisons of the attitudes of the groups shown on Table 2 indicates that blacks were higher in radicalism and prisonization, while whites reported a stronger need to assert themselves to protect their interests in interactions with others. There were no differences between the groups on staff identification or fear of injury while in prison.

Table 2 also shows that blacks reported being more depressed than whites but that there were no differences between the groups in anxiety. For conflicts with others, blacks reported more conflicts with guards; in contrast, whites reported more conflict with other inmates. There were no differences between groups in control of events in prison.

EXPERIENCE WITH THE CRIMINAL JUSTICE SYSTEM AND RACE

In order to examine whether past experience with prison and the criminal justice system differentially influenced black and white prisoners in their attitudes and adjustment to prison, a general linear regression analysis was performed. In the model, age, prior convictions and time served were entered as covariates with race, and the interaction of each with race was examined. An interaction would suggest different patterns of adjustment for whites and blacks depending upon past experiences. Table 3 illustrates significant interactions of race with prior convictions in predicting radicalism and prisonization, and a borderline interaction of prior convictions and race for staff identification attitudes.[9]

Follow-up analyses run separately for whites and blacks with age, prior convictions and time served revealed that prior convictions were not significant in predicting radicalism, prisonization, or staff identification for blacks. In contrast, prior convictions did significantly predict these attitudes for whites. Whites who had been convicted of more felony offenses previously were more radical $F(7,722) = 3.56$, $p < 0.001$ ($\beta = 0.64$), more prisonized $F(7,725)=7.69$, $p<0.001$ ($\beta=1.11$), and identified less with staff $F(7,723)=9.88$, $p<0.001$ ($\beta=-0.97$).

The results of t tests comparing whites with 0, 1 and 2 or more convictions with the mean level for blacks on radicalism, prisonization and staff identification are shown in Table 4. Although whites increased in radicalism as a function of the number of prior convictions, even after two or more convictions they were significantly less radical than blacks, t (1007)=4.68, $p<0.01$. In contrast, there were no significant differences on prisonization between whites and blacks if whites had been previously convicted one or more times. However, whites who had never before been convicted of a felony offense were less prisonized than blacks, t (1066)=5.38, $p<0.01$. In addition, whites without any previous convictions identified with staff more than did blacks, $t(1066)=2.08$, $p<0.05$. They did not differ from blacks if they had one prior conviction but they identified less with staff than did blacks if they had two or more convictions, $t(1007)=3.71$, $p<0.01$.

For those adjustment variables for which no interactions occurred with race, a covariance analysis without interactions was run to examine racial differences when the effects of age, prior convictions and time served were partialled out. As shown in Table 5, the racial groups significantly differed after the effects of the covariates were partialled out on the two conflict scales, depression and assertive interactions, and there was a borderline difference on event control. No differences were found for the groups on either fear or anxiety. Except for event control, these results and the direction of the differences are similar to the results of the t tests reported in Table 2. Thus, after controlling for age, prior convictions and time served, whites continued to report more conflict with prisoners and to score higher on the assertive interaction scale, while blacks reported more conflict with guards and more depression.

Examination of the borderline difference in event control revealed that after the effects of the covariates were partialled out, whites (adjusted mean = 16.03) reported more control than blacks (adjusted mean = 16.54). Separate analyses with each covariate and race suggested that this borderline difference occurred for race when either the effects of prior convictions, $F(1,1505)=3.00$, $p<0.09$ or time served, $F(1,1406)=2.72$, $p<0.10$ were controlled.[10]

SOCIOECONOMIC FACTORS AND RACE

To examine whether socioeconomic factors differentially influenced the two racial groups, covariance analyses were run with education, city size and prosocial activities as covariates, with race and the interactions predicting the adjustment and attitudinal variables. As indicated in Table 6, there were significant interactions of race with city size predicting both conflicts with guards and conflicts with inmates. Also, there were border-line interactions of race with city size predicting staff identification and of race with prosocial activities predicting depression.

Follow-up analyses were run separately for each race with the three background variables to examine the interactions of race and city size. The results indicated that the larger the city the white inmates came from the more conflicts they reported with guards $F(1,795)=12.08$, $p<0.001$ ($\beta = -0.32$), and with other inmates $F(1,797)=4.55$, $p<0.05$ ($\beta=-0.22$). There were no significant differences in conflicts for black inmates as a function of the size of their home city or town. In contrast, black inmates significantly differed in staff identification as a function of the size of the city or town $F(1,685)=8.35$, $p<0.01$ ($\beta=0.44$), but white inmates did not. The smaller the home city or town of the black inmates, the more they identified with the staff. Shown in Table 4 are the mean conflict scores as a function of town size (grouped into 3 sizes) for whites compared to the mean level of these scores for blacks. As can be seen, only whites from small towns or rural areas were significantly lower than blacks in conflicts with guards, $t(980)=4.71$, $p<0.01$. However, whites from large and small cities reported significantly more conflict with inmates in comparison to black inmates, $t(1114)=3.35$, $p<0.01$ and $t(970)=4.15$, $p<0.01$, respectively. Comparisons of the mean staff identification at each of the three levels of city size indicated that only blacks from small cities were significantly higher than whites, $t(922)=2.25$, $p<0.05$. Although the mean level of identification with staff for blacks from rural areas was higher than for whites, the combination of the large standard deviation and low number of blacks in this cell ($n=30$) resulted in no significant difference.

To examine the significant interaction of race with prosocial activities in predicting depression, separate analyses by race were run. They revealed that white inmates who had been less involved in prosocial activities were more depressed $F(1,685)=9.93$, $p<0.01$ ($\beta= 0.57$) while prosocial activities were not significant in predicting depression for the black inmates.

A comparison of the mean depression scores reported by white inmates who differed in extent of prosocial activities compared to black inmates revealed that only whites who had been involved in full time activities prior to incarceration were less depressed than were black (Table 4). Whites with full-time involvement were significantly less depressed than were whites who had no involvement, $t(722)=3.18$, $p<0.01$, but did not differ from whites with part-time commitments.

Shown in Table 7 are the results of the covariance analyses of those variables for which no interactions were found with race (Education $\times$ City Size $\times$ Prosocial Activities $\times$ Race). Race differences were examined after the effects of the covariates were partialled out. As found in the *t* tests reported in Table 2, there were no significant differences by race for either fear or anxiety. Significant differences by race on the radicalism and assertive interactions scales also reflected the *t* tests reported earlier. In contrast with the earlier *t* test results, there were no differences by race on prisonization after the effects of the covariates were partialled out (blacks, adjusted mean=27.14; whites adjusted mean=26.93). Separate analyses with each of the covariates were run to examine whether the effect of one particular covariate was the relevant factor in eliminating the racial difference in prisonization. The results indicated that when the effect of city size was controlled, there were no racial differences in prisonization. Controlling for the other covariates did not have this effect. When the covariates were partialled out, there was also a significant difference between blacks and whites in the event control scale which had not been found in the *t* tests (blacks, adjusted mean=16.61; whites, adjusted mean=15.92). Blacks reported less control of events. Separate analyses of each covariate with race suggested that city size was the variable that significantly changed the mean differences between whites and blacks on event control.[11]

DISCUSSION OF RESULTS

Oppositional Attitudes to Authority

Findings from the present study suggest that largely due to differential cultural backgrounds, the process through which prisonized attitudes develop is somewhat different for blacks than for whites. As predicted, when no covariates are entered, blacks manifest significantly higher levels of prisonization. However, when the factors of education, prosocial commitment, and home city or town are controlled, ethnic differences in prisonization are no longer found. Moreover, the crucial control variable in these analyses is home city or town, indicating that urban blacks and whites tend to be highly prisonized, rural blacks and whites less so. These findings suggest that one's preprison experiences, in particular one's exposure to events in an urban neighborhood, may predispose an individual, black or white, to approach prison authorities with suspicion and opposition. Because blacks are so much more likely to come to prison from urban environments, most also enter prison already espousing prisonized attitudes.

This picture, of most blacks already prisonized when they enter prison and whites more variable, is supported by the analysis predicting prisonization when age, prior felony convictions, and time served were entered as covariates. In their development of prisonized attitudes, white prisoners are found to be significantly affected by the extent of their involvement with the criminal justice system. Their degree of prisonization increases as their number of prior felony convictions increases from zero to one and from one to two or more. Blacks, on the other hand, remain consistent in their degree of prisonization, regardless of their experiences with conviction and incarceration.

The fact that blacks appear to be more highly predisposed than whites to attitudes in opposition to authority is also evident in the results of the radicalism scale. Again, whites appear to become more radical with more felony convictions (and assumedly more incarcerations) while the degree of radicalism expressed by blacks remains at a constant level regardless of their experience with the criminal justice system. Hence blacks apparently enter prison with certain radical attitudes, while whites are influenced by the prison culture in the development of their radical perspective. The process of white prisoners becoming more radical and beginning to identify themselves as members of a larger group of political prisoners as they spend more time in prison is vividly described by Abbott (1982).

These results, as well as the parallel finding that whites reduce their staff identification with more felony convictions to a greater extent than do blacks, may aid our understanding of the inmate social system. When it comes to attitudes concerning authority figures within the prison, both black and white prisoners subscribe to a norm of opposition to correctional staff. The groups differ only to the extent that most blacks enter prison subscribing to this norm while many whites internalize it after exposure to prison culture. These findings support the results of a study of three maximum security prisons by Fox (1982), indicating few differences among racial groups with respect to subscription to the convict code. The results of the present study also corroborate those of Alpert (1979) and Jensen and Jones (1976), who found whites to be more affected by their exposure to the prison culture than blacks in their development of prisonized attitudes.

It is noteworthy that despite whites' increasing radicalism with more criminal justice system exposure, their scores never reached those of blacks'. Moreover, whites' scores remained lower despite the introduction of controls for cultural/socioeconomic factors. This finding suggests that there is an additional force operating on black prisoners which contributes to their development and maintenance of radicalism. It is reasonable that blacks' status as members of a minority group and the concommitant discriminatory reactions of others to that ascribed status characteristic may contribute to blacks' heightened radicalism. Moreover, it is logical that black prisoners would be more radical than whites but not more prisonized (after appropriate controls are introduced). This is because as prisoners blacks and whites largely share in the same types of degradations and deprivations perpetrated by correctional staff and endemic to total institutional living (Goffman, 1961; Sykes, 1956). However, as members of a caste who are liable to be the recipients of discrimination both inside the prison and out, blacks may attribute their differential treatment to a dynamic more pervasive and general than the behavior of correctional staff, such as discrimination and racism fostered by society at large.

Violence and Aggression

With respect to inmate attitudes toward authority figures, most black and white prisoners appear to be unified in their opposition once appropriate controls have been introduced. Findings from the present study suggest, however, that within the inmate population, there may be conflicts along racially defined lines. Specifically, our data indicate that white prisoners report higher levels of prisoner/prisoner conflict and score higher on the assertive interactions scale. Thus, whites may perceive a greater need than blacks to present themselves as willing to confront another inmate rather than backing down.

We had hypothesized, based on our review of the literature, that blacks should report higher levels of conflict than whites, and we found precisely the opposite. However, given that the conflict scale used in the present study did not specify direction, that is whether the inmate was victim or aggressor, these results are reasonable. It may be that whites, perceiving themselves as more isolated and less a part of a social support network, attempt to ward off potential threats by posturing an assertive stance with other prisoners. This self presentation may be accompanied by a higher level of involvement in conflicts—both instigated directly by the inmate and as an indirect result of the reactions of other inmates to this assertive posturing. It is interesting to speculate that the victimization of whites by blacks found in other studies may not be expressions of rage and retaliation by blacks for past discrimination. Instead, this may be a response of blacks to assertive posturing by whites who are not backed up by a cohesive support group.

That the higher level of prisoner/prisoner conflict is related to whites' greater preoccupation with assertive self presentation rather than actual physical aggression or victimization finds support in inmates' responses to the fear of victimization scale. Even with the introduction of all of the control variables, whites reported no greater fear for their physical safety than did blacks. This finding may in part reflect inmates' unwillingness to admit to fear, even on a confidential questionnaire. However, it also supports the contention that whites' higher levels of prisoner conflict reflects attempts to maintain their position in the inmate social system rather than actual physical confrontation.

Unfortunately, we have no data on the degree to which inmates perceive themselves as part of an informal support network, but we do know that blacks report having more friends in prison whom they had known outside than whites. As others have suggested (Moore, 1978; Carroll, 1974) it may be primarily this group of "homeboys" that provides blacks with their informal support network.

Results from the present study concerning inmate conflicts with guards merit a different interpretation. Here, blacks report a higher level of conflict, although this result can be attributed to an interaction between race and town size. That is, blacks do not differ in their extent of guard conflict as a function of town size while whites from urban areas report higher levels of conflict than whites from rural areas. This pattern of results indicates that for whites, coming from an urban environment implies a higher probability of conflict with guards. Like blacks, urban whites have similar attitudes opposing prison authority, as evidenced by their higher prisonization scores. These attitudes may be manifested in their conduct toward correctional officers leading to a higher level of conflict with guards than their rural counterparts. Why should rural blacks, who do not differ from whites with respect to their prisonization scores, not have lower scores than urban blacks on the guard conflict scale as well? The authors suggest that this finding may reflect the additive effects of two processes: (1) harsher and more discriminatory treatment by guards toward blacks and (2) reactions by guards to a generally more oppositional stance among blacks to authority figures (reflected in the larger number of blacks who are more radical and prisonized). Informal interviews conducted by the investigators in the various prisons studied corroborated this picture, with black prisoners and several staff representatives attesting to discriminatory treatment by a minority of correctional officers toward blacks.

Event Control

The results of this research indicate no overall differences in control of events for blacks and whites. However, when factors related to experience with the criminal justice system or sociocultural background were controlled, a racial difference occurred. Although the effect was borderline for criminal justice system experience, in both cases whites reported more control of events than did blacks.

These results lend no support to the position that the shared cultural background of blacks resulting in more group solidarity and experience with violent subcultures may enable them to successfully exert more control of events in prisons than is possible for white inmates. Rather they suggest that blacks' lowered ability to control events in prison is a reflection of discriminatory treatment in the institution, as previous research has suggested (Held, et al., 1979; Carroll, 1974). An examination of the items in the scale suggests that most are related to methods of control that depend upon the legitimate institutional structure, such as getting to see a counselor quickly or getting a job change. It is reasonable, presuming some degree of differential treatment of blacks by institutional staff, for whites to perceive that they have greater access to staff in key positions and, hence, more personal control over these events. Possibly if the scale had been constructed to focus on the ability of inmates to influence illegitimate activities, such as, obtaining a weapon or drugs, there would have been no racial difference or blacks might have scored higher than whites.

Anxiety and Depression

Surprisingly, results from the present study do not corroborate results of several studies (Fagan and Lira, 1978; Oldroyd and Howell, 1977) that whites experience more psychological stress and depression in prison than blacks. Respondents' scores on the anxiety scale did not differ by race, either before or after the introduction of controls for sociocultural and criminal justice system experience factors.

Moreover, overall results from the depression scale were in direct contradiction to our hypothesis, with blacks experiencing higher levels of depression than whites. However, this result can be explained by the interaction of race and prosocial behavior, such that whites who had worked full time prior to entering prison were significantly less depressed than all blacks, as well as whites who had not worked at all.

These results do not support Johnson's (1976) contention that being part of an informal social support network reduces inmates' stress levels. It could be inferred that, with more prison friends from the outside than whites, blacks are more likely to perceive themselves a part of a support network. Yet they report anxiety and depression levels which are at least equal to those reported by white inmates.

In addition, our data do not support the hypothesis proposed by Johnson (1976) and Carroll (1974) that white prisoners are socioculturally less prepared for prison life and hence encounter greater coping difficulties. The results of the present study do document sociocultural differences between black and white prisoners, with whites more likely than blacks to come from rural areas and to have been involved in full-time prosocial activities. However, these differences were not reflected in differential levels of inmate stress. In fact, the one interaction effect found for stress related variables was for prosocial whites to be less depressed than other inmate groups, suggesting the potential value of self efficacy in mediating against the stressful effects of prison life (Bandura, 1977).

To what factor can the lack of overall racial differences on anxiety and depression be attributed? It may be that the experience of psychological stress in prison is linked to the perception of oneself as a victim, as Toch (1977) and Lockwood (1980) have suggested. In our sample, white prisoners were no more likely to perceive themselves as potential victims than were blacks, as evidenced by their scores on the fear of violence scale. Hence, it would be reasonable that white and black prisoners report the same overall levels of anxiety and depression.

It could be argued that inmates are reluctant to admit to experiencing coping problems in prison even if they are having difficulties, and that the lack of racial differences on the anxiety scale may be due to a social desirability effect causing an artificial flattening of all scores. If this were the case, one would expect artificially low scores, indicating low levels of anxiety for all inmates. In our sample, however, inmates' scores were generally higher than the norms presented by the scale's developers, higher even than norms reported for other prisoner samples (Spielberger *et al.*, 1970), suggesting that this interpretation does not explain the racial differences found.

CONCLUSIONS AND IMPLICATIONS

Certainly our tentative conclusions should be further explored and corroborated or refined through analyses of data from other prisons. Additionally, analyses in the present study were performed on pooled inmate samples from five correctional institutions which differed with respect to the proportions of blacks and whites in the respective inmate populations. In the present exploration of racial differences, the potential impact of relative racial group representation on inmate adjustment was not investigated.[12] As Carroll (1974) has suggested, it may be the case that differential modes of adjustment for blacks and whites are manifested depending upon their racial group's relative dominance with the inmate population. This question should also be addressed in subsequent research on ethnic and racial differences on prisoner adjustment.

Notes

[1] Toch's (1977) finding that white inmates are more satisfied with prison than black inmates provides a contradictory note to the literature presented in this section.

[2] Since both time served and number of prior incarcerations are related to age, it is necessary to remove the effects of age before the effects of these variables or race on the

dependent variable can be examined. Otherwise, age would be hopelessly confounded with the control variables.

3 Data were collected over a one-year period. Population figures are mean estimates for this period of time.

4 Samples were drawn three different times in Stillwater, Stateville, and Logan and two times in Somers and Algoa over a one-year period. Inmates who had previously participated in the study were eliminated at successive visits. While there are no confirmatory data available on this point, it appeared to the investigators that blacks and whites were equally likely to decline to participate in the study.

5 The proportions of white and black inmates of the total sample (including others) at the various institutions studied were as follows: Somers-47.2% white, 41.0% black; Stillwater-69.2% white, 20.0% black; Stateville-10.5% white, 77.4% black; Logan-42.4% white, 51.6% black; and Algoa-68.0% white, 28.5% black.

6 Inmates requiring assistance were orally administered the questionnaire by a a research assistant in small groups. The proportion of respondents receiving this procedure is estimated at no more than two percent.

7 Coefficient alphas are based on data collected from the first visits to each prison and included approximately 750 inmates in all.

8 For the classified variables X^2 tests were also run. Results were consistent with the conclusions drawn on the basis of mean differences.

9 Previous analyses indicated that time served may have a curvilinear trend. Therefore, it was run as a blocked variable in these analyses.

10 An examination of the effects of the covariates entered in hierarchical order (age, prior convictions, time served) in the analyses shown in Tables 3 and 4 revealed that age was significantly related ($p < .05$) to fear, radicalism, prisonized attitudes, anxiety, depression, assertiveness in interactions and conflicts with both inmates and guards and positively related ($p < .05$) with staff identification and event control. After the effect of age had been partialled out, prior convictions was positively related ($p < .05$) to radicalism, prisonization, assertive interactions and conflicts with guards and inversely related to staff identification. This latter finding is due to the interaction of prior convictions and race, discussed above. Time served was positively ($p < .05$) related to conflicts with inmates and guards and inversely ($p < .05$) related to staff identification after the effects of age and prior convictions were partialled out.

11 As shown in Tables 6 and 7 educational attainment (entered first in the model) was positively related ($p < .05$) to inmate and guard conflict and event control and negatively related ($p < .05$) to inmate identification and depression. When the effect of education was controlled, the size of the home city or town was positively related ($p < .05$) to radicalism, prisonization, and conflict with guards. This latter finding is attributible to the city size by race interaction, discussed earlier. After education and city size were controlled, involvement in prosocial activities was significantly and inversely related ($p < .05$) to prisonization and assertive interactions and positively related to identification with staff and depression. This latter finding is due to the race by prosocial interaction reported earlier.

12 In addition to relative racial proportions, it is conceivable that differential custody levels or degrees of gang involvement in the five prisons studied may promote differential patterns of adjustment among black and white inmates. Other research performed by the authors (Goostein and MacKenzie, 1982) indicates that the racial differences in inmate adjustment reported in this chapter are consistent across the prisons studied. Hence, it appears that white and black inmates respond to prison consistently, regardless of their relative numerical dominance, custody level of the prison or degree of gang activity. These results support the generalizability of the findings reported in this chapter.

References

Abbott, J. In the Belly of the Beast. New York: Vintage, 1982.

Akers, R.L.; Hayner, N.S.; Gruninger, W. "Prisonization in five countries: type of prison and inmate characteristics," Criminology 14 (4):527-554, 1977.

Alpert, G. P. "Prisons as formal organizations: compliance theory in action," Sociology and Social Research 63(1):112-130, 1978.

_____, "Patterns of change in prisonization: a longitudinal analysis," Criminal Justice and Behavior 6(2):159-173, 1979.

Atchley, R.C.; McCabe, P.M. "Socialization in correctional communities: a reaplication," American Sociological Review 33:774-785, 1968.

Bandura, A. (1977) "Self efficacy: toward a unified theory of behavioral change," Psychological Review 84:191-215, 1977.

Bartollas, C.; S. Miller; S. Dinitz. Juvenile Victimization: The Institutional Paradox. New York: Halstead Press, 1976.

Berk, B. "Organizational goals and inmate organization," American Journal of Sociology 71:522-534, 1966.

Berman, J. J. "Parolees' perception of the justice system: black-white differences," Criminology 13(4):507-520, 1976.

"Blacks and the law," The Annals of the American Academy of Political and Social Science 407, 1973.

Carroll, L. Hacks, Blacks and Cons: Race Relations in a Maximum Security Prison. Lexington, MA: D.C. Health, 1974.

Christianson, S. "Our black prisons," Crime and Delinquency 27(3):364-375, 1981.

Clemmer, D. The Prison Community. New York: Holt, Rinehart and Winston, 1940.

Davidson, T. R. Chicano Prisoners, The Key to San Quentin. New York: Holt, Rinehart and Winston, 1974.

Davis, A.J. "Sexual Assaults in the Philadelphia Prison System and Sheriff's Vans," Trans-Action 6:8-16, 1968.

Edinger, J.D.; K.G. Bailey; F.T. Lira. "Effects of team play on racial prejudice," Psychological Reports 40:887-898, 1977.

Fagan, T.J.; F.T. Lira, "Profile of mood states: racial differences in a delinquent population," Psychological Reports (43):348-350, 1978.

Faine, J.R. "A self-consistency approach to prisonization," Sociological Quarterly 14:576-588, 1973.

Fox, J. G. "Black time—white time: race and the prisoner social system." Presented at the annual meeting of the Society for the Study of Social Problems, San Francisco, California, 1982.

Fuller, D.; T. Orsagh. "Violence and victimization within a state prison system," Criminal Justice Review 2(2):35-55, 1977.

Garabedian, P. "Social Roles and Processes of Socialization in the Prison Community," Social Problems 11:139-152, 1963.

Glaser, Daniel. The Effectiveness of a Prison and Parole System. Indianapolis: Bobbs-Merrill, 1964.

Goffman, E. Asylums. New York: Doubleday, 1961.

Goodstein, L.; D. MacKenzie. Race and Inmate Adjustment in Five Prisons. Unpublished manuscript, 1982.

Grier, W.; P. Cobbs; Black Rage. New York: Basic Books, 1968.

Held, B.S.; D. Levine; and V.D. Swartz. "Interpersonal aspects of dangerousness," Criminal Justice and Behavior 6(1):49-58, 1979.

Hepburn, J.R.; J.R. Stratton. "Total institutions and inmate self-esteem," British Journal of Criminology 17(3):237-250, 1977.

Irwin, J. "The Changing Social Structure of the Men's Prison" in D.F. Greenberg, ed., Corrections and Punishment. Beverly Hills: Sage, 1977.

_____, Prisons in Turmoil. Boston: Little, Brown, 1980.

_____; D.R. Cressey. "Thieves, Convicts and the Inmate Culture," Social Problems 10:142-155, 1962.

Jacobs, J. "Street gangs behind bars," Social Problems 21:395-409, 1974.

_____, "Stratification and conflict among prison inmates," Journal of Criminal Law and Criminology 66:476-482, 1976.

_____, Stateville, The Penitentiary in Mass Society. Chicago: University of Chicago Press, 1977.

Jensen, G.F.; D. Jones. "Perspectives on inmate culture: a study of women in prison," Social Forces 54:590-603, 1976.

Johnson, R. Culture and Crisis in Confinement. Lexington, MA: D.C. Heath, 1976.

Lockwood, D. Prison Sexual Violence. New York: Elsevier North Holland, 1980.

McCorkle, L.W.; R. Korn. "Resocialization within walls," The Annals of the American Academy of Political and Social Science 293:88-98, 1954.

Moore, J. (1978) Homeboys: Gangs, Drugs and Prison in the Barrios of Los Angeles. Philadelphia: Temple University Press, 1978.

Morris, T.; P. Morris. Pentonville, A Study of an English Prison. London: Routledge and Kegan Paul, 1963.

Oldroyd, R.J.; R.J. Howell. "Personality, intellectual and behavioral differences between black, chicano, and white prison inmates in the Utah state prison," Psychological Reports 41:187-191, 1977.

Owens, C. E. "Minority offenders: a new challenge in corrections," in Roberg, R.R.; V.J. Webb, eds., Critical Issues in Corrections. St. Paul, MN: West, 1981.

Reasons, C. "Racism, prisons, and prisoners' rights," Issues in Criminology 9(2):3-20, 1974.

Roberg, R.R.; V.J. Webb. Critical Issues in Corrections; Problems, Trends and Prospects. St. Paul, MN: West, 1981.

Scacco, A.M. Rape in Prison. Springfield, IL: Charles C. Thomas, 1975.

Schrag, C. "Leadership among prison inmates," American Sociological Review 19:37-42, 1954.

————, "A preliminary criminal typology," Pacific Sociological Review 4:11-16, 1961.

Shoemaker, D.J.; G.A. Hillary. "Violence and Commitment in Custodial Settings," Criminology 18(1):94-102, 1980.

Spielberger, C.D.; R.L. Gorsuch; R.E. Lushene. STAI Manual for the State-Trait Anxiety Inventory. Palo Alto, CA: Consulting Psychologists Press, 1970.

Sykes, G. "Men, merchants and toughs: a study of reactions to imprisonment," Social Problems 4:130-138, 1956.

————, The Society of Captives. New York: Atheneum, 1966.

————; S.L. Messinger. "The inmate social system," in R. Cloward, ed., Theoretical Studies in the Social Organization of the Prison. New York: Social Science Research Council, 1960.

Thomas, C. W. "Toward a more inclusive model of the inmate contraculture," Criminology 8:251-262, 1970.

————, "Prisonization or resocialization? a study of external factors associated with the impact of imprisonment," Journal of Research in Crime and Delinquency 10:13-21, 1973.

————; S. C. Foster. "Prisonization in the inmate contraculture," Social Problems 20:229-239, 1972.

————, "The importation model perspective on inmate social roles: an empirical test," Sociological Quarterly 14:226-234.

————; D. M. Peterson. Prison Organization and Inmate Subcultures. Indianapolis: Bobbs-Merrill, 1977.

Thornberry, T. P. (1973) "Race, socioeconomic status and sentencing in the juvenile system," The Journal of Criminal Law and Criminology 64:90-98, 1973.

————, "Sentencing disparities in the juvenile justice system," Journal of Criminal Law and Criminology 70(2):164-171, 1979.

Tittle, C. R. Society of Subordinates: Inmate Organization in a Narcotic Hospital. Bloomington: Indiana University Press, 1972.

Toch, H. "A psychological view of prison violence," in Cohen, Cole & Bailey, eds., Prison Violence. Lexington, Ma.: D. C. Heath, 1976.

————, Living in Prison. New York: Macmillan, 1977.

Uhlman, T. M. Racial Justice. Lexington, Ma.: Lexington, 1979.

Wellford, C. "Factors Associated With Adoption of the Inmate Code: A Study of Normative Socialization," Journal of Criminal Law, Criminology and Police Science 58:197-203, 1967.

Wheeler, S. "Socialization in correctional communities," American Sociological Review 26:-697-712, 1961.

Wolfgang, M.E.; B. Cohen. Crime and Race: Conceptions and Misconceptions. New York: Institute of Human Relations Press, 1970.

_____; F. Ferracuti. The Subculture of Violence. London: Tavistock, 1967.

Appendix

Assertive Interactions

1. *It would be pretty hard for anyone to ever make me mad enough to fight him.
2. You can't let someone push you around because if you do you'll get pushed around from then on.
3. If you ever do have to fight, you're smart to do a good enough job on the other guy that he'll never come back for more.
4. One inmate should never inform on another inmate to the staff.
5. I try to stay out of trouble but nobody is going to push me around and get away with it.
6. The other men are right when they say, "don't do anything more than you have to."
7. When inmates stick together it's easier to do time.
8. You can't really expect people to think much of you if you're willing to back away from trouble.
9. It's better to tell the staff what they want to hear than to tell them the truth if you want to get out soon.

Fear of Victimization

10. The odds of getting hurt while you're pulling time here are pretty high.
11. I worry a lot about getting beaten up or attacked before I get out of here.
12. One of the worst things about being in prison is that you never know when somebody might try to really hurt you.
13. You can't help feeling like a caged animal in a place like this.

Radicalism

14. The government has no right to put poor people in prison when all they have done is try to survive in an unjust system.
15. Most inmates are nothing more than victims of an unjust society.

---

* Denotes reversals

16. The solution to the problem of crime is to tear down the prisons and rebuild the whole society that forces people into crime.
17. I shouldn't be in prison for doing something that I had to do to survive.
18. When a man deals with staff, he should stick up for his own beliefs and not let the staff tell him what's good and what's not.
19. If you reveal too much of yourself to a staff member the information will probably be used against you.

Staff Identification

20. I have more in common with people on the staff than I do with most of the men.
21. I probably spend more of my free time talking with people on the staff than most of the other men do.
22. If I have personal difficulties the best people to talk them over with are the staff.
23. Most of the people on the staff here are willing to go out of their way to help an inmate.
24. *In an institution, generally the only persons you really want to talk things over with are inmate friends.
25. *Resident Dooley gets cut in a knife fight with another resident. Dooley is called before the disciplinary committee. The committee asks him to tell them who he was fighting with. He refused to name the other inmate. HOW DO YOU PERSONALLY FEEL ABOUT DOOLEY'S ACTION?
26. *Anyone who talks about his personal problems with people on the staff is weak.

Depression

27. At times I worry too much about things that don't really matter.
28. Sometimes, recently, I have worried about losing my mind.
29. I often feel angry these days.
30. In the past few weeks, I have felt depressed and very unhappy.
31. These days I can't help wondering if anything is worthwhile anymore.

Event Control

32. *If you wanted to* could you:
a. Find a way to make an emergency phone call.

---

* Denotes reversals

b. Change jobs in here.
c. Get to see the doctor quickly.
d. Get your clothes pressed well.
e. Get someone on the staff to do something about a complaint you have.
f. Get to see a counselor quickly.

Table 1   Mean Differences between Whites and Blacks on Cultural/Socioeconomic Variables and Experience with the Criminal Justice System

	White	(n)	Black	(n)	t value	df
Cultural/Socioeconomic Variables						
Education	11.3	(835)	11.24	(751)	0.61	1578
Prosocial Activities Score[b]	1.54	(830)	1.66	(755)	2.78**	1583
Home City or Town[b]	3.13	(832)	1.58	(746)	20.40**	1414[a]
Experience with the Criminal Justice System						
Age	28.04	(837)	27.62	(759)	1.01	1565[a]
Prior Convictions Score[b]	0.93	(811)	0.87	(729)	1.35	1538
Time Served Score[b]	3.39	(770)	3.61	(681)	2.90**	1449

[a]Satterthwaite's degrees of freedom approximation for heterogeneous variances.
[b]Prior convictions classified: 0, 1, and 2 or more.
Time served classified into 6 categories.
Prosocial activities classified: (1) full time, (2) part time, (3) none.
Home city or town classified into 6 categories.
**$p < 0.01$

Table 2   Mean Differences between Whites and Blacks on Attitudes, Stress, Conflicts and Control of Events

	White	(n)	Black	(n)	t value	df
Attitudes						
Staff Identification	17.73	(830)	17.95	(745)	.93	1573
Radicalism	18.16	(829)	20.33	(744)	9.75**	1437[a]
Prisonization	26.78	(834)	27.33	(753)	2.42*	1585
Fearfulness	13.40	(838)	13.58	(761)	1.11	1549[a]
Assertive Instructions	32.1	(836)	31.24	(756)	2.84**	1590
Stress						
Anxiety	53.47	(830)	53.82	(716)	.66	1542[a]
Depression	10.58	(714)	11.02	(588)	1.99*	1300
Conflicts With Others						
Inmates	12.88	(828)	11.88	(752	3.48**	1578
Guards	9.88	(825)	10.67	(745)	2.94**	1473[a]
Control						
Event Control	16.07	(829)	16.45	(745)	1.49	1516[a]

[a]Satterthwaite's degrees of freedom approximation for heterogeneous variances.
*Significant at $p < 0.05$.
**Significant at $p < 0.01$.

Table 3   Results of Models Predicting Staff Identification, Radicalism, and Prisonization with Individual Variables[a]

	Staff Identification		Radicalism		Prisonization	
	F	(df)	F	(df)	F	(df)
Total Analysis	5.78***	(15,1341)	8.84***	(15,1338)	4.28***	(15,1347)
Age	8.75***		10.77***		8.67***	
Prior Convictions	23.30***		3.89**		24.52***	
Time Served	8.58***		1.77		1.97	
Race	3.12*		99.43***		4.66**	
Age x Race	0.76		0.02		0.36	
Prior Convictions x Race	3.45*		6.16***		10.77***	
Time Served x Race	1.12		0.64		1.15	

[a]Variables entered in hierarchial order and interactions entered last after the effects of all other variables were partialled out.

*$p < 0.07$
**$p < 0.05$
***$p < 0.01$

Table 4   **Mean Differences in Attitudes and Adjustment Variables for the Racial Group**

| Attitudes and Adjustment Variables | Whites—Prior Convictions[a] | | | | | | Blacks | |
| | None | | One | | Two or More | | | |
	M	(n)	M	(n)	M	(n)	M	(n)
Radicalism	17.68**	(339)	17.85**	(192)	18.92**	(280)	20.37	(729)
Prisonization	25.85**	(339)	26.76	(192)	27.96	(280)	27.37	(729)
Identification	18.57*	(339)	17.70	(192)	16.72**	(280)	17.94	(729)

| | Whites—Prosocial Activities[a] | | | | | | Blacks | |
| | Full Time | | Part Time | | None | | | |
	M	(n)	M	(n)	M	(n)	M	(n)
Depression	10.29**	(552)	10.91	(106)	11.43	(172)	11.02	(155)

| | Whites—City or Town Size[a] | | | | | | Blacks | |
| | Large or Medium City | | Suburb or Small City | | Small Town or Rural | | | |
	M	(n)	M	(n)	M	(n)	M	(n)
Conflict-Guards	10.25	(370)	10.18	(226)	9.03**	(236)	10.60	(746)
Conflict-Inmates	13.00**	(370)	13.61**	(226)	12.00	(236)	11.78	(746)

| | Blacks—City or Town Size[b] | | | | | | Whites | |
| | Large or Medium City | | Suburb or Small City | | Small Town or Rural | | | |
	M	(n)	M	(n)	M	(n)	M	(n)
Staff Identification	17.71	(624)	18.88*	(92)	19.57	(30)	17.71	(832)

[a] Whites at each level compared with blacks' mean level.
[b] Blacks at each level compared with whites' mean level.
* $p < 0.05$
** $p < 0.01$

Table 5   Results of Covariance Analyses Predicting Conflict with Inmates, Conflicts with Guards, Anxiety, Depression, Fear Interactions, and Event Control

	Conflicts with Inmates F (df)	Conflicts with Guards F (df)	Anxiety F (df)	Depression F (df)	Fear F (df)	Assertive Interactions F (df)	Event Control F (df)
Total Analysis	16.87***(8,1351)	11.96***(8,1348)	2.72***(8,1329)	5.57***(8,1099)	2.42*(8,1361)	8.88***(8,1357)	3.33***(8,1345)
Age	83.12***	39.14***	15.90***	37.39***	9.55***	44.92***	14.03***
Prior Convictions	3.29	5.64**	.27	.39	0.00	15.30***	6.58**
Time Served	6.29***	9.18***	.92	.27	1.57	0.58	0.50
Race	17.10***	5.01**	.98	5.42**	1.96	7.87	3.48*

$* \ p < 0.07$
$** \ p < 0.05$
$*** \ p < 0.01$

Table 6   Results of Models Predicting Staff Identification, Depression, Conflicts with Guards[a] and Conflicts with Inmates with Individual Variables[a]

	Staff Identification		Depression		Conflicts with Guards		Conflicts with Inmates	
	F	(df)	F	(df)	F	(df)	F	(df)
Total Analysis	3.90***(7,1484)		3.64***(7,1217)		3.38***(7,1477)		4.70***(7,1484)	
Education	5.04**		8.91***		4.82**		5.98**	
Town or City	2.83		0.15		9.35***		0.61	
Prosocial Activities	9.44***		4.23**		0.13		3.19	
Race	4.41**		2.63		1.56		16.36***	
Education × Race	0.03		2.49		0.01		1.53	
City × Race	3.64*		0.68		7.72***		5.59**	
Prosocial Activities × Race	2.01		5.56**		0.02		0.08	

[a] Variables entered in hierarchical order and interactions entered last after the effects of all other variables were partialled out.
* $p < 0.06$
** $p < 0.05$
*** $p < 0.01$

Table 7   Results of Covariance Analyses Predicting Radicalism, Prisonization, Assertive Interactions, Fear, Event Control, and Anxiety

| | Radicalism | | Prisonization | | Assertive Interactions | | Fear | | Event Control | | Anxiety | |
	F	df	F	df	F	df	F	df	F	df	F	df
Total Analysis	22.20**(4,1481)		5.81**(4,1493)		4.63**(4,1495)		2.16 (4,1503)		3.49*(4,1484)		1.32 (4,1464)	
Education	0.01		2.48		2.57				7.78**			
Town or City Size	26.46**		8.96**		0.42				0.72			
Prosocial Activities	2.23		11.12**		6.45*				0.00			
Race	60.10**		0.69		9.06**				5.47*			

* $p < 0.05$
** $p < 0.01$

18

The Role of Education in Prison and the Black Inmate

Arthur Black*

A large majority of prison inmates lack even a basic educational background. Many come from lower-class, deprived neighborhoods where educational development has been thwarted by bad schools, impoverished lives, broken families, and a general sense of hopelessness felt by children and adults alike. Educational programs in prison, then, face the enormous task of instilling a sense of personal responsibility and self worth that will open inmates to the learning process. But the difficulties of working with grown adults who have never experienced the rigors of an educational regimen, who have never had the real opportunity to develop job skills or pursue a profession, are constant reminders that rehabilitation is the most problematic of prison objectives. Even though there is virtually universal agreement that prisons may offer the only opportunity some inmates may have to receive an education, controversy surrounds the types of programs—their structure, content, and extent of commitment—prisons should develop. How far should a prison go to see that inmates are given a fair chance to learn and develop as potentially useful citizens? How should a program be designed to meet the diverse needs of the inmate population? What about those inmates who have been so hardened by deprived lives that education may seem to be "too late?" These questions are just a few that accompany the endless discussions and debates concerning the purposes of imprisonment and the meaning of criminal justice.

Society hopes to achieve at least four major objectives through the use of imprisonment. First, there is the goal of retribution, reflecting society's belief that the criminal must be made to suffer for the wrongdoing (Sykes and Drabeh, 1969:355). Second, there is the goal of deterrence, for the individual who is in prison or for those on the outside who have not yet broken the law (Sykes and Drabeh, 1969:355). Third, it is hoped that somehow imprisonment can lead to rehabilitation so that in the future the law is obeyed gladly rather than from fear (Sykes and Drabeh, 1969:355).

* Dr. Black is the Associate Superintendent of Education for School District #428. He is also the director of Adult Education for the Illinois Department of Corrections.

Fourth, there is the idea that if we can accomplish nothing else we can at least keep the criminal out of circulation (Sykes and Drabeh, 1969:355).

Unfortunately, these goals are rarely achieved because of a conflict in the day-to-day operation of the prison system and, foremost, because of confusion as to what the institutional goals are and how they can be met.

The concept of rehabilitation in prison is a myth. It is a myth not because rehabilitation is impossible, but because many prisoners have never been part of the dominant social order. What is attempted, then, is more a matter of acculturation rather than rehabilitation. Rehabilitation, implies that one was once whole, lost that wholeness, and, through rehabilitative efforts, is on the path to being restored to his or her original state. In relation to a majority of prisoners, particularly black prisoners, this is simply not the case.

Americans must acknowledge that poverty produces sets of rules and norms that are not consistent with those of the dominant culture. This difference goes a far way in explaining crime. For example, the poor are forced to place primary emphasis on securing the fundamentals of living—shelter, food, clothes—while more advantaged classes, secure in these basic requirements, can pursue with relative ease avenues that promote personal and cultural development. Individuals who are not only unemployed but uneducated do not share the same experience of security and self-satisfaction endemic to the dominant culture. Instead, lacking a sense of belonging and sensing the unfairness of living deprived and unfulfilled lives, underprivileged individuals can easily become hostile and resentful. An abandonment of social conscience is not an especially difficult relinquishment for those whose lives are rendered meaningless by poverty.

PRISON EDUCATION

American prisons have always held a disproportionate number of blacks and the trend may become even worse (Keves, 1981:21). In New York prisons, 56 percent of the prisoners are black and an additional 16 percent other minorities. This leaves only 27 percent white, or more than twice as many blacks as whites imprisoned (Keves, 1981:71).

There are indications that the lack of education and job skills may be significant causal factors in anti-social behavior (U.S. Department of Justice, 1979:1). Certainly, the measurable educational levels of inmates are not high:

—   The Federal Bureau of Prisons estimates that up to 50 percent of adults in federal and state facilities can neither read not write
—   90 percent of all inmates have not completed high school

— 85 percent of inmates dropped out of school before their 16th birthday
— The average inmate functions 2-3 grades below the actual number of school years he/she has completed
— Two-thirds of inmates have had no vocational training of any kind

The recognition that the correctional system in this country has not been successful on any level, and that the lack of educational and job skills among inmate populations is unusually high, has caused some penologists to look at education as one practical and powerful solution to both of these ills.

Educational programs began in response to the need to train prisoners to perform particular tasks in the maintenance and operation of the facility. The first teachers or trainers were usually prison officials who were assigned particular duties in the maintenance and operation of the facility or inmates who were skilled and achieved status within the prison environment.

Formal educational programs of any significance in this country are a recent prison innovation. The first school system for all prisoners was established in Maryland in the 1830s, followed by a New York law of 1847 appointing instructors to its prisons (Roberto, 1981:15). Although illiteracy was common among prisoners and was considered to be an important factor leading to incarceration, the growth of prison education was slow. Austin H. MacCormick, who visited nearly all state and federal correctional institutions in 1927-1928, noted that "not a single complete and well-rounded educational program, adequately financed and staffed, was encountered in all the prisons in the country (Roberto, 1981:15). The establishment of the American Prison Association's Committee on Education provided the catalyst for the broad development of educational programs across the country (Roberto, 1981:15).

A long-time handicap to prison teaching staffs has been their "stepchildren" status in the average prison (Keves, 1981:232). In the traditional educational environment, the concept of education is the central theme of the institution. In the prison environment, the central theme is confinement and security; educators must function within the stated objective of security within the institution.

There are several ways to organize educational programs in the prison setting that would provide education with the appropriate status and structure. Illinois and Maryland have established, by statute, correction school district boards of education with the independent powers requisite to serve such a function (Keves, 1981:233). Other states have adopted educational structures that serve the same function as the structure adopted by Illinois and Maryland. In Connecticut and Tennessee the corrections school districts are simply under the direction of the corrections commissioner who delegates the academic program responsibility to a key subordinate with academic credentials (Keves, 1981:232).

Today, education is being viewed more than ever before as a weapon against crime. The large number of individuals being imprisoned who are uneducated and unskilled have provided an awareness of the tremendous need for education in the prison setting. Chief Justice Warren Burger pointed out in his recent address to the American Bar Association:

> We must accept the reality that to confine offenders behind walls without trying to change them is an expensive folly with short term benefits—a winning of battles while losing the war (U.S. Department of Education, 1981:5).

In order for an educational program to be successful in prison, a formal written structure must be established where consistency in function and in operation is possible. The Illinois structure is one example of such a program. The role and responsibility of the different components of the Illinois system are well defined and established. The prison educational structure of Illinois is virtually a mirror image of educational systems found in any other school district in the state. The only difference in the corrections school district and the free world school district is that the correctional school district overlaps other school districts in order to serve the prison, and it contracts with post-secondary institutions for the purpose of providing advanced academic and educational opportunities for the inmates.

The Illinois system has a school board. The school board is responsible for implementing state law, developing policy where necessary to implement the law, and, in the absence of specific law, to serve as a legislative body. The system also has a superintendent; he is the executive officer of the board. His realm is the executive function, while the board is the legislative policymaking body. The superintendent has an executive staff of associate superintendents, an assistant superintendent, and other central office staff designed to carry out the function of administering the school programs. At each correctional center, an educational administrator (in adult facilities) or principal (in juvenile facilities) is responsible for administering the educational program at that site. The educational administrator reports both to the local administrator for institutional responsibilities and to the school district for educational policies. Also at each center is a staff of teachers (academic and vocational); counselors; contractual educators (junior college and college); and clerical personnel that the educational administrator is responsible for. The role of the educational administrator should coincide with the institution's philosophy concerning security and programs. The educational administrator can influence the philosophy of the institution as it relates to education by establishing close working relationships with both security and program staff at the center. The educational administrator, in other words, must be a salesman for education in the prison.

Prison history has been filled with educational success stories. Robert Stroud, the "Birdman of Alcatraz," is the obvious example of the value of education in the prison setting. Stroud dropped out of school at the sixth grade level. He was sentenced to prison at the age of 18. While in prison, he earned diplomas in mechanical drawing, engineering, music, theology, and mathematics from Kansas State Agriculture College. Later Stroud became interested in birds, and dedicated the rest of his life to raising birds and studying their diseases. In this effort he became very knowledgeable as well as in pharmacology, chemistry, medicine, and bacteriology. In 1933, he published a manuscript entitled *Diseases of Canaries* and in 1942, he published *Digest on the Diseases of Birds*. By the time of his death, Robert Stroud was recognized as the world's leading authority on the diseases of birds. Mr. Stroud is by no means the lone example of prison education. Malcolm X, an ex-offender who dropped out of school after the eighth grade, considered to be illiterate at the time of his incarceration, educated himself behind prison bars and consequently became one of the most influential black men of his time. Michael Hogan, a poet and ex-offender from Arizona, is another example of the value of prison education. The fact is, education can and does flourish in prisons where the programs are seriously supported and promoted as a positive aim of the institution.

EDUCATIONAL OPPORTUNITIES AND PROCEDURES IN THE PRISON SETTING FROM A BLACK PERSPECTIVE

Sentencing is only the first step in the imprisonment process. Once a person is sentenced to prison, he/she must go through a reception process. This process includes, along with other activities, a comprehensive psychological and physical checkup and orientation to the prison and housing assignment. The orientation phase of the reception process is often the point where the inmate becomes aware of the educational opportunities available within the institution.

The availability of inmates to participate in educational programs is directly affected by the assignment and adjustment processes in the prison. The assignment process (known as an assignment committee in Illinois) has the responsibility of assigning inmates to programs at the correctional facilities. The racial makeup of this committee is important to the opportunity for fair and equal assignments in the prison. Not only race but

program background is important in the assignment process as well. Individuals with educational backgrounds would generally support assigning inmates to the educational program. The adjustment process (known
as the adjustment committee in Illinois) serves as the judicial body for the
institution. This body can withdraw program opportunities from the inmate or it can award inmates for acts and deeds that are considered by the
institution to be acts reflective of successful rehabilitative efforts. The
racial makeup of this committee and educational background of the members forming this committee directly affect the availability of programs for
the black and minority inmates.

Either of these two programs or committees can slow down the assignment process or make it so complicated that the inmate will lose interest
in enrolling in the educational program at the facility. The role of these two
committees is often overlooked and their importance oversimplified. In the
prison setting, because of the limited physical environment, the racial
makeup of the staff is a significant factor in the assignment of or access
to programs and the successful completion of the program. Black educators
working with the black inmate tend to establish understandings more
quickly. Also, there tends to be less questioning of the black instructor's
reasons as opposed to the white instructor in the educational process. Black
instructors at the facility serve as role models, whether they intended to
serve in that capacity or not.

In order for any educational program to be successful in prison, it is of
utmost importance to establish a sound and consistent testing and placement program. The purposes of the testing and placement program should
be explained very clearly to the inmate. In explaining the process to the
inmate, it is important to stress that the purpose of the testing is not to see
how dumb he/she is, but rather to place him/her in the proper program
to insure the maximum opportunity for success. Another important part
of the testing and placement process is the interpretation of the test results
to the inmate. The test interpretation must be sensitive to the need to
explain the test results in a positive rather than negative manner. It is at
this point that the inmate can gain confidence in his/her ability to compete
successfully in the educational program.

In states where inmates are transferred from institution to institution,
it is important for the educational program to establish a common testing
instrument. A common and consistent testing program can add consistency
to the educational placement of inmates as well as reduce the amount of
testing necessary for proper placement of inmates into the educational
program. There are a number of good as well as bad testing instruments
on the market today. The instrument that is used in the assessment process
should respond to the program's ability to administer it and interpret the

results to the inmate. When an inmate is transferred from one institution to another, his educational records should follow him.

The educational level of the black inmate upon entry to the correctional educational program appears to be lower than that of the white inmate. Substantially more black inmates than white inmates are placed in the ABE program (lower academic program) based on placement test results. Generally more white inmates are placed in the GED program (higher academic program) based on the placement test results. However, the ability to learn appears to be no different. The black inmates are successfully completing the ABE program and continuing on to complete the GED program. The lower academic performance on standardized tests by the black inmate appears to be the result of environment rather than innate ability.

A sound and comprehensive educational program that respects the worth and dignity of the individual is a new experience for a majority of the black inmates. Most of the black inmates dropped out of school before finishing the eighth grade. As a result of leaving school at such an early age, most never tested their academic or vocational ability in a structured environment.

Once the black inmate experiences success in the program, a sense of pride and self confidence often replaces feelings of hostility or inadequacy. The fear of failure loses its strength and learning prowess assumes a powerful, positive status. A common phenomenon observed by many educators and administrators in prison is the emergence of learning characteristics and habits normally assigned to the white middle-class student. For example, it is not uncommon for ambitious black inmates to ask for extra work or complete outside assignments under the impetus of past success.

Because education in prison does not compete with the basic needs of clothing, shelter, and food, as it does in the slum-ghetto environment, well-thought out programs and responsible administration have the potential to give black inmates a new sense of hope and self determination. Until the value of educational programs in prison is recognized, and programs are developed to respond to the special needs and characteristics of minorities, the future of this country's correctional system remains problematic.

References

Brameld, Theodore. The Use of Explosive Ideas in Education. Pittsburgh, Pennsylvania, 1965.

Harton, Paul B. and Hunt, Chester L. Sociology (2nd ed.). New York: McGraw-Hill and Boah Company, 1968.

Keves, Paul W. Corrections. New York: John Wiley and Sons, 1981.

Roberto, Albert R. Readings in Prison Education. Springfield, IL: Charles C. Thomas, 1981.

Rubington, Earl and Weinberg, Martin S. *Deviance.* (3rd ed.). New York: MacMillan, 1978.

Sykes, Graham and Drubeh, Thomas E. Law and the Lawless: A Reader in Criminology. New York: Random House, 1969.

U.S. Department of Education. "Education: A Weapon Against Crime." These proceedings were presented at a forum on prisoner education corrections program, March 26, 1981.

U.S. Department of Justice. "Correctional Education Programs for Inmates." National Evaluation Program Phase I Report. Washington, D.C., U.S. Government Printing Office, June 1979.

19

Discrimination and the Decision to Incarcerate

Sherwood Zimmerman and Bruce C. Frederick

The impact of race and ethnicity on criminal justice processing is a matter of great ethical concern because it goes to the core of our ability as a society to dispense justice in a fair and evenhanded manner. A basic principle of justice in the United States is the equality of individuals in the eyes of the law, and a finding that the criminal justice system discriminates against any group would be a serious indictment of society's ability to function according to the principles we espouse. This concern, and the growing political influence of minorities, has forced criminal justice practitioners and researchers to begin addressing the issue of discrimination. The specific question at issue is whether criminal justice decision makers (police, prosecutors, judges) systematically discriminate against minorities and thereby produce more intrusive or negative consequences than are imposed on similarly situated non-minorities.

It is easy to understand how perceptions of discrimination by the criminal justice system arise. The United States has a long history of discrimination against minorities. Discrimination historically has pervaded virtually every important aspect of society from economic opportunities to interpersonal relations, and the justice system is no exception (Long, et al., 1975; Knowles and Prewitt, 1969). Attempts to eliminate discrimination over the past thirty years have been at least partially successful in areas such as employment and education (Wilson, 1980). There has also been progress toward eliminating discrimination from the criminal justice system, but the amount of progress is a subject of considerable debate (Reasons and Kuykendall, 1972). The debate is fueled both by dramatic incidents of discriminatory behavior and by data concerning the system's routine processing of minority defendants. This chapter addresses the latter issue using data from a cohort of 1980 New York State felony convictions.

DISPROPORTIONALITY AS EVIDENCE FOR DISCRIMINATION

If one examines the number of minority and non-minority persons processed by the criminal justice system, it is immediately apparent that the
number of minorities in the system is disproportional to their numbers in
the overall population. For example, although blacks constituted only
about 12 percent of the U.S. population, they accounted for almost 35
percent of those who were arrested in 1979 (Sourcebook, 1981:352). The
rate at which blacks are incarcerated in state and federal prisons is even
more dramatic: the rate of incarceration per 100,000 population is approximately seven times greater for blacks than for whites (Blumstein, 1982).
This disproportionality has been interpreted by some as evidence of racial
discrimination (Dunbaugh, 1979; Christianson, 1981). Such direct interpretations of these data are not appropriate, however.

As Blumstein (1982) has pointed out, the fact that a group is disproportionately represented at some point in the criminal justice system cannot
directly be interpreted as evidence of discrimination. In the context of
routine criminal justice processing, discrimination is an ethical judgment
made about disproportionality: discrimination is disproportionality that is
not considered justifiable. There are, in fact, many types of individuals
who are disproportionally processed by the system. The normative label
of discrimination is not usually applied because there are acceptable reasons for the differences. For example, males constituted about 96 percent
of the national prison population in 1979, although females comprised over
half of the total U.S. population (Blumstein 1982). The overwhelming
preponderance of males in prisons is not usually viewed as ethically unacceptable because males commit more crimes and generally more serious
crimes than do females (Nettler, 1974). Thus, there are rational and acceptable reasons for their disproportional presence in prison populations. Similarly, persons between 16 and 18 years of age constituted about 17 percent
of all arrests in 1979, but only about 6 percent of the U.S. population
(Sourcebook, 1981:346). The reason 16 to 18 year olds were arrested at such
a high rate is that they committed functionally arrestable criminal acts at
a higher rate than other age groupings (Nettler, 1974), and it would be
inappropriate to infer from these data that they were being discriminated
against by criminal justice decision makers. The problem is whether it is
appropriate to attribute the differential presence of minorities to discriminatory decision making within the system.

Blumstein (1982) examined this issue by comparing the national distributions of arrest rates and incarceration rates for blacks and whites. He
identified the offenses for which individuals were imprisoned and compared the proportions of white and black prisoners with their proportions
in the same offenses at arrest. If post-arrest decisions were highly dis-

criminatory, one would expect large differences between the proportion of black and white offenders arrested for a given offense and the proportion imprisoned for that offense. If processing decisions were not discriminatory, the proportions would be nearly identical for each offense type. Blumstein found that 80 percent of the disproportionality in prison populations could be accounted for by differential arrest rates. That is, blacks were disproportionately arrested for the crimes that typically result in prison sentences (homicide, robbery, assault, burglary), and this arrest differential largely accounted for the racial composition of prison populations. He also found that this relationship was stable from 1970-79.

Blumstein's study demonstrated that the primary component of racial disproportionality in the justice system is the differential created at arrest. Initial racial differences are perpetuated at other decision points, thus creating a system whose clients are predominately minorities. Blumstein suggested a number of other factors that might account for the remaining disproportionality not explained by the arrest charges (the 20%). Racial discrimination in post-arrest processing was one of the possibilities he suggested. For example, racial factors might have influenced prosecutors in deciding who to prosecute and how vigorously to pursue prosecutions. Similarly, racial factors might have influenced sentencing decisions. Although racial discrimination may have been responsible for some of the observed differences, it is not likely to have been the only factor involved; as Blumstein pointed out, arguably legitimate factors such as prior criminal record might also account for a portion of the unexplained 20 percent.

Finally, Blumstein's analysis examined only the initial inputs to the system (arrests) and a single outcome of system processing (prison populations). This type of analysis could not address the possibility that discrimination at one decision point was compensated for in other decisions. Conley and Zimmerman (1982), for example, found that the voting patterns of some Oklahoma Parole Board members systematically favored the release of black inmates. They suggested that this may have been an attempt to redress perceived racial inequities in Oklahoma judges' sentencing decisions. There is clearly a need to examine intervening processing decisions and to account for the effects of other legitimate factors before making judgments about the impact of minority status on criminal justice decisionmaking.

DISCRIMINATION IN SENTENCING

One processing decision of considerable importance is sentencing. Sentencing decisions influenced by a defendant's race or ethnicity are ethically and legally inappropriate. A body of empirical research has addressed the question of discrimination in sentencing decisions, but findings of the research are ambiguous and sometimes contradictory. Some studies have found that minority status (primarily race) had an effect on sentencing, but these studies have been criticized for methodological deficiencies such as the failure to adequately control the effects of other legitimate factors (McNeely and Pope, 1981). Studies that attempted to control for these factors typically have failed to identify minority status as an important element in sentencing decisions (McNeely and Pope, 1981).

Even methodologically sophisticated studies often are conducted in ways that tend to limit the generalizability of their findings. For example, in their analysis of sentencing decisions in Chicago, Newark, and Phoenix, Zimmerman and Tracy (1981) found no significant race effect. This study examined three large metropolitan areas with homogeneous court systems and, presumably, with established processing norms in the felony courts. These more urban courts routinely deal with a larger number of minority defendants than other courts in their respective states. Their routine involvement with minority defendants may lead to the evolution of processing norms quite different from those in non-urban courts where minority defendants are less frequently encountered. Also, community attitudes toward minorities in the metropolitan areas may differ from those in the suburbs, small towns, or rural areas. Generalizing the Zimmerman and Tracy findings to Illinois, New Jersey, and Arizona would almost certainly lead to inaccurate impressions about sentencing outside of Chicago, Newark, and Phoenix.

The current inability to answer questions definitively about sentencing discrimination does not imply that empirical studies are without value. There has been progress toward addressing the issue more rigorously, and each thoughtful study helps in understanding how better to ask and answer the central questions. There have been studies in several specific jurisdictions that were sufficiently rigorous to support valid conclusions about discrimination (or the lack of discrimination). The remainder of this chapter presents the results of a recent analysis that contributes to this growing body of knowledge. This study used relatively refined methods to examine sentencing decisions in New York State.

THE DECISION TO INCARCERATE IN NEW YORK STATE

Data for the New York State study were obtained from the New York State Computerized Criminal History/Offender-Based Transaction Statistics (CCH/OBTS) data base. From the CCH/OBTS files, a group of cases was selected involving probation-eligible offenders who were convicted of felony offenses in 1980. The resulting 11,098 cases[1] constituted the study cohort that supported this empirical analysis of sentencing decisions by New York State judges.

The focus of the analysis was the decision about whether or not a convicted defendant should be incarcerated (the "In/Out" decision). Judicial decisions about the length of confinement were excluded from this analysis. For felons convicted in New York State, the In/Out decision actually involves three basic alternatives or combinations thereof: state prison, county jails, and no incarceration (probation, fines, etc.). County jail sentences of one year or less are possible for probation eligible felons, and the state provides reimbursement to counties for housing convicted felons. Defendants sentenced to county jail received a sentence involving incarceration, so they, along with those sentenced to state prison, were classified as "In" decisions for this analysis. It should also be emphasized that the 11,098 cases involved only defendants who were eligible to receive a probation sentence: defendants for whom prison was mandatory, based on either conviction offense or prior felony convictions, were excluded. These cases were excluded because when mandatory prison sentences were involved, the judges did not make an IN/OUT decision; they only decided on the sentence length.[2] For this analysis, defendants for whom incarceration was not mandatory were referred to as "probation eligible" defendants.

PRELIMINARY ANALYSIS

The racial/ethnic composition of the total cohort of 11,098 probation eligible defendants is displayed in Table 1. Almost 53 percent of the defendants belonged to a minority group for which discriminatory sentencing has been raised as an issue. About 40 percent of the defendants in the cohort were Black, and about 13 percent were Hispanic. Thus, minority defendants slightly outnumbered White defendants.[3] As had been expected from the literature, minority defendants were sentenced to incarceration at a higher rate than Whites. Statewide, almost 53 percent of all probation eligible defendants were incarcerated, but only about 49 percent of the White and Other defendants received jail or prison sentences. About 52 percent of the Hispanic defendants and 58 percent of the Black defendants were incarcerated. The percentage of each group sentenced to state prison was lower but the pattern was similar. These data raise the possibility of discrimination in the sentencing of minority defendants.

As discussed earlier, there are other factors that need to be examined before attributing the differences between the White and minority defendants to discrimination. One factor is regional differences in sentencing patterns. For example, there may have been equitable but more severe treatment of *all* defendants in regions with large numbers of minority defendants. There may also have been discriminatory sentencing in one area of the State and non-discriminatory sentencing patterns in other areas. It was previously suggested that there may be less discrimination against minority defendants in highly urban areas, such as New York City, than in less urban areas of a jurisdiction.

To explore this possibility, the state of New York was divided into three areas and the proportion of incarcerative sentences was calculated for each. Table 2 shows the results of this analysis. Judges incarcerated the highest proportion of defendants in the New York City suburbs (62%) and the lowest proportion Upstate (47%). This analysis also indicated that the majority of probation eligible cases during 1980 came from New York City. The proportion of defendants sentenced to state prison was 24 percent in New York City and about 15 percent in both the Suburban and upstate areas. These data indicate that there were differences in sentencing outcomes among the three regions, and it is thus important to examine the distribution of sentences for each racial/ethnic group within each region separately.

Table 3 shows the result of this cross-classification. Three-quarters of the New York City defendants were minorities; 53% were Black and 22 percent were Hispanic. The New York City judges incarcerated about half of the White and Hispanic defendants, and 55 percent of the Blacks. Although the differences in incarceration rates among racial/ethnic groups were small in New York City, the disproportionality was substantial in the other areas of the State. In both the Suburban and Upstate areas there were very few Hispanic defendants. White defendants predominated in both areas and Whites were much less likely to be incarcerated than Blacks. Blacks were 13 percentage points more likely than Whites to be incarcerated in the Suburban area (71% to 58%) and 17 percentage points more likely to be incarcerated Upstate (61% to 44%). Thus, the complexion of disproportionality between minorities and Whites was different in the three areas of New York, and the statewide distribution (Table 1) masked these differences.

Other Factors Related to Incarceration Rates

One legitimate factor consistently found to influence the decision to incarcerate is the defendant's prior criminal record. In fact, prior criminal activity has usually been found to be the most important influence on IN/OUT decisions (Gottfredson and Gottfredson, 1980). In New York State, defendants with prior *felony* convictions who are subsequently convicted of another felony generally are not eligible for probation and, therefore, would not have been included in these analyses. However, other features of a defendant's criminal history may still have influenced the In/Out decision for these probation eligible defendants. Therefore, a composite scale was created to indicate the intensity of prior involvement with the criminal justice system. The scale ranged from 0 to 3, with 0 indicating no prior criminal history and 3 indicating substantial prior involvement with the justice system. Defendants in this study were given one point for each of the following elements contained in their prior criminal record: one or more prior felony arrests; one or more prior misdemeanor convictions; three or more prior misdemeanor arrests.

As seen in Table 4, the majority of probation eligible defendants had no prior criminal history or only one point on the prior record scale; about 60 percent of the defendants in each region had little or no prior contact with the criminal justice system. The categories of the scale have dramatically increasing percentages of defendants incarcerated as prior criminal involvement becomes more serious. The influence of prior record is the greatest in New York City, where there was a 56 percentage point difference between defendants with no prior record (28% were incarcerated) and defendants with the most serious prior record (84% were incarcerated). Even Upstate, where the range was attenuated, there was a 42 percentage point difference in the incarceration rates of defendants at the two extremes on this scale. Prior record was clearly an important factor in these decisions and it must be considered when analyzing the influence of minority status in sentencing.

Another legitimate factor that has been shown to be an influence on sentencing decisions is the crime for which the defendant was convicted (Gottfredson and Gottfredson, 1980). This factor is often important because it helps explain why defendants with similar prior records can face different risks of being incarcerated. For example, about 32 percent of the New York State defendants who had no prior criminal record were still incarcerated. One reason why these individuals were incarcerated may have been that they committed serious crimes. Conversely, about 18 percent of the defendants with the most serious prior records were not incarcerated, perhaps because they were convicted of relatively minor offenses. One way to examine this issue is to classify the most serious conviction offense in each case according to the type of crime involved. Table 5 shows the distributions of defendants incarcerated when the conviction offenses are categorized into Personal, Property, Drug, and Public Order crimes.

Most of the convictions in New York City involved a Personal crime as the most serious charge (65%). Property offenses were the dominant crime type in the rest of the State, constituting about 60 percent of the conviction offenses. There were differences in the percentage of defendants incarcerated for each offense type, but the differences were much smaller than those related to prior record. In the Suburban and Upstate regions, defendants convicted of Public Order crimes had the lowest likelihood of incarceration, and those convicted of Personal crimes had the highest. In both of these regions there was about a 25 percentage point difference between the rate of incarceration for Public Order and Personal crimes.

The situation in New York City was more complex. About 47 percent of the defendants convicted of Drug and Public Order crimes were incarcerated. The highest rate of incarceration was for Property crimes (59%), and 51 percent of the defendants convicted of Personal crimes were incarcerated. This pattern seems counterintuitive, but may again reflect a joint effect with prior record. For example, there may have been a large number of New York City defendants who committed Property crimes and who also had a serious prior criminal record. It is also possible that interactions between prior record and crime type were operating in other ways that account for the seeming irrationality of the crime type distribution. It is possible, for example, that defendants with extensive prior records and who were convicted of Personal crimes had an even higher likelihood of incarceration than would be suggested from the independent presence of each condition.

The data presented so far make it clear that it is important to examine simultaneously the prior records and conviction offenses of defendants within each region before it is possible to determine whether minority status had a differential impact on sentencing. There are a number of other normatively and legally acceptable factors that can affect sentencing decisions. To the extent that any such factors are wholly or partially confounded with minority status, it could appear that decisions are made on the basis of race or ethnicity. For example, if in a particular jurisdiction Personal crimes are more apt to result in incarcerative sentences than Property crimes, and if in that same jurisdiction the crimes categorized as "person offenses" are more apt to have been committed by minority offenders, then the focus on crime type will tend to result in a disproportionate number of minority defendants being incarcerated. In that case, however, the disproportionality would not necessarily be viewed as discriminatory. To the extent that observed disproportionality can be explained (empirically) on the basis of normatively and legally acceptable factors, the case for discrimination is weakened, at least in the absence of more direct evidence of discriminatory intent. The remainder of this chapter examines the magnitude of the influence of minority statues on the In/Out decision, after controlling the joint influence of a number of legitimate factors.

SIMULTANEOUS CONTROL FOR LEGITIMATE FACTORS

Controlling the joint influence of additional factors could be accomplished by extending the crosstabulations already presented, but tabular analyses involving more than two or three dimensions are difficult to present and confusing to interpret. The preferred method for assessing the joint influence of a large number of variables is to apply simultaneous mathematical controls using multivariate statistical techniques. One such technique that is appropriate for examining the effect of race/ethnicity on the In/Out decision is binary logit analysis (Zimmerman and Tracy, 1981).

Binary logit analysis is a technique for assessing the relationship between a set of "independent" explanatory or predictor variables and a dichotomous "dependent" variable. In the present study, the independent variables are race/ethnicity and the more legitimate control factors such as crime type and prior record. The dependent variable is the dichotomous IN/OUT decision. The result of a binary logit analysis is a mathematical equation, or "model," that specifies the optimum weight given each independent variable in the effort to explain or predict outcomes. In this case, the model equation specifies the relative influence of race/ethnicity and each legitimate control factor on the probability of incarceration.[4]

A list of the variables included in the logit analysis is presented in Table 6. Logit equations were constructed for each region, so the distributions of the variables are also reported separately for each. The regions were analyzed separately because it was believed that there were likely to be such different sentencing patterns in each region that a statewide analysis would mask important differences. Specifically, sentencing patterns in New York City might have resulted in underestimating the influence of race statewide because of the large number of cases in New York City and the apparent lack of sentencing disproportionality there (cf. Table 3).

The prior record scale was treated as a single interval variable (labeled BADGUY). Three of the crime types were treated as separate dichotomous variables. They were coded: personal crime or not (PERS), property crime or not (PROP), and drug crime or not (DRUG). Public order offenses were designated indirectly as not PERS, PROP, or DRUG, and the effects of the public order offenses were therefore absorbed in the equations' "constant" terms.

The statutory class of the conviction offense was included as another index of crime seriousness. In general, the most serious crimes are included in statuatory class A, and the most severe penalties are permitted for these crimes. Subsequent statutory groupings involve increasingly less serious crimes and less severe penalties as sentencing options. Class E offenses are the least serious felonies in New York State. Because there were so few class A, B and C felonies in this probation eligible cohort, these statutory classifications were grouped as one category for this analysis (CLASABC). These serious crimes constituted less than 10 percent of the conviction offenses in all three regions. Class D offenses were treated as a distinct group (CLASD), and constituted the most frequently occuring conviction class in each region. Class E felonies were identified indirectly as not CLASABC or CLASD, and their contribution to the probability of incarceration was absorbed in the constant terms along with that of the Public Order offenses.

Charge reductions were captured in the variable DOWN. This variable indicated the number of statuatory classes that charges were reduced from arrest to conviction, and it was treated as an interval variable in this analysis. DOWN provided a rough indication of the seriousness of the arrest charge (which was likely to be more consistent with the actual offense than the conviction charge), and the type of deal achieved through charge negotiation. This variable was included because it provided information about the seriousness of the arrest offense and about plea bargaining.

Defendants between the ages of 20 and 30 have the highest rates of incarceration of any group (Blumstein, Cohen and Miller, 1980). The variable AGERISK was included in the analysis to determine whether minority defendants have differential incarceration rates when age is (statistically) held constant. Thirty to forty percent of the defendants in the three regions were in this age group. Finally, male defendants were identified by the variable DEFSEX. Males constituted over 90 percent of the probation eligible defendants in the cohort and generally have higher incarceration rates than females. This variable was included to determine whether there were differential sentencing patterns for male and female minority defendants.

The four terms designated in Table 6 as cross products among individual variables (BADXPERS, BADXPROP, BADXDRUG, and PERSXABC) were included to capture effects that may differ from one subgroup to another. BADXPERS was included to investigate the possibility that prior record may have more (or less) influence on IN/OUT decisions for offenders convicted of Personal crimes than for offenders convicted of some other type of crime (or equivalently, that the distinction between Personal and Other crimes matters more for offenders with particular prior record scores). The interactions BADXPROP and BADDRUG were included for similar reasons. The interaction term PERSXABC was also included because it was believed that serious Personal crimes may have had an impact beyond that expected from a simple additive combination of the PERS and CLASABC effects.

For the New York City cases, race was coded so as to reflect separately, any differences between Blacks and Whites and between Hispanics and Whites. The Hispanic-white contrast was expected to have negligible effects in the Suburban and Upstate equations due to the small number of Hispanics in these regions. Consequently, for the regions outside New York City, race was treated as a single variable contrasting Blacks and Hispanics with Whites and Others.

RESULTS OF THE LOGIT ANALYSES

There are at least two related types of inferences that can be drawn from the results of the logit analyses. First, it can be determined whether including race in the statistical model reliably improves the precision with which one can ascertain the probability of incarceration, beyond the precision that would be obtained from considering only the more legitimate "control" factors. Second, the independent contribution of each variable to the overall probability of incarceration is reflected in the relative magnitudes of the coefficients in the model equations. Thus, one can determine the magnitude of the differences that race makes in the probability of incarceration when the other factors included in the model are held constant.

The results of the logit analyses are presented in Table 7. The percent of cases that would be correctly classified by each model suggests that the models do have appreciable explanatory value. The variation in sentencing left unexplained by the models may be due to the influence of factors that were not available for analysis or simply due to unsystematic variation in judicial decision making. The asterisks attached to the race coefficients indicate that eliminating race from consideration would significantly decrease the ability to explain the probability of incarceration in the Suburban and Upstate regions, but would not make a statistically significant difference for explaining the outcomes of the New York City cases.

The magnitudes of the weighting coefficients indicate that individual variables tend to have different relative influences in different regions.[5] For example, although the degree of charge reduction (DOWN) was among the more influential variables in the Upstate and Suburban regions, its relative impact appears to have been much less in New York City. Also, although prior record (BADGUY) was the most influential variable in all three regions,[6] its relative impact was substantially greater in New York City.

The magnitude of the race effect, adjusting statistically for the influence of other factors, was negligible in New York City, but appreciable in the Upstate and Suburban regions. Although race was less important than prior record, it appears to have been more important than, for example, whether the offender was in a high risk age group.

The magnitudes of the weighting coefficients have a known relationship to the probabilities of incarceration. If, for a specific type of case, the corresponding codes for each variable are inserted into the model equations, the equations can then be used to calculate a composite risk score for cases of that type. The risk score is expressed as the natural logarithm of an odds ratio, and can be easily converted to a probability statement. For example, a case with a risk score of zero has a 50 percent chance of incarceration (1:1 odds). In order to illustrate the expected magnitudes of race effects in the three regions, the probability of incarceration was calculated for several hypothetical case studies.

CASE STUDIES

The probabilities of incarceration in each region are presented in Table 8 for six hypothetical case studies. *CASE 1-W* assumes a White defendant between the ages of 20 and 30 with a prior record score of "1," arrested for a class D person offense and convicted of a class E Person offense. *CASE 1-B* has the same characteristics as CASE 1-W, except that the defendant is assumed to be Black. *CASE 2-W* and *CASE 2-B* refer respectively to White and Black defendants *not* in the high risk age group with prior record scores equal to "1," arrested for a class B Person offense and convicted of a person offense one class lower than the arrest offense. *CASE 3-W* and *CASE 3-B* refer to defendants not in the high risk age group with prior record scores equal to "0," arrested for a class C Property offense and convicted of a class D Property offense.

The probabilities of incarceration for these six cases indicate that even similarly situated defendants face systematically different risks of incarceration depending on the region in which the case is decided,[7] and whether the defendants are Black or White. The case studies also illustrate the magnitudes of these differences, and show that Black defendants face a greater risk of incarceration than Whites, especially in the Suburban and Upstate regions, and especially in the middle range where the outcome is a "toss up" and the greatest discretion is exercised. Among the case studies examined, race makes the greatest difference for a (probably young) Property offender with *no* prior record whose case is decided in the Suburban region.

CONCLUSION

It is clear that the empirical analysis of racial discrimination in criminal justice decision making is complex. Limiting the analysis to gross population comparisons will overstate the problem, and can produce misleading information as to whether discriminatory decision making exists. It should also be noted that analyses of formal processing decisions ignore many less visible decisions in which discrimination might operate. Harassment of minorities by system personnel, less desirable work assignments, and indifference to important cultural needs could exist, but not be systematically reflected in formal processing decisions.

Even the relatively refined analysis of the more restricted questions examined in this chapter cannot indicate conclusively whether racial discrimination is a factor in the IN/OUT decision. Although the analysis did control for most of the obvious legitimate influences on sentencing decisions, other potentially important factors were not available for study (e.g., weapons use or injury to victims). If influential factors not included in the study happen to be correlated with race, then some of the disproportionality that is due to the omitted factors will be attributed to race. For example, long-term unemployment is generally thought to help predict criminal recidivism, and, therefore, may influence judges' sentencing decisions. Since the unemployment rate tends to be much higher among blacks, when employment status is considered at sentencing it tends to produce disproportionate incarceration rates for black defendants. Depending on one's ethical judgments about its legitimacy, attending to non-criminal attributes that help predict recidivism may or may not be considered discriminatory. In either case, however, it would not be possible to determine conclusively whether the observed disproportionality was due to race per se.

On the other hand, conclusive proof is not required for some purposes. Kaye (1982) has recently reviewed the use of statistical evidence in court cases alleging discrimination in jury selection and employment decisions. He suggested that statistically reliable evidence of grossly disparate impact may be sufficient to establish the existence of discrimination. In the Suburban and Upstate regions of New York State, the disparate impact of race on the IN/OUT decision was statistically significant. Moreover, race was nearly as influential as other more legitimate factors. A definitive conclusion about the effect of race in these sentences would require in-depth studies of judges' sentencing decisions. Such studies would have to include a variety of factors not available in the data supporting the research presented here. From the data presented, however, it can be concluded that there is a prima facie case that race plays an important role in sentencing defendants from the Suburban and Upstate regions of New York State.

Notes

[1] It is estimated that between 20% and 30% of the final court dispositions had not been reported at the time the data were extracted from the CCH/OBTS file.

2 It is interesting to note that the 2,206 probation eligible felons sentenced to New York State prisons in 1980 represented only about one-third of all those who received prison sentences. That is, about two-thirds of those sentenced to prison were incarcerated due to mandatory sentencing statutes. This suggests the powerful influence that mandatory sentencing laws had on prison populations.

3 The category containing White defendants also included a few "Other" individuals such as orientals, American Indians, etc. Because those groups were so sparsely represented, and because they seemed to be treated similarly to White defendants, they were combined with Whites to form a "White and Other" category.

4 Readers who are interested in a more complete introduction to binary logit analysis and relate techniques should refer to an intermediate level statistics textbook, for example, Hanushek and Jackson (1977).

5 Because the constant term is different for each region, direct comparisons of coefficients across equations can be somewhat complex. Comparisons of relative within-region contributions will be generally less misleading.

6 Because BADGUY is a four-point scale and most of the other variables are dichotomous, one should approximately double the BADGUY coefficients to assess the relative impact of prior record.

7 Analyses not reported here suggest that the higher risk of incarceration outside New York City is due largely to jail rather than prison sentences.

References

Blumstein, Alfred. "On the racial disproportionality of the United States prison population," Journal of Criminal Law and Criminology 73(3), 1982.

——————— Jacqueline Cohen and Harold D. Miller. "Demographically disaggregated projections of prison populations," Journal of Criminal Justice 8(1), 1980.

Christianson, Scott and Richard Dehais. "The black incarceration rate in the United States: a nationwide problem," Draft Report: Training Program in Criminal Justice Education, School of Criminal Justice, State University of New York at Albany, August 1980.

Conley, John A. and Sherwood E. Zimmerman. "Decision making by a part-time parole board: an observational and empirical study," Criminal Justice and Behavior 9(4), 1982.

Dunbaugh, Frank M. "Racially disproportionate rates of incarceration in the United States," Prison Law Monitor 2(9), 1979.

Flanagan, Timothy J., David J. van Alstyne, and Michael R. Gottfredson, eds. Sourcebook of Criminal Justice Statistics—1981. Albany, NY: Criminal Justice Research Center, 1981.

Gottfredson, Michael R. and Don M. Gottfredson. Decisionmaking in Criminal Justice: Toward the Rational Exercise of Discretion. Cambridge, MA: Ballinger, 1980.

Hanushek, Eric and John Jackson. Statistical Methods for Social Scientists. New York: Academic Press, 1977.

Kaye, David. "Statistical evidence of discrimination," Journal of the American Statistical Association 77(380), 1982.

Knowles, Lewis and Kenneth Prewitt. Institutional Racism in America. Englewood Cliffs, NJ: Prentice-Hall, 1975.

Long, Elton, et al. American Minorities: The Justice Issues. Englewood Cliffs, NJ: Prentice-Hall, 1975.

McNeely R.L. and Carl E. Pope. "Race, crime and criminal justice: an overview," in McNeely and Pope, Race, Crime and Criminal Justice. Beverly Hills, CA: Sage Publications, 1981.

Nettler, Gwynn. Explaining Crime. New York: McGraw-Hill, 1974.

Reasons, Charles R. and Jack L. Kuykendall. Race, Crime and Justice. Pacific Palisades, CA: Goodyear Publishing Company, 1972.

Wilson, William J. The Declining Significance of Race: Blacks and Changing American Institutions. Chicago: University of Chicago Press, 1980.

Zimmerman, Sherwood E. and Ronald L. Tracy. "Models of sentencing behavior," paper presented at the Criminal Sentencing Panel of CORS-TIMS-ORSA, Joint National Meeting, May 1981.

Table 1   Distribution of Sentences by Race/Ethnicity

Race/Ethnicity	Number		% Incarcerated	% Prison
Black	4,416	(39.8%)	58.0%	24.2%
Hispanic	1,409	(12.7%)	52.2%	19.9%
White & Other	5,273	(47.5%)	48.7%	16.2%
TOTAL New York State	11,098	(100%)	52.9%	19.9%

Table 2   Distribution of Sentences by Region

Region	Number		% Incarcerated
New York City	6,078	(54.8%)	53.2%
Suburban	1,735	(15.6%)	62.5%
Upstate	3,285	(29.6%)	47.2%
TOTAL New York State	11,098	(100%)	52.9%

Table 3   Distribution of Sentences by Race/Ethnicity within Region

Region	Race/Ethnicity	Number		% Incarcerated
New York City	Black	3,231	(53.2%)	55.2%
	Hispanic	1,357	(22.3%)	50.9%
	White & Other	1,490	(24.5%)	50.2%
Suburban	Black	580	(33.4%)	70.7%
	Hispanic	37	(2.1%)	62.2%
	White & Other	1,118	(64.4%)	58.3%
Upstate	Black	605	(18.4%)	60.8%
	Hispanic	15	(0.4%)	60.0%
	White & Other	2,665	(81.1%)	43.9%

Table 4   Distribution of Sentences by Prior Criminal Involvement within Region

Region	Prior Scale	Number		% Incarcerated
New York City	0	2,188	(36.0%)	28.1%
	1	1,390	(22.9%)	53.7%
	2	1,663	(27.4%)	70.2%
	3	837	(13.8%)	84.2%
Suburban	0	648	(37.3%)	42.3%
	1	405	(23.3%)	69.1%
	2	405	(23.3%)	74.3%
	3	277	(16.0%)	83.0%
Upstate	0	1,506	(47.5%)	32.5%
	1	809	(24.6%)	54.5%
	2	563	(17.1%)	60.2%
	3	353	(10.7%)	74.2%
TOTAL New York State	0	4,396	(39.6%)	31.7%
	1	2,604	(23.5%)	56.3%
	2	2,631	(23.7%)	68.7%
	3	1,467	(13.2%)	81.6%

Table 5   Distribution of Sentences by Conviction Crime Type within Region

Region	Crime Type	Number		% Incarcerated
New York City	Personal	3,344	(55.0%)	51.4%
	Property	1,981	(32.6%)	58.6%
	Drug	573	(9.4%)	47.1%
	Public Order	180	(3.0%)	46.7%
Suburban	Personal	388	(22.4%)	68.3%
	Property	1,044	(60.2%)	65.5%
	Drug	111	(6.4%)	50.5%
	Public Order	192	(11.1%)	41.7%
Upstate	Personal	587	(17.9%)	59.8%
	Property	1,946	(59.2%)	47.6%
	Drug	123	(3.7%)	44.7%
	Public Order	629	(19.1%)	34.3%
TOTAL New York State	Personal	4,319	(38.9%)	54.1%
	Property	4,971	(44.8%)	55.7%
	Drug	807	(7.3%)	47.2%
	Public Order	1,000	(9.0%)	38.0%

Table 6   Variables Used in the Logit Analysis

Variable Name	Variable Description	New York City (N=6078)	Suburban (N=1735)	Upstate (N=3285)
BADGUY[a]	Prior Record Scale	X̄=1.1890	X̄=1.1793	X̄=.9114
PERS[b]	Convicted of Personal Crime	55.0%	22.4%	17.9%
PROP[b]	Convicted of Property Crime	32.6%	60.2%	59.2%
DRUG[b]	Convicted of Drug Crime	9.4%	6.4%	3.7%
CLASABC[b]	Convicted of Class A, B, or C Felony	9.1%	5.4%	3.4%
CLASD[b]	Convicted of Class D Felony	52.5%	39.5%	46.1%
DOWN[c]	Number of Classes Charge Reduced	X̄=1.0535	X̄=.7372	X̄=.5306
AGERISK[b]	Defendant's Age Between 20 & 30	41.1%	31.2%	36.3%
DEFSEX[b]	Male Defendants	93.6%	92.6%	93.3%
BADXPERS[d]	BADGUY X PERS Interaction	—	—	—
BADXPROP[d]	BADGUY X PROP Interaction	—	—	—
BADXDRUG[d]	BADGUY X DRUG Interaction	—	—	—
PERSXABC[d]	PERS X CLASABC Interaction	—	—	—
RACE[b]	Black	53.2%	35.5%	18.8%
	Hispanic	22.3%		
IN/OUT	Defendants Incarcerated (dependent variable)	53.2%	62.5%	47.2%

a = coded 0, 1, 2, or 3
b = coded +1 = yes; −1 = no
c = coded 0, 1, or 2
d = calculated as the products of the component

Table 7   Results of Logit Analyses

		Logit Coefficients	
Variable Name	New York City	Suburban	Upstate
CONSTANT	−1.524	−0.253	−0.106
BADGUY	1.109**	0.641**	0.461**
PERS	−0.232	0.411*	0.542**
PROP	−0.336**	0.289	0.120
DRUG	−0.389**	0.238	0.219
CLASABC	0.181**	0.282*	0.738**
CLASD	0.280**	0.191**	0.263**
DOWN	0.072	0.399**	0.361**
AGERISK	0.100**	0.087	0.063
DEFSEX	0.346**	0.538**	0.454**
BADXPERS	0.238**	0.039	−0.054
BADXPROP	0.342**	0.158	0.065
BADXDRUG	0.183*	−0.085	−0.160
PERSXABC	0.041	0.035	0.233*
RACE: BLACK	0.073		
HISPANIC	0.033	0.210**	0.153**
Cases Correctly Classified:	70.0%	73.4%	70.1%

* Significant at .05 level.
** Significant at .01 level.

Table 8   Probabilities of Incarceration of Six Hypothetical Case Studies

				Case Characteristics					Probabilities		
Case	Race	Age 20-30	Prior Record Score	Arrest Class	Arrest Type	Conviction Class	Conviction Type		New York City[a]	Suburban	Upstate
CASE1-W	White	Yes	1	D	PERS	E	PERS		.43	.63	.52
CASE1-B	Black	Yes	1	E	PERS	E	PERS		.47	.72	.60
								DIFFERENCE	.04[a]	.09	.08
CASE2-W	White	No	1	B	PERS	C	PERS		.49	.73	.87
CASE2-B	Black	No	1	B	PERS	C	PERS		.53	.81	.90
								DIFFERENCE	.04[a]	.08	.03
CASE3-W	White	No	0	C	PROP	D	PROP		.29	.49	.40
CASE3-B	Black	No	0	C	PROP	D	PROP		.33	.60	.48
								DIFFERENCE	.04[a]	.11	.08

[a] The race coefficients for New York City were not statistically significant, therefore, the differences in probabilities displayed for New York City should be viewed as unreliable.

Conclusion

20

An Uncertain Future

Daniel Georges-Abeyie

The Reagan Administration has saddled "affirmative action" with the misnomer "reverse discrimination" and has declared a war on crime that will probably result in the continued abrogation of the rights of America's black minority. Law without justice and attempted enforcement of judicial and social order without social conscience demean this country's notion of democratic ideals. Nevertheless, this trend is likely to continue if the American correctional and law enforcement policies first advocated by former Attorney General Smith and the Reagan Task Force Recommendation on Violent Crime become the legal-social reality of the 1980s. America's "black prisons" are becoming "blacker" and the renewed demand for more severe sentences, capital punishment, bail "reform," and revisions in the exclusionary rule in regard to admissible evidence highlight an American obsession with "law and order" rather than justice.

Law without justice and the attempted enforcement of judicial and social order without social conscience have been well documented American social realities.[1] These social realities have taken the form of political trials[2] cultural bias,[3] vigilante and collective violence,[4] prejudicial enforcement of law in both the police and court functions,[5] prejudicial laws,[6] post-trial practices and procedures,[7] and corrections.[8] What remains a chronic uncertainty for America's black minority is the possibility of equal justice under the law.

The issue of justice, much less equal justice under the law, is of crucial significance when one is made aware of the preponderance of blacks as clients within the American criminal justice process as well as black and white attitudes about criminal justice fairness and efficiency.

BLACKS AS CRIMINAL JUSTICE CLIENTS

The 1982 FBI *Uniform Crime Reports, Crime in the United States* (F.B.I., 1983:38) reports the occurrence of 12,857,200 Crime Index Offenses, a three percent decline from 1981, the first significant annual decrease since 1977. Howev-

337

er, if one considers a longer time frame, the 1982 total was up 15 percent over the 1978 figure and 47 percent higher than that for 1973. That Index Offenses remain a too common reality is without dispute. Of special significance to us, as students of the relationship of crime and race, are the following facts:

(1)   murder and non-negligent manslaughter remain as intraracial crime;

(2)   blacks are disproportionately represented in both the victim and offender categories;

(3)   blacks in 1982 comprised 35.6 percent of those arrested for index offenses; or more specifically, blacks comprised 46.7 percent of those arrested for violent crimes (i.e., murder and non-negligent manslaughter, forcible rape, robbery and aggravated assaults); and 32.7 percent of those arrested for the following property crimes; larceny-theft motor vehicle theft and arson;

(4)   blacks in 1982 comprised 38.2 percent of those arrested within cities (F.B.I., 1983), 26.9 percent of those arrested within suburban counties (F.B.I., 1982), and 19.3 percent of those arrested within rural counties (F.B.I., 1982).

In brief, the 1982 *Uniform Crime Reports* (F.B.I., 1983) documents the high visibility of blacks as clients of the American criminal justice system. This fact is especially important, and disturbing when we note the American public's fear of crime and of being criminally victimized (see Flanagan and McLeod, *Sourcebook of Criminal Justice Statistics—1982* (1983:210-222). It should be noted that these fears are much more widespread than the patterns of crime commission and likely criminal victimization (Harries, 1974; Georges-Abeyie and Harries, 1980).

CRIME CONTROL AND "LAW AND ORDER"

This apparent American obsession with crime, and fear of crime and criminal victimization has been translated into repressive suggestions for reform of the American criminal justice process and the ever increasing demand, especially by whites, for greater severity in the treatment of criminals. These concerns, fears, reforms, and "insights" can be summarized as follows:

(1)   the majority of white Americans sampled favor capital punishment (Flanagan and McLeod, 1983:264);

(2)   the majority of white Americans believe that judges should have

the right to prohibit newspapers from printing information about certain criminal cases (Hindelang, Gottfredson, Flanagan, 1980:182);

(3) 53 percent of Americans believe that the press and the public should be excluded from some trials, although the U.S. Constitution says that court trials should be public (Hindelang, Gottfredson, Flanagan, 1980:182);

(4) the majority of Americans approve of a policeman's right to strike a citizen under certain circumstances;

(5) only 25 percent of the American public has "a great deal" of confidence in the U.S. Supreme Court (Flanagan and McLeod, 1982:246-247);

(6) 83 percent of the U.S. public believes that the courts, in general, in their own area, do *not* deal harshly enough with criminals (Flanagan and McLeod, 1982:248-249).

But perhaps the most disturbing translation of the American citizenry's fear of and concern with crime has come from the government itself, in the form of statements by former Attorney General William French Smith and the report of the Reagan Administration's 44-point crime bill entitled *Task Force Recommendation on Violent Crime* (Bell and Thompson, 1981) chaired by former U.S. Attorney General Griffin Bell and Illinois Republican Governor James Thompson.

Time Magazine (September 18, 1981:28) notes that Attorney General Smith has declared violent crime the Justice Department's top priority; and accordingly, the department, this fall may push Congress for a federal death penalty; a loosening of the "exclusionary rule" that makes illegally obtained evidence inadmissible at trials; and stricter bail laws, including the right to refuse bail to dangerous offenders—actions liable to infringe upon the life and liberty of the poor and the black more heavily than upon white middle-class America. According to Ira Glasser, Executive Director of the American Civil Liberties Union, these reforms are harmful to civil liberties and they won't have any impact on crime (*Time Magazine,* September 28, 1981:28). More specifically, the Reagan Task Force on Violent Crime included the following recommendations:

(1) The construction of more jails, with Washington paying 75 percent of the construction costs over the next four years (some $20 billion) with states assuming the remaining cost.

(2) Bail reform which allows judges to consider the "dangerousness" of a defendant before placing him on bail; thus a movement away from the setting of bail supposedly based *solely* on the likelihood that the accused will flee.

(3)   The establishment of uniform guidelines for sentencing and the abolishment of parole; criminals convicted of federal crimes would serve full terms.

(4)   The "patch up" of a loophole in the 1968 Gun Control Act that allows parts for "saturday night specials"—though not the guns themselves—to be imported. This "patchup" of the 1968 Gun Act would also require a waiting period for prospective gun buyers so that police authorities could check for criminal records.

(5)   The loosening of the exclusionary rule under which illegally obtained evidence is found inadmissible. The Task Force recommendation suggests that illegally obtained evidence be admissible to court if the police can show they were acting "in good faith" when the evidence was seized.

(6)   Limiting habeas corpus petitions which allow prisoners to try repeatedly to get their convictions dismissed on constitutional grounds.

(7)   The curtailment of the insanity defense, making it applicable only to a person who is unable to appreciate the nature or wrongness of his acts. A defendant would have to prove he was insane at the time of the crime instead of the prosecution having to prove that he was sane, as is now the case. The new law would eliminate expert testimony on the defendant's condition at the time of the crime.

If one couples the Reagan *Task Force Recommendation on Violent Crime* with statements and policy initiatives by Attorney General Smith and President Reagan, one is forced to note a bleak future for blacks who become clients of the justice system. Also, there seems to be a headlong executive department rush away from the principles of affirmative action; note the appointment of federal judges. *Time Magazine* (September 28, 1981:28) states that almost all the judges recruited by the Justice Department have been white and male. Of the 47 judges selected only one is black and two are women. Jimmy Carter, by contrast, chose 41 women and 37 blacks among his 281 federal judges. One should also be aware of the overrepresentation of blacks in American prisons, an imbalance that is growing worse, not better. This prison population racial imbalance coupled with the dearth of black judges and the continued disproportionate (and increasing) representation of blacks on death row should alarm America's black minority. And if execution rates are examined, by offense and by percent distribution by race, the shocking reality is that from 1930 to 1981, 53 percent of the individuals executed were black and that an even higher percentage of blacks have been executed for crimes other than murder.

The assurance of justice for blacks under the law, and not just law enforcement against black law violators, is questionable at best, under a presidency that has sacked U.S. Civil Rights Commissioners for being too outspoken in support of affirmative action; and has, in fact, appointed a female Hispanic who publicly states that the U.S. Civil Rights Commission will challenge mandatory affirmative action guidelines and laws as well as equal pay for comparable work guidelines and laws championed by past U.S. Civil Rights Commissions. This uncertainty about the possibility of equal justice for blacks under the law is perhaps most eloquently voiced by New York City Supreme Court Justice Bruce Wright in the interview presented in Chapter 21.

Notes

[1] See, Leon Wilmer and Paul B. Weston, *American Minorities: The Justice Issue* (Englewood Cliffs, NJ: Prentice-Hall, 1975); Isaac D. Balbus, *The Dialectics of Legal Repression* (New York: Russell Sage Foundation, 1973); Derrick Bell Jr., *Race, Racism and American Law* (Boston: Little, Brown and Company, 1973); Gilbert Ware, *From the Black Bar* (New York: G.P. Putnam's Sons, 1976); Charles E. Reasons and Jack L. Kuykendall, *Race, Crime and Justice* (Pacific Palisades, CA: Goodyear Publishing Company, Inc., 1972); Scott Christianson, *Index to Minorities and Criminal Justice: 1981 Cumulative Edition* (Albany, NY: Research Foundation of the State University of New York at Albany, 1981).

[2] See, Haywood Burns, "Political Uses of the Law." In Gilbert Ware, *From the Black Bar.*

[3] See Daniel H. Swett, "Cultural Bias in the American Legal System." In Reasons and Kuykendall, *Race, Crime and Justice;* Louis A. Radelet, *The Police and the Community* (Encino, CA; Glencoe Publishing Co., 1980).

[4] See Arthur F. Raper, *The Tragedy of Lynching* (New York: Arno Press and The New York Times, 1969); Joe R. Feagin, and Harlan Hahn, *Ghetto Revolts* (New York: MacMillan Publishing Co., Inc., 1973); Joseph Boskin, *Urban Racial Violence* (Beverly Hills, CA: Glencoe Press, 1976); Willard A. Heaps, *Riots USA 1765-1970* (New York: Seabury Press, 1970); Anthony M. Platt, *The Politics of Riot Commissions* (New York: Macmillan Company, 1971); Louis H. Masotti and Don R. Bowen, *Civil Violence in the Urban Community* (Beverly Hills: Sage, 1968); Hugh D. Graham and Ted R. Gurr, *The History of Violence in America* (New York: Bantam Books, 1970); Otto Kerner, *The Report of the National Advisory Commission on Civil Rights* (New York: Bantam Books, 1968).

[5] See Reasons and Kuykendall *Race, Crime and Justice;* Ware, *From the Black Bar;* Christianson, *Index to Minorities.*

[6] See Bell, *Race and Racism;* George Crockett Jr., "Racism in the Law." In Reasons and Kuykendall, *Race, Crime and Justice;* Haywood Burns, "Political Uses of the Law." In Ware, *From the Black Bar;* Christianson, *Index to Minorities.*

[7] Ware, *From the Black Bar;* Christianson, *Index to Minorities.*

[8] See Christianson's article in this volume; also see Georges-Abeyie, "Blacks, Crime and Criminal Justice: An Overview" in this volume; Christianson, *Index to Minorities.*

References

Balbus, Isaac, D. The Dialectics of Legal Repression. New York: Russell Sage Foundation, 1973.

Bell, Derrick, A., Jr. Race, Racism and American Law. Boston: Little, Brown and Company, 1973.

Bell, Griffen and James Thompson (Chairman). Task Force on Violent Crime. Washington, DC: U.S. Government Printing Office, 1980.

Boskin, Joseph. Urban Racial Violence. Beverly Hills, CA: Glencoe Press, 1976.

Burns, Haywood. "Political uses of the law," in Gilbert Ware (ed.), From the Black Bar. New York: G.P. Putnam; 1976:18-31.

Christianson, Scott. Index to Minorities and Criminal Justice: 1981 Cumulative Edition. Albany, NY: Research Foundation of the State University of New York at Albany, 1981.

Christianson, Scott. "Our black prisons." In Daniel Georges-Abeyie (ed.), Blacks, Crime, and Criminal Justice. New York: Clark Boardman Company, Ltd., 1984.

Crockett, George W., Jr. "Racism in the law," in Charles Reasons and Jack Kuykendall (eds.), Race, Crime and Justice. Pacific Palisades, CA: Goodyear Publishing Company, 1972: 104-109.

Feagin, Joe R. and Harlan Hahn. Ghetto Revolts. New York: Macmillan, 1973.

Federal Bureau of Investigation. Crime in the United States: Uniform Crime Report—1982. Washington, DC: U.S. Government Printing Office, 1983.

Flanagan, Timothy and Maureen McLeod (eds.). Sourcebook of Criminal Justice Statistics—1982. Albany, NY: Criminal Justice Research Center, 1983.

Georges-Abeyie, Daniel E. and K.D. Harries (eds.). Crime: A Spatial Perspective. New York: Columbia University Press, 1980.

Georges-Abeyie, Daniel E. "The Criminal Justice System and Minorities-A Review of the Literature," In Georges-Abeyie (ed.), Criminal Justice System and Blacks. New York: Clark Boardman Company, Ltd., 1984.

Graham, Hugh D. and Ted R. Gurr. The History of Violence in America. New York: Bantam Books, 1970.

Harries, K.D. The Geography of Crime and Justice. New York: McGraw-Hill, 1974.

Heaps, Willard A. Riots U.S.A. 1765-1970. New York: Seabury Press, 1970.

Hindelang, Michael J., Michael R. Gottfredson, and Timothy J. Flanagan (eds.). Sourcebook of Criminal Justice Statistics—1980. Albany, NY; Criminal Justice Research Center, 1981.

Kerner, Otto. The Report of the National Advisory Commission on Civil Rights. New York: Bantam Books, 1968.

Long, Elton; James Long; Wilmer Leon; and Paul B. Weston. American Minorities: The Justice Issue. Englewood Cliffs, NJ: Prentice-Hall, 1975.

Masotti, Louis H. and Don R. Bowen. Civil Violence in the Urban Community. Beverly Hills, CA: Sage Publications, 1968.

Platt, Anthony M. The Politics of Riot Commissions. New York: Macmillan, 1971.

Radelet, Louis A. The Police and the Community. Encino, CA: Glencoe, 1980.

Raper, Arthur F. The Tragedy of Lynching. New York: Arno Press and the New York Times, 1969.

Reasons, Charles E. and Jack L. Kuykendall (eds.). Race, Crime and Justice. Pacific Palisades, CA: Goodyear Publishing Company, 1972.

Swett, Daniel H. "Cultural bias in the American legal system," in Charles E. Reasons and Jack L. Kuykendall (eds.), Race, Crime and Justice. Pacific Palisades, CA: Goodyear Publishing Company, 1972:28-55.

Time Magazine. September 28, 1981:28.

U.S. Department of Justice. Uniform Crime Reports: Crime in the United States 1982. Washington, DC: U.S. Government Printing Office, 1983.

U.S. Department of Justice. Capital Punishment—1981. Washington, DC: U.S. Government Printing Office, 1982.

Ware, Gilbert (ed.). From the Black Bar. New York: G.P. Putnam, 1976.

Wright, Bruce. "A View from the bench," in Gilbert Ware (ed.), From the Black Bar. New York: G.P. Putnam, 1976:85-103.

21

Interview with Judge
Bruce McM. Wright*

Judge Wright believes that judges are inadequately trained for the complicated legal as well as human task of determining guilt or innocence. He contends that the typical judge lacks training in black and hispanic culture (or any minority racial or ethnic group culture or history) as well as training in sociology, psychology, psychoanalysis, psychiatry, and sociological jurisprudence. Judge Wright reveals his views on the criminal justice system, recognizing that the system has great potential, but that it has yet to fulfill its promise. This interview touches on a number of controversial issues surrounding black judges, black defendants and inmates, and the failure of the system to adequately address the true causes of crime and those blacks and other minority groups which have been victimized by poverty and a heritage of subjugation.

Question: What are your general views on the effects of racism on the criminal justice system?

Answer: I think that the system can lead to just outcomes, but not often. I especially believe that juries are a very difficult aspect of the system. For instance, Dr. Harry Kalven of the University of Chicago did an indepth study on northern juries judging blacks. He concluded that those juries generally felt that black defendants must have done something wrong, perhaps something worse than what they are accused of. In regard to racism in the system—many scholars in this country have indicted the system as racist. Derrick Bell has written one of the most effective books, I think. It's in plain and simple, blunt, language. He details instances of racism in the American judicial system. Judge Leon Higgenbotham has done an even more scholarly work, citing research in the matter of color and the roots of racism in the system itself.

The people who say that the criminal justice system is satisfactory are the same people who are proud that we were in Vietnam and who are as equally proud of our involvement in Lebanon and other places abroad. They're the people who believe that the government never lies. Of course we have racism in our system—racism which is reflected by the limited number of black judges on any bench and by the eighty-five to ninety

---

* Interview conducted December 7, 1983.

percent of the people who appear before the criminal bars of our urban areas who are black or who may be hispanic. I also point to a system where the police are taught to characterize any person with a Spanish name as white when he stands before the bench; I certainly resent the long-standing discrimination of the police which used to be dominated here in New York and in Boston by the Irish and Catholics. The Irish at one time were known as the "white niggers" in this city. And they competed with blacks for the lowest, meanest jobs that were available in those days. One of the lowest being the so-called night soil tax, that is emptying outhouses before modern plumbing. The system is also corrupt in a way because it deliberately excludes black women from the bench. It does not try to attract them to the profession—to that extent I suppose it's black sexist. And the system is gravely deficient in my view because of our reluctance to train judges. I think that in a city such as New York where there is a large non-white population judges who have not been trained in sociology and judges who know nothing of social work, black history, the black struggle, or hispanic culture; they will judge us as aliens.

Question: In terms of the background training for judges in general, what's necessary in terms of treating blacks more fairly before the bench? What types of programs would you initiate to correct the training of judges in general?

Answer: I have urged more comprehensive training of judges over a period of years in many of my speeches; only Georgetown University's Law School indicated some interest in that concept, but they could not get the funding. Judging is a kind of arrogance. You sit in judgment of your fellow human beings as though you have committed no sins. Therefore, judges should be adequately trained and prepared for "sitting in judgment." We are not prepared in New York. Our preparation is to go around to the courts where the older judges are functioning to see how they perform their job. To me, this is simply perpetuating errors. Another reason I say judges should be educated is because we're taught contracts. We're taught torts. We're taught trust and estates, commercial paper, creditors and debtors rights. We are taught, in short, to perpetuate the system as it now is. It's part of the capitalist system. We are taught what we should support—it's good, it's America. As Calvin Coolidge said, "the business of America is business." That's what we're taught. We're taught very little about human values, very little about sociological jurisprudence which Roscoe Pound brought out of the so-called middle country of Nebraska many years ago before he became Dean of the Harvard Law School. We're taught nothing about human values, and sociological jurisprudence seems to have failed. We aren't taught that the Fourteenth Amendment, for example, should be used as a focus on the human element in the law. There are no yardsticks for measuring the human character as we know it except through psychology, psychoanalysis, and psychiatry. But judges certainly aren't trained in those areas. I've long suggested that a psychiatrist should sit on the bench with the judge. Judges need lots of support—we're not gods despite the fact that some people put on the black robe and think they are automatically transformed into a diety of some kind. And we do need help in coping with human problems. We know, for example, that most of the murders in this country are between people who have always known each other and perhaps have been lovers. In a fit of temper, which is vastly different from premeditation, they kill the person they love. These are things here that go beyond a simple resolution of the facts—human emotions, sensitivities that judges cannot, or should not, overlook. There is a great gap in our training, which is impersonal, purely legalistic and most people, despite the old cliche about being presumed to know the law, do not know the law. If you're a trial judge as I am you see many lawyers who apparently do not know the law or how to express it. So it is very important to have patience. It is important that judging should not deteriorate into the statistics of a baseball game. And yet what do the criminal courts do here in New York state, and in New York City? They circulate every week a report stating what judge handled how many cases. How many were disposed of in the shortest possible period of time. That's not justice. That may be law but it certainly has nothing to do with justice.

Question: Do you believe that the criminal justice system was designed to ensure justice?

Answer: In my view, the system was created by the establishment to protect the establishment. In British philosophy either Hobbs or Hume had it: "To keep each of us from the throat of the other." Certainly to keep the peasants from the throats of their leaders. You know that all religion in every system is to give you the hope of some better life so that you won't rebel in this one. Peasants of India have been controlled by that kind of belief for years. You don't see the rich coming into court without a lawyer. Consequently, you don't see the rich going to jail. The rich do not go to the electric chair. The rich are not hung, nor do they go to the scaffold. One of the greatest pieces of research was done on the case of *Furman v. Georgia,* when for a short period of time the court declared the death penalty unconstitutional. Thurgood Marshall had the legal defense committee do regular research and if you saw the footnotes on that case you know as well as I that of the 3,000 and some people who have been sentenced to death almost 2,000 were black, five hundred were non-white, all were poor. Marshall also makes the point about the death penalty being disproportionately applied against the poor and seldom if ever against women. So the system is deficient in many ways and no one is really working to change it.

Question: What do you think the hiring of more minorities and women would bring to the criminal justice system.

Answer: First, I don't see that happening, not unless blacks start voting. For example, it's a marvelous opportunity now to intimidate Republicans and Democrats simply by voting for Jesse Jackson. Marvelous opportunity —this could be the only valid demonstration of today's black power in this country. We can't be guerrillas. We can't fight the establishment with might—we don't have it. In addition to which, we have too many middle-class, self-annointed bourgeois blacks who are nothing more than Afrosaxons who believe they have it made. I tell people all the time that it really makes no difference who is in the White House; Republicans believe in a democratic form of government, and Democrats believe in a republican form of government. Now we have an opportunity. We didn't take it with Shirley Chisolm, so we should take it now.

Question: Do you think the criminal justice system will improve in the future? Do you think it can evolve into a truly just, truly democratic system from the black point of view?

Answer: No, and I'll tell you why. Because there's so much money around and blacks have so much of it, at least I'm told our spending power is billions a year. These blacks think they have it made. They want to protect what little they do have, and to that extent they're protecting the system.

The people who recognize the injustices practiced against them are looking for some charismatic leader, somebody to trust, somebody who will speak to white authority in a way that they can't or are unable to do for any number of reasons. They tell me this. I don't see why more of us don't speak out, unless too many are complacent, as I just pointed out, or just afraid. It's a tragedy that we have so few blacks in the state legislature, in the city council. The power is in the legislature, that's where we could be effective. The legislature is where you can really do your brokering and trading.

Question: One possibility of bringing about change is for blacks to vote as independents. What about third parties?

Answer: I believe we should start a black party. I'm wholeheartedly in favor of a national black political party. But the only place any effective organization has taken place is in the South. I wish it would catch on. I think it would be healthy for this country. The only trouble is that many blacks want the same things that whites want; sometimes we get diverted from the needs of the black race in this country and forget, too soon, that there's been a 300 year black holocaust in this country. We tend to forget, and that's the tragedy.

Question: You once commented that black judges must be "consciously black" on the bench. What does this mean to you?

Answer: This means that black judges should treat blacks with a special understanding, the understanding that springs from their own experience and from their experience with American history. And then, of course, you lean over backwards to be fair to whites.

Question: You've argued that a black accused is treated as if he were guilty until he is proven innocent. Judge Crockett, Milton Allen, and a number of other black jurists have agreed with this view. Do you still argue that basically when a person comes before the court for a criminal offense, a felony offense, and he's poor, black, hispanic, or some other racial minority member, that the person is guilty until proven innocent?

Answer: I'm convinced of this. There are all kinds of preconceived notions that undermine basic criminal justice principles. No, it's not innocent until proven guilty when it comes to minorities. It is almost impossible to get an impartial jury because of white preconceptions concerning blacks. And in order to guarantee conviction, the D.A. will do everything in his power to exercise challenges for cause to keep blacks and Puerto Ricans off if a black is being tried. There is a great dispute between Burt Roberts and me as to when the presumption of innocence begins. I say at the moment of arrest; he asserts that it's only when the trial begins.

Question: What about bail policy?

Answer: I view my bail policy to be constitutional and proper under the statutes of New York. The Eighth Amendment says that bail should not be excessive, which gives the judge a great deal of discretion. If somebody has a job or is a student who has never been out of the city, who is not as wealthy as Vesco, who can't flee anywhere, I see no reason to hold him in jail until his trial, which can be eighteen months later, or to inflict upon him the kind of punishment he would get if he had already been found guilty.

In 1970 the state legislature in New York rejected preventive detention —rejected it. Our code of criminal procedure has many different ways in which you can release somebody before trial. Now the judges want preventive detention, an issue currently in fashion in the newspapers, which continually run features pointing to the need to protect society from dangerous characters. They seem to forget that these so-called dangerous characters have yet to be convicted. This is all a perfect example of the "guilty until proven innocent" principle at work. And preventive detention is practiced not only on the city level but on the federal level as well. Several years ago the *New York Times* had an article in which the FBI and CIA admitted that they kept arresting and rearresting black militants for fear that a new Martin Luther King, Jr. would come to the surface to lead the black people. This kind of thinking, this reliance on preventive detention for a number of reasons far from serving the requisites of justice, is one reason why our prisons are bulging with blacks and hispanics. And who are the caretakers in the rural prisons where many of these inmates go? Rural white, redneck, Ku Klux Klan, hinterlanders—these are the ones who are in charge of blacks and hispanics.

Question: What about the early release programs initiated by the federal courts under Judge Lasker? It seems as if everybody is up in arms, calling for the scalps of both the releasees and Judge Lasker.

Answer: They're not calling for Judge Lasker's scalp, are they? If I had initiated such a program, though, I wouldn't have a scalp or head! I do think that Judge Lasker can't be faulted for what he did. If you could have seen some of the things that went on in the tombs—roach infested mattresses, rats coming up out of the toilets. Of course conditions were unconstitutional. It all gets right back to what I said earlier. If you dehumanize people you have to expect them to go back to their way of life. It's like training felons to make mailbags and license plates. Where else can you make those things but in prison?

Question: How common is police brutality?

Answer: I think brutality occurs whenever white police can get away with it. I used to hear my mother's five brothers, all of whom were police officers, talk about how they beat heads and threw people against walls . . . of course there's police brutality. And it's well known that blacks can be accused of resisting arrest simply because of the way they looked at an officer.

Question: In closing, what are your general ideas on crime and the purposes of criminal justice?

Answer: Let me first refer to the views of Dr. Bauman who teaches at Union College. He teaches philosophy and was trained as a lawyer. He says unless this country is willing to bring about a redistribution of wealth, the poor people are going to do it by larcenies. They always have, and they always will. When you're exposed to riches, you want a share. George Bernard Shaw talks about the greatest of crime, the greatest of evils— poverty. In regard to the criminal justice system, it is of primary importance to recognize that there is not going to be any rehabilitation. We work on custody. That's the whole theory of the criminal justice system— custody, not rehabilitation. We don't have time for that. I heard one of the Attica survivors one night over the radio practically cry when he said, "How the hell we going to be rehabilitated when we've never been habilitated in the first place." I agree.